# Contents

صلى الله عليه وسلم

# MUHAMMAD

## his life based on the earliest sources

*by*

**Martin Lings**

ابو بكر سراج الدّين

THE ISLAMIC TEXTS SOCIETY

First published by George Allen & Unwin 1983, reprinted 1986, 1988
This edition published by
The Islamic Texts Society 1991
Miller's House
Kings Mill Lane
Great Shelford
Cambridge CB22 5EN, U.K.



Reprinted in 1995, 1997, 2001, 2002, 2004, 2005, 200 , 2009, 2010,
2011,2012, 2013, 2014, 2015, 2016, 2017

British Library Cataloguing-in-Publication Data.
A catalogue record for this book
is available from The British Library.

ISBN: 978 0946621 25 5 cloth
ISBN: 978 0946621 33 0 paper



Printed by Mega Printing in Turkey

# I

# *The House of God*

THE Book of Genesis tells us that Abraham was childless, without hope of children, and that one night God summoned him out of his tent and said to him: "Look now towards heaven, and count the stars if thou art able to number them." And as Abraham gazed up at the stars he heard the voice say: "So shall thy seed be."[1]

Abraham's wife Sarah was then seventy-six years old, he being eighty-five, and long past the age of child-bearing, so she gave him her handmaid Hagar, an Egyptian, that he might take her as his second wife. But bitterness of feeling arose between the mistress and the handmaid, and Hagar fled from the anger of Sarah and cried out to God in her distress. And He sent to her an Angel with the message: "I will multiply thy seed exceedingly, that it shall not be numbered for multitude." The Angel also said to her: "Behold, thou art with child, and shalt bear a son, and shalt call his name Ishmael; because the Lord hath heard thy affliction."[2] Then Hagar returned to Abraham and Sarah and told them what the Angel had said; and when the birth took place, Abraham named his son Ishmael, which means "God shall hear".

When Abraham had reached his hundredth year, and Sarah was ninety years old, God spoke again to Abraham and promised him that Sarah also should bear him a son who must be called Isaac. Fearing that his elder son might thereby lose favour in the sight of God, Abraham prayed: "*O that Ishmael might live before Thee!*" And God said to him: "*As for Ishmael, I have heard thee. Behold, I have blessed him . . . and I will make him a great nation. But My covenant will I establish with Isaac, which Sarah shall bear unto thee at this set time in the next year.*[3]

Sarah gave birth to Isaac and it was she herself who suckled him; and when he was weaned she told Abraham that Hagar and her son must no longer remain in their household. And Abraham was deeply grieved at this, on account of his love for Ishmael; but again God spoke to him, and told him to follow the counsel of Sarah, and not to grieve; and again He promised him that Ishmael should be blessed.

Not one but two great nations were to look back to Abraham as their father – two great nations, that is, two guided powers, two instruments to work the Will of Heaven, for God does not promise as a blessing that which is profane, nor is there any greatness before God except greatness in the Spirit. Abraham was thus the fountain-head of two spiritual streams,

[1] 15: 5. [2] 16: 10–11. [3] 17: 20–1.

which must not flow together, but each in its own course; and he entrusted Hagar and Ishmael to the blessing of God and the care of His Angels in the certainty that all would be well with them.

Two spiritual streams, two religions, two worlds for God; two circles, therefore two centres. A place is never holy through the choice of man, but because it has been chosen in Heaven. There were two holy centres within the orbit of Abraham: one of these was at hand, the other perhaps he did not yet know; and it was to the other that Hagar and Ishmael were guided, in a barren valley of Arabia, some forty camel days south of Canaan. The valley was named Becca, some say on account of its narrowness: hills surround it on all sides except for three passes, one to the north, one to the south, and one opening towards the Red Sea which is fifty miles to the west. The Books do not tell us how Hagar and her son reached Becca;[1] perhaps some travellers took care of them, for the valley was on one of the great caravan routes, sometimes called "the incense route", because perfumes and incense and such wares were brought that way from South Arabia to the Mediterranean; and no doubt Hagar was guided to leave the caravan, once the place was reached. It was not long before both mother and son were overcome by thirst, to the point that Hagar feared Ishmael was dying. According to the traditions of their descendants, he cried out to God from where he lay in the sand, and his mother stood on a rock at the foot of a nearby eminence to see if any help was in sight. Seeing no one, she hastened to another point of vantage, but from there likewise not a soul was to be seen. Half distraught, she passed seven times in all between the two points, until at the end of her seventh course, as she sat for rest on the further rock, the Angel spoke to her. In the words of Genesis:

> *And God heard the voice of the lad; and the angel of God called to Hagar out of heaven and said to her: What aileth thee, Hagar? Fear not, for God hath heard the voice of the lad where he is. Arise and lift up the lad and hold him in thy hand, for I will make him a great nation. And God opened her eyes, and she saw a well of water.*[2]

The water was a spring which God caused to well up from the sand at the touch of Ishmael's heel; and thereafter the valley soon became a halt for caravans by reason of the excellence and abundance of the water; and the well was named Zamzam.

As to Genesis, it is the book of Isaac and his descendants, not of Abraham's other line. Of Ishmael it tells us: *And God was with the lad; and he grew and dwelt in the wilderness and became an archer.*[3] After that it scarcely mentions his name, except to inform us that the two brothers Isaac and Ishmael together buried their father in Hebron, and that some years later Esau married his cousin, the daughter of Ishmael. But there is indirect praise of Ishmael and his mother in the Psalm which opens *How amiable are Thy tabernacles, O Lord of hosts*, and which tells of the miracle of Zamzam as having been caused by their passing through the valley: *Blessed is the man whose strength is in Thee; in whose heart are the ways of them who passing through the valley of Baca make it a well.*[4]

[1] According to the traditions of the Arabs, accepted by most Muslims, Ishmael was still a babe in arms when Hagar brought him to the valley of Becca.

[2] 21: 17–20. [3] ibid. [4] Psalm 84: 5–6.

When Hagar and Ishmael reached their destination Abraham had still seventy-five years to live, and he visited his son in the holy place to which Hagar had been guided. The Koran tells us that God showed him the exact site, near to the well of Zamzam, upon which he and Ishmael must build a sanctuary;[1] and they were told how it must be built. Its name, Ka'bah, cube, is in virtue of its shape which is approximately cubic; its four corners are towards the four points of the compass. But the most holy object in that holy place is a celestial stone which, it is said, was brought by an Angel to Abraham from the nearby hill Abū Qubays, where it had been preserved ever since it had reached the earth. "It descended from Paradise whiter than milk, but the sins of the sons of Adam made it black."[2] This black stone they built into the eastern corner of the Ka'bah; and when the sanctuary was completed, God spoke again to Abraham and bade him institute the rite of the Pilgrimage to Becca – or Mecca, as it later came to be called: *Purify My House for those who go the rounds of it and who stand beside it and bow and make prostration. And proclaim unto men the pilgrimage, that they may come unto thee on foot and on every lean camel out of every deep ravine.*[3]

Now Hagar had told Abraham of her search for help, and he made it part of the rite of the Pilgrimage that the pilgrims should pass seven times between Ṣafā and Marwah, for so the two eminences between which she had passed had come to be named.

And later Abraham prayed, perhaps in Canaan, looking round him at the rich pastures and fields of corn and wheat: *Verily I have settled a line of mine offspring in a tilthless valley at Thy Holy House . . . Therefore incline unto them men's hearts, and sustain them with fruits that they may be thankful.*[4]

[1] XXII, 26. [2] Saying of the Prophet, Tir. VII, 49. (See *Key to References*, p. 349.)
[3] K. XXII, 26-7. [4] K. XIV, 37.

# II

# *A Great Loss*

ABRAHAM'S prayer was answered, and rich gifts were continually brought to Mecca by the pilgrims who came to visit the Holy House in increasing numbers from all parts of Arabia and beyond. The Greater Pilgrimage was made once a year; but the Ka'bah could also be honoured through a lesser pilgrimage at any time; and these rites continued to be performed with fervour and devotion according to the rules which Abraham and Ishmael had established. The descendants of Isaac also venerated the Ka'bah, as a temple that had been raised by Abraham. For them it counted as one of the outlying tabernacles of the Lord. But as the centuries passed the purity of the worship of the One God came to be contaminated. The descendants of Ishmael became too numerous to live all in the valley of Mecca; and those who went to settle elsewhere took with them stones from the holy precinct and performed rites in honour of them. Later, through the influence of neighbouring pagan tribes, idols came to be added to the stones; and finally pilgrims began to bring idols to Mecca. These were set up in the vicinity of the Ka'bah, and it was then that the Jews ceased to visit the temple of Abraham.[1]

The idolaters claimed that their idols were powers which acted as mediators between God and men. As a result, their approach to God became less and less direct, and the remoter He seemed, the dimmer became their sense of the reality of the World-to-come, until many of them ceased to believe in life after death. But in their midst, for those who could interpret it, there was a clear sign that they had fallen away from the truth: they no longer had access to the Well of Zamzam, and they had even forgotten where it lay. The Jurhumites who had come from the Yemen were directly responsible. They had established themselves in control of Mecca, and the descendants of Abraham had tolerated this because Ishmael's second wife was a kinswoman of Jurhum; but the time came when the Jurhumites began to commit all sorts of injustices, for which they were finally driven out; and before they left they buried the Well of Zamzam. No doubt they did this by way of revenge, but it was also likely that they hoped to return and enrich themselves from it, for they filled it up with part of the treasure of the sanctuary, offerings of pilgrims which had accumulated in the Ka'bah over the years; then they covered it with sand.

Their place as lords of Mecca was taken by Khuzā'ah[2], an Arab tribe

[1] I.I., 15.

[2] See index for note on pronunciation of Arabic names, p. 348.

descended from Ishmael which had migrated to the Yemen and then returned northwards. But the Khuzā'ites now made no attempt to find the waters that had been miraculously given to their ancestor. Since his day other wells had been dug in Mecca, God's gift was no longer a necessity, and the Holy Well became a half forgotten memory.

Khuzā'ah thus shared the guilt of Jurhum. They were also to blame in other respects: a chieftain of theirs, on his way back from a journey to Syria, had asked the Moabites to give him one of their idols. They gave him Hubal, which he brought back to the Sanctuary, setting it up within the Ka'bah itself; and it became the chief idol of Mecca.

# III

# *Quraysh of the Hollow*

ANOTHER of the most powerful Arab tribes of Abrahamic descent was Quraysh; and about four hundred years after Christ, a man of Quraysh named Quṣayy married a daughter of Ḥulayl who was then chief of Khuzā'ah. Ḥulayl preferred his son-in-law to his own sons, for Quṣayy was outstanding amongst Arabs of his time, and on the death of Ḥulayl, after a fierce battle which ended in arbitration, it was agreed that Quṣayy should rule over Mecca and be the guardian of the Ka'bah.

He thereupon brought those of Quraysh who were his nearest of kin and settled them in the valley, beside the Sanctuary – his brother Zuhrah; his uncle Taym; Makhzūm, the son of another uncle; and one or two cousins who were less close. These and their posterity were known as Quraysh of the Hollow, whereas Quṣayy's more remote kinsmen settled in the ravines of the surrounding hills and in the countryside beyond and were known as Quraysh of the Outskirts. Quṣayy ruled over them all as king, with undisputed power, and they paid him a tax every year on their flocks, so that he might feed those of the pilgrims who were too poor to provide for themselves. Until then the keepers of the Sanctuary had lived round it in tents. But Quṣayy now told them to build themselves houses, having already built himself a spacious dwelling which was known as the House of Assembly.

All was harmonious, but seeds of discord were about to be sown. It was a marked characteristic of Quṣayy's line that in each generation there would be one man who was altogether pre-eminent. Amongst Quṣayy's four sons, this man was 'Abdu Manāf, who was already honoured in his father's lifetime. But Quṣayy preferred his first-born, 'Abd ad-Dār, although he was the least capable of all; and shortly before his death he said to him: "My son, I will set thee level with the others in despite of men's honouring them more than thee. None shall enter the Ka'bah except thou open it for him, and no hand but thine shall knot for Quraysh their ensign of war, nor shall any pilgrim draw water for drink in Mecca except thou give him the right thereto, nor shall he eat food except it be of thy providing, nor shall Quraysh resolve upon any matter except it be in thy house."[1] Having thus invested him with all his rights and powers, he transferred to him the ownership of the House of Assembly.

Out of filial piety 'Abdu Manāf accepted without question his father's wishes; but in the next generation half of Quraysh gathered round 'Abdu Manāf's son Hāshim, clearly the foremost man of his day, and demanded that the rights be transferred from the clan of 'Abd ad-Dār to his clan. Those who supported Hāshim and his brothers were the descendants of Zuhrah and Taym, and all Qusayy's descendants except those of the eldest line. The descendants of Makhzūm and of the other remoter cousins maintained that the rights should remain in the family of 'Abd ad-Dār. Feeling rose so high that the women of the clan of 'Abdu Manāf brought a bowl of rich perfume and placed it beside the Ka'bah; and Hāshim and his brothers and all their allies dipped their hands in it and swore a solemn oath that they would never abandon one another, rubbing their scented hands over the stones of the Ka'bah in confirmation of their pact. Thus it was that this group of clans were known as the Scented Ones. The allies of 'Abd ad-Dār likewise swore an oath of union, and they were known as the Confederates. Violence was strictly forbidden not only in the Sanctuary itself but also within a wide circle round Mecca, several miles in diameter; and the two sides were about to leave this sacred precinct in order to fight a battle to the death when a compromise was suggested, and it was agreed that the sons of 'Abdu Manāf should have the rights of levying the tax and providing the pilgrims with food and drink, whereas the sons of 'Abd ad-Dār should retain the keys of the Ka'bah and their other rights, and that their house should continue to be the House of Assembly.

Hāshim's brothers agreed that he should have the responsibility of providing for the pilgrims. When the time of the Pilgrimage drew near he would rise in the Assembly and say: "O men of Quraysh, ye are God's neighbours, the people of His House; and at this feast there come unto you God's visitors, the pilgrims to His House. They are God's guests, and no guests have such claim on your generosity as His guests. If my own wealth could compass it, I would not lay this burden upon you."[2]

Hāshim was held in much honour, both at home and abroad. It was he who established the two great caravan journeys from Mecca, the Caravan of Winter to the Yemen and the Caravan of Summer to north-west Arabia, and beyond it to Palestine and Syria, which was then under Byzantine rule as part of the Roman Empire. Both journeys lay along the ancient incense route; and one of the first main halts of the summer caravans was the oasis of Yathrib, eleven camel days north of Mecca. This oasis had at one time been chiefly inhabited by Jews, but an Arab tribe from South Arabia was now in control of it. The Jews none the less continued to live there in considerable prosperity, taking part in the general life of the community while maintaining their own religion. As to the Arabs of Yathrib, they had certain matriarchal traditions and were collectively known as the children of Qaylah after one of their ancestresses. But they had now branched into

[1] I.I. 83. Throughout this book, everything between quotation marks has been translated from traditional sources.

[2] I.I. 87.

two tribes which were named Aws and Khazraj after Qaylah's two sons.

One of the most influential women of Khazraj was Salmà the daughter of 'Amr, of the clan of Najjār, and Hāshim asked her to marry him. She consented on condition that the control of her affairs should remain entirely in her own hands; and when she bore him a son she kept the boy with her in Yathrib until he was fourteen years old or more. Hāshim was not averse to this, for despite the oasis fever, which was more of a danger to newcomers than to the inhabitants, the climate was healthier than that of Mecca. Moreover he often went to Syria and would stay with Salmà and his son on the way there and on his return. But Hāshim's life was not destined to be a long one, and during one of his journeys he fell ill at Gaza in Palestine and died there.

He had two full brothers, 'Abdu Shams and Muṭṭalib,[1] and one half-brother, Nawfal. But 'Abdu Shams was exceedingly busied with trade in the Yemen, and later also in Syria, whereas Nawfal was no less busied with trade in Iraq, and both would be absent from Mecca for long periods. For these and perhaps for other reasons also, Hāshim's younger brother Muṭṭalib took over the rights of watering the pilgrims and of levying the tax to feed them; and he now felt it his duty to give thought to the question of his own successor. Hāshim had had three sons by wives other than Salmà. But if all that was said were true, none of these – and for that matter none of Muṭṭalib's own sons – could be compared with Salmà's son. Despite his youth, Shaybah – for so she had named him – already showed distinct promise of gifts for leadership, and excellent reports of him were continually brought to Mecca by travellers who passed through the oasis. Finally Muṭṭalib went to see for himself, and what he saw prompted him to ask Salmà to entrust his nephew to his care. Salmà was unwilling to let her son go, and the boy refused to leave his mother without her consent. But Muṭṭalib was not to be discouraged, and he pointed out to both mother and son that the possibilities which Yathrib had to offer were not to be compared with those of Mecca. As guardians of the Holy House, the great centre of pilgrimage for all Arabia, Quraysh ranked higher in dignity than any other Arab tribe; and there was a strong likelihood that Shaybah would one day hold the office which his father had held and so become one of the chiefs of Quraysh. But for this he must first be integrated into his people. No mere exile from outside could hope to attain to such honour. Salmà was impressed by his arguments, and if her son went to Mecca it would be easy for her to visit him there and for him to visit her, so she agreed to let him go. Muṭṭalib took his nephew with him on the back of his camel; and as they rode into Mecca he heard some of the bystanders say as they looked at the young stranger: "'Abd al-Muṭṭalib", that is, "al-Muṭṭalib's slave". "Out upon you," he said, "he is no less than the son of my brother Hāshim." The laughter with which his words were greeted was but a prelude to the merriment that was caused throughout the city as the story

[1] The name is al-Muṭṭalib, except in the vocative case where the "al-" must be omitted. But since this prefix (the definite article) is cumbersome in transcription, the vocative form has been extended here throughout to most cases of proper names which begin with the article.

of the blunder ran from mouth to mouth; and from that day the youth was affectionately known as 'Abd al-Muṭṭalib.

Not long after his arrival he was involved in a dispute about his father's estate with his uncle Nawfal: but with the help of his guardian uncle, and pressure brought to bear from Yathrib, 'Abd al-Muṭṭalib was able to secure his rights. Nor did he disappoint the hopes that had been encouraged by his early promise; and when, after several years, Muṭṭalib died, no one disputed his nephew's qualifications to succeed to the heavy responsibility of feeding and watering the pilgrims. It was even said that he surpassed both his father and his uncle in his fulfilment of this task.

# IV

# *The Recovery of a Loss*

ADJOINING the north-west side of the Ka'bah there is a small precinct surrounded by a low semicircular wall. The two ends of the wall stop short of the north and west corners of the House, leaving a passage for pilgrims. But many pilgrims make wide their circle at this point and include the precinct within their orbit, passing round the outside of the low wall. The space within it is named Ḥijr Ismā'īl, because the tombs of Ishmael and Hagar lie beneath the stones which pave it.

'Abd al-Muṭṭalib so loved to be near the Ka'bah that he would sometimes order a couch to be spread for him in the Ḥijr; and one night when he was sleeping there a shadowy figure came to him in a vision and said: "Dig sweet clarity." "What is sweet clarity?" he asked, but the speaker vanished. He none the less felt such happiness and peace of soul when he woke that he determined to spend the next night in the same place. The visitant returned and said: "Dig beneficence." But again his question received no answer. The third night he was told: "Dig the treasured hoard", and yet again the speaker vanished at his questioning. But the fourth night the command was: "Dig Zamzam"; and this time when he said "What is Zamzam?" the speaker said:

"Dig her, thou shalt not regret,
For she is thine inheritance
From thy greatest ancestor.
Dry she never will, nor fail
To water all the pilgrim throng."

Then the speaker told him to look for a place where there was blood and dung, an ants' nest, and pecking ravens. Finally he was told to pray "for clear full flowing water that will water God's pilgrims throughout their pilgrimage".[1]

When dawn was breaking 'Abd al-Muṭṭalib rose and left the Ḥijr at the north corner of the Holy House which is called the Iraqi Corner. Then he walked along the north-east wall, at the other end of which is the door of the Ka'bah; and passing this he stopped, a few feet beyond it, at the east

[1] I.I. 93.

corner, where he reverently kissed the Black Stone. From there he began the rite of the rounds, going back past the door to the Iraqi Corner, across the Ḥijr to the west corner – the Syrian Corner – and thence to the Yemenite Corner which is towards the south. The children of Abraham, alike the lines of Ishmael and Isaac, go round their sanctuaries with a movement opposite to that of the sun. As he walked from the Yemenite Corner to the Black Stone, he could see the dark slope of Abū Qubays and beyond it the further eastern hills, sharply outlined against the yellow light. Seven times he went the round, and each time the light was appreciably brighter, for in Arabia the dawns and the dusks are brief. Having fulfilled the rite he went from the Black Stone to the door and, taking hold of the metal ring which hung from the lock, he prayed the prayer which he had been told to pray.

There was a sound of wings and a bird alighted in the sand behind him. Then another bird alighted and having finished his supplication he turned and watched them strut with their raven's gait towards two statuesque rocks which were about a hundred yards away, almost opposite the door. These had been adopted as idols, and it was between them that Quraysh sacrificed their victims. ʻAbd al-Muṭṭalib knew well, as did the ravens, that there was always blood in the sand at that place. There was also dung; and, going up to it, he now saw that there was an ants' nest.

He went to his house and took two pickaxes, one of which was for his son Ḥārith whom he brought with him to the place where he knew that he must dig. The thud of the tools in the sand and the unusual sight – for the courtyard could be seen from all sides – soon attracted a crowd; and despite the respect generally felt for ʻAbd al-Muṭṭalib, it was not long before some of them protested that it was a sacrilege to dig at the place of sacrifice between the idols, and that he must stop. He said he would not, and told Ḥārith to stand by him and see that no one interfered with his digging. It was a tense moment, and the outcome could have been unpleasant. But the two Hāshimites were determined and united, whereas the onlookers had been taken by surprise. Nor did these idols, Isāf and Nā'ilah, hold a high rank among the idols of Mecca, and some even said that they were a Jurhumite man and woman who had been turned to stone for profaning the Kaʻbah. So ʻAbd al-Muṭṭalib continued to dig without any actual move being made to stop him; and some of the people were already leaving the sanctuary when suddenly he struck the well's stone covering and uttered a cry of thanksgiving to God. The crowd reassembled and increased; and when he began to dig out the treasure which Jurhum had buried there, everyone claimed the right to a share in it. ʻAbd al-Muṭṭalib agreed that lots should be cast for each object, as to whether it should be kept in the sanctuary or go to him personally or be divided amongst the tribe. This had become the recognised way of deciding an issue of doubt, and it was done by means of divining arrows inside the Kaʻbah, in front of the Moabite idol Hubal. In this instance some of the treasure went to the Kaʻbah and some to ʻAbd al-Muṭṭalib, but none of it to Quraysh in general. It was also agreed that the clan of Hāshim should have charge of Zamzam itself, since in any case it was their function to water the pilgrims.

# V

# *The Vow to Sacrifice a Son*

'ABD al-Muṭṭalib was respected by Quraysh for his generosity, his reliability and his wisdom. He was also a very handsome man, with a most commanding presence. His wealth was yet another reason why he should consider himself fortunate; and now all this was crowned by the honour of being the chosen instrument through which Zamzam had been restored. He was deeply grateful to God for these blessings; but his soul was still troubled by thoughts of the moment when he had been told to stop digging, and when everything had seemed to hang in the balance. All had gone well, praise be to God! But never before had he felt so keenly his poverty – for so it seemed to him – in having only one son. His cousin Umayyah, for example, the head of the clan of 'Abdu Shams, was blessed with many sons; and if the digger had been Mughīrah, the chief of Makhzūm, his sons could have made a large and powerful circle round him. But he himself, although he had more than one wife, had only one son to uphold him. He was already half resigned to this; but God who had given him Zamzam could also increase him in other respects; and encouraged by the favour he had just received he prayed God to give him more sons, adding to his prayer the vow that if He would bless him with ten sons and let them all grow to manhood, he would sacrifice one of them to Him at the Ka'bah.

His prayer was answered: the years passed and nine sons were born to him. When he made his vow, it had seemed to refer to a very far-off possibility. But the time came when all his sons were grown up except the youngest, 'Abd Allāh, and his vow began to dominate his thoughts. He was proud of all his sons, but he had never been equally fond of them all, and it had long been clear to him that 'Abd Allāh was the one he loved most. Perhaps God also preferred this same son, whom He had endowed with remarkable beauty, and perhaps He would choose him to be sacrificed. However that might be, 'Abd al-Muṭṭalib was a man of his word. The thought of breaking his oath did not enter his head. He was also a man of justice, with a deep sense of responsibility, which meant that he knew what responsibilities were to be avoided. He was not going to place upon himself the burden of deciding which son he would sacrifice. So when it was no longer possible to consider 'Abd Allāh as a mere stripling he gathered his ten sons together, told them of his pact with God, and called on them to help him keep his word. They had no choice but to agree; their father's vow was their vow; and they asked him what they were to do. He told them to make each his mark on an arrow. Meanwhile he had sent word to the official arrow-diviner of Quraysh, asking him to be present at the Ka'bah. He then took his sons to the Sanctuary and led them into the Holy House, where he told the diviner about his vow. Each son produced his arrow, and 'Abd al-Muṭṭalib took his stand beside Hubal, drew out a large knife which he had brought with him, and prayed to God. The lots were cast, and it was 'Abd Allāh's arrow that came out. His father took him by the hand, and with the knife in his other hand he led him to the door, intending to make straight for the place of sacrifice, as if afraid to give himself time to think.

But he had not reckoned with the women of his household, and in particular with 'Abd Allāh's mother, Fāṭimah. His other wives were from outlying tribes and had relatively little influence in Mecca. But Fāṭimah was a woman of Quraysh, of the powerful clan of Makhzūm, while on her mother's side she was descended from 'Abd, one of the son's of Quṣayy. All her family were at hand, within easy reach, ready to help her if need be. Three of the ten sons were hers, Zubayr, Abū Ṭālib and 'Abd Allāh. She was also the mother of 'Abd al-Muṭṭalib's five daughters, who were devoted to their brothers. These women had not been idle, and no doubt the other wives had sought Fāṭimah's help in view of the danger that hung over the heads of all the ten sons, one of whom was the owner of the arrow of sacrifice.

By the time the lots had been cast, a large gathering had assembled in the courtyard of the Sanctuary. When 'Abd al-Muṭṭalib and 'Abd Allāh appeared on the threshold of the Ka'bah, both as pale as death, a murmur arose from the Makhzūmites as they realised that one of their sister's sons was the intended victim. "Wherefore that knife?" called a voice, and others reiterated the question, though they all knew the answer. 'Abd al-Muṭṭalib began to tell them of his vow but he was cut short by Mughīrah, the chief of Makhzūm: "Sacrifice him thou shalt not; but offer a sacrifice in his stead, and though his ransom be all the property of the sons of Makhzūm we will redeem him." 'Abd Allāh's brothers had by this time come out from the Holy House. None of them had spoken, but now they turned to their father and begged him to let their brother live and to offer some other sacrifice by way of expiation. There was not one man present who did not take their part, and 'Abd al-Muṭṭalib longed to be persuaded, but he was filled with scruples. Finally, however, he agreed to consult a certain wise woman in Yathrib who could tell him whether an expiation was possible in this case, and if so what form it should take.

Taking with him 'Abd Allāh and one or two other sons, 'Abd al-Muṭṭalib rode to the country of his birth only to learn that the woman had gone to Khaybar, a wealthy Jewish settlement in a fertile valley almost a hundred miles north of Yathrib. So they continued their journey, and when they had found the woman and told her the facts she promised to consult her familiar spirit, and bade them return the following day. 'Abd al-Muṭṭalib prayed to God, and the next morning the woman said: "Word hath come to me. What is the blood-wite amongst you?" They answered that it was ten camels. "Return to your country," she said, "and put your man and ten camels side by side and cast lots between them. If the arrow fall against your man, add more camels and cast lots again; and if need be add more camels until your Lord accepts them and the arrow falls against them. Then sacrifice the camels and let the man live."

They returned to Mecca forthwith, and solemnly led 'Abd Allāh and ten camels to the courtyard of the Ka'bah. 'Abd al-Muṭṭalib went inside the Holy House, and standing beside Hubal he prayed to God to accept what they were doing. Then they cast lots, and the arrow fell against 'Abd Allāh. Another ten camels were added, but again the arrow said that the camels should live and that the man should die. They went on adding camels, ten at a time, and casting lots with the same result until the number of camels had reached a hundred. Only then did the arrow fall against them. But 'Abd al-Muṭṭalib was exceedingly scrupulous: for him the evidence of one arrow was not enough to decide so great an issue. He insisted that they should cast lots a second and a third time, which they did, and each time the arrow fell against the camels. At last he was certain that God had accepted his expiation, and the camels were duly sacrificed.

# VI

# *The Need for a Prophet*

'ABD al-Muṭṭalib did not pray to Hubal; he always prayed to God – to *Allāh*. But the Moabite idol had been for generations inside the House of God and had become for Quraysh a kind of personification of the *barakah*, that is the blessing, the spiritual influence, which pervaded that greatest of all sanctuaries. There were other lesser sanctuaries throughout Arabia and the most important of these in the Ḥijāz were the temples of three "daughters of God" as some of their worshippers claimed them to be, al-Lāt, al-'Uzzah and Manāt. From his earliest years, like the rest of the Arabs of Yathrib, 'Abd al-Muṭṭalib had been brought up to revere Manāt whose temple was at Qudayd on the Red Sea, almost due west of the oasis. More important for Quraysh was the shrine of al-'Uzzah in the valley of Nakhlah, a camel day's journey south of Mecca. Another day's journey in the same direction brought the devotee to Ṭā'if, a walled town on a luxuriant green tableland, inhabited by Thaqīf, a branch of the great Arab tribe of Hawāzin. Al-Lāt was "the lady of Ṭā'if", and her idol was housed in a rich temple. As guardians of this, Thaqīf liked to think of themselves as the counterpart of Quraysh; and Quraysh went so far as to speak currently of "the two cities" when they meant Mecca and Ṭā'if. But despite the wonderful climate and fertility of "the Garden of the Ḥijāz", as Ṭā'if was called, its people were not unjealous of the barren valley to their north, for they knew in their hearts that their temple, however much they might promote it, could never compare with the House of God. Nor did they altogether wish it were otherwise, for they too were descended from Ishmael and had roots in Mecca. Their sentiments were mixed and sometimes conflicting. Quraysh on the other hand were jealous of no one. They knew that they lived at the centre of the world and that they had in their midst a magnet capable of drawing pilgrims from all points of the compass. It was up to them to do nothing that might diminish the good relationship which had been established between themselves and the outlying tribes.

'Abd al-Muṭṭalib's office as host of pilgrims to the Ka'bah imposed on him an acute awareness of these things. His function was an intertribal one, and it was shared to a certain extent by all Quraysh. The pilgrims must be made to feel that Mecca was a home from home, and welcoming them meant welcoming what they worshipped and never failing to show honour to the idols they brought with them. The justification and authority for accepting idols and believing in their efficacy was that of tradition: their fathers and grandfathers and great-grandfathers had done so. None the less, God was, for 'Abd al-Muṭṭalib, the great reality; and he was no doubt nearer to the religion of Abraham than most of his contemporaries of Quraysh and Khuzā'ah and Hawāzin and other Arab tribes.

But there were – and always had been – a few who maintained the full purity of Abrahamic worship. They alone realised that far from being traditional, idol worship was an innovation – a danger to be guarded against. It only needed a longer view of history to see that Hubal was no better than the golden calf of the son's of Israel. These Ḥunafā',[1] as they called themselves, would have nothing to do with the idols, whose presence in Mecca they looked on as a profanation and a pollution. Their refusal to compromise and their frequent outspokenness relegated them to the fringe of Meccan society where they were respected, tolerated or ill-treated, partly according to their personalities and partly according to whether their clans were prepared to protect them or not.

'Abd al-Muṭṭalib knew four of the Ḥunafā', and one of the more respected of them, Waraqah by name, was the son of his second cousin Nawfal,[2] of the clan of Asad. Waraqah had become a Christian; and there was a belief among Christians of those parts that the coming of a Prophet was imminent. This belief may not have been widespread, but it was supported by one or two venerable dignitaries of eastern churches and also by the astrologers and soothsayers. As to the Jews, for whom such a belief was easier, since for them the line of Prophets ended only with the Messiah, they were almost unanimous in their expectancy of a Prophet. Their rabbis and other wise men assured them that one was at hand; many of the predicted signs of his coming had already been fulfilled; and he would, of course, be a Jew, for they were the chosen people. The Christians, Waraqah amongst them, had their doubts about this; they saw no reason why he should not be an Arab. The Arabs stood in need of a Prophet even more than the Jews, who at least still followed the religion of Abraham inasmuch as they worshipped the One God and did not have idols; and who but a Prophet would be capable of ridding the Arabs of their worship of false gods? In a wide circle round the Ka'bah, at some distance from it, there were 360 idols; and in addition to these almost every house in Mecca had its god, an idol large or small which was the centre of the household. As his last act on leaving the premises, especially if it was for a journey, a man would go to the idol and stroke it in order to obtain blessings from it, and such was the first act on returning home. Nor was Mecca exceptional in this respect, for these practices prevailed throughout most of Arabia. There were, it was true, some well established Arab Christian communities to the south, in Najran and the Yemen, as well as to the north near the frontiers of Syria; but God's latest intervention, which had transformed the Mediterranean and vast tracts of Europe, had made, in nearly six

[1] The word *ḥanīf*, plural *ḥunafā'*, has the sense of "orthodox". See K. VI, 161.

[2] Not to be confused with Hashim's brother Nawfal, after whom the clan of Nawfal was named.

hundred years, practically no impact on the pagan society which centred on the Meccan shrine. The Arabs of the Ḥijāz and of the great plain of Najd to its east seemed impervious to the message of the Gospels.

Not that Quraysh and the other pagan tribes were hostile to Christianity. Christians sometimes came to do honour to the Sanctuary of Abraham, and they were made welcome like all the rest. Moreover one Christian had been allowed and even encouraged to paint an icon of the Virgin Mary and the child Christ on an inside wall of the Ka'bah, where it sharply contrasted with all the other paintings. But Quraysh were more or less insensitive to this contrast: for them it was simply a question of increasing the multitude of idols by another two; and it was partly their tolerance that made them so impenetrable.

Unlike most of his tribe, Waraqah could read and had made a study of the scriptures and of theology. He was therefore capable of seeing that in one of Christ's promises, generally interpreted by Christians as referring to the miracle of Pentecost, there were none the less certain elements which did not fit that miracle and must be taken to refer to something else – something which had not yet been fulfilled. But the language was cryptic: what was the meaning of the words: *he shall not speak of himself, but whatsoever he shall hear, that shall he speak.*[1]

Waraqah had a sister named Qutaylah who was very close to him. He often spoke to her about these things, and his words had made so great an impression on her that thoughts of the expected Prophet were often in her mind. Could it be that he was already in their midst?

Once the sacrifice of the camels had been accepted, 'Abd al-Muṭṭalib made up his mind to find a wife for his reprieved son, and after some consideration the choice fell on Āminah, the daughter of Wahb, a grandson of Zuhrah, the brother of Quṣayy.

Wahb had been chief of Zuhrah but had died some years previously and Āminah was now a ward of his brother Wuhayb, who had succeeded him as chief of the clan. Wuhayb himself also had a daughter of marriageable age, Hālah by name, and when 'Abd al-Muṭṭalib had arranged that his son should marry Āminah, he asked that Hālah should be given in marriage to himself. Wuhayb agreed, and all preparations were made for the double wedding to take place at the same time. On the appointed day, 'Abd al-Muṭṭalib took his son by the hand, and they set off together for the dwellings of the Bani Zuhrah.[2] On the way they had to pass the dwellings of the Bani Asad; and it so happened that Qutaylah, the sister of Waraqah, was standing at the entrance to her house, perhaps deliberately in order to see what could be seen, for everyone in Mecca knew of the great wedding which was about to take place. 'Abd al-Muṭṭalib was now over seventy years old, but he was still remarkably young for his age in every respect; and the slow approach of the two bridegrooms, their natural grace enhanced by the solemnity of the occasion, was indeed an impressive sight. But as they drew near, Qutaylah had eyes only for the younger man. 'Abd Allāh was, for beauty, the Joseph of his times. Even the oldest men and

[1] St John 16: 13.

[2] The sons (i.e. descendants) of Zuhrah; *bani* is the plural of *ibn*, son.

women of Quraysh could not remember having seen his equal. He was now in his twenty-fifth year, in the full flower of his youth. But Qutaylah was struck above all – as she had been on other occasions, but never so much as now – by the radiance which lit his face and which seemed to her to shine from beyond this world. Could it be that 'Abd Allāh was the expected Prophet? Or was he to be the father of the Prophet?

They had now just passed her, and overcome by a sudden impulse she said "O 'Abd Allāh". His father let go his hand as if to tell him to speak to his cousin. 'Abd Allāh turned back to face her, and she asked him where he was going. "With my father," he said simply, not out of reticence but because he felt sure that she must know that he was on his way to his wedding. "Take me here and now as thy wife," she said, "and thou shalt have as many camels as those that were sacrificed in thy stead." "I am with my father," he replied. "I cannot act against his wishes, and I cannot leave him."[1]

The marriages took place according to plan, and the two couples stayed for some days in the house of Wuhayb. During that time 'Abd Allāh went to fetch something from his own house, and again he met Qutaylah, the sister of Waraqah. Her eyes searched his face with such earnestness that he stopped beside her, expecting her to speak. When she remained silent, he asked her why she did not say to him what she had said the day before. She answered him, saying: "The light hath left thee that was with thee yesterday. Today thou canst not fulfil the need I had of thee."[2]

The year of the marriages was AD 569. The year following this has been known ever since as the Year of the Elephant, and it was momentous for more than one reason.

[1] I.I. 100. [2] I.I. 101.

# VII

# *The Year of the Elephant*

AT that time the Yemen was under the rule of Abyssinia, and an Abyssinian named Abrahah was vice-regent. He built a magnificent cathedral in San'ā', hoping thereby to make it supersede Mecca as the great place of pilgrimage for all Arabia. He had marble brought to it from one of the derelict palaces of the Queen of Sheba, and he set up crosses in it of gold and of silver, and pulpits of ivory and ebony, and he wrote to his master, the Negus: "I have built thee a church, O King, the like of which was never built for any king before thee; and I shall not rest until I have diverted unto it the pilgrimage of the Arabs." Nor did he make any secret of his intention, and great was the anger of the tribes throughout Ḥijāz and Najd. Finally a man of Kinānah, a tribe akin to Quraysh, went to San'ā' for the deliberate purpose of defiling the church, which he did one night and then returned safely to his people.

When Abrahah heard of this he vowed that in revenge he would raze the Ka'bah to the ground; and having made his preparations he set off for Mecca with a large army, in the van of which he placed an elephant. Some of the Arab tribes north of San'ā' attempted to bar his way, but the Abyssinians put them to flight and captured their leader, Nufayl of the tribe of Khath'am. By way of ransom for his life, he offered to act as guide.

When the army reached Ṭā'if, the men of Thaqīf came out to meet them, afraid that Abrahah might destroy their temple of al-Lāt in mistake for the Ka'bah. They hastened to point out to him that he had not yet reached his goal, and they offered him a guide for the remainder of his march. Although he already had Nufayl, he accepted their offer, but the man died on the way, about two miles from Mecca, at a place called Mughammis, and they buried him. Afterwards the Arabs took to stoning his grave, and the people who live there still stone it to this day.

Abrahah halted at Mughammis, and sent on a detachment of horse to the outskirts of Mecca. They took what they could on the way, and sent back their plunder to Abrahah, including two hundred camels which were the property of 'Abd al-Muṭṭalib. Quraysh and other neighbouring tribes held a council of war, and decided that it was useless to try to resist the enemy. Meanwhile Abrahah sent a messenger to Mecca, bidding him to ask for the chief man there. He was to tell him they had not come to fight but only to destroy the temple, and if he wished to avoid all bloodshed he must come to the Abyssinian camp.

There had been no official chief of Quraysh since the time when their privileges and responsibilities had been divided between the houses of 'Abd ad-Dār and 'Abdu Manāf. But most people had their opinion as to which of the chiefs of the clans was in fact if not by right the leading man of Mecca, and on this occasion the messenger was directed to the house of 'Abd al-Muṭṭalib who, together with one of his sons, went back with the messenger to the camp. When Abrahah saw him he was so impressed by his appearance that he rose from his royal seat to greet him and then sat beside him on the carpet, telling his interpretor to inquire if he had a favour to ask. 'Abd al-Muṭṭalib replied that the army had taken two hundred of his camels and he asked that they should be returned to him. Abrahah was somewhat surprised at the request, and said that he was disappointed in him, that he should be thinking of his camels rather than his religion which they had now come to destroy. 'Abd al-Muṭṭalib replied: "I am the lord of the camels, and the temple likewise hath a lord who will defend it." "He cannot defend it against me," said Abrahah. "We shall see," said 'Abd al-Muṭṭalib. "But give me my camels." And Abrahah gave orders for the camels to be returned.

'Abd al-Muṭṭalib returned to Quraysh and advised them to withdraw to the hills above the town. Then he went with some of his family and others to the Sanctuary. They stood beside him, praying to God for His help against Abrahah and his army, and he himself took hold of the metal ring in the middle of the Ka'bah door and said: "O God, thy slave protecteth his house. Protect Thou Thy House!" Having thus prayed, he went with the others to join the rest of Quraysh in the hills at points where they could see what took place in the valley below.

The next morning Abrahah made ready to march into the town, intending to destroy the Ka'bah and then return to San'ā' by the way they had come. The elephant, richly caparisoned, was led into the front of the army, which was already drawn up; and when the mighty animal reached his position his keeper Unays turned him the same way as the troops were turned, that is towards Mecca. But Nufayl, the reluctant guide, had marched most of the way in the van of the army with Unays, and had learned from him some of the words of command which the elephant understood; and while the head of Unays was turned to watch for the signal to advance, Nufayl took hold of the great ear and conveyed into it a subdued but intense imperative to kneel. Thereupon, to the surprise and dismay of Abrahah and the troops, the elephant slowly and deliberately knelt himself down to the ground. Unays ordered him to rise, but Nufayl's word had coincided with a command more powerful than that of any man, and the elephant would not move. They did everything they could to bring him to his feet; they even beat him about the head with iron bars and stuck iron hooks into his belly, but he remained like a rock. Then they tried the strategem of making the whole army turn about and march a few paces in the direction of the Yemen. He at once rose to his feet, turned round and followed them. Hopefully they turned round about again, and he also turned, but no sooner was he facing Mecca than again he knelt.

This was the clearest of portents not to move one step further forward, but Abrahah was blinded by his personal ambition for the sanctuary he had built and by his determination to destroy its great rival. If they had turned back then, perhaps they would all have escaped disaster. But suddenly it was too late: the western sky grew black, and a strange sound was heard; its volume increased as a great wave of darkness swept upon them from the direction of the sea, and the air above their heads, as high as they could see, was full of birds. Survivors said that they flew with a flight like that of swifts, and each bird had three pebbles the size of dried peas, one in its beak and one between the claws of each foot. They swooped to and fro over the ranks, pelting as they swooped, and the pebbles were so hard and launched with such velocity that they pierced even coats of mail. Every stone found its mark and killed its man, for as soon as a body was struck its flesh began to rot, quickly in some cases, more gradually in others. Not everyone was hit, and amongst those spared were Unays and the elephant, but all were terror-stricken. A few remained in the Ḥijāz and earned a livelihood by shepherding and other work. But the main part of the army returned in disorder to San'ā': Many died by the wayside, and many others, Abrahah included, died soon after their return. As to Nufayl, he had slipped away from the army while all attention was concentrated on the elephant, and he made his way unscathed to the hills above Mecca.

After that day Quraysh were called by the Arabs "the people of God", and they were held in even greater respect than before, because God had answered their prayers and saved the Ka'bah from destruction. They are still honoured, but rather on account of a second event – no doubt not unconnected with the first – which took place in that same Year of the Elephant.

'Abd Allāh, the son of 'Abd al-Muṭṭalib, was not in Mecca at the time of the miracle of the birds. He had gone for trade to Palestine and Syria with one of the caravans; and on his way home he had lodged with his grandmother's family in Yathrib, and there he had fallen ill. The caravan went on without him to Mecca and when it brought the news of his illness 'Abd al-Muṭṭalib sent Ḥārith to accompany his brother home as soon as he should be well enough to travel. But when Ḥārith arrived at the house of his Yathrib cousins they answered his greetings with commiserations, and he knew at once that his brother was dead.

There was great grief in Mecca when Ḥārith returned. Āminah's one consolation was the unborn child of her dead husband, and her solace increased as the time of her delivery drew near. She was conscious of a light within her, and one day it shone forth from her so intensely that she could see the castles of Bostra in Syria. And she heard a voice say to her: "Thou carriest in thy womb the lord of this people; and when he is born say: 'I place him beneath the protection of the One, from the evil of every envier'; then name him Muḥammad."[1]

Some weeks later the child was born. Āminah was in the home of her uncle, and she sent word to 'Abd al-Muṭṭalib, asking him to come to see his

[1] I.I. 102.

grandson. He took the boy in his arms and carried him to the Sanctuary and into the Holy House, where he prayed a prayer of thanksgiving to God for this gift. Then he brought him once more to his mother, but on the way he showed him to his own household. He himself was shortly to have another son, by Āminah's cousin Hālah. At the moment his youngest son was the three-year-old 'Abbās who now met him at the door of his house. "This is thy brother; kiss him," he said, holding out to him the new-born babe, and 'Abbās kissed him.

# VIII
# *The Desert*

IT was the custom of all the great families of Arab towns to send their sons, soon after their birth, into the desert, to be suckled and weaned and spend part of their childhood amongst one of the Bedouin tribes. Nor had Mecca any reason for being an exception, since epidemics were not infrequent and the rate of infant mortality was high. But it was not only the desert's fresh air that they wished their sons to imbibe. That was for their bodies, but the desert had also its bounty for souls. Quraysh had only recently taken to the sedentary life. Until Quṣayy had told them to build themselves houses round the Sanctuary they had been more or less nomadic. Fixed settlements were perhaps inevitable, but they were dangerous. Their ancestors' way of life had been the nobler one, the life of tent-dwellers, often on the move. Nobility and freedom were inseparable, and the nomad was free. In the desert a man was conscious of being the lord of space, and in virtue of that lordship he escaped in a sense from the domination of time. By striking camp he sloughed off his yesterdays; and tomorrow seemed less of a fatality if its where as well as its when had yet to come. But the townsman was a prisoner; and to be fixed in one place, – yesterday, today, tomorrow – was to be a target for time, the ruiner of all things. Towns were places of corruption. Sloth and slovenliness lurked in the shadow of their walls, ready to take the edge off a man's alertness and vigilance. Everything decayed there, even language, one of man's most precious possessions. Few of the Arabs could read, but beauty of speech was a virtue which all Arab parents desired for their children. A man's worth was largely assessed by his eloquence, and the crown of eloquence was poetry. To have a great poet in the family was indeed something to be proud of; and the best poets were nearly always from one or another of the desert tribes, for it was in the desert that the spoken language was nearest to poetry.

So the bond with the desert had to be renewed in every generation – fresh air for the breast, pure Arabic for the tongue, freedom for the soul; and many of the sons of Quraysh were kept as long as eight years in the desert, so that it might make a lasting impression upon them, though a lesser number of years was enough for that.

Some of the tribes had a high reputation for nursing and rearing children, and amongst these were the Bani Sa'd ibn Bakr, an outlying branch of Hawāzin, whose territory lay to the south-east of Mecca. Āminah was in favour of entrusting her son to the care of a woman of this tribe. They came periodically to Quraysh for nurselings, and some were expected shortly. Their journey to Mecca on this occasion was described in after-years by one of their number, Ḥalīmah, the daughter of Abū Dhu'ayb, who was accompanied by her husband, Ḥārith, and a recently born son of their own whom she was nursing. "It was a year of drought," she said, "and we had nothing left. I set forth on a grey she-ass of mine, and we had with us an old she-camel which could not yield one drop of milk. We were kept awake all night by our son who was wailing for hunger, for I had not enough in my breasts to feed him; and that ass of mine was so weak and so emaciated that I often kept the others waiting."

She told how they went on their way with nothing to hope for except a fall of rain which would enable the camel and the ass to graze enough for their udders to swell a little, but by the time they reached Mecca no rain had fallen. Once there they set about looking for nurselings, and Āminah offered her son first to one and then to another until finally she had tried them all and they had all refused. "That", said Ḥalīmah, "was because we hoped for some favour from the boy's father. 'An orphan!' we said. 'What will his mother and his grandfather be able to do for us?'" Not that they would have wanted direct payment for their services, since it was considered dishonourable for a woman to take a fee for suckling a child. The recompense they hoped for, though less direct and less immediate, was of a far wider scope. This interchange of benefits between townsman and nomad was in the nature of things, for each was poor where the other was rich, and rich where the other was poor. The nomad had the age-old God-given way of life to offer, the way of Abel. The sons of Cain – for it was Cain who built the first villages – had possessions and power. The advantage for the Bedouin was to make an enduring link with one of the great families. The foster-mother gained a new son who would look on her as a second mother and feel a filial duty to her for the rest of his life. He would also feel himself a brother to her own children. Nor was the relationship merely a nominal one. The Arabs hold that the breast is one of the channels of heredity and that a suckling drinks qualities into his nature from the nurse who suckles him. But little or nothing could be expected from the foster-child himself until he grew up, and meantime his father could normally be relied on to fulfil the duties of his son. A grandfather was too remote; and in this case they would have known that 'Abd al-Muṭṭalib was an old man who could not reasonably be expected to live much longer. When he died, his sons, not his grandson, would be his heirs. As to Āminah, she was poor; and as to the boy himself, his father had been too young to have acquired wealth. He had left his son no more than five camels, a small flock of sheep and goats, and one slave girl. 'Abd Allāh's son was indeed a child of one of the great families; but he was by far the poorest nurseling that these women were offered that year.

On the other side, though the foster-parents were not expected to be rich, they must not be too poverty-stricken, and it was evident that Ḥalīmah and her husband were poorer than any of their companions. Whenever the choice lay between her and another, the other was preferred and chosen; and it was not long before every one of the Bani Sa'd women except Ḥalīmah had been entrusted with a babe. Only the poorest nurse was without a nurseling; and only the poorest nurseling was without a nurse.

"When we decided to leave Mecca," said Ḥalīmah, "I told my husband: 'I hate to return in the company of my friends without having taken a babe to suckle. I shall go to that orphan and take him.' 'As thou wilt,' he said. 'It may be that God will bless us in him.' So I went and took him, for no reason save that I could find none but him. I carried him back to where our mounts were stationed, and no sooner had I put him in my bosom than my breasts overflowed with milk for him. He drank his fill, and with him his foster-brother drank likewise his fill. Then they both slept; and my husband went to that old she-camel of ours, and lo! her udders were full. He milked her and drank of her milk and I drank with him until we could drink no more and our hunger was satisfied. We spent the best of nights, and in the morning my husband said to me: 'By God, Ḥalīmah, it is a blessed creature that thou hast taken.' 'That is indeed my hope,' I said. Then we set out, and I rode my ass and carried him with me on her back. She outstripped the whole troop, nor could any of their asses keep pace with her. 'Confound thee!' they said to me, 'Wait for us! Is not this ass of thine the same ass that thou didst come on?' 'Yea by God,' I said, 'she is the very same.' 'Some wonder hath befallen her,' they said.

"We reached our tents in the Bani Sa'd country, and I know of no place on God's earth more barren than that then was. But after we brought him to live with us, my flock would come home to me replete at every eventide and full of milk. We milked them and drank, when others had no drop of milk; and our neighbours would say to their shepherds: 'Out upon you, go graze your flocks where he grazeth his,' meaning my shepherd. Yet still their flocks came hungry home, yielding no milk, while mine came well fed, with milk in plenty; and we ceased not to enjoy this increase and this bounty from God until the babe's two years had passed, and I weaned him.[1]

"He was growing well," she continued, "and none of the other boys could match him for growth. By the time he was two years old he was a well made child, and we took him again to his mother, although we were eager that he should stay with us for the blessings he brought us. So I said to her: 'Leave my little son with me until he grow stronger, for I fear lest he be stricken with the plague of Mecca.' And we importuned her until she gave him once more into our keeping and we brought him again to our home.

"One day, several months after our return, when he and his brother were with some lambs of ours behind our tents, his brother came running to us and said: 'That Qurayshite brother of mine! Two men clothed in white have taken him and have laid him down and opened his breast and they are stirring it with their hands.' So I and his father went to him and we found him standing, but his face was very pale. We drew him to us and said: 'What aileth thee, my son?' He said: 'Two men clothed in white came to me and laid me down and opened my breast and searched it for I know not what.'"[2]

Ḥalīmah and Ḥārith her husband looked this way and that, but there

[1] I.I. 105. [2] ibid.

was no sign of the men; nor was there any blood or any wound to bear out what the two boys had said. No amount of questioning would make them take back their words or modify them in any respect. Yet there was not even the trace of a scar on the breast of their foster-child nor any blemish on his perfect little body. The only unusual feature was in the middle of his back between his shoulders: a small but distinct oval mark where the flesh was slightly raised, as it were from the impress of a cupping glass; but that had been there at his birth.

In after-years he was able to describe the event more fully: "There came unto me two men, clothed in white, with a gold basin full of snow. Then they laid hold upon me, and splitting open my breast they brought forth my heart. This likewise they split open and took from it a black clot which they cast away. Then they washed my heart and my breast with the snow."[1] He also said: "Satan toucheth every son of Adam the day his mother beareth him, save only Mary and her son."[2]

[1] I.S. I/1, 96 [2] B. LX, 54.

# IX

# *Two Bereavements*

HALĪMAH and Ḥārith were convinced that the boys had been speaking the truth, and they were exceedingly shaken in consequence. Ḥārith feared that their foster-son had been possessed by an evil spirit or smitten by some spell, and he told his wife to take him with all speed to his mother before the harm he had suffered became apparent in him. So Ḥalīmah took him once more to Mecca, intending to say nothing about the real reason for her change of mind. But the change was too abrupt and Āminah, not to be deceived, finally compelled her to recount the whole story. Having heard it, she dismissed Ḥalīmah's fears, saying: "Great things are in store for my little son." Then she told her of her pregnancy, and of the light she had been conscious of carrying within her. Ḥalīmah was reassured, but this time Āminah decided to keep her son. "Leave him with me," she said, "and a good journey home."

The boy lived happily in Mecca with his mother for about three years, winning the affection of his grandfather and his uncles and aunts, and his many cousins with whom he played. Particularly dear to him were Ḥamzah and Ṣafiyyah, the children of 'Abd al-Muṭṭalib's last marriage which had taken place on the same day as that of Muḥammad's parents. Ḥamzah was his own age, Ṣafiyyah a little younger – his uncle and his aunt through his father, his cousins through his mother – and a powerful and lasting bond was formed between the three of them.

When he was six years old, his mother decided to take him on a visit to his kinsmen in Yathrib. They joined one of the northbound caravans, riding on two camels, Āminah on one of them and he on the other with his devoted slave girl, Barakah. In later life he recounted how he learned to swim in a pool which belonged to his Khazrajite kinsmen with whom they stayed, and how the boys taught him to fly a kite. But not long after they had set out on their return journey Āminah fell ill and they were obliged to halt, letting the caravan go on without them. After some days she died – it was at Abwā', not far from Yathrib – and there she was buried. Barakah did what she could to console the boy, now doubly an orphan, and in the company of some travellers she brought him once more to Mecca.

His grandfather now took complete charge of him, and it soon became clear that his special love for 'Abd Allāh had been transferred to 'Abd Allāh's son. 'Abd al-Muṭṭalib was always happy to be near the Ka'bah, as when it had been his wont to sleep in the Ḥijr at the time when he had been ordered to dig Zamzam. So his family used to spread him a couch every day in the shadow of the Holy House, and out of respect for their father none of his sons, not even Ḥamzah, would ever venture to sit on it; but his little grandson had no such scruples, and when his uncles told him to sit elsewhere ʿAbd al-Muṭṭalib said: "Let my son be. For by God, a great future is his." He would seat him beside him on the couch, and stroke his back; and it always pleased him to watch what he was doing. Almost every day they could be seen together, hand in hand, at the Kaʿbah or elsewhere in Mecca. ʿAbd al-Muṭṭalib even took Muḥammad with him when he went to attend the Assembly where the chief men of the town, all over forty, would meet to discuss various matters, nor did the eighty-year-old man refrain from asking the seven-year-old boy his opinion on this or that; and when called to question by his fellow dignitaries, he would always say: "A great future is in store for my son."

Two years after the death of his mother, the orphan was bereaved of his grandfather. When he was dying, ʿAbd al-Muṭṭalib entrusted his grandson to Abū Ṭālib, who was full brother to the boy's father; and Abū Ṭālib prolonged the affection and the kindness that his nephew had received from the old man. Henceforth he was as one of his own sons, and his wife Fāṭimah[1] did all she could to replace the boy's mother. In after-years Muḥammad used to say of her that she would have let her own children go hungry rather than him.

[1] Like Abū Ṭālib she was a grandchild of Hāshim, the daughter of his son Asad, half-brother of ʿAbd al-Muṭṭalib.

# X

# *Baḥīrà the Monk*

THE fortunes of 'Abd al-Muṭṭalib had waned during the last part of his life, and what he left at his death amounted to no more than a small legacy for each of his sons. Some of them, especially 'Abd al-'Uzzah who was known as Abū Lahab, had acquired wealth of their own. But Abū Ṭālib was poor, and his nephew felt obliged to do what he could to earn his own livelihood. This he did mostly by pasturing sheep and goats, and he would thus spend day after day alone in the hills above Mecca or on the slopes of the valleys beyond. But his uncle took him sometimes with him on his travels and on one occasion when Muḥammad was nine, or according to others twelve, they went with a merchant caravan as far as Syria. At Bostra, near one of the halts where the Meccan caravan always stopped, there was a cell which had been lived in by a Christian monk for generation after generation. When one died, another took his place and inherited all that was in the cell including some old manuscripts. Amongst these was one which contained the prediction of the coming of a Prophet to the Arabs; and Baḥīrà, the monk who now lived in the cell, was well versed in the contents of this book, which interested him all the more because, like Waraqah, he too felt that the coming of the prophet would be in his lifetime.

He had often seen the Meccan caravan approach and halt not far from his cell, but as this one came in sight his attention was struck by something the like of which he had never seen before: a small low-hanging cloud moved slowly above their heads so that it was always between the sun and one or two of the travellers. With intense interest he watched them draw near. But suddenly his interest changed to amazement, for as soon as they halted the cloud ceased to move, remaining stationary over the tree beneath which they took shelter, while the tree itself lowered its branches over them, so that they were doubly in the shade. Baḥīrà knew that such a portent, though unobtrusive, was of high significance. Only some great spiritual presence could explain it, and immediately he thought of the expected Prophet. Could it be that he had at last come, and was amongst these travellers?

The cell had recently been stocked with provisions, and putting together all he had, he sent word to the caravan: "Men of Quraysh, I have prepared food for you, and I would that ye should come to me, every one of you, young and old, bondman and freeman." So they came to his cell, but despite what he had said they left Muḥammad to look after their camels and their baggage. As they approached, Baḥīrà scanned their faces one by one. But he could see nothing which corresponded to the description in his book, nor did there seem to be any man amongst them who was adequate to the greatness of the two miracles. Perhaps they had not all come. "Men of Quraysh," he said, "let none of you stay behind." "There is not one that hath been left behind," they answered, "save only a boy, the youngest of us all." "Treat him not so" said Baḥīrà, "but call him to come, and let him be present with us at this meal." Abū Ṭālib and the others reproached themselves for their thoughtlessness. "We are indeed to blame," said one of them, "that the son of 'Abd Allāh should have been left behind and not brought to share this feast with us," whereupon he went to him and embraced him and brought him to sit with the people.

One glance at the boy's face was enough to explain the miracles to Baḥīrà; and looking at him attentively throughout the meal he noticed many features of both face and body which corresponded to what was in his book. So when they had finished eating, the monk went to his youngest guest and asked him questions about his way of life and about his sleep, and about his affairs in general. Muḥammad readily informed him of these things for the man was venerable and the questions were courteous and benevolent; nor did he hesitate to draw off his cloak when finally the monk asked if he might see his back. Baḥīrà had already felt certain, but now he was doubly so, for there, between his shoulders, was the very mark he expected to see, the seal of prophethood even as it was described in his book, in the selfsame place. He turned to Abū Ṭālib: "What kinship hath this boy with thee?" he said. "He is my son," said Abū Ṭālib. "He is not thy son," said the monk; "it cannot be that this boy's father is alive." "He is my brother's son," said Abū Ṭālib. "Then what of his father?" said the monk. "He died," said the other, "when the boy was still in his mother's womb." "That is the truth," said Baḥīrà. "Take thy brother's son back to his country, and guard him against the Jews, for by God, if they see him and know of him that which I know, they will contrive evil against him. Great things are in store for this brother's son of thine."[1]

[1] I.I. 115–7.

# XI

# *A Pact of Chivalry*

WHEN he had finished his trading in Syria, Abū Ṭālib returned to Mecca with his nephew, who continued his solitary life as before. But his uncles saw to it that he, as also 'Abbās and Ḥamzah, had some training in the use of weapons of war. Ḥamzah was clearly destined to be a man of mighty stature, endowed with great physical strength. He was already a good swordsman and a good wrestler. Muḥammad was of average height and average strength. He had a marked aptitude for archery, and gave every promise of being an excellent bowman, like his great ancestors, Abraham and Ishmael. A powerful asset for this lay in the strength of his eyesight: he was reputed to be able to count no less than twelve of the stars of the constellation of the Pleiades.

In those years Quraysh were not involved in any fighting except for a spasmodic and intermittent conflict which came to be known as the sacrilegious war because it had started in one of the sacred months. A profligate of Kinānah had treacherously murdered a man of 'Āmir, one of the Hawāzin tribes of Najd, and had taken refuge in the impregnable fortress township of Khaybar. The sequence of events followed the usual desert pattern: honour demanded revenge, so the tribe of the murdered man attacked Kinānah, the tribe of the murderer, and Quraysh were involved, somewhat ingloriously, as allies of Kinānah. The conflict dragged on for three or four years in which there were only five days of actual fighting. The head of the clan of Hāshim was at that time Zubayr, full brother, like Abū Ṭālib, of Muḥammad's father. Zubayr and Abū Ṭālib took their nephew with them to one of the first battles, but they said he was too young to fight. He was none the less allowed to help by gathering enemy arrows that had missed their mark and handing them to his uncles so that they could shoot them back.[1] But at one of the subsequent battles, where Quraysh and their allies had the worst of the day, he was allowed to show his skill as a bowman and was praised for his valour.[2]

The war helped to fan the growing discontent which every sedentary community tends to feel with the law of the desert. Most of the leading men of Quraysh had travelled to Syria and had seen for themselves the relative justice which prevailed in the Roman Empire. It was also possible in Abyssinia to have justice without recourse to fighting. But in Arabia there was no comparable system of law by which a victim of crime, or his family, might obtain redress; and it was natural that the sacrilegious war, like

[1] I.H. 119. [2] I.S. I/1, 81.

other conflicts before it, should have set many minds thinking of ways and means to prevent the same thing from happening again. But this time the result was more than mere thoughts and words: as far as Quraysh were concerned, there was now a widespread readiness to take action; and their sense of justice was put to the test by a scandalous incident which took place in Mecca in the first few weeks after the end of the fighting.

A merchant from the Yemeni port of Zabīd had sold some valuable goods to a notable of the clan of Sahm. Having taken possession of these, the Sahmite refused to pay the promised price. The wronged merchant, as his wronger well knew, was a stranger to Mecca, and had no confederate or patron in all the city to whom he might go for help. But he was not to be overawed by the other man's insolent self-assurance; and, taking his stand on the slope of Abū Qubays, he appealed to Quraysh as a whole, with loud and vehement eloquence, to see that justice was done. An immediate response came from most of those clans which had no traditional alliance with Sahm. Quraysh were bent above all on being united, regardless of clan; but within that union there was still an acute consciousness of the rift which had divided them, over the legacy of Quṣayy, into two groups, the Scented Ones and the Confederates, and Sahm were of the Confederates. One of the leaders of the other group, and one of the wealthiest men in Mecca at this time, was the chief of Taym, 'Abd Allāh ibn Jud'ān, and he now offered his large house as a meeting-place for all lovers of justice. From amongst the Scented Ones, only the clans of 'Abdu Shams and Nawfal were absent. Hāshim, Muṭṭalib, Zuhrah, Asad and Taym were all well represented, and they were joined by 'Adī, which had been one of the Confederates. Having decided, after an earnest discussion, that it was imperative to found an order of chivalry for the furtherance of justice and the protection of the weak, they went in a body to the Ka'bah where they poured water over the Black Stone, letting it flow into a receptacle. Then each man drank of the thus hallowed water; and with their right hands raised above their heads they vowed that henceforth, at every act of oppression in Mecca, they would stand together as one man on the side of the oppressed against the oppressor until justice was done, whether the oppressed were a man of Quraysh or one who had come from abroad. The Sahmite was thereupon compelled to pay his debt, nor did any of those clans which had abstained from the pact offer him their assistance.

Together with the chief of Taym, Zubayr of Hāshim was one of the founders of this order, and he brought with him his nephew Muḥammad, who took part in the oath and who said in after-years: "I was present in the house of 'Abd Allāh ibn Jud'ān at so excellent a pact that I would not exchange my part in it for a herd of red camels; and if now, in Islam, I were summoned unto it, I would gladly respond."[1] Another of those present was their host's first cousin, Abū Quhāfah of Taym, together with his son Abū Bakr, who was a year or two younger than Muḥammad and who was to become his closest friend.

[1] I.I. 86.

# XII

# *Questions of Marriage*

MUHAMMAD had now passed his twentieth year, and as time went on he received more and more invitations to join one or another of his kinsmen on their travels abroad. Finally the day came when he was asked to take charge of the goods of a merchant who was unable to travel himself, and his success in this capacity led to other similar engagements. He was thus able to earn a better livelihood, and marriage became a possibility.

His uncle and guardian Abū Ṭālib had at that time three sons: the eldest, Ṭālib, was about the same age as Muḥammad himself; 'Aqīl was thirteen or fourteen; and Ja'far was a boy of four. Muḥammad was fond of children and liked to play with them; and he grew especially attached to Ja'far who was a beautiful and intelligent child, and who responded to his cousin's love with a devotion that proved to be lasting. Abū Ṭālib also had daughters, and one of these was already of marriageable age. Her name was Fākhitah, but later she was called Umm Hāni', and it is by that name that she is always known. A great affection had grown up between her and Muḥammad, who now asked his uncle to let him marry her. But Abū Ṭālib had other plans for his daughter: his cousin Hubayrah, the son of his mother's brother, of the clan of Makhzūm, had likewise asked for the hand of Umm Hāni'; and Hubayrah was not only a man of some substance but he was also, like Abū Ṭālib himself, a gifted poet. Moreover the power of Makhzūm in Mecca was as much on the increase as that of Hāshim was on the wane; and it was to Hubayrah that Abū Ṭālib married Umm Hāni'. When his nephew mildly reproached him, he simply replied: "They have given us their daughters in marriage" – no doubt referring to his own mother – "and a generous man must requite generosity."[1] The answer was unconvincing inasmuch as 'Abd al-Muṭṭalib had already more than repaid the debt in question by marrying two of his daughters, 'Ātikah and Barrah, to men of Makhzūm. Muḥammad no doubt took his uncle's words as a courteous and kindly substitute for telling him plainly that he was not yet in a position to marry. That, at any rate, is what he now decided for

[1] I.S. VIII, 108.

himself; but unexpected circumstances were soon to induce him to change his mind.

One of the richer merchants of Mecca was a woman – Khadījah, daughter of Khuwaylid, of the clan of Asad. She was first cousin to Waraqah, the Christian, and his sister Qutaylah, and like them she was a distant cousin to the sons of Hāshim. She had already been married twice, and since the death of her second husband it had been her custom to hire men to trade on her behalf. Now Muḥammad had come to be known throughout Mecca as al-Amīn, the Reliable, the Trustworthy, the Honest, and this was initially owing to the reports of those who had entrusted their merchandise to him on various occasions. Khadījah had also heard much good of him from family sources; and one day she sent word to him, asking him to take some of her merchandise to Syria. His fee would be the double of the highest she had ever paid to a man of Quraysh; and she offered him, for the journey, the services of a lad of hers named Maysarah. He accepted what she proposed and accompanied by the lad he set off with her goods for the north.

When they reached Bostra in the South of Syria, Muḥammad took shelter beneath the shadow of a tree not far from the cell of a monk named Nestor. Since travellers' halts often remain unchanged, it could have been the selfsame tree under which he had sheltered some fifteen years previously on his way through Bostra with his uncle. Perhaps Baḥīrā had died and been replaced by Nestor. However that may be – for we only know what Maysarah reported – the monk came out of his cell and asked the lad: "Who is the man beneath that tree?" "He is a man of Quraysh," said Maysarah, adding by way of explanation: "of the people who have guardianship of the Sanctuary." "None other than a Prophet is sitting beneath that tree," said Nestor.[1]

As they went on further into Syria, the words of Nestor sank deep into the soul of Maysarah, but they did not greatly surprise him, for he had become aware throughout the journey that he was in the company of a man unlike any other he had ever met. This was still further confirmed by something he saw on his way home: he had often noticed that the heat was strangely unoppressive, and one day towards noon it was given to him to have a brief but clear vision of two Angels shading Muḥammad from the sun's rays.

On reaching Mecca they went to Khadījah's house with the goods they had bought in the markets of Syria for the price of what they had sold. Khadījah sat listening to Muḥammad as he described the journey and told her of the transactions he had made. These proved to be very profitable, for

[1] I.S. I/1, 83. According to Islamic tradition Muḥammad is none other than the mysterious Shiloh, to whom would be transferred, "in the latter days", the spiritual authority which until then had remained the prerogative of the Jews, Jesus himself having been the last Prophet of the line of Judah. The prophecy in question was made by Jacob immediately before his death: *And Jacob called unto his sons and said, Gather yourselves together, that I may tell you that which shall befall you in the last days . . . The sceptre shall not depart from Judah, nor a lawgiver from between his feet, until Shiloh come; and unto him shall the gathering of the people be.* (Genesis 49: 1, 10).

she was able to sell her newly acquired assets for almost the double of what had been paid for them. But such considerations were far from her thoughts, for all her attention was concentrated on the speaker himself. Muḥammad was twenty-five years old. He was of medium stature, inclined to slimness, with a large head, broad shoulders and the rest of his body perfectly proportioned. His hair and beard were thick and black, not altogether straight but slightly curled. His hair reached midway between the lobes of his ears and his shoulders, and his beard was of a length to match. He had a noble breadth of forehead and the ovals of his large eyes were wide, with exceptionally long lashes and extensive brows, slightly arched but not joined. In most of the earliest descriptions his eyes are said to have been black, but according to one or two of these they were brown, or even light brown. His nose was aquiline and his mouth was wide and finely shaped – a comeliness always visible for although he let his beard grow, he never allowed the hair of his moustache to protrude over his upper lip. His skin was white, but tanned by the sun. In addition to his natural beauty there was a light on his face – the same which had shone from his father, but in the son it was more powerful – and this light was especially apparent on his broad forehead, and in his eyes, which were remarkably luminous. Khadījah knew that she herself was still beautiful, but she was fifteen years his elder. Would he none the less be prepared to marry her?

As soon as he had gone, she consulted a woman friend of hers named Nufaysah, who offered to approach him on her behalf and, if possible, to arrange a marriage between them. Maysarah now came to his mistress and told her about the two Angels, and what the monk had said, whereupon she went to her cousin Waraqah and repeated these things to him. "If this be true, Khadījah," he said, "then is Muḥammad the prophet of our people. Long have I known that a prophet is to be expected, and his time hath now come."[1]

Meanwhile Nufaysah came to Muḥammad and asked him why he did not marry. "I have not the means to marry," he answered. "But if thou wert given the means," she said, "and if thou wert bidden to an alliance where there is beauty and property and nobility and abundance, wouldst thou not consent?" "Who is she?" he said. "Khadījah," said Nufaysah. "And how could such a marriage be mine?" he said. "Leave that to me!" was her answer. "For my part," he said, "I am willing."[2] Nufaysah returned with these tidings to Khadījah, who then sent word to Muḥammad asking him to come to her; and when he came she said to him: "Son of mine uncle, I love thee for thy kinship with me, and for that thou art ever in the centre, not being a partisan amongst the people for this or for that; and I love thee for thy trustworthiness and for the beauty of thy character and the truth of thy speech."[3] Then she offered herself in marriage to him, and they agreed that he should speak to his uncles and she would speak to her uncle 'Amr, the son of Asad, for Khuwaylid her father had died. It was Ḥamzah, despite his relative youth, whom the Hāshimites delegated to represent them on this occasion, no doubt because he was the

[1] I.I. 121. [2] I.S. I/1, 84. [3] I.I. 120.

most closely connected of them with the clan of Asad, for his full sister Ṣafiyyah had recently married Khadījah's brother 'Awwām. So Ḥamzah went with his nephew to 'Amr and asked for the hand of Khadījah; and it was agreed between them that Muḥammad should give her twenty she-camels as dowry.

# XIII
# *The Household*

THE bridegroom left his uncle's house and went to live in the house of his bride. As well as being a wife, Khadījah was also a friend to her husband, the sharer of his inclinations and ideals to a remarkable degree. Their marriage was wondrously blessed, and fraught with great happiness, though not without sorrows of bereavement. She bore him six children, two sons and four daughters. Their eldest child was a son named Qāsim, and Muḥammad came to be known as Abū l-Qāsim, the father of Qāsim; but the boy died before his second birthday. The next child was a daughter whom they named Zaynab; and she was followed by three other daughters, Ruqayyah, Umm Kulthūm, and Fāṭimah, and finally by another short-lived son.

On the day of his marriage, Muḥammad set free Barakah, the faithful slave he had inherited from his father; and on the same day Khadījah made him a gift of one of her own slaves, a youth of fifteen named Zayd. As to Barakah, they married her to a man of Yathrib to whom she bore a son, after whom she came to be known as Umm Ayman, the mother of Ayman. As to Zayd, he and some other youths had recently been bought at the great fair of 'Ukāẓ by Khadījah's nephew Ḥakīm, the son of her brother Ḥizām; and the next time his aunt visited him Ḥakīm had sent for his newly acquired slaves and invited her to choose one of them for herself. It was Zayd that she had chosen.

Zayd was proud of his ancestry: his father Ḥārithah was of the great northern tribe of Kalb whose territory lay on the plains between Syria and Iraq: his mother was a woman of the no less illustrious neighbouring tribe of Ṭayy, one of whose chieftains at that time was the poet-knight Ḥātim, famous throughout Arabia for his chivalry and his fabulous generosity. Several years had now passed since Zayd had been taken by his mother to visit her family, and the village where they were staying had been raided by some horsemen of the Bani Qayn, who had carried the boy off and sold him into slavery. Ḥārithah, his father, had searched for him in vain; nor had Zayd seen any travellers from Kalb who could take a message from him to his parents. But the Ka'bah drew pilgrims from all parts of Arabia, and one day during the holy season, several months after he had become Muḥammad's slave, he saw some men and women of his own tribe and clan in the streets of Mecca. If he had seen them the previous year, his feelings would have been very different. He had yearned for such an encounter; yet now that it had at last come it placed him in a quandary. He could not deliberately leave his family in ignorance of his whereabouts. But what message could he send them? Whatever its gist, he knew, as a son of the desert, that nothing less than a poem would be adequate for such an occasion. He composed some verses which expressed something of his mind, but implied more than they expressed. Then he accosted the Kalbite pilgrims and, having told them who he was, he said: "Speak unto my family these lines, for well I know that they have sorrowed for me:

> Though I myself be far, yet take my words
> Unto my people: at the Holy House
> I dwell, amidst the places God hath hallowed.
> Set then aside the sorrows ye have grieved,
> Weary not camels, scouring the earth for me,
> For I, praise be to God, am in the best
> Of noble families, great in all its line."

When the pilgrims returned home with their tidings, Ḥārithah at once set off for Mecca with his brother, Ka 'b; and going to Muḥammad they begged him to allow them to ransom Zayd, for as high a price as he might ask. "Let him choose," said Muḥammad, "and if he choose you, he is yours without ransom; and if he choose me, I am not the man to set any other above him who chooseth me." Then he called Zayd and asked him if he knew the two men. "This is my father," said the youth, "and this is mine uncle." "Me thou knowest," said Muḥammad, "and thou hast seen my companionship unto thee, so choose thou between me and them." But Zayd's choice was already made and he said at once: "I would not choose any man in preference to thee. Thou art unto me as my father and my mother." "Out upon thee, O Zayd!" exclaimed the men of Kalb. "Wilt thou choose slavery above freedom, and above thy father and thine uncle and thy family?" "It is even so," said Zayd, "for I have seen from this man such things that I could never choose another above him."

All further talk was cut short by Muḥammad, who now bade them come with him to the Ka'bah; and, standing in the Ḥijr, he said in a loud voice: "All ye who are present, bear witness that Zayd is my son; I am his heir and he is mine."[1]

The father and the uncle had thus to return with their purpose unachieved. But the tale they had to tell their tribe, of the deep mutual love which had brought about this adoption, was not an inglorious one; and when they saw that Zayd was free, and established in honour, with what promised to be a high standing amongst the people of the Sanctuary such as might benefit his brothers and other kinsmen in years to come, they were reconciled and went their way without bitterness. From that day the new Hāshimite was known in Mecca as Zayd ibn Muḥammad.

Among the most frequent visitors to the house was Ṣafiyyah, now Khadījah's sister-in-law, the youngest of Muḥammad's aunts, younger even than himself; and with her she would bring her little son Zubayr, whom she had named after her elder brother. Zubayr was thus well acquainted with his cousins, the daughters of Muḥammad, from his earliest years. With Ṣafiyyah came also her faithful retainer Salmà, who

[1] I.S. III/1, 28.

had delivered Khadījah of all her children, and who considered herself to be one of the household.

As the years passed there were occasional visits from Ḥalīmah, Muḥammad's foster-mother, and Khadījah was always generous to her. One of these visits was at a time of severe and widespread drought through which Ḥalīmah's flocks had been seriously depleted, and Khadījah made her a gift of forty sheep and a howdah camel.[1] This same drought, which produced something like a famine in the Ḥijāz, was the cause of a very important addition to the household.

Abū Ṭālib had more children than he could easily support, and the famine weighed heavily upon him. Muḥammad noticed this and felt that something should be done. The wealthiest of his uncles was Abū Lahab but he was somewhat remote from the rest of the family, partly no doubt because he had never had any full brothers or sisters amongst them, being the only child of his mother. Muḥammad preferred to ask for the help of 'Abbās, who could well afford it, being a successful merchant, and who was close to him because they had been brought up together. Equally close, or even closer, was 'Abbās's wife, Umm al-Faḍl, who loved him dearly and who always made him welcome at their house. So he went to them now, and suggested that each of their two households should take charge of one of Abū Ṭālib's sons until his circumstances improved. They readily agreed, and the two men went to Abū Ṭālib, who said when he heard their proposal: "Do what ye will, but leave me 'Aqīl and Ṭālib." Ja'far was now about fifteen, and he was no longer the youngest of the family. His mother Fāṭimah had borne yet another son to Abū Ṭālib, some ten years younger, and they had named him 'Alī. 'Abbās said he would take charge of Ja'far, whereupon Muḥammad agreed to do the same for 'Alī. It was about this time that Khadījah had borne her last child, a son named 'Abd Allāh, but the babe had died at an even earlier age than Qāsim. In a sense he was replaced by 'Alī, who was brought up as a brother to his four girl cousins, being about the same age as Ruqayyah and Umm Kulthūm, somewhat younger than Zaynab and somewhat older than Fāṭimah. These five, together with Zayd, formed the immediate family of Muḥammad and Khadījah. But there were many other relatives for whom he felt a deep attachment, and who have a part to play, large or small, in the history which here is chronicled.

Muḥammad's eldest uncle, Ḥārith, who was now dead, had left many children, and one of the sons, his cousin Abū Sufyān, was also his foster-brother, having been nursed by Ḥalīmah amongst the Bani Sa'd a few years after himself. People would say that Abū Sufyān was of those who bore the closest family likeness to Muḥammad; and amongst the characteristics they had in common was eloquence. But Abū Sufyān was a gifted poet – perhaps more gifted than his uncles Zubayr and Abū Ṭālib – whereas Muḥammad had never shown any inclination to compose a poem, though he was unsurpassed in his mastery of Arabic, and in the beauty of his speech.

In Abū Sufyān, who was more or less his own age, he had something of a friend and a companion. A little closer by blood kinship were the numer-

[1] I.S. I/1, 71.

ous children of his father's full sisters, that is, of 'Abd al-Muṭṭalib's five eldest daughters. Amongst the eldest of these cousins were the children of his aunt Umaymah who had married a man named Jahsh, of the North Arabian tribe of Asad.[1] He had a house in Mecca, and it was possible for a man who lived amongst a tribe other than his own to become, by mutual alliance, the confederate of a member of that tribe, into which he thus became partly integrated, sharing up to a point its responsibilities and its privileges. Ḥarb, now chief of the Umayyad[2] branch of the clan of 'Abdu Shams, had made Jaḥsh his confederate, so that by marrying him Umaymah could almost be said to have married a Shamsite. Their eldest son, named after her brother 'Abd Allāh, was some twelve years younger than Muḥammad, and the two cousins had a great affection for each other. Umaymah's daughter Zaynab, several years younger than her brother, a girl of outstanding beauty, was included in this bond. Muḥammad had known and loved them both from their earliest childhood; and the same was true of others, in particular of Abū Salamah, the son of his aunt Barrah.

The powerful attraction which centred on al-Amīn – as he was so often called – went far beyond his own family; and Khadījah was with him at that centre, loved and honoured by all who came within the wide circle of their radiance, a circle which also included many of her own relations. Particularly close to her was her sister Hālah whose son, Abū l-'Āṣ, was a frequent visitor to the house. Khadījah loved this nephew as if he had been her own son; and in due course – for she was continually sought after for help and advice – Hālah asked her to find a wife for him. When Khadījah consulted her husband, he suggested their daughter Zaynab, who would soon be of marriageable age; and when the time came they were married.

The hopes of Hāshim and Muṭṭalib – the two clans counted politically as one – were set upon Muḥammad for the recovery of their waning influence. But beyond all question of clan, he had come to be considered by the chiefs of Quraysh as one of the most capable men of the generation which would succeed them and which would have, after them, the task of maintaining the honour and the power of the tribe throughout Arabia. The praise of al-Amīn was continually upon men's lips; and it was perhaps because of this that Abū Lahab now came to his nephew with the proposal that Ruqayyah and Umm Kulthūm should be betrothed to his sons 'Utbah and 'Utaybah. Muḥammad agreed, for he thought well of these two cousins, and the betrothals took place.

It was about this time that Umm Ayman became once more a member of the household. It is not recorded whether she returned as a widow, or whether her husband had divorced her. But she had no doubt that her place was there, and for his part Muḥammad would sometimes address her as "mother", and would say of her to others: "She is all that is left me of the people of my house."[3]

[1] Asad ibn Khuzaymah, a tribe to the north-east of Mecca, whose territory lay at the northern extremity of the plain of Najd. It is not to be confused with the Quraysh clan of Asad.

[2] Named after Ḥarb's father Umayyah, son of 'Abdu Shams.

[3] I.S. VIII, 162.

# XIV

# *The Rebuilding of the Ka'bah*

SOMEWHAT before these last-mentioned happenings, about the time when 'Alī was taken into the household, when Muḥammad was thirty-five years old, Quraysh decided to rebuild the Ka'bah. As it then stood the walls were just above the height of a man, and there was no roof, which meant that even when the door was locked access was easy; and recently there had been a theft of some of its treasure which was stowed in a vault that had been dug inside the building for that purpose. They already had all the wood that was needed for the roof: the ship of a Greek merchant had been driven ashore and wrecked beyond repair at Jeddah, so they had taken its timbers to serve as rafters; and there happened to be in Mecca at that time a Copt who was a skilled carpenter.

But such was their awe of the Ka'bah that they hesitated to lay hands on it. Their plan was to demolish its walls which were built of loose stones and to rebuild it altogether; but they were afraid of incurring the guilt of sacrilege, and their hesitation was greatly increased by the appearance of a large snake which had taken to coming every day out of the vault to sun itself against a wall of the Ka'bah. If anyone approached, it would rear its head and hiss with gaping jaws, and they were terrified of it. But one day, while it was sunning itself, God sent against it an eagle, which seized it and flew away with it. So Quraysh said among themselves: "Now we may indeed hope that God is pleased with our intent. We have a craftsman whose heart is with us, and we have wood; and God hath rid us of the serpent."

The first man to lift a stone from the top of one of the walls was the Makhzūmite Abū Wahb, the brother of Fāṭimah, Muḥammad's grandmother; but no sooner had it been lifted than the stone leapt from his hand and returned to its place, whereupon they all drew back from the Ka'bah, afraid to proceed with the work. Then the chief of Makhzūm, Walīd the son of the now dead Mughīrah, took up a pickaxe and said: "I will begin the razing for you"; and going to the Ka'bah he said: "O God, fear not, O God, we intend nought but good." Thereupon he knocked down part of the wall between the Black Stone and the Yemenite Corner, that is, the south-easterly wall; but the rest of the people held back. "Let us wait and see," they said. "If he be smitten we will raze no more of it, but restore it even as it was; but if he be not smitten, then is God pleased with our work, and we will raze it all to the ground." The night passed without mishap and Walīd was again at work early next morning, so the others joined him; and when the walls were all down as far as the foundation of Abraham they came upon large greenish cobble-stones like the humps of camels placed side by side. A man put a crowbar between two of these stones to lever one of them out; but at the first movement of the stone a quaking shudder ran through the whole of Mecca, and they took it as a sign that they must leave that foundation undisturbed.

Inside the Corner of the Black Stone they had found a piece of writing in Syriac. They kept it, not knowing what it was, until one of the Jews read it to them: "I am God, the Lord of Becca. I created her the day I created the heavens and the earth, the day I formed the sun and the moon, and I placed round about her seven inviolable angels. She shall stand so long as her two hills stand, blessed for her people with milk and water." Another piece of writing was found beneath the Station of Abraham, a small rock near the door of the Ka'bah which bears the miraculous print of his foot: "Mecca is the holy house of God. Her sustenance cometh unto her from three directions. Let not her people be the first to profane her."

Quraysh now gathered more stones, in addition to those they already had, so as to increase the height of the building. They worked separately, clan by clan, until the walls were high enough for the Black Stone to be built once more into its corner. Then a violent disagreement broke out amongst them, for each clan wanted the honour of lifting it into its place. The deadlock lasted for four or five days and the tension had increased to the point of alliances being made and preparations for battle begun, when the oldest man present proposed a solution. "O men of Quraysh," he said, "take as arbiter between you, about that wherein ye differ, the first man who shall enter in through the gate of this Mosque."[1] The precinct round the Ka'bah was called a mosque, in Arabic *masjid*, a place of prostration, because the rite of prostrating oneself to God in the direction of the Holy House had been performed there since the time of Abraham and Ishmael. They agreed to follow the old man's counsel; and the first man to enter the Mosque was Muḥammad, who had just returned to Mecca after an absence. The sight of him produced an immediate and spontaneous recognition that here was the right person for the task, and his arrival was greeted by exclamations and murmurs of satisfaction. "It is al-Amīn," said some. "We accept his judgement," said others, "it is Muḥammad." When they explained the matter to him, he said: "Bring me a cloak." And when they brought it, he spread it on the ground, and taking up the Black Stone he laid it on the middle of the garment. "Let each clan take hold of the border of the cloak," he said. "Then lift it up, all of you together." And when they had raised it to the right height he took the stone and placed it in the corner with his own hands; and the building was continued and completed above it.

[1] I.I. 125.

# XV
# *The First Revelations*

IT was not long after this outward sign of his authority and his mission that he began to experience powerful inward signs, in addition to those of which he had already been conscious. When asked about these he spoke of "true visions" which came to him in his sleep and he said that they were "like the breaking of the light of dawn."[1] The immediate result of these visions was that solitude became dear to him, and he would go for spiritual retreats to a cave in Mount Ḥirā' not far from the outskirts of Mecca. There was nothing in this that would have struck Quraysh as particularly strange, for retreat had been a traditional practice amongst the descendants of Ishmael, and in each generation there had been one or two who would withdraw to a solitary place from time to time so that they might have a period that was uncontaminated by the world of men. In accordance with this age-old practice, Muḥammad would take with him provisions and consecrate a certain number of nights to the worship of God. Then he would return to his family, and sometimes on his return he took more provisions and went again to the mountain. During these few years it often happened that after he had left the town and was approaching his hermitage he would hear clearly the words "Peace be on thee, O Messenger of God",[2] and he would turn and look for the speaker but no one was in sight, and it was as if the words had come from a tree or a stone.

Ramadan was the traditional month of retreat, and it was one night towards the end of Ramadan, in his fortieth year, when he was alone in the cave, that there came to him an Angel in the form of a man. The Angel said to him: "Recite!" and he said: "I am not a reciter," whereupon, as he himself told it, "the Angel took me and whelmed me in his embrace until he had reached the limit of mine endurance. Then he released me and said: 'Recite!' I said: 'I am not a reciter,' and again he took me and whelmed me in his embrace, and again when he had reached the limit of mine endurance he released me and said: 'Recite!', and again I said 'I am not a reciter.' Then a third time he whelmed me as before, then released me and said:

[1] B. I, 3. [2] I.I. 151.

*Recite in the name of thy Lord who created!*
*He createth man from a clot of blood.*
*Recite; and thy Lord is the Most Bountiful,*
*He who hath taught by the pen,*
*taught man what he knew not.*[1]"[2]

He recited these words after the Angel, who thereupon left him; and he said; "It was as though the words were written on my heart."[3] But he feared that this might mean he had become a jinn-inspired poet or a man possessed. So he fled from the cave, and when he was half-way down the slope of the mountain he heard a voice above him saying: "O Muḥammad, thou art the Messenger of God, and I am Gabriel." He raised his eyes heavenwards and there was his visitant, still recognisable but now clearly an Angel, filling the whole horizon, and again he said: "O Muḥammad, thou art the Messenger of God, and I am Gabriel." The Prophet stood gazing at the Angel; then he turned away from him, but whichever way he looked the Angel was always there, astride the horizon, whether it was to the north, to the south, to the east or to the west. Finally the Angel turned away, and the Prophet descended the slope and went to his house. "Cover me! Cover me!"[4] he said to Khadījah as with still quaking heart he laid himself on his couch. Alarmed, yet not daring to question him, she quickly brought a cloak and spread it over him. But when the intensity of his awe had abated he told her what he had seen and heard; and having spoken to him words of reassurance she went to tell her cousin Waraqah, who was now an old man, and blind. "Holy! Holy!", he said. "By Him in whose hand is the soul of Waraqah, there hath come unto Muḥammad the greatest Nāmūs,[5] even he that would come unto Moses. Verily Muḥammad is the Prophet of this people. Bid him rest assured." So Khadījah went home and repeated these words to the Prophet, who now returned in peace of mind to the cave, that he might fulfil the number of days he had dedicated to God for his retreat. When this was completed, he went straight to the Ka'bah, according to his wont, and performed the rite of the rounds, after which he greeted the old and the blind Waraqah whom he had noticed amongst those who were sitting in the Mosque; and Waraqah said to him: "Tell me, O son of my brother, what thou hast seen and heard." The Prophet told him, and the old man said again what he had said to Khadījah. But this time he added: "Thou wilt be called a liar, and ill-treated, and they will cast thee out and make war upon thee; and if I live to see that day, God knoweth I will help His cause."[6] Then he leaned towards him and kissed his forehead, and the Prophet returned to his home.

The reassurances of Khadījah and Waraqah were followed by a reassurance from Heaven in the form of a second Revelation. The manner of its coming is not recorded, but when asked how Revelation came to him the Prophet mentioned two ways: "Sometimes it cometh unto me like the

[1] K. XCVI, 1–5. [2] B. I, 3. [3] I.I. 153. [4] B. I, 3.
[5] The Greek *Nomos*, in the sense of Divine Law or Scripture, here identified with the Angel of Revelation.
[6] I.I. 153–4.

reverberations of a bell, and that is the hardest upon me; the reverberations abate when I am aware of their message. And sometimes the Angel taketh the form of a man and speaketh unto me, and I am aware of what he saith."[1]

The Revelation, this second time, began with a single letter, the earliest instance of those cryptic letters with which several of the Koranic messages begin. The letter was followed by a Divine oath, sworn *by the pen* which had already been mentioned in the first Revelation as the primary means of God's teaching men His wisdom. When questioned about the pen, the Prophet said: "The first thing God created was the pen. He created the tablet and said to the pen: "Write!" And the pen answered: "What shall I write?" He said: "Write My knowledge of My creation till the day of resurrection." Then the pen traced what had been ordained."[2] The oath *by the pen* is followed by a second oath, *by that which they write*; and amongst what they, that is the Angels, write in Heaven with lesser pens on lesser tablets is the Koran's celestial archetype, which subsequent Revelations refer to as *a glorious recitation (qur'ān)*[3] *on an inviolable tablet*[4] and as *the mother of the book*.[5] The two oaths are followed by the Divine reassurance:

> *Nūn. By the pen, and by that which they write, no madman art thou, through the grace of thy Lord unto thee, and thine shall be a meed unfailing, and verily of an immense magnitude is thy nature.*[6]

After the first Messages had come there was a period of silence, until the Prophet began to fear that he had incurred in some way the displeasure of Heaven, though Khadījah continually told him that this was not possible. Then at last the silence was broken, and there came a further reassurance, and with it the first command directly related to his mission:

> *By the morning brightness, and by the night when it is still, thy Lord hath not forsaken thee nor doth He hate thee, and the last shall be better for thee than the first, and thy Lord shall give and give unto thee, and thou shalt be satisfied. Hath He not found thee an orphan and sheltered thee, and found thee astray and guided thee, and found thee needy and enriched thee? So for the orphan, oppress him not, and for the beggar, repel him not, and for the bountiful grace of thy Lord, proclaim it!*[7]

[1] B. I, 3. [2] Tir. 44.
[3] It is from this that the Divine Revelation on which Islam is based takes its name.
[4] LXXXV, 21–2. [5] XIII, 39. [6] LXVIII, 1–4. [7] XCIII.

# XVI
# *Worship*

IN accordance with these last two words he now began to speak about the Angel and the Revelations to those who, after his wife, were the nearest and dearest to him. As yet he had no demands to make upon them, except that they should not divulge his secret. But this situation did not last long: Gabriel came to him one day on the high ground above Mecca, and struck with his heel the turf of the hillside, whereupon a spring gushed forth from it. Then he performed the ritual ablution to show the Prophet how to purify himself for worship, and the Prophet followed his example. Then he showed him the postures and movements of the prayer, the standing, the inclining, the prostrating and the sitting, with the repeated magnification, that is, the words *Allāhu Akbar*, *God is Most Great*, and the final greeting *as-Salāmu 'alaykum*, *Peace be on you*, and again the Prophet followed his example. Then the Angel left him, and the Prophet returned to his house, and taught Khadījah all that he had learnt, and they prayed together.

The religion was now established on the basis of the ritual purification and prayer; and after Khadījah the first to embrace it were 'Alī and Zayd and the Prophet's friend Abū Bakr of the clan of Taym. 'Alī was only ten years old, and Zayd had as yet no influence in Mecca, but Abū Bakr was liked and respected, for he was a man of wide knowledge, easy manners and an agreeable presence. Many would come to consult him about this or that, and he now began to confide in all those whom he felt he could trust, urging them to follow the Prophet. Many responses took place through him; and two of the earliest to respond to the call were a man of Zuhrah, 'Abdu 'Amr, the son of 'Awf, a distant kinsman of the Prophet's mother, and Abū 'Ubaydah the son of al-Jarrāḥ of the Bani l-Ḥārith.[1]

In connection with the first of these, 'Abdu 'Amr, a precedent of importance was established. Amongst the most striking features of the Revelation were the two Divine Names *ar-Raḥmān* and *ar-Raḥīm*. The word *raḥīm*, an intensive form of *rāḥim*, merciful, was current in the sense of very merciful or boundlessly merciful. The still more intensive *raḥmān*, for lack of any concept to fit it, had fallen into disuse. The Revelation revived it in accordance with the new religion's basic need to dwell on the heights of Transcendence. Being stronger even than *ar-Raḥīm* (the All-Merciful), the Name *ar-Raḥmān* refers to the very essence or root of Mercy, that is, to the Infinite Beneficence or Goodness of God, and the

[1] See genealogical tree, p. 347.

Koran expressly makes it an equivalent of *Allāh: Invoke God (Allāh) or invoke the Infinitely Good (ar-Raḥmān), whichever ye invoke, His are the names most Beautiful.*[1] This Name of Goodness was very dear to the Prophet, and since the name 'Abdu 'Amr, the slave of 'Amr, was too pagan, he changed the new believer's name to 'Abd ar-Raḥmān, the slave of the Infinitely Good. Nor was the son of 'Awf the only man whose name he changed to 'Abd ar-Raḥmān.

Some of the earliest responses were promoted initially by motives which could not be ascribed to any human attempt to persuade. Abū Bakr had long been known throughout Mecca for his ability to interpret dreams; and one morning he had an unexpected visit from Khālid, the son of a powerful Shamsite, Sa'id ibn al-'Āṣ. The young man's face still showed signs of having been recently aghast at some terrifying experience; and he hastened to explain that during the night he had had a dream which he knew must be significant though what it meant he did not understand. Could Abū Bakr tell him the meaning of it? He had dreamed that he was standing at the edge of a great pit in which was a raging fire so vast that he could see no end to it. Then his father came, and tried to push him into it; and as they were struggling on the brink, at the moment of his greatest terror, he felt round his waist the firm clasp of two hands which held him back despite all his father's efforts. Looking round, he saw that his saviour was al-Amīn, Muḥammad the son of 'Abd Allāh, and at that moment he awoke. "I wish thee joy," said Abū Bakr. "This man who saved thee is the Messenger of God, so follow him – nay, follow him thou shalt, and shalt enter through him into Islam which shall safeguard thee against falling into the fire." Khālid went straight to the Prophet, and having told him of his dream he asked him what his message was, and what he should do. The Prophet instructed him, and Khālid entered Islam, keeping it a secret from his family.[2]

It was about the same time that another man of 'Abdu Shams, a merchant on his way home from Syria, was awoken one night by a voice crying in the desert: "Sleepers, awake, for verily Aḥmad hath come forth in Mecca."[3] The merchant was 'Uthmān, son of the Umayyad 'Affān, and grandson, through his mother, of one of 'Abd al-Muṭṭalib's daughters, Umm Ḥakīm al-Bayḍā', the Prophet's aunt. The words sank into his heart, though he did not understand what was meant by "coming forth", nor did he recognise that the superlative Aḥmad "most glorified" stood for Muḥammad, "glorified". But before reaching Mecca he was overtaken by a man of Taym named Ṭalḥah, a cousin of Abū Bakr; and Ṭalḥah had passed through Bostra, where he had been asked by a monk if Aḥmad had yet appeared amongst the people of the Sanctuary. "Who is Ahmad?" said Ṭalḥah. "The son of 'Abd al-Muṭṭalib's son 'Abd Allāh," answered the monk. "This is his month, in which he shall come forth; and he is the last of the Prophets." Ṭalḥah repeated these words to 'Uthmān, who told him of his own experience, and on their return Ṭalḥah suggested that they should

[1] XVII, 110. In what follows, the Names of Mercy will sometimes be rendered "the Good, the Merciful" for sake of having a single word as in Arabic, and relying on the definite article to denote the Absolute. The same practice is also followed with other Divine Names.

[2] I.S. IV/1, 68. [3] I.S. III/1, 37.

go to his cousin Abū Bakr, who was known to be the closest friend of the man now uppermost in their minds. So they went to Abū Bakr, and when they told him what they had heard he took them at once to the Prophet so that they could repeat to him the words of the monk and the words of the desert voice. Having done this, they made their professions of faith.

A fourth conversion, no less remarkable than these in the way it took place, was that of ʻAbd Allāh ibn Masʻūd, a young confederate of Zuhrah. Telling of it himself, he said: "I was at that time a youth just grown into manhood, and I was pasturing the flocks of ʻUqbah ibn Abī Muʻayt, when one day the Prophet and Abū Bakr passed by. The Prophet asked me if I had any milk to give them to drink. I replied that the flocks were not mine but entrusted to my care and I could not give them to drink. The Prophet said: 'Hast thou a young ewe that no ram hath ever leaped?' I said I had, and brought her to them. Having tethered her, the Prophet put his hand to her udder and prayed, whereupon the udder swelled with milk, and Abū Bakr brought a boulder which was hollowed like a cup. The Prophet milked her into it, and we all drank. Then he said to the udder: 'Dry,' and it dried."[1] A few days later ʻAbd Allāh went to the Prophet and entered Islam. Nor was it long before he had learned from him seventy sūrahs[2] by heart, being exceptionally gifted in that way; and he soon became one of the best and most authoritative reciters of the Koran.

The Prophet had been distressed by the period of silence from Heaven; yet his soul still shrank from receiving the tremendous impact of the Divine Word, which itself affirmed in a not yet revealed verse: *If We sent down this Koran upon a mountain, thou wouldst see it prostrate in humility, rent asunder through fear of God.*[3] The impulse which had prompted him to cry out "cover me, cover me" still came to him at times; and one night when he was lying wrapped in his cloak there broke in upon his seclusion a Divine Command more stern and urgent than any he had yet received, bidding him warn men of the Day of Judgement: *O thou who art wrapped in thy cloak, arise and warn! Thy Lord magnify! Thy raiment purify! Defilement shun! . . . For when the trumpet shall be blown, that shall be a day of anguish, not of ease, for disbelievers.*[4] Another night soon after this, he was aroused by further commands telling him of the intensity of worship expected from him and his followers, and fully confirming his apprehensions of a great burden of responsibility that was to be laid upon him: *O thou who art wrapped in thy raiment, keep vigil all the night save a little, half the night or lessen than half a little, or add to it, and with care and clarity chant the Koran. Verily We shall load thee with a word of heavy weight.*[5] In the same passage was also the command: *And invoke in remembrance the name of thy Lord, and devote thyself unto Him with an utter devotion. Lord of the east and of the west – no god but He. Him*

[1] I.S. III/1, 107.

[2] The Koran consists of 114 sūrahs, of unequal length. The longest sūrah has 285 verses, the shortest only three.

[3] LIX, 21. The sudden change from first to third person *We . . . God*, is frequent in the Koran.

[4] LXXIV, 1–10. [5] LXXIII, 1–5.

*therefore take, on Him place thy reliance!*[1] There came also other Revelations, more gentle in tone, which confirmed and increased the reassurances already given to the Prophet; and on one occasion, visible to him alone, as was normally the case, the Angel said to him: "Give unto Khadījah greetings of Peace from her Lord." So he said to her: "O Khadījah, here is Gabriel who greeteth thee with Peace from thy Lord." And when Khadījah could find words to speak, she answered; "God is Peace, and from Him is Peace, and on Gabriel be Peace!"[2]

The first adherents of the new religion took the commands addressed to the Prophet as applying to themselves, so like him they would keep long vigils. As to the ritual prayer, they were now careful not only to perform the ablution in preparation for it but also to make sure that their garments were free from all defilement; and they were quick to learn by heart all that had been revealed of the Koran, so that they might chant it as part of their worship. The Revelations now began to come more copiously. They were immediately transmitted by the Prophet to those who were with him, then passed from mouth to mouth, memorised and recited – a long and rapidly increasing litany which told of the ephemeral nature of all earthly things, of death and of the certainty of the Resurrection and the Last Judgement, followed by Hell or Paradise. But above all it told of the Glory of God, of His Indivisible Oneness, his Truth, Wisdom, Goodness, Mercy, Bounty and Power; and by extension it continually referred to His Signs, the marvels of nature, and to their harmonious working together which testified so eloquently to the Oneness of their Sole Originator. Harmony is the imprint of Oneness upon multiplicity, and the Koran draws attention to that harmony as a theme for man's meditation.

When uninhibited by the presence of hostile disbelievers, the believers greeted each other with the words given to the Prophet by Gabriel as the greeting of the people of Paradise, "Peace be on you!", to which the answer is "And on you be Peace!", the plural being used to include the two guardian Angels of the person greeted. The revealed verses of consecration and of thanksgiving also played an increasingly significant part in their lives and their outlook. The Koran insists on the need for gratitude, and the sacrament of thanksgiving is to say *Praise be to God the Lord of the worlds*, whereas that of consecration or dedication is to say *In the Name of God, the Infinitely Good, the All-Merciful.* This was the first verse of every *sūrah*[3] of the Koran, and following the example of the Prophet they used it to inaugurate every Koranic recital, and by extension every other rite, and by further extension every act or initiative. The new religion admitted of nothing profane.

[1] LXXIII, 8–9. [2] I.H. 156.

[3] Only one *sūrah*, IX (see p. 323) begins without the mention of the Names of Mercy, but that had not yet been revealed.

# XVII

# "Warn Thy Family"

NO summons to Islam had yet been made in public, but there was an ever-increasing group of devout believers and intense worshippers, both men and women, most of them young. Amongst the first to come, apart from those already mentioned, were the Prophet's cousins Ja'far and Zubayr; then came other cousins, his and theirs, the sons of their aunt Umaymah, 'Abd Allāh ibn Jahsh and his brother 'Ubayd Allāh, and the son of their aunt Barrah, Abū Salamah. There were also two cousins on his mother's side, Sa'd the son of Abu Waqqāṣ of Zuhrah and his younger brother 'Umayr. But not one of the Prophet's four uncles showed any inclination to follow him: Abū Ṭālib made no objection to the Islam of his two sons Ja'far and 'Alī, but for himself he said he was not prepared to forsake the religion of his forefathers; 'Abbās was evasive and Ḥamzah uncomprehending, though both assured him of their unfailing affection for him personally; but Abū Lahab showed plainly his conviction that his nephew was self-deceived, if not a deceiver.

After the revelation of the verse *Warn thy family who are thy nearest of kin*[1] the Prophet called 'Alī to him, and said: "God hath commanded me to warn my family, my nearest of kin, and the task is beyond my strength. But make ready food, with a leg of mutton, and fill a cup with milk, and assemble together the Bani 'Abd al-Muṭṭalib, that I may tell them that which I have been commanded to say." 'Alī did exactly as he had been told, neither more nor less, and most of the clan of Hāshim came to the meal, about forty men. "When they were assembled," said 'Alī, "the Prophet told me to bring in the food which I had made ready. Then he took a piece of meat, bit upon it, and cast it again into the dish, saying: 'Take it in the Name of God.' The men ate in relays, several at a time, until not one of them could eat any more. But," said 'Alī, "I could see no change in the food, except that it had been stirred by men's hands; and by my life, if they had been but one man, he could have eaten all that I had put before them. Then the Prophet said: 'Give them to drink', so I brought the cup, and each drank his fill, though one man alone could have emptied that cup. But when the Prophet was about to address them, Abū Lahab forestalled him and said: 'Your host hath placed a spell upon you' whereat they dispersed before he could speak."

The next day the Prophet told 'Alī to do exactly as he had done the previous day. So another similar meal was prepared and everything went as before, except that this time the Prophet was on his guard and made sure

[1] XXVI, 214.

of addressing them. "O sons of 'Abd al-Muṭṭalib," he said, "I know of no Arab who hath come to his people with a nobler message than mine. I bring you the best of this world and the next. God hath commanded me to call you unto Him. Which of you, then, will help me in this, and be my brother, mine executor and my successor amongst you?" There was silence throughout the clan. Ja'far and Zayd could both have spoken, but they knew that their Islam was not in question and that the purpose of the gathering was to bring in others than themselves. But when the silence remained unbroken, the thirteen-year-old 'Alī felt impelled to speak, and said: "O Prophet of God, I will be thy helper in this." The Prophet laid his hand on the back of 'Alī's neck and said: "This is my brother, mine executor and my successor amongst you. Hearken unto him, and obey him." The men rose to their feet, laughing and saying to Abū Ṭālib: "He hath ordered thee to hearken unto thy son and to obey him."[1]

As to the Prophet's aunts, Ṣafiyyah had no hesitation in following him as her son Zubayr had done, but her five sisters could not bring themselves to make any decision. Arwà's attitude was typical of them all: "I am waiting to see what my sisters will do," she would say. On the other hand, his aunt by marriage, Umm al-Faḍl, the wife of the hesitant 'Abbas, was the first woman to enter Islam after Khadījah; and she was soon able to bring three of her sisters to the Prophet – Maymūnah, her full sister, and two half-sisters, Salmà and Asmā'. It was in the household of Umm al-Faḍl that Ja'far had been brought up, and it was there that he had come to know and to love Asmā', whom he had recently married; and Ḥamzah had married her sister Salmà. Another of the first to respond was Umm Ayman. The Prophet said of her: "He that would marry a woman of the people of Paradise, let him marry Umm Ayman"[2] and this remark was overheard by Zayd, who took it deeply to heart. She was much older than he was, but that did not deter him, and he spoke his mind to the Prophet, who had no difficulty in persuading Umm Ayman to agree to the marriage. She bore Zayd a son whom they named Usāmah, and he was brought up as the grandson of the Prophet, who dearly loved him.

[1] Ṭab. 1171. [2] I.S. VIII, 162.

# XVIII

# *Quraysh Take Action*

IN these early days of Islam the Companions of the Prophet would often go out together in groups to the glens outside Mecca where they could pray the ritual prayer together without being seen. But one day a number of idolaters came upon them while they were praying and rudely interrupted them with ridicule. Finally they came to blows, and Sa'd of Zuhrah struck one of the disbelievers with the jawbone of a camel and wounded him. This was the first blood shed in Islam. But after that they decided to refrain from violence until God should decide otherwise, for the Revelation continually enjoined patience upon the Prophet and therefore upon them. *Bear with patience what they say, and part from them with a courteous farewell,*[1] and also *Deal gently with the disbelievers, give them respite for a while.*[2]

This case of violence had been something of an exception on both sides, for Quraysh as a whole were disposed to tolerate the new religion, even after the Prophet had openly proclaimed it, until they saw that it was directed against their gods, their principles and their inveterate practices. Once they had realised this, however, some of their leading men went in a body to Abū Ṭālib, to insist that he should restrain his nephew's activities. He put them off with a conciliatory answer; but when they saw that he had done nothing they came to him again and said: "O Abū Ṭālib, thine is a high and honourable position amongst us, and we have asked thee to hold in check thy brother's son, but thou hast not done so. By God, we will not suffer our fathers to be insulted, our ways scoffed at, and our gods reviled. Either make him desist, or we will fight you both." Then they left him, and in great distress he sent for his nephew, and having told him what they had threatened, he said: "O son of my brother, spare me and spare thyself. Lay not upon me a burden greater than I can bear." But the Prophet answered him saying: "I swear by God, if they put the sun in my right hand and the moon in my left on condition that I abandon this course before He hath made it victorious, or I have perished therein, I would not abandon it."[3] Then, with tears in his eyes, he rose to his feet and turned to go, but his uncle called him back: "Son of my brother," he said, "go thou and say what thou wilt, for by God I will never forsake thee on any account."

[1] LXXIII, 10. [2] LXXXVI, 17. [3] I.I. 168.

When they found that their words had achieved nothing with Abū Ṭālib, Quraysh still hesitated to attack his nephew directly, for, as a chief of clan, Abū Ṭālib had power to grant inviolate protection, and it was in the interests of every other chief of clan in Mecca to see that the rights of chieftaincy were duly respected. So they confined themselves for the moment to organising a widespread persecution of all those adherents of the new religion who had no one to protect them.

Meantime they consulted together in an attempt to form a common policy about the cause of their trouble. The situation was exceedingly grave: the time of the Pilgrimage would soon be upon them and Arabs would come to Mecca from all over Arabia. They, Quraysh, had a high reputation for hospitality, not only as regards food and drink but also because they made every man welcome, both him and his gods. But this year pilgrims would hear their gods insulted by Muḥammad and his followers, and they would be urged to forsake the religion of their forefathers and to adopt a new religion which appeared to have numerous disadvantages. No doubt many of them would not come to Mecca again, which would not only be bad for trade but would also diminish the honour in which the guardians of the Sanctuary were now held. At the worst, the Arabs might league together to drive them out of Mecca and to establish another tribe or group of tribes in their place – as they themselves had previously done with Khuzā'ah, and as Khuzā'ah had done with Jurhum. It was therefore imperative that the visiting Arabs should be told that Muḥammad in no way represented Quraysh. But although it was easy to deny his prophethood, that was merely to express an opinion and indirectly to invite others to listen to his claims and judge for themselves. Something else needed to be said in addition; and here lay their weakness, for some had taken to saying that he was a soothsayer, others that he was possessed, others that he was a poet, yet others that he was a sorcerer. They consulted Walīd the son of Mughīrah, probably the most influential man of the tribe at that time, as to which of these accusations would be best likely to convince, and he rejected them all as wide of the mark; but on second thoughts he decided that although the man in question was certainly not a sorcerer, he had at least one thing in common with sorcerers: he had the power to separate a man from his father or from his brother or from his wife or from his family in general. He advised them therefore to let their unanimous accusation be along those lines, namely that Muḥammad was a dangerous sorcerer, to be avoided at all costs. Having readily agreed to follow his advice, they decided that outside the town all the roads by which Mecca was approached must be manned, and that visitors must be warned in advance to be on their guard against Muḥammad, for they knew from their own experience how winning he could be. Had he not been, before he began preaching, one of the best loved men in Mecca? Nor had his tongue lost any of its eloquence, nor his presence anything of its compelling majesty.

They carried out their plans with zeal and thoroughness. In at least one particular case, however, they were doomed to failure from the outset. A man of the Bani Ghifār named Abū Dharr – his tribe lived to the north-west of Mecca, not far from the Red Sea – had already heard of the

Prophet and of the opposition to him. Like most of his tribesmen, Abū Dharr was a highwayman; but unlike them he was a firm believer in the Oneness of God, and he refused to pay any respect to idols. His brother Unays went to Mecca for some reason, and on his return he told Abū Dharr that there was a man of Quraysh who claimed to be a Prophet and who said *there is no god but God*, and his people had disowned him in consequence. Abū Dharr immediately set off for Mecca, in the certainty that here was a true Prophet, and on his arrival those of the Quraysh who manned the approaches told him all he wished to know before he had time to ask. Without difficulty he found his way to the Prophet's house. The Prophet was lying asleep on a bench in the courtyard, with his face covered by a fold of his cloak. Abū Dharr woke him and wished him good morning. "On thee be Peace!" said the Prophet. "Declaim unto me thine utterances," said the Bedouin. "I am no poet," said the Prophet, "but what I utter is the Koran, and it is not I who speak but God who speaketh." "Recite for me," said Abū Dharr, and he recited to him a *sūrah*, whereupon Abū Dharr said: "I testify that there is no god but God, and that Muḥammad is the messenger of God." "Who are thy people?" said the Prophet, and at the man's answer he looked him up and down in amazement and said: "Verily God guideth whom He will."[1] It was well known that the Bani Ghifār were mostly robbers. Having instructed him in Islam the Prophet told him to return to his people and await his orders. So he returned to the Bani Ghifār, many of whom entered Islam through him. Meantime he continued his calling as highwayman, with special attention to the caravans of Quraysh. But when he had despoiled a caravan he would offer to give back what he had taken on condition that they would testify to the Oneness of God and the prophethood of Muḥammad.

Another encounter with the Prophet had the result of bringing Islam to the Bani Daws, who were also, like Ghifār, an outlying western tribe. Ṭufayl, a man of Daws, told afterwards how he had been warned on his arrival in Mecca against speaking to the sorcerer Muḥammad or even listening to him lest he should find himself separated from his people. Ṭufayl was a poet and a man of considerable standing in his tribe. Quraysh were therefore especially insistent in their warning, and they made him so afraid of being bewitched that before going into the Mosque he stuffed his ears with cotton wool. The Prophet was there, having just taken up his stance for prayer between the Yemeni Corner and the Black Stone as was his wont, facing towards Jerusalem, with the south-east wall of the Ka'bah immediately in front of him. His recitation of Koranic verses was not very loud, but some of it none the less penetrated Ṭufayl's ears. "God would not have it", he said, "but that He should make me hear something of what was recited, and I heard beautiful words. So I said to myself: I am a man of insight, a poet, and not ignorant of the difference between the fair and the foul. Why then should I not hear what this man is saying? If it be fair I will accept it, and if foul, reject it. I stayed until the Prophet went away, whereupon I followed him and when he entered his house I entered it upon his heels and said: 'O Muḥammad thy people told me this and that and

[1] I.S. IV, 164.

they so frightened me about thy state that I stuffed mine ears lest I should hear thy speech. But God would not have it but that He should make me hear thee. So tell me thou the truth of what thou art.'"

The Prophet explained Islam to him and recited the Koran, and Ṭufayl made his profession of faith. Then he returned to his people, determined to convert them. His father and his wife followed him into Islam, but the rest of Daws held back, and he returned to Mecca in great disappointment and anger, demanding that the Prophet should put a curse on them. But instead the Prophet prayed for their guidance and said to Ṭufayl: "Return to thy people, call them to Islam, and deal gently with them."[1] These instructions he faithfully followed, and as the years passed more and more families of Daws were converted.

Before meeting the Prophet, Ṭufayl had only met his enemies; but other pilgrims met also his followers who told them a story very different from what the enemies told them, and each believed what his nature prompted him to believe. As a result the new religion was spoken of, well or ill, throughout all Arabia; but nowhere was it more a theme of talk than in the oasis of Yathrib.

1 I.I. 252–4.

# XIX

# *Aws and Khazraj*

THE tribes of Aws and Khazraj had alliances with some of the Jewish tribes who lived beside them in Yathrib. But relations between them were often strained and fraught with ill feeling, not least because the monotheistic Jews, conscious of being God's chosen people, despised the polytheistic Arabs, while having to pay them a certain respect because of their greater strength. In moments of acrimony and frustration, the Jews had been known to say: "The time of a Prophet who is to be sent is now at hand, with him we shall slay you, even as 'Ād and Iram[1] were slain." And their rabbis and soothsayers, when asked whence the Prophet would come, had always pointed in the direction of the Yemen which was also, for them, the direction of Mecca. So when the Yathrib Arabs heard that a man in Mecca had now in fact declared himself to be a Prophet, they opened their ears; and they were still more interested when they were told something about his message, for they were already familiar with many of the principles of orthodox religion. In more friendly moments, the Jews often spoke to them of the Oneness of God, and of man's final ends, and they would discuss these questions together. The idea that they would rise from the dead was especially difficult for the polytheists to accept; and noticing this, one of the rabbis pointed to the south and said that thence a Prophet was about to come who would affirm the truth of the Resurrection.

But their deepest preparation for the news from Mecca had come, indirectly, from a Jew named Ibn al-Hayyabān who had migrated from Syria, and who on more than one occasion had saved the oasis from drought through his prayers for rain. This saintly man had died about the time that the Prophet had received his first Revelation; and when he had felt himself at the point of death – as Aws and Khazraj were subsequently told – he had said to those about him: "O Jews, what was it, think ye, that made me leave a land of bread and wine for a land of hardship and hunger?" "Thou best knowest," they said. "I came to this country," he answered, "in expectation of the coming forth of a Prophet whose time is near. To this country he will migrate. I had hopes that he would be sent in time for me to follow him. His hour is close upon you."[2] These words were taken greatly to heart by some Jewish youths who heard them and who were enabled by them, when the time came, to accept the Prophet even though he was not a Jew.

[1] Ancient Arab tribes, suddenly destroyed for their refusal to obey the Prophets who were sent to them.

[2] I.I. 136.

But generally speaking, whereas the Arabs were in favour of the man but against the message, the Jews were in favour of the message but against the man. For how could God send a Prophet who was not one of the chosen people? None the less, when the pilgrims brought news of the Prophet to Yathrib, the Jews were interested despite themselves and eagerly questioned them for more details; and when the Arabs of the oasis sensed this eagerness, and when they saw how the monotheistic nature of the message increased the interest of the rabbis tenfold, they could not fail to be impressed, as were the bearers of the tidings themselves.

Apart from such considerations, the tribe of Khazraj was fully aware of its strong links of kinship with the very man who now claimed to be a Prophet, and who had visited Yathrib with his mother as a child, and since then, more than once, on his way to Syria. As to Aws, one of their leading men, Abū Qays, had married a Meccan who was the aunt of Waraqah and also of Khadījah. Abū Qays had often stayed with his wife's family, and he respected Waraqah's opinion of the new Prophet.

All these factors, supplemented by continuous reports of pilgrims and other visitors from Mecca, now began to work upon the people of the oasis. But for the moment most of their attention was centred upon the urgent problems of their own internal affairs. A quarrel ending in bloodshed between an Awsite and a Khazrajite had gradually involved more and more clans of the two tribes. Even the Jews had taken sides. Three battles had already been fought, but instead of being decisive these had inflamed the souls of men still further, and multiplied the needs for revenge. A fourth battle on a larger scale than the others seemed inevitable; and it was in view of this that the leaders of Aws had the idea of sending a delegation to Mecca to ask Quraysh for their help against Khazraj.

While they were waiting for an answer, the Prophet went to them and asked them if they would like something better than what they had come for. They asked what that might be, and he told them of his mission and of the religion he had been commanded to preach. Then he recited to them some of the Koran, and when he had finished a young man named Iyās, son of Mu'ādh, exclaimed: "People, by God this is better than that ye came for!" But the leader of the delegation took a handful of earth and threw it in the youth's face, saying: "Let that be all from thee! By my life, we have come for other than this." Iyās relapsed into silence, and the Prophet left them. Quraysh refused their request for help, and they returned to Medina. Shortly after this Iyās died, and those who were present at his death said that they heard him continually testifying to the Oneness of God and magnifying, praising and glorifying Him until the end. He is thus counted as the first man of Yathrib to enter Islam.

# XX

# *Abū Jahl and Ḥamzah*

IN Mecca the steady increase in the number of believers brought with it a corresponding increase in the hostility of the disbelievers; and one day when some of the chief men of Quraysh were gathered together in the Ḥijr, bitterly stirring up each others' anger against the Prophet, it so happened that the Prophet himself entered the Sanctuary. Going to the east corner of the Ka'bah, he kissed the Black Stone and began to make the seven rounds. As he passed the Ḥijr they raised their voices in slanderous calumny against him, and it was clear from his face that he had heard what they said. He passed them again on his second round, and again they slandered him. But when they did the same as he was passing them the third time he stopped and said: 'O Quraysh, will ye hear me? Verily by Him who holdeth my soul in His Hand, I bring you slaughter!"[1] This word and the way he said it seemed to bind them as by a spell. Not one of them moved or spoke, until the silence was finally broken by one of those who had been most violent, saying in all gentleness: 'Go thy way, O Abu l-Qāsim, for by God thou art not an ignorant fool." But the respite did not last long, for they soon began to blame themselves for having been so unaccountably overawed, and they vowed that in the future they would make amends for this momentary weakness.

One of the worst enemies of Islam was a man of Makhzūm named 'Amr and known to his family and friends as Abu l-Ḥakam, which the Muslims were not slow to change into Abū Jahl, "the father of ignorance". He was a grandson of Mughīrah and nephew of the now elderly Walīd who was chief of the clan. Abū Jahl felt sure of succeeding his uncle, and he had already established for himself a certain position in Mecca through his wealth and his ostentatious hospitality, and partly also through making himself feared on account of his ruthlessness and his readiness to take revenge on anyone who opposed him. He had been the most indefatigable of all those men who had manned the approaches to Mecca during the recent Pilgrimage, and the most vociferous in his denunciation of the Prophet as a dangerous sorcerer. He was also the most active in persecuting the more helpless believers of his own clan, and in urging other clans to

[1] I.I. 183.

do the same. But one day, despite himself, he indirectly did the new religion a great service.

The Prophet was sitting outside the Mosque near the Ṣafā Gate, so named because the pilgrims go out through it to perform the rite of passing seven times between the hill of Ṣafā which is near the gate and the hill of Marwah some 450 yards to the north. A rock near the foot of Ṣafā marks the starting point of the ancient rite, and the Prophet was alone at this hallowed place when Abū Jahl came past. Here was an opportunity for the Makhzūmite to show that he at least was not overawed; and standing in front of the Prophet he proceeded to revile him with all the abuse he could muster. The Prophet merely looked at him, but spoke no word; and finally, having heaped upon him the worst insults he could think of, Abū Jahl entered the Mosque to join those of Quraysh who were assembled in the Ḥijr. The Prophet sadly rose to his feet and returned to his home.

Scarcely had he gone than Ḥamzah came in sight from the opposite direction on his way from the chase, with his bow slung over his shoulder. It was his custom, whenever he came back from hunting, to do honour to the Holy House before he joined his family. Seeing him approach, a woman came out of her house near the Ṣafā Gate and addressed him. She was a freedwoman of the household of the now dead 'Abd Allāh ibn Jud'ān of Taym, the man who twenty years previously had been one of the chief inaugurators of the chivalric pact, Ḥilf al-Fuḍūl. The Jud'ān family were cousins of Abū Bakr, and she herself, being well disposed to the Prophet and his religion, had been outraged by Abū Jahl's insults, every word of which she had overheard. "Abū 'Umārah,"[1] she said to Ḥamzah, "if only thou hadst seen how Muḥammad, thy brother's son, was treated even now by Abū l-Ḥakam, the son of Hishām. He found him sitting here, and most odiously reviled him and abused him. Then he left him" – she pointed towards the Mosque to indicate where he had gone – "and Muḥammad answered not a word." Ḥamzah was of a friendly nature and an easy disposition. He was none the less the most stalwart man of Quraysh, and when roused he was the most formidable and the most unyielding. His mighty frame now shook with anger such as he had never felt, and his anger set free something in his soul, and brought to completion an already half formed resolve. Striding into the Mosque he made straight for Abū Jahl; and, standing over him, he raised his bow and brought it down with all his force on his back. "Wilt thou insult him," he said "now that I am of his religion, and now that I avouch what he avoucheth? Strike me blow for blow, if thou canst." Abū Jahl was not lacking in courage, but on this occasion he evidently felt that it was better that the incident should be closed. So when some of the Makhzūmites present rose to their feet as if to help him he motioned them to be seated, saying: "Let Abū 'Umārah be, for by God I reviled his brother's son with a right ugly reviling."

[1] 'Umārah was Ḥamzah's daughter. The politest form of address among the Arabs is to name a man "Father (Abū) of so-and-so" and a woman "Mother (Umm) of so-and-so".

# XXI

# *Quraysh Make Offers and Demands*

FROM that day Ḥamzah faithfully maintained his Islam and followed all the Prophet's behests. Nor did his conversion fail to have its effect upon Quraysh, who were now more hesitant to harass the Prophet directly, knowing that Ḥamzah would protect him. On the other hand, this totally unexpected event made them all the more conscious of what they considered to be the gravity of the situation; and it increased their sense of the need to find a solution and to stop a movement which, so it seemed to them, could only end in the ruin of their high standing among the Arabs. In view of this danger they agreed to change their tactics and to follow a suggestion which was now made in the assembly by one of the leading men of 'Abdu Shams, 'Utbah ibn Rabī'ah. "Why should I not go to Muḥammad," he said, "and make certain offers to him, some of which he might accept? And what he accepteth, that will we give him, on condition that he leave us in peace." Word now came that the Prophet was sitting alone beside the Ka'bah, so 'Utbah left the assembly forthwith and went to the Mosque. He had proposed himself for this task partly because he was a grandson of 'Abdu Shams, the brother of Hāshim; and though the clans named after these two sons of 'Abdu Manāf, son of the great Quṣayy, had drifted apart, their differences could easily be sunk in virtue of their common ancestor. Moreover, 'Utbah was of a less violent and more conciliatory nature than most of Quraysh; and he was also more intelligent.

"Son of my brother," he said to the Prophet, "thou art as thou knowest a noble of the tribe and thy lineage assureth thee of a place of honour. And now thou hast brought to thy people a matter of grave concern, whereby thou hast rifted their community, declared their way of life to be foolish, spoken shamefully of their gods and their religion, and called their forefathers infidels. So hear what I propose, and see if any of it be acceptable to thee. If it be wealth thou seekest, we will put together a fortune for thee from our various properties that thou mayst be the richest man amongst us. If it be honour thou seekest, we will make thee our overlord and take no decision without thy consent; and if thou wouldst have kingship, we will make thee our king; and if thyself thou canst not rid thee of this sprite that appeareth unto thee, we will find thee a physician and spend our wealth until thy cure be complete." When he had finished speaking, the Prophet said to him: "Now hear thou me, O Father of Walīd." "I will," said 'Utbah, whereupon the Prophet recited to him part of a Revelation which he had recently received.

'Utbah was prepared to make at least a semblance of heeding, out of policy towards a man he hoped to win, but after a few sentences all such thoughts had changed to wonderment at the words themselves. He sat there with his hands behind his back, leaning upon them as he listened, amazed at the beauty of the language that flowed into his ears. The signs[1] that were recited spoke of the Revelation itself, and of the creation of the earth and the firmament. Then it told of the Prophets and of the peoples of old who, having resisted them, had been destroyed and doomed to Hell. Then came a passage which spoke of the believers, promising them the protection of the Angels in this life and the satisfaction of every desire in the Hereafter. The Prophet ended his recitation with the words: *And of His signs are the night and the day and the sun and the moon. Bow not down in adoration unto the sun nor unto the moon, but bow down in adoration unto God their Creator, if Him indeed ye worship*[2] – whereupon he placed his forehead on the ground in prostration. Then he said: "Thou hast heard what thou hast heard, O Abu l-Walīd, and all is now between thee and that."

When 'Utbah returned to his companions they were so struck by the change of expression on his face that they exclaimed: "What hath befallen thee, O Abu l-Walīd?" He answered them saying: "I have heard an utterance the like of which I have never yet heard. It is not poetry, by God, neither is it sorcery nor sooth saying. Men of Quraysh, hearken unto me, and do as I say. Come not between this man and what he is about, but let him be, for by God the words that I have heard from him will be received as great tidings. If the Arabs strike him down ye will be rid of him at the hands of others, and if he overcome the Arabs, then his sovereignty will be your sovereignty and his might will be your might, and ye will be the most fortunate of men." But they mocked at him saying: "He hath bewitched thee with his tongue." "I have given you my opinion," he answered, "so do what ye think is best." He opposed them no further, nor was the impact made on him by the Koranic verses more than a fleeting impression. Meantime, since he had not brought back an answer to any of the questions he had put, one of the others said: "Let us send for Muḥammad and talk to him and argue with him, so that we cannot be blamed for having left any way unattempted." So they sent for him saying: "The nobles of thy people are gathered together that they may speak with thee," and he went to them with all speed, thinking that they must have been prevailed upon to change their attitude. He longed to guide them to the truth, but his hopes faded as soon as they began repeating the offers already made to him. When they had finished he said to them: "I am not possessed, neither seek I honour amongst you, nor kingship over you. But

[1] Each verse of the Koran is called a 'sign' that is, a miracle, in view of its direct revelation.

[2] XLI, 37.

God hath sent me to you as a messenger and revealed to me a book and commanded me that I should be for you a teller of good tidings and a warner. Even so have I conveyed to you the message of my Lord, and I have given you good counsel. If ye accept from me what I have brought you, that is your good fortune in this world and the next; but if ye reject what I have brought, then will I patiently await God's judgement between us."[1]

Their only reply was to go back to where they had left off, and to say that if he would not accept their offers, then let him do something which would prove to them that he was a messenger from God, and which would at the same time make life easier for them. "Ask thy Lord to remove from us these mountains which hem us round and to flatten for us our land and to make rivers flow through it even as the rivers of Syria and Iraq; and to raise for us some of our forefathers, Quṣayy amongst them, that we may ask them if what thou sayest be true or false. Or if thou wilt not do these things for us, then ask favours for thyself. Ask God to send with thee an Angel who shall confirm thy words and give us the lie. And ask Him to bestow on thee gardens and palaces and treasures of gold and silver, that we may know how well thou standest with thy Lord." The Prophet answered them, saying: "I am not one to ask of his Lord the like of such things, nor was I sent for that, but God hath sent me to warn and give good tidings." Refusing to listen, they said: "Then make fall the sky in pieces on our heads," in scornful reference to the already revealed verse: *If We will, We shall make the earth gape and swallow them, or make fall the firmament in pieces upon them.*[2] "That is for God to decide," he said. "If He will, He will do it."

Without answering, except by mutual glances of derision, they went to another point. For them, one of the most puzzling features of the Revelation was the constant recurrence of the strange name *Raḥmān*,[3] apparently related to the source of the Prophet's inspiration. One of the Revelations began with the words *The Infinitely Good (ar-Raḥmān) taught the Koran*,[4] and because it pleased them to accept the rumour that Muḥammad was taught his utterances by a man in Yamāmah, their final retort on this occasion was to say: "We have heard that all this is taught thee by a man in Yamāmah called Raḥmān, and in Raḥmān will we never believe!" The Prophet remained silent, and they continued: "We have now justified ourselves before thee, Muḥammad; and we swear by God that we will not leave thee in peace nor desist from our present treatment of thee until we destroy thee or until thou destroy us." And one of them added: "We will not believe in thee until thou bring us God and the Angels as a warrant." At these words the Prophet rose to his feet, and as he was about to leave them 'Abd Allāh, the son of Abū Umayyah of Makhzūm, also rose and said to him: "I will not believe in thee ever, nay, not until thou takest a ladder and I see thee mount on it up to heaven, and until thou bringest four Angels to testify that thou art what thou claimest to be; and even then I think I would not believe thee." Now this 'Abd Allāh, on his father's side, was first cousin to Abū Jahl; but his mother was 'Ātikah, daughter of 'Abd al-Muṭṭalib, and she had named her son after her brother, the Prophet's father. So the

[1] I.I. 188. [2] XXXIV, 9. [3] See above, pp. 46–9. [4] LV, 1.

Prophet went home with the sadness at hearing such words from so near a kinsman added to his general sorrow at the great distance which now lay between himself and the leaders of his people.

Yet from the clan of Makhzūm, where so much hatred seemed to be concentrated, he had at least the devotion of Abū Salamah, the son of his aunt Barrah; and now from that direction there came an unexpected help and strength for the new religion. Abū Salamah had a rich cousin on his father's side named Arqam – their Makhzūmite grandfathers were brothers – and Arqam came to the Prophet and pronounced the two testifications *lā ilāha illā Llāh*, there is no god but God, and *Muḥammadun rasūlu Llāh*, Muḥammad is the Messenger of God. Then he placed his large house near the foot of Mount Ṣafā at the service of Islam. From henceforth the believers had a refuge in the very centre of Mecca where they could meet and pray together without fear of being seen or disturbed.

# XXII

# *Leaders of Quraysh*

THE followers of the Prophet were continually increasing, but whenever a new convert came to him and pledged his or her allegiance, it was more often than not a slave, or a freed slave, or a member of Quraysh of the Outskirts or else a young man or woman from Quraysh of the Hollow, of influential family but of no influence in themselves, whose conversion would increase tenfold the hostility of their parents and elder kinsmen. 'Abd ar-Raḥmān, Ḥamzah and Arqam had been exceptions, but they were far from being leaders; and the Prophet longed to win over some of the chiefs, not one of whom, not even his uncle Abū Ṭālib, had shown any inclination to join him. It would greatly help him to spread his message if he had the support of a man like Abū Jahl's uncle, Walīd, who was not only chief of Makhzūm but also, if it were possible to say such a thing, the unofficial leader of Quraysh. He was, moreover, a man who seemed more open to argument than many of the others; and one day an opportunity came for the Prophet to speak with Walīd alone. But when they were deep in converse a blind man came past, one who had recently entered Islam, and hearing the Prophet's voice he begged him to recite to him some of the Koran. When asked to be patient and wait for a better moment, the blind man became so importunate that in the end the Prophet frowned and turned away. His conversation had been ruined; but the interruption was not the cause of any loss, for Walīd was in fact no more open to the message than those whose case seemed hopeless.

A new *sūrah* was revealed almost immediately, and it began with the words: *He frowned and turned away, because the blind man came to him.* The Revelation continued: *As to him who sufficeth unto himself, with him thou art engrossed, yet is it no concern of thine if purified he be not. But as for him who cometh unto thee in eager earnestness and in fear of God, from him thou art drawn away.*[1]

Not long after this, Walīd was to betray his own self-satisfaction by saying: "Are revelations sent to Muḥammad and not to me, when I am the chief man of Quraysh and their lord? Are they sent neither to me nor to Abū Mas'ūd, the lord of Thaqīf, when we are the two great men of the two townships?"[2] The reaction of Abū Jahl was less coldly confident and more passionate. The possibility that Muḥammad might be a Prophet was too intolerable to be entertained for one moment. "We and the sons of 'Abdū

[1] LXXX, 5–10. [2] I.I. 238; see K. XLIII, 31.

Manāf," he said, "have vied for honour, the one with the other. They have fed food, and we have fed food. They have borne others' burdens, and we have borne others' burdens. They have given, and we have given, until, when we were running equal, knee unto knee, like two mares in a race, they say: 'One of our men is a Prophet; Revelations come to him from Heaven!' And when shall we attain to the like of this? By God, we will never believe in him, never admit him to be a speaker of truth." As to the Shamsite 'Utbah, his reaction was less negative, but almost equally lacking in sense of proportion; for his first thought was not that Muḥammad must be followed if he were a Prophet but that his prophethood would bring honour to the sons of 'Abdu Manāf. So one day, when Abū Jahl pointed derisively at the object of his hatred and said to 'Utbah: "There is your prophet, O sons of 'Abdu Manāf," 'Utbah rejoined sharply: "And why shouldst thou take it amiss if we have a prophet, or a king?" This last word was a reference to Quṣayy, and a subtle reminder to the Makhzūmite that 'Abdu Manāf was Quṣayy's son, whereas Makhzūm was only his cousin. The Prophet was near enough to hear this altercation and he came to them and said: "O 'Utbah, thou wast not vexed for the sake of God, nor for the sake of His messenger, but for thine own sake. And as for thee, Abū Jahl, a calamity shall come upon thee. Little shalt thou laugh, and much shalt thou weep."[1]

The fortunes of the various clans of Quraysh were continually fluctuating. Two of the most powerful at this time were 'Abdu Shams and Makhzūm. 'Utbah and his brother Shaybah were the leaders of one branch of the Shamsite clan. Their cousin Ḥarb, the former leader of its Umayyad branch, had been succeeded on his death by his son Abū Sufyān, who had married, amongst other wives, 'Utbah's daughter Hind. Abū Sufyān's success, both in politics and in trade, was partly due to his reserve of judgement and his capacity for cold and patient deliberation – and also forbearance, if his astute sense of opportunity saw that an advantage could thereby be gained. His cool-headedness was a frequent cause of exasperation for the impetuous and quick-tempered Hind, but he seldom if ever allowed her to sway him once his mind was made up. As might have been expected, he was less violent than Abū Jahl in his hostility towards the Prophet.

But if the leaders of Quraysh differed somewhat from each other in their attitude towards the Messenger, they were unanimous in their rejection of the message itself. Having all attained a certain success in life – though the younger men hoped that for them this was merely the beginning – they had by common consent achieved something of what had come to be accepted in Arabia as the ideal of human greatness. Wealth was not held to be an aspect of that greatness, but it was in fact almost a necessity as a means to the end. A great man must be greatly in demand as an ally and a protector, which meant that he must himself have reliable allies. This he could partly contrive by weaving for himself, through his own marriages and the marriages of his sons and his daughters, a network of powerful and formidable connections. Much in this respect could be achieved by wealth,

[1] Ṭab. 1203, 3.

which the great man also needed in his capacity as host. The virtues were an essential aspect of the ideal in question, especially the virtue of generosity, but not with a view to any heavenly reward. To be extolled by men, throughout all Arabia and perhaps beyond, for lavish bounty, for leonine courage, for unfailing fidelity to one's word, whether it had been given for alliance, protection, guarantee or any other purpose – to be extolled for these virtues in life and after death was the honour and the immortality which seemed to them to give life its meaning. Men like Walīd felt certain of such greatness; and this generated in them a complacence which made them deaf to a message that stressed the vanity of earthly life – the vanity of the very setting where their own success had taken place. Their immortality depended on Arabia remaining as it was, on Arab ideals being perpetuated from the past into the future. They were all sensitive, in varying degrees, to the beauty of the language of the Revelation; but as to its meaning, their souls spontaneously closed themselves to such verses as the following, which told them that they and their honoured forefathers had achieved nothing, and that all their efforts had been misplaced: *This lower life is but a diversion and a game; and verily the abode of the Hereafter, that, that is Life, did they but know.*[1]

[1] XXIX, 64.

# XXIII

# *Wondermen t and Hope*

THE young and the less successful did not by any means all accept the Divine message forthwith; but at least complacency had not blocked their hearing against the sharpness and vehemence of the summons, which had broken upon their little world as with the notes of a clarion. The voice that 'Uthmān had heard crying in the desert "Sleepers awake" was akin to the message itself and for those who now accepted the message it was indeed as if they had awakened from a sleep and had entered upon a new life.

The disbelievers' attitude, past and present, was summed up in the words: *There is naught but the life of this world . . . and we shall not be raised.*[1] To this came the Divine answers: *Not in play did We create the heavens and the earth and all that is between them*[2] and *Deem ye that We did but create you in vain and that ye shall not be brought back unto Us?*[3] For those in whom disbelief had not crystallised, these words rang with truth; and so it was with the Revelation as a whole, which described itself as being a light and having in itself the power to guide. A parallel imperative cause for accepting the message was the Messenger himself, a man who was, they were certain, too full of truth to deceive and too full of wisdom to be self-deceived. The Message contained a warning and a promise: the warning impelled them to take action, and the promise filled them with joy.

> *Verily those who say: "Our Lord is God", and who then follow straight His path, on them descend the Angels saying: "Fear not nor grieve, but hearken to good tidings of the Paradise which ye are promised. We are your protecting friends in this lower life, and in the Hereafter wherein ye shall be given that which your souls long for, that which ye pray for, in bounty from Him who is All-Forgiving, All-Merciful."*[4]

Another of the many verses about Paradise which had now been revealed was one which spoke of *the Garden of Immortality which is promised to*

[1] VI, 29. [2] XXI, 16; XLIV, 38. [3] XXIII, 115. [4] XLI, 30–2.

*the pious*. Of this it said: *For them therein is that which they desire, for ever and ever – a promise that thy Lord hath bound Himself to fulfil.*[1]

The true believers are defined as *they who set their hopes on meeting Us*, whereas the disbelievers are *they who set not their hopes on meeting Us, and who are satisfied with this lower life and find their deepest peace therein, and fail to treat Our signs as signs.*[2] The believer's attitude must be the opposite in every way. An aspect of the dreamlike illusion in which the infidels were sunk was to take for granted the blessings of nature. To be awake to reality meant not only shifting one's hopes from this world to the next but also marvelling in this world at the signs of God which here are manifest. *Blessed is He who hath placed in the heavens the constellations of the zodiac, and hath placed therein a lamp and a light-giving moon. And He it is who hath made the night and the day to succeed one the other, as a sign for him who would reflect or give thanks.*[3]

The leaders of Quraysh had asked defiantly for signs such as the descent of an Angel to confirm the prophethood of Muḥammad, and the rising of Muḥammad up to Heaven. On one occasion, a night of the full moon, not long after it had risen, when it was to be seen hanging in the sky above Mount Ḥirā', a body of disbelievers approached the Prophet and asked him to split the moon in two as a sign that he was indeed the Messenger of God. Many others were also present, including believers and hesitants, and when the demand was made all eyes were turned towards the luminary. Great was their amazement to see it divide into two halves which drew away from each other until there was a half moon shining brightly on either side of the mountain. "Bear ye witness," the Prophet said.[4] But those who had made the demand rejected this optic miracle as mere magic,[5] saying that he had cast a spell over them. The believers, on the other hand, rejoiced, and some of the hesitants entered Islam, while others came nearer to doing so.

This immediate heavenly response to a derisive challenge was an exception. Others of the signs demanded by Quraysh were in fact given, but not exactly as they had asked, and not in their time but in God's. There were also many lesser miracles which only the believers witnessed. But such wonders were never allowed to stand in the centre, for the revealed Book itself was the central miracle of the Divine intervention now taking place, just as Christ had been the central miracle of the preceding intervention. According to the Koran, Jesus is both *Messenger of God* and also *His Word which He cast unto Mary, and a Spirit from Him*;[6] and as it had been with the Word-made-flesh, so now analogously, it was through the Divine Presence in this world of the Word-made-book that Islam was a religion in the true sense of bond or link with the Hereafter. One of the functions of the Word-made-book, with a view to the primordial religion that Islam claimed to be,[7] was to reawaken in man his primeval sense of wonderment which, with the passage of time, had become dimmed or misdirected. Therefore when Quraysh ask for marvels the Koran's main response is to point to those which they have always had before their eyes without seeing the wonder of them:

1 XXV, 15–16. 2 X, 7. 3 XXV, 61–2. 4 B. LXI, 24.
5 K. LIV, 1–2. 6 IV, 171. 7 XXX, 30.

*Will they not behold the camels, how they are created?*
*And the firmament, how it is raised aloft?*
*And the mountains, how they are established?*
*And the earth, how it is spread?*[1]

The wonderment and hope demanded of the believer are both attitudes of return to God. The sacrament of thanksgiving, to say *Praise be to God the Lord of the worlds*, includes wonder and takes the thing praised, and with it the praiser, back to the Transcendent Origin of all good. The sacrament of consecration, to say *In the Name of God, the Infinitely Good, the All-Merciful*, precipitates the soul in the same direction upon the stream of hope. On this path of return the basic prayer of Islam is centred, *al-Fātiḥah*, the Opening, so called because it is the first chapter[2] of the Koran:

*Praise be to God, the Lord of the worlds,*
*The Infinitely Good, the All-Merciful,*
*Master of the day of judgement.*
*Thee we worship, and in Thee we seek help.*
*Guide us upon the straight path,*
*the path of those on whom Thy grace is,*
*not those on whom Thine anger is,*
*nor those who are astray.*[3]

Also basic as a perfect and concentrated expression of the doctrine of Islam is the *Sūrat al-Ikhlāṣ*, the Chapter of Sincerity, which is placed at the end of the Koran, the last *sūrah* but two, and which was revealed when an idolater asked the Prophet to describe his Lord:

*Say: He, God, is One,*
*God, the Self-Sufficient Besought of all.*
*He begetteth not, nor is begotten,*
*and none is like Him.*[4]

[1] LXXXVIII, 17–20.
[2] First in order of final arrangement but not of revelation. Its place in the Islamic liturgy ensures that it is recited at least seventeen times every day.
[3] I, 2–7. [4] CXII.

# XXIV
# *Family Divisions*

TĀLIB and 'Aqīl, the elder sons of Abū Ṭālib, had not followed the example of their younger brothers Ja'far and 'Alī, but had remained like their father unconverted yet tolerant. Very different was the attitude of Abū Lahab: since the recent confrontation with the leaders of Quraysh he had become openly hostile; and his wife Umm Jamīl, the sister of the Shamsite leader Abū Sufyān, had conceived a hatred for the Prophet. Between them they compelled their two sons to repudiate Ruqayyah and Umm Kulthūm – it is not certain whether the marriages had already taken place, or whether they were still only betrothed. But Umm Jamīl's satisfaction at this rupture was diminished when she heard that her wealthy Umayyad cousin, 'Uthmān ibn 'Affān, had asked for the hand of Ruqayyah and had married her. This marriage was most pleasing to the Prophet and Khadījah. Their daughter was happy and their new son-in-law was devoted to her and to them. There was also another consideration which impelled them to give thanks: Ruqayyah was the most beautiful of their daughters and one of the most beautiful women of her generation throughout all Mecca; and 'Uthmān was a remarkably handsome man. To see the two of them together was in itself a reason for rejoicing. "God is Beautiful and he loveth beauty".[1] Not long after their marriage, when they were both absent from Mecca, the Prophet sent them a messenger, who returned considerably later than he was expected. When he began to proffer his excuses the Prophet cut him short, saying: "I will tell thee, if thou wilt, what hath kept thee: thou didst stand there gazing at 'Uthmān and Ruqayyah and marvelling at their beauty."[2]

The Prophet's aunt Arwà now made up her mind to enter Islam. The immediate cause of her decision was her son Ṭulayb, a youth of fifteen, who had recently made his profession of faith in the house of Arqam. When he told his mother she said: "If we could do what men can do, we would protect our brother's son." But Ṭulayb refused to accept such vagueness. "What preventeth thee," he said, "from entering Islam and following him? Thy brother Ḥamzah hath done so." And when she made her usual excuse about waiting for her sisters he cut her short, saying: "I beg thee by God to go and greet him and say thou believest in him and testify that *There is no god but God.*" She did what he had said; and, having done so, she took courage, and rebuked her brother Abū Lahab for his treatment of their nephew.

[1] Saying of the Prophet, A.H. IV, 133–4. [2] S. 205.

As to Khadījah's relatives, no sooner had Islam become known in Mecca than her half brother Nawfal became one of its worst and most violent enemies. This did not, however, prevent his son Aswad from entering the religion which was for Khadījah a compensation for Nawfal's enmity. But it was a disappointment that her favourite nephew, the Shamsite Abu l-'Āṣ, already for some years her son-in-law, had not entered Islam as his wife Zaynab had done; and great presssure was now being put upon him by the leaders of his clan and others to divorce her. They went so far as to suggest that he should look for the richest, best-connected and most beautiful bride available in Mecca, and they promised, on condition of his divorce, that they would unite their efforts towards arranging the marriage in question. But Zaynab and Abu l-'Āṣ loved each other deeply: she always hoped and prayed that he would join her in Islam; and he, for his part, firmly told his clansmen that he already had the wife of his choice and that he wanted none other. Ḥakīm, another of Khadījah's nephews – her brother Ḥizām's son who nearly twenty years previously had made her a present of Zayd – retained like Abu l-'Āṣ his affection for his aunt and her household without renouncing the gods of Quraysh; but Ḥakīm's brother Khālid entered Islam.

*Verily thou guidest not whom thou lovest, but God guideth whom He will.*[1] The truth expressed in this verse is repeated continually through the Koran. But if such Revelations helped to ease the weight of the Prophet's sense of responsibility, they did not prevent him from being sad at the averseness of his Makhzūmite cousin 'Abd Allāh; and another such case, which perhaps caused him even more sadness was that of his uncle Ḥārith's son, Abū Sufyān, his foster-brother, cousin and one-time friend. He had hoped that he would respond to his message, whereas on the contrary the message made a rift between them, and Abū Sufyān's aloofness and coldness increased as time went on, perhaps through the influence of their uncle Abū Lahab. Others also were made to feel the truth of the above-quoted verse: Abū Bakr had been followed into Islam by his wife Umm Rūmān, and by 'Abd Allāh and Asmā', his son and daughter by another wife presumably now dead. Umm Rūmān had just borne him a second daughter whom they named 'Ā'ishah and who was, like Zayd's son Usāmah, one of the first children to be born into Islam. But although Abū Bakr had been responsible for so many conversions he was unable to convert his own eldest son, 'Abd al-Ka'bah, who resisted all the attempts of his father and his mother – he was Umm Rūmān's son – to persuade him to enter their religion.

If the believers had disappointments, their opponents had the vexation of feeling themselves face to face with a new and incalculable presence in Mecca which threatened to disrupt their way of life and frustrate all their projects for the future, especially those which related to planning the marriages of their children. The Bani Makhzūm had been gratified when their clansmen 'Abd Allāh had so sharply opposed his cousin Muḥammad in the Assembly. 'Abd Allāh's brother Zuhayr, though somewhat less hostile to the new religion, had also refused to enter it. Like 'Abd Allāh, he

[1] XXVIII, 56.

was the son of ʿĀtikah, the daughter of ʿAbd al-Muṭṭalib, but their now dead father had had a second wife also named ʿAtikah, who had borne him a daughter. Hind, for so she was named, was a woman of great beauty, now in her nineteenth year, and she had not long been married to the cousin of her two half-brothers, Abū Salamah of the other branch of Makhzūm. The whole clan was pleased at this link between their two branches. Great, therefore, was their dismay when Abū Salamah's Islam became known; and this dismay was doubled when Hind – or Umm Salamah, as she is always called – instead of leaving her husband became like him one of the most devoted followers of the Prophet.

On the death of Abū Salamah's father, his mother Barrah had married a man of the Quraysh clan of ʿĀmir by whom she had had a second son, known as Abū Ṣabrah. Suhayl, the chief of ʿĀmir, had recently given Abū Ṣabrah his daughter Umm Kulthūm in marriage. Barrah, unlike her sister Arwà, had not yet entered Islam; but Abū Sabrah was subject to its influence not only through his half-brother Abū Salamah but also through his stepmother, his father's second wife Maymūnah. It was to Maymūnah and her three sisters, the wives of ʿAbbās, Ḥamzah and Jaʿfar, that the Prophet referred when he said: "Verily the sisters are true believers";[1] and Maymūnah's marriage brought to the clan of ʿĀmir a powerful presence of faith.

Suhayl had another daughter, Sahlah, whom he had given to Abū Hudhayfah, the son of the Shamsite leader ʿUtbah. ʿĀmir had of late been rapidly increasing in power, and this marriage was thought to be an advantageous one by both the clans concerned. Not long afterwards, however, the couple entered Islam; they were followed, or preceded, by the other couple, Abū Ṣabrah and Umm Kulthūm. Suhayl thus lost two daughters to the new religion, and two carefully chosen sons-in-law. He likewise lost his three brothers, Ḥāṭib, Salīṭ and Sakrān, and Sakrān's wife, their cousin Sawdah. But, worst of all from Suhayl's point of view, his eldest son, ʿAbd Allāh, also became a devout follower of the Prophet. ʿAbd Allāh had hopes that his father might one day join them, and these hopes were shared by the Prophet himself, for Suhayl was a man of more piety and intelligence than most of the other leaders, and had even been known to make spiritual retreats. But as yet he showed himself hostile to the new faith, not violently but none the less resolutely, and his children's disobedience seemed to have a hardening effect upon him.

In ʿAbdu Shams, Abū Hudhayfah was not the only son of a leader to defy parental authority. Khālid, who had dreamed of the Prophet saving him from the fire, had kept his Islam secret, but his father heard of it and ordered him to renounce it. Khālid said: "I will die sooner than forsake the religion of Muḥammad",[2] whereupon he was beaten unmercifully and imprisoned in a room without food or drink. But after three days he escaped, and his father disowned him without taking further action. ʿUtbah was characteristically less violent and more patient with Abū Hudhayfah, who for his part was attached to his father and hoped that he would come to see the errors of idolatry.

1 I.S. VIII, 203. 2 I.S. IV 1, 68.

As to the Umayyad branch of 'Abdu Shams, in addition to the Islam of 'Uthmān and his marriage to Ruqayyah, there were other serious losses. Many of their confederates of the Bani Asad ibn Khuzaymah had likewise professed their faith in the new religion, fourteen in number including the Jaḥsh family who, as cousins of the Prophet, were no doubt the leaders. With these valued confederates Abu Sufyān the Umayyad chief lost also his own daughter, Umm Ḥabībah, whom he had married to 'Ubayd Allāh ibn Jaḥsh, the younger brother of 'Abd Allāh.

In the clan of 'Adī, in one of its chief families, the power of the tie of truth to break lesser ties had been prefigured in the last generation. Nufayl had had two sons, Khaṭṭāb and 'Amr, by two different wives; and on the death of Nufayl the mother of Khaṭṭāb married her stepson 'Amr and bore him a son whom they named Zayd. Khaṭṭāb and Zayd were thus half-brothers on their mother's side. Zayd was one of the few men who, like Waraqah, saw the idolatrous practices of Quraysh for what they were; and not only did he refuse to take part in them himself, but he even refused to eat anything that had been sacrificed to idols. He proclaimed that he worshipped the God of Abraham, and he did not hesitate to rebuke his people in public. Khaṭṭāb, on the other hand, was a staunch adherent of the inveterate practices of Quraysh and he was scandalised by Zayd's disrespect for the gods and goddesses that they worshipped. So he persecuted him to the point of forcing him to leave the hollow of Mecca and to live in the hills above it; and he even organised a band of young men whom he instructed not to allow Zayd to approach the Sanctuary. The outcast thereupon left the Ḥijāz and went as far as Mosul in the north of Iraq and from there south-west into Syria, always questioning monks and rabbis about the religion of Abraham, until finally he met a monk who told him that the time was now near when there would come forth, in the very country he had left, a Prophet who would preach the religion he was seeking. Zayd then retraced his steps, but on his way through the territory of Lakhm on the southern border of Syria he was attacked and killed. When Waraqah heard of his death, he wrote an elegy in praise of him. The Prophet also praised him and said that on the day of the Resurrection "he will be raised as having, in himself alone, the worth of a whole people."[1]

Many years had now passed since Zayd's death: Khaṭṭāb also was dead, and his son 'Umar was on good terms with Zayd's son Sa'īd, who had married 'Umar's sister Fāṭimah. The rift between the two branches of the family had closed. But with the coming of Islam Sa'īd was one of the first to join it, whereas 'Umar, whose mother was the sister of Abū Jahl, became one of its fiercest opponents. Fāṭimah followed her husband, but they did not dare to tell her brother, knowing his violent nature. 'Umar was beset by Islam on another side also: his wife Zaynab was the sister of 'Uthmān the son of Maẓ'ūn of the clan of Jumaḥ; and this 'Uthmān was by nature an ascetic and had had tendencies towards monotheism before the descent of the Revelation. He and his two brothers were among the first to respond to it; and they and Zaynab had also three nephews who had entered Islam. Of Zaynab herself, 'Umar's wife, nothing is recorded at this stage, no doubt

[1] I.I. 145.

because, wherever her sympathies lay, she had powerful reasons for keeping them a secret. Her brother 'Uthmān was even more uncompromising than 'Umar, though he was less violent.

Zaynab and her brothers were younger cousins of the chief of their clan, Umayyah ibn Khalaf, who was one of the most implacable enemies of Islam, as were his immediate family. It was his brother Ubayy who one day took a decayed bone to the Prophet and said: "Claimest though, Muḥammad, that God can bring this to life?" Then with a disdainful smile he crumbled the bone in his hand and blew the fragments into the face of the Messenger, who said: "Even so, that do I claim: He will raise it, and thee too when thou art as that now is; then will He enter thee into the fire."[1] It is to Ubayy that the following Revelation refers: *He forgot his own createdness and said: Who will give life to bones when they are rotten? Say: He who gave them being the first time will give them life again.*[2]

[1] I.I. 239. [2] XXXVI, 78.

# XXV

# *The Hour*

ONE of the disbelievers' most frequent contentions was that if God had truly had a message for them he would have sent an Angel. To this the Koran replied: *If the angels walked at their ease upon earth, verily We had sent down upon them an angel messenger.*[1] The descent of Gabriel from time to time did not make him a Messenger in the Koranic sense of the term. For that, it was necessary to be stationed upon earth amongst the people to whom the message was to be unfolded. The Revelation also said: *They who place not their hopes in meeting Us say: Why are the angels not sent down unto us? Or why see we not our Lord? Verily they are proud with pride in themselves, and arrogant with a great arrogance. The day they behold the angels, on that day there will be no good tidings for the evil-doers, and they will say: A barrier that bars!*[2] That is, they will call, but in vain, for the barrier to be put back between Heaven and earth. That will be the end, when the direct contact with Heaven will cause the earthly conditions of time and space to be obliterated and the earth itself to disintegrate. *The day men shall be like scattered moths, and the mountains float like tufts of wool.*[3] And *A day that shall turn the hair of children grey.*[4] This end is continually heralded throughout the Koran. It is *the Hour*, which is near at hand – *the heavens and the earth are pregnant with it.*[5] Its moment has not yet come, and when the scriptures speak of it as *near* it must be remembered that *verily a day in the sight of thy Lord is as a thousand years of what ye count.*[6] But the period of the message is none the less an anticipation of the Hour.

This is according to the nature of things, not of earthly things in themselves, but in a wider context. For if there is a Divine intervention to establish a new religion there is necessarily a passage through the barrier between Heaven and earth, not so great an opening as would transform earthly conditions but enough to make the time of the Prophet's mission altogether exceptional, as had been the times of Jesus and Moses and Abraham and Noah. The Koran says of the Night of Worth, *Laylat al-Qadr*, the night when Gabriel came to Muḥammad in the cave on Mount Ḥirā': *The Night of Worth is better than a thousand months. In it the angels descend, and the Spirit.*[7] And something of that peerlessness necessarily overflowed into the whole period of the intercourse between the Prophet and the Archangel.

[1] XVII, 95. [2] XXV, 21–2. [3] CI, 4–5. [4] LXXIII, 17.
[5] VII, 187. [6] XXII, 47. [7] XCVII, 3–4.

To anticipate the Hour is to anticipate the Judgement: and the Koran had recently declared itself to be *al-Furqān*,[1] the Criterion, the Discrimination. The same must apply to every revealed Scripture for a Revelation is a presence of the Eternal in the ephemeral, and that otherworldly presence precipitates something of a final judgement. This meant that in many cases, quite independently of what the Prophet himself might prophesy, the ultimate destinies of Paradise or Hell became clearly apparent. Hidden depths of good and evil were summoned to the surface. The presence of the Messenger was also bound to work a parallel effect, for the attractive power of his guidance measured out the full perversity of those who resisted it, while drawing those who accepted it into the very orbit of his own perfection.

It was immediately understandable that the Revelation should cause the good to excel themselves. But it was not only distressing but also perplexing to many of the believers that some of those whom they had always looked on as not bad should suddenly become unquestionably evil. The Koran tells them that they must expect this, for its verses increase the opposition of its worst opponents.

> *Verily We have given them in this Koran ample reason to take heed, yet it doth but increase them in aversion.*[2]
>
> *We give them cause to fear, yet it doth but increase them in monstrous outrage.*[3]

No one had been previously aware of the fundamental nature of Abū Lahab; and, to take another example, ʻAbd ar-Raḥmān ibn ʻAwf had even been something of a friend of the chief of Jumaḥ, Umayyah ibn Khalaf. The Koran offers an exalted parallel in telling how Noah complained to God that his message only served to widen the gap between himself and the majority of his people, and to lead them yet further astray.[4]

[1] This is the title of Sūrah XXV.

[2] XVII, 41. [3] XVII, 60. [4] LXXI, 6.

# XXVI

# *Three Questions*

AT every assembly of Quraysh there was at least some discussion of what seemed to them their greatest problem; and they now decided to send to Yathrib to consult the Jewish rabbis: "Ask them about Muḥammad," they said to their two envoys. "Describe him to them, and tell them what he says; for they are the people of the first scripture, and they have knowledge of the Prophets which we have not." The rabbis sent back the answer: "Question him about three things wherein we will instruct you. If he tell you of them, then is he a Prophet sent by God, but if he tell you not, then is the man a forger of falsehood. Ask him of some young men who left their folk in the days of old, how it was with them, for theirs is a tale of wonder; and ask him tidings of a far traveller who reached the ends of the earth in the east and in the west; and ask him of the Spirit, what it is. If he tell you of these things, then follow him, for he is a Prophet."

When the envoys returned to Mecca with their news, the leaders of Quraysh sent to the Prophet and asked him the three questions. He said: "Tomorrow I will tell you," but he did not say "if God will"; and when they came for the answers he had to put them off, and so it went on day by day until fifteen nights had passed and still he had received no Revelation of any kind, neither had Gabriel come to him since they had questioned him. The people of Mecca taunted him, and he was distressed by what they said and greatly saddened that he had not received the help he had hoped for. Then Gabriel brought him a Revelation reproaching him for his distress on account of what his people said, and telling him the answers to their three questions. The long wait he had had to endure was explained in the words: *And say not of anything: verily I shall do that tomorrow, except thou sayest: if God will.*[1]

But the delay of this Revelation, although painful to the Prophet and his followers, was in reality an added strength. His worst enemies refused to draw conclusions from it, but for those many of Quraysh who were in two minds it was a powerful corroboration of his claim that the Revelation came to him from Heaven and that he had no part in it and no control over it. Was it conceivable that if Muḥammad had invented the earlier Revelations he could have delayed so long before inventing this latest one, especially when so much appeared to be at stake?

The believers drew strength also, as always, from the Revelation itself.

[1] XVIII, 23–4.

When Quraysh asked for the story of the youths who left their folk in the days of old – a story which no one in Mecca had ever heard – they did not know that it would have a bearing on the present situation, to their own discredit and to the credit of the believers. It is often called the story of the sleepers of Ephesus, for it was there, in the middle of the third century AD, that some young men had remained faithful to the worship of the One God when their people had fallen away into idolatry and were persecuting them for not following them. To escape from this persecution they took refuge in a cave, where they were miraculously put to sleep for over 300 years.

In addition to what the Jews already knew, the Koranic narrative[1] told of details that no human eye had seen, such as how the sleepers looked as they slept their unwitnessed sleep in their cave throughout the centuries, and how their faithful dog lay with his front paws stretched over the threshold.

As to the second question, the great traveller is named Dhu l-Qarnayn, *he of the two horns*. The Revelation mentions his journey to the far west and to the far east, and then, answering more than was asked, it tells of a mysterious third journey to a place between two mountains where the people begged him to make a barrier that would protect them from Gog and Magog and other jinn who were devastating their land; and God gave him power to confine the evil spirits within a space from which they will not emerge until a divinely appointed day,[2] when, according to the Prophet, they will work terrible destruction over the face of the earth. Their breaking forth would take place before the final Hour, but it would be one of the signs that the end was near.

In answer to the third question, the Revelation affirmed the Spirit's transcendence over the mind of man, which is incapable of grasping it: *They will question thee concerning the Spirit. Say: the Spirit proceedeth from the command of my Lord; and ye have not been given knowledge, save only a little.*[3]

The Jews had been very eager to hear what answers Muḥammad had given to their questions; and, with regard to this last sentence about knowledge, they asked him, at their first opportunity, if it referred to his people or to them. "To both of you," said the Prophet, whereupon they protested that they had been given knowledge of all things, for they had read the Torah in which was *an exposition of everything*, as the Koran itself affirmed.[4] The Prophet answered: "That all is but little in respect of God's Own Knowledge; yet have ye therein enough for your needs, if ye would but practise it."[5] It was then that there came the Revelation about *the Words of God*, which express merely a part of His knowledge: *If all the trees in the earth were pens, and if the sea eked out by seven seas more were ink, the Words of God could not be written out unto their end.*[6]

The leaders of Quraysh had not bound themselves to take the advice of the rabbis, nor did the rabbis themselves recognise the Prophet, despite his having answered their questions beyond all their expectations. But the answers served to convert others; and the more his followers increased, the more his opponents felt that their community and their way of life was in

[1] XVIII, 9–25. [2] XVIII, 93–9. [3] XVII, 85.
[4] VI, 154. [5] I.I. 198. [6] XXXI, 27.

danger, and the more resolutely they organised their persecution of all those converts who could be ill-treated with impunity. Each clan dealt with its own Muslims: they would imprison them and torment them with beating and hunger and thirst; and they would stretch them out on the sun-baked earth of Mecca when the heat was at its height, to make them renounce their religion.

The chief of Jumaḥ, Umayyah, had an African slave named Bilāl who was a firm believer. Umayyah would take him out at noon into an open space, and would have him pinned to the ground with a large rock on his chest, swearing that he should stay like that until he died, or until he renounced Muḥammad and worshipped al-Lāt and al-'Uzzah. While he endured this Bilāl would say "One, One"; and it happened that the aged Waraqah came past when he was suffering this torment and repeating "One, One." "It is indeed One, One, O Bilāl," said Waraqah. Then, turning to Umayyah, he said: "I swear by God that if ye kill him thus I will make his grave a shrine."

Not every man of Quraysh lived amongst his own clan, and Abū Bakr had acquired a house amongst the dwellings of the Bani Jumaḥ. This meant that they had more opportunities of seeing the Prophet than most other clans, for he used to visit Abū Bakr every afternoon; and it is said that part of a Prophet's message is always written on his face. The face of Abū Bakr was also something of a book; and his presence in that quarter of Mecca, previously welcomed as an asset by the whole clan, was now a source of anxiety to its leaders. It was through him that Bilāl had entered Islam; and, when he saw how they were torturing him, he said to Umayyah: "Hast thou no fear of God, to treat this poor man thus?" "It is thou who hast corrupted him," retorted Umayyah, "so save him from what thou seest." "I will," said Abū Bakr. "I have a black youth who is tougher and sturdier than he, a man of thy religion. Him will I give thee for Bilāl." Umayyah agreed, and Abū Bakr took Bilāl and set him free.

He had already set free six others, the first one being 'Āmir ibn Fuhayrah, a man of great spiritual strength, who had been one of the earliest converts. 'Āmir was a shepherd and after he was freed he took charge of Abū Bakr's flocks. Another of those whom he set free was a slave girl belonging to 'Umar. She had entered Islam, and 'Umar was beating her to make her renounce it, when Abū Bakr happened to pass by and asked him if he would sell her to him. 'Umar agreed, whereupon Abū Bakr bought her and set her free.

Among the most relentless of the persecutors was Abū Jahl. If a convert had a powerful family to defend him, Abū Jahl would merely insult him and promise to ruin his reputation and make him a laughing-stock. If he were a merchant he would threaten to stop his trade by organising a general boycott of his goods so that he would be ruined. If he were weak and unprotected and of his own clan he would have him tortured; and he had powerful allies in many other clans whom he could persuade to do the same with their own weak and unprotected converts.

It was through him that his clansmen tortured three of their poorer confederates, Yāsir and Sumayyah and their son 'Ammār. They refused to renounce Islam, and Sumayyah died under the sufferings they inflicted on her. But some of the victims of Makhzūm and of other clans could not endure what they were made to suffer, and their persecutors reduced them to a state when they could agree to anything. It was said to them: "Are not al-Lāt and al-'Uzzah your gods as well as Allāh?" They would say yes; and if a beetle crawled past them and they were asked "Is not this beetle your god as well as Allāh?" they would say yes simply in order to escape from a pain they could not endure.

These recantations were on the lips, not in the heart. But those who had made them could no longer practise Islam except in the greatest privacy, and some of them had no privacy at all. There was, however, an example for them in the recently revealed story of the young men who had left their people and taken refuge in God rather than submit to worshipping other gods. And when the Prophet saw that although he escaped persecution himself many of his followers did not, he said to them: "If ye went to the country of the Abyssinians, ye would find there a king under whom none suffereth wrong. It is a land of sincerity in religion. Until such time as God shall make for you a means of relief from what ye now are suffering."[1] So some of his companions set off for Abyssinia; and this was the first emigration in Islam.

[1] I.I. 208.

# XXVII
# *Abyssinia*

THE emigrants were well received in Abyssinia, and were allowed complete freedom of worship. In all, not counting the small children they took with them, they were about eighty in number; but they did not all go at the same time. Their flight was secretly planned and carried out unobtrusively in small groups. Their families would and could have stopped it, if they had known about it; but the move had been totally unexpected, and they failed to realise what had happened until the believers had all reached their destination. The leaders of Quraysh, however, were none the less determined that they should not be left in peace, to establish there, beyond their control, a dangerous community which might be increased tenfold if other converts joined them. So they speedily thought out a plan, and made ready a quantity of presents of a kind that the Abyssinians were known to value most. Leatherwork they prized above all, so a large number of fine skins were collected, enough to make a rich bribe for every one of the Negus's generals. There were also rich gifts for the Negus himself. Then they carefully chose two men, one of whom was 'Amr ibn al-'Āṣ, of the clan of Sahm. Quraysh told them exactly what to do: they were to approach each of the generals separately, give him his present, and say: "Some foolish young men and women of our people have taken refuge in this kingdom. They have left their own religion, not for yours, but for one they have invented, one that is unknown to us and to yourselves. The nobles of their people have sent us to your king on their account, that he may send them home. So when we speak to him about them, counsel him to deliver them into our hands and have no words with them; for their people see best how it is with them." The generals all agreed, and the two men of Quraysh took their presents to the Negus, asking that the emigrants should be given into their hands and explaining the reason as they had done to the generals, and finally adding: "The nobles of their people, who are their fathers, their uncles and their kinsmen, beg thee to restore them unto them." The generals were present at the audience, and now with one voice they urged the Negus to comply with their request and give up the refugees, inasmuch as kinsmen are the best judges of the affairs of their kinsmen. But the Negus was displeased and said: "Nay, by God, they shall not be betrayed – a people that have sought my protection and made my country their abode and chosen me above all others! Give them up I will not, until I have summoned them and questioned them concerning what these men say of them. If it be as they have said, then will I deliver them unto them, that they may restore them to their own people. But if not, then will I be their good protector so long as they seek my protection."

Then he sent for the companions of the Prophet, and at the same time he assembled his bishops, who brought with them their sacred books and spread them open round about the throne. 'Amr and his fellow envoy had hoped to prevent this meeting between the Negus and the refugees, and it was indeed in their interests to prevent it, even more so than they realised. For they were unaware that while the Abyssinians tolerated them for commercial and political reasons they looked down on them as heathens and were conscious of a barrier between them. They themselves were Christians, many of them devout; they had been baptised, they worshipped the One God, and they carried in their flesh the sacrament of the Eucharist. As such they were sensitive to the difference between the sacred and the profane, and they were keenly conscious of the profanity of men like 'Amr. So much the more were they receptive – none more than the Negus himself – to the impression of holy earnestness and depth which was made on them by the company of believers who were now ushered into the throne room, and a murmur of wonderment arose from the bishops and others as they recognised that here were men and women more akin to themselves than to such of Quraysh as they had previously encountered. Moreover, most of them were young, and in many of them their piety of demeanour was enhanced by a great natural beauty.

Not for all of them had the emigration been a necessity. 'Uthmān's family had given up trying to make him recant, but the Prophet none the less allowed him to go and to take with him Ruqayyah. Their presence was a source of strength to the community of exiles. Another couple very pleasing to look upon were Ja'far and his wife Asmā'. They were well protected by Abū Ṭālib; but the refugees needed a spokesman and Ja'far was an eloquent speaker. He was also most winning in his person, and the Prophet said to him on one occasion: "Thou art like me in looks and in character."[1] It was Ja'far he had chosen to preside over the community of exiles; and his qualities of attraction and intelligence were amply seconded by Muṣ'ab of 'Abd ad-Dār, a young man whom the Prophet was later to entrust with a mission of immense importance in virtue of his natural gifts. Likewise remarkable was a young Makhzūmite known as Shammās, whose mother was the sister of 'Utbah. His name, which means "deacon", was given him because on one occasion Mecca had been visited by a Christian dignitary of that rank, a man so exceptionally handsome as to arouse general admiration, whereupon 'Utbah had said "I will show you a *shammās* more beautiful than he," and he went and brought before them his sister's son. Zubayr, Ṣafiyyah's son, was also present, and there were other cousins of the Prophet: Ṭulayb the son of Arwà; two sons of Umaymah, 'Abd Allāh ibn Jahsh and 'Ubayd Allāh together with 'Ubayd Allāh's Umayyad wife Umm Ḥabibah; and the two sons of Barrah, Abū Salamah and Abū Ṣabrah, both with their wives. It is from the beautiful Umm Salamah that most of the accounts of this first emigration have come down.

[1] I.S. IV/1, 24.

When they were all assembled, the Negus spoke to them and said: "What is this religion wherein ye have become separate from your people, though ye have not entered my religion nor that of any other of the folk that surround us?" And Ja'far answered him saying: "O King, we were a people steeped in ignorance, worshipping idols, eating unsacrificed carrion, committing abominations, and the strong would devour the weak. Thus we were, until God sent us a Messenger from out of our midst, one whose lineage we knew, and his veracity and his worthiness of trust and his integrity. He called us unto God, that we should testify to His Oneness and worship Him and renounce what we and our fathers had worshipped in the way of stones and idols; and he commanded us to speak truly, to fulfil our promises, to respect the ties of kinship and the rights of our neighbours, and to refrain from crimes and from bloodshed. So we worship God alone, setting naught beside Him, counting as forbidden what He hath forbidden and as licit what He hath allowed. For these reasons have our people turned against us, and have persecuted us to make us forsake our religion and revert from the worship of God to the worship of idols. That is why we have come to thy country, having chosen thee above all others; and we have been happy in thy protection, and it is our hope, O King, that here, with thee, we shall not suffer wrong."

The royal interpreters translated all that he had said. The Negus then asked if they had with them any Revelation that their Prophet had brought them from God and, when Ja'far answered that they had, he said: "Then recite it to me," whereupon Ja'far recited a passage from the *Sūrah* of Mary, which had been revealed shortly before their departure:

> *And make mention of Mary in the Book, when she withdrew from her people unto a place towards the east, and secluded herself from them; and We sent unto her Our Spirit, and it appeared unto her in the likeness of a perfect man. She said: I take refuge from thee in the Infinitely Good, if any piety thou hast. He said: I am none other than a messenger from thy Lord, that I may bestow on thee a son most pure. She said: How can there be for me a son, when no man hath touched me, nor am I unchaste? He said: Even so shall it be; thy Lord saith: It is easy for Me. That We may make him a sign for mankind and a mercy from Us; and it is a thing ordained.*[1]

The Negus wept, and his bishops wept also, when they heard him recite, and when it was translated they wept again, and the Negus said: "This hath truly come from the same source as that which Jesus brought." Then he turned to the two envoys of Quraysh and said: "Ye may go, for by God I will not deliver them unto you; they shall not be betrayed."

But when they had withdrawn from the royal presence, 'Amr said to his companion: "Tomorrow I will tell him a thing that shall tear up this green growing prosperity of theirs by the roots. I will tell him that they aver that Jesus the son of Mary is a slave." So the next morning he went to the Negus and said: "O King, they utter an enormous lie about Jesus the son of Mary.

[1] XIX, 16–21.

Do but send to them, and ask them what they say of him." So he sent them word to come to him again and to tell him what they said of Jesus, whereupon they were troubled, for nothing of this kind had ever yet befallen them. They consulted together as to what they should reply when the question was put to them, though they all knew that they had no choice but to say what God had said. So when they entered the royal presence, and it was said to them: "What say ye of Jesus, the son of Mary?" Ja'far answered: "We say of him what our Prophet brought unto us, that he is the slave of God and His Messenger and His Spirit and His Word which He cast unto Mary the blessed virgin." The Negus took up a piece of wood and said: "Jesus the son of Mary exceedeth not what thou hast said by the length of this stick." And when the generals round him snorted, he added: "For all your snorting." Then he turned to Ja'far and his companions and said: "Go your ways, for ye are safe in my land. Not for mountains of gold would I harm a single man of you"; and with a movement of his hand towards the envoys of Quraysh, he said to his attendant: "Return unto these two men their gifts, for I have no use for them." So 'Amr and the other man went back ignominiously to Mecca.

Meantime the news of what the Negus had said about Jesus spread among the people, and they were troubled and came out against him, asking for an explanation, and accusing him of having left their religion. He thereupon sent to Ja'far and his companions and made ready boats for them and told them to embark and be ready to set sail if necessary. Then he took a parchment and wrote on it: "He testifieth that there is no god but God and that Muḥammad is His slave and His Messenger and that Jesus the son of Mary is His slave and His Messenger and His Spirit and His Word which He cast unto Mary." Then he put it beneath his gown and went out to his people who were assembled to meet him. And he said to them: "Abyssinians, have I not the best claim to be your king?" They said that he had. "Then what think ye of my life amongst you?" "It hath been the best of lives," they answered. "Then what is it that troubleth you?" he said. "Thou hast left our religion," they said, "and hast maintained that Jesus is a slave." "Then what say ye of Jesus?" he asked. "We say that he is the son of God," they answered. Then he put his hand on his breast, pointing to where the parchment was hidden, and testified to his belief in "this", which they took to refer to their words.[1] So they were satisfied and went away, for they were happy under his rule, and only wished to be reassured; and the Negus sent word to Ja'far and his companions that they could disembark and go back to their dwellings, where they went on living as before, in comfort and security.

[1] I.I. 224.

# XXVIII
# *'Umar*

WHEN the two envoys returned to Mecca with the news that they had been rebuffed and that the Muslims had been established in the favour of the Negus, Quraysh were indignant and dismayed. They immediately set about intensifying their repression and persecution of the believers, largely under the direction of Abu Jahl, whose nephew 'Umar was one of the most violent and unrestrained in carrying out his instructions. 'Umar was at this time about twenty-six years old, a headstrong young man, not easily deterred, and of great resolution. But unlike his uncle he was pious, and here in fact lay his chief motive for opposing the new religion. Khaṭṭāb had brought him up to venerate the Ka'bah and to respect everything that had come to be inseparably connected with it in the way of gods and goddesses. It was all woven together for him into a sacred unity that was not to be questioned and still less tampered with. Quraysh also had been one; but Mecca was now a city of two religions and two communities. He saw clearly, moreover, that the trouble had one cause only. Remove the man who was that cause, and everything would soon be as it had been before. There was no other remedy, but that would be a certain remedy. He continued to brood along these lines, and eventually the day came – it was soon after the return of the unsuccessful envoys from Abyssinia – when a sudden wave of anger goaded him to action, and taking up his sword he set out from his house. No sooner had he left it than he came face to face with Nu'aym ibn 'Abd Allāh, one of his fellow clansmen. Nu'aym had entered Islam, but he kept this a secret in fear of 'Umar and others of his people. The grim expression which he now saw on 'Umar's face prompted him to ask him where he was going. "I am going to Muḥammad, that renegade, who hath split Quraysh into two," said 'Umar, "and I shall kill him." Nu'aym tried to stop him by pointing out that he himself would certainly be killed. But when he saw that 'Umar was deaf to such an argument he thought of another way by which he might at least delay him, in time to give the alarm. This would mean betraying a secret of fellow Muslims who, like himself, were concealing their Islam; but he knew that they would forgive him, and even applaud him, in the circumstances. "O 'Umar," he said, "why not first go back to the people of thine own house, and set them to rights." "What people of my house?" said 'Umar. "Thy brother-in-law Sa'īd and thy sister Fāṭimah," said Nu'aym. "They are both followers of Muḥammad in his religion. On thy head may it fall if thou let them be." Without a word 'Umar turned and made straight for his sister's house. Now there was a poor confederate of

Zuhrah named Khabbāb who often came to recite the Koran to Sa'īd and Fāṭimah; and he was with them at that moment with some written pages of the Sūrah named *Ṭā-Hā*[1] which had just been revealed and which they were reading together. When they heard the voice of 'Umar angrily calling out his sister's name as he approached, Khabbāb hid in a corner of the house, and Fāṭimah took the manuscript and put it under her gown. But 'Umar had heard the sound of their reading, and when he came in he said to them: "What was that jibbering I heard?" They tried to assure him he had heard nothing. "Hear it I did," he said, "and I am told that ye both have become followers of Muḥammad." Then he set upon his brother-in-law Sa'īd and grappled with him, and when Fāṭimah went to the defence of her husband, 'Umar struck her a blow which broke the skin. "It is even so," they said, "we are Muslims and we believe in God and in His Messenger. So do what thou wilt." Fāṭimah's wound was bleeding, and when 'Umar saw the blood he was sorry for what he had done. A change came over him, and he said to his sister: "Give me that script that I even now heard you reading, that I may see what it is that Muḥammad hath brought." Like them, 'Umar could read; but when he asked for the script she said, "We fear to trust thee with it." "Fear not," he said, and, unbuckling his sword-belt and laying down his sword, he swore by his gods that he would give it back when he had read it. She could see that he was softened, and she was filled with longing that he should enter Islam. "O my brother," she said, "thou art impure in thine idolatry, and only the pure may touch it." Thereupon 'Umar went and washed himself, and she gave him the page on which was written the opening of *Ṭā-Hā*. He began to read it, and when he had read a passage he said: "How beautiful and how noble are these words!" When Khabbāb heard this he came out from his hiding-place and said: "'Umar, I have hope that God hath chosen thee through the prayer of His Prophet, whom yesterday I heard pray: 'O God, strengthen Islam with Abū l-Ḥakam the son of Hishām or with 'Umar the son of Khaṭṭāb!'" "O Khabbāb," said 'Umar, "where will Muḥammad now be, that I may go to him and enter Islam?" Khabbāb told him that he was at the house of Arqam near the Ṣafā Gate with many of his companions; and 'Umar girt on his sword again and went to Ṣafā, knocked at the door of the house, and said who he was. They had been warned by Nu'aym, so that his coming was not unexpected, but they were struck by the subdued tone of his voice. One of the companions went to the door and looked through a chink and came back in some dismay. "O Messenger of God," he said, "it is indeed 'Umar and he is girt with his sword." "Let him come in," said Ḥamzah. "If he hath come with good intent, we will give him a wealth of good; and if his intent be evil, we will slay him with his own sword." The Prophet agreed that he should be admitted and, advancing to meet him, he seized him by the belt and pulled him into the middle of the room, saying: "What hath brought thee here, O son of Khaṭṭāb? I cannot see thee desisting until God send down some calamity upon thee." "O Messenger of God," said 'Umar, "I have come to thee that I may declare my faith in God, and in His Messenger and in what he hath brought from God." "*Allāhu Akbar* (God

[1] XX.

*is Most Great*)," said the Prophet, in such a way that every man and woman in the house knew that 'Umar had entered Islam; and they all rejoiced.[1]

There was no question of 'Umar's keeping his Islam secret. He wished to tell everyone, in particular those who were most hostile to the Prophet. In after years he used to say: "When I entered Islam that night, I thought to myself: Which of the people in Mecca is the most violent in enmity against God's Messenger, that I may go to him and tell him I have become a Muslim? My answer was: Abū Jahl. So the next morning I went and knocked at his door, and Abū Jahl came out and said: "The best of welcomes to my sister's son! What hath brought thee here?" I answered: "I came to tell thee that I believe in God and in His Messenger Muḥammad; and I testify to the truth of that which he hath brought." "God curse thee!" he said, "and may His curse be on the tidings thou hast brought!" Then he slammed the door in my face."[2]

[1] I.I. 227. [2] I.I. 230.

# XXIX

# *The Ban and its Annulment*

IT was not tolerable to ʿUmar that Quraysh should worship their gods openly at the Kaʿbah, while the believers worshipped God in secret. So he used to pray in front of the Kaʿbah and he would encourage other Muslims to pray with him. Sometimes he and Ḥamzah would go with a large body of the faithful to the sanctuary, and on such occasions the leaders of Quraysh kept away. It would have been a loss of dignity for them to stand by and let this happen, yet if they resisted they knew that ʿUmar would stop at nothing. They were none the less determined not to allow this young man to imagine that he had defeated them, and under pressure from Abū Jahl they decided that the best solution would be to place an interdiction on the whole clan of Hāshim who, with the exception of Abū Lahab, were resolved to protect their kinsman whether they believed him to be a Prophet or not. A document was drawn up according to which it was undertaken that no one would marry a woman of Hāshim or give his daughter in marriage to a man of Hāshim; and no one was to sell anything to them, or buy anything from them. This was to continue until the clan of Hāshim themselves outlawed Muḥammad, or until he renounced his claim to prophethood. No less than forty leaders of Quraysh set their seal to this agreement though not all of them were equally in favour of it, and some of them had to be won over. The clan of Muṭṭalib refused to forsake their Hāshimite cousins, and they were included in the ban. The document was solemnly placed inside the Kaʿbah.

For the sake of mutual security the Bani Hāshim gathered round Abū Ṭālib in that quarter of the hollow of Mecca where he and most of the clan lived. At the arrival of the Prophet and Khadījah with their household, Abū Lahab and his wife moved away and went to live in a house which he owned elsewhere, to demonstrate their solidarity with Quraysh as a whole.

The ban was not always rigorously enforced, nor was it possible to close all the loopholes owing to the fact that a woman was still a member of her own family after marrying into another clan. Abū Jahl was continually on the watch, but he could not always impose his will. One day he met Khadījah's nephew Ḥakīm with a slave carrying a bag of flour, and they appeared to be making for the dwellings of the Bani Hāshim. He accused them of taking food to the enemy and threatened to denounce Ḥakīm before Quraysh. While they were arguing, Abu l-Bakhtarī, another man of Asad, came and asked what was the matter, and when it was explained to him he said to Abū Jahl: "It is his aunt's flour and she hath sent to him for it. Let the man go on his way." Neither Ḥakīm nor Abu l-Bakhtarī were Muslims, but the passing of this bag of flour from one member of the clan of Asad to another could concern no one outside that clan. The interference of the Makhzūmite was outrageous and intolerable; and when Abū Jahl persisted Abu l-Bakhtari picked up a camel's jawbone and brought it down on his head with such force that he was half stunned and fell to the ground, whereupon they trampled him heavily underfoot, to the gratification of Ḥamzah who happened to come by at that moment.

Ḥakīm was within his rights, but others simply defied the ban out of sympathy for its victims. Hishām ibn 'Amr of 'Āmir had no Hāshimite blood, but his family had close marriage connections with the clan; and under cover of the night he would often bring a camel laden with food to the entrance to Abū Ṭālib's quarter. Then he would take off its halter and strike it a blow on the flank so that it would go past their houses; and another night he would load it with clothes and other gifts.

Apart from such help from unbelievers, the Muslims themselves of the other clans, especially Abū Bakr and 'Umar, contrived various ways of thwarting the interdiction. When two years had passed, Abū Bakr could no longer be counted as a wealthy man. But despite such help there was perpetual shortage of food amongst the two victimised clans, and sometimes the shortage bordered on famine.

During the sacred months, when they could leave their retreat and go about freely without fear of being molested, the Prophet frequently went to the Sanctuary, and the leaders of Quraysh took advantage of his presence there to insult him and to satirise him. Sometimes when he recited Revelations warning Quraysh of what had happened to former peoples, Naḍr of 'Abd ad-Dār would rise to his feet and say: "By God, Muḥammad is no better as a speaker than I am. His talk is but tales of the men of old. They have been written out for him even as mine have been written out for me." Then he would tell them tales of Rustum and Isfandiyār and the kings of Persia. In this connection was revealed one of the many verses which refer to the heart as the faculty by which man has sight of supernatural realities. The eye of the heart, though closed in fallen man, is able to take in a glimmering of light and this is faith. But an evil way of living causes a covering like rust to accumulate over the heart so that it cannot sense the Divine origin of God's Message: *When Our Revelations are recited unto him, he saith: Tales of the men of old. Nay, but their earnings are even as rust over their hearts.*[1] As to the opposite state of this, the supreme possibility of insight, the Prophet affirmed of himself on more than one occasion that the eye of his heart was open even in sleep: "Mine eye sleepeth, but my heart is awake."[2]

Another Revelation, one of the very few that mentions by name any contemporary of the Prophet, had now come affirming that Abū Lahab and his wife were destined for Hell.[3] Umm Jamīl heard of this, and she went

[1] LXXXIII, 13–14. [2] I.I. 375; B. XIX, 16, etc. [3] XCI.

to the Mosque with a stone pestle in her hand in search of the Prophet, who was sitting with Abū Bakr. She came up to Abū Bakr and said to him: "Where is thy companion?" He knew that she meant the Prophet who was there in front of her, and he was too amazed to speak. "I have heard," she said, "that he hath lampooned me, and by God, if I had found him I would have shattered his mouth with this pestle." Then she said: "As for me, I am a poetess indeed," and she uttered a rhyme about the Prophet:

"We disobey the reprobate,
Flout the commands he doth dictate,
And his religion hate."

When she had gone, Abū Bakr asked the Prophet if she had not seen him. "She saw me not," he said. "God took away her sight from me." As to "Reprobate" – in Arabic *mudhammam*, blamed, the exact opposite of *muḥammad*, praised, glorified – some of Quraysh had taken to calling him that by way of revilement. He would say to his companions: "Is it not wondrous how God turneth away from me the injuries of Quraysh? They revile Mudhammam, whereas I am Muḥammad."[1]

The ban on Hāshim and Muṭṭalib had lasted two years or more and showed no signs of having any of the desired effects. It had moreover the undesired and unforeseen effect of drawing further attention to the Prophet and of causing the new religion to be talked of more than ever throughout Arabia. But independently of these considerations, many of Quraysh began to have second thoughts about the ban, especially those who had close relatives amongst its victims. The time had come for a change of mind to take place, and the first man to act was that same Hishām who had so often sent his camel with food and clothes for the Hāshimites. But he knew that he could achieve nothing by himself, so he went to the Makhzūmite Zuhayr, one of the two sons of the Prophet's aunt 'Ātikah, and said to him: "Art thou content to eat food and wear clothes and marry women when thou knowest how it is with thy mother's kinsmen. They can neither buy nor sell, neither marry nor give in marriage; and I swear by God that if they were the brethren of the mother of Abū l-Ḥakam" – he meant Abū Jahl – "and thou hadst called upon him to do what he hath called on thee to do, he would never have done it." "Confound thee, Hishām," said Zuhayr. "What can I do? I am but a single man. If I had with me another man, I would not rest until I had annulled it." "I have found a man," said Hishām. "Who is he?" "Myself." "Find us a third," said Zuhayr. So Hishām went to Muṭ'im ibn 'Adī, one of the leading men of the clan of Nawfal – a grandson of Nawfal himself, brother of Hāshim and Muṭṭalib. "Is it thy will," he said, "that two of the sons of 'Abdu Manāf should perish whilst thou lookest on in approval of Quraysh? By God, if ye enable them to do this ye will soon find them doing the like to you." Muṭ'im asked for a fourth man, so Hishām went to Abu l-Bakhtarī of Asad, the man who had struck Abū Jahl on account of Khadījah's bag of flour, and when he asked for a fifth man Hishām went to

[1] I.I. 234.

another Asadite, Zam'ah ibn al-Aswad, who agreed to be the fifth without asking for a sixth. They all undertook to meet that night at the outskirts of Hajūn, above Mecca, and there they agreed on their plan of action and bound themselves not to let drop the matter of the document until they had had it annulled. "I am the most nearly concerned," said Zuhayr, "so I will be the first to speak."

Early the next day they joined the gathering of the people in the Mosque and Zuhayr, clad in a long robe, went round the Ka'bah seven times. Then he turned to face the assembly and said: "O people of Mecca, are we to eat food and wear clothes, while the sons of Hāshim perish, unable to buy and unable to sell? By God, I will not be seated until this iniquitous ban be torn up." "Thou liest!" said his cousin Abū Jahl. "It shall not be torn up." "Thou art the better liar," said Zam'ah. "We were not in favour of its being written, when it was written." "Zam'ah is right," said Abu l-Bakhtarī. "We are not in favour of what is written in it, neither do we hold with it." "Ye are both right," said Muṭ'im, "and he that saith no is a liar. We call God to witness our innocence of it and of what is written in it." Hishām said much the same, and when Abū Jahl began to accuse them of having plotted it all overnight, Muṭ'im cut him short by going into the Ka'bah to fetch the document. He came out in triumph with a small piece of vellum in his hand: the worms had eaten the ban, all but the opening words "In Thy Name, O God".

Most of Quraysh had been virtually won over already, and this unquestionable omen was a final and altogether decisive argument. Abū Jahl and one or two like-minded men knew that it would be vain to resist. The ban was formally revoked, and a body of Quraysh went to give the good news to the Bani Hāshim and the Bani l-Muṭṭalib.

There was much relief in Mecca after the ban was lifted, and for the moment hostilities against the Muslims were relaxed. Exaggerated reports of this soon reached Abyssinia, whereupon some of the exiles immediately set about making preparations to return to Mecca while others, Ja'far amongst them, decided to remain for a while where they were.

Meantime the leaders of Quraysh concentrated their efforts on trying to persuade the Prophet to agree to a compromise. This was the nearest approach they had yet made to him. Walīd and other chiefs proposed that they should all practise both religions. The Prophet was saved the trouble of formulating his refusal by an immediate answer which came directly from Heaven in a *sūrah* of six verses:

> *Say: O disbelievers, I shall not worship that which ye worship, nor will ye worship that which I worship, nor have I worshipped that which ye worship, nor have ye worshipped that which I worship. For you your religion and for me mine.*[1]

As a result, the momentary good will had already much diminished by the time the returning exiles reached the edge of the sacred precinct.

[1] CIX.

Except for Ja'far and 'Ubayd Allāh ibn Jahsh, all the Prophet's cousins returned. With them came also 'Uthmān and Ruqayyah. Another Shamsite who returned with 'Uthmān was Abū Hudhayfah. He could rely on his father 'Utbah to protect him. But Abū Salamah and Umm Salamah could hope for nothing but persecution from their own clan, so before they entered Mecca Abū Salamah sent word to his Hāshimite uncle Abū Ṭālib, asking for his protection which he agreed to give, much to the indignation of Makhzūm. "Thou hast protected from us thy nephew Muḥammad," they said, "but why art thou protecting our own clansman?" "He is my sister's son," said Abū Ṭālib. "If I did not protect my sister's son, I could not protect my brother's son." They had no choice but to allow him his rights of chieftaincy. Moreover, on this occasion Abū Lahab supported his brother, and Makhzūm knew that he was one of their most powerful allies against the Prophet, so they did not wish to offend him. For his part, he perhaps regretted having manifested so clearly, at the time of the ban, the implacable hatred which he felt for his nephew. Not that his hatred was diminished in any sense; but he wished to be on better terms with his family for the reason that after his elder brother's death he might normally hope to take his place as chief of the clan; and it may be that he now saw in Abū Ṭālib signs that he had not much longer to live.

# XXX

# *Paradise and Eternity*

ANOTHER returned emigrant who required help against his own people was 'Umar's brother-in-law, 'Uthmān ibn Maẓ'ūn of Jumaḥ, for he knew well that his cousins Umayyah and Ubayy would persecute him. This time it was Makhzūm who safeguarded a man of another clan: Walīd himself took 'Uthmān under his protection; but, when 'Uthmān saw his fellow Muslims being persecuted while he remained safe, he went to Walīd and renounced his protection. "Son of my brother," said the old man, "hath any of my people harmed thee?" "Not so," said 'Uthmān, "but I would have protection of God and I desire not the protection of any but Him". So he went with Walīd to the Mosque and publicly absolved him of his protection.

Some days later it happened that the poet Labīd was reciting to Quraysh, and 'Uthmān was present at the large gathering which had assembled to hear him. At a level somewhat higher than that of the general giftedness of the Arabs for poetry, there were the many distinctly gifted poets like Abū Ṭālib and Hubayrah and Abū Sufyān the son of Ḥārith. But beyond these there were the few who were counted as great; and Labīd was by common consent one of them. He was perhaps the greatest living Arab poet, and Quraysh felt privileged to have him amongst them. One of the verses he now recited began:

"Lo, everything save God is naught"

"Thou hast spoken true," said 'Uthmān. Labīd went on:

"And all delights away shall vanish."

"Thou liest," exclaimed 'Uthmān. "The delight of Paradise shall never vanish." Labīd was not accustomed to being interrupted; as to Quraysh, they were not only astonished and outraged but also exceedingly embarrassed, for the poet was their guest. "O men of Quraysh," he said, "they who sat with you as friends were never wont to be ill-treated. Since when is this?" One of the gathering rose to proffer the tribe's excuses. "This man is but a dolt," he said, "one of a band of dolts that have left our religion. Let not thy soul be moved by what he saith." 'Uthmān retorted with such vehemence that the speaker came and hit him over the eye, so that his brow turned green; and Walīd, who was sitting nearby, remarked to him that his eye need never have suffered if he had remained under his protection.

"Nay," said 'Uthmān, "my good eye is indeed a pauper for want of what hath befallen her sister in the way of God. I am under His protection who is mightier and more determining than thou." "Come, son of my brother," said Walīd, "renew thy pact with me." But 'Uthmān declined.

The Prophet was not present at the gathering. But he heard of the poem of Labīd and of what had ensued. His only recorded comment was: "The truest word that poet ever spake is: "Lo, everything save God is naught."[1] He did not blame Labīd for the words which immediately followed. The poet could be credited with meaning that "all earthly delights away shall vanish"; and on the other hand, all Paradises and Delights which are Eternal can be thought of as included in God or in *the Face of God*. There had come, about this time, the Revelation: *Everything perisheth but His Face*[2] and in an earlier Revelation are the words: *Eternal is the Face of thy Lord in Its Majesty and Bounty.*[3] Where this Eternal Bounty is, there its recipients must be, and also their delights.

There now came a more explicit Revelation which contained the following passage. The first verse refers to the Judgement: *On the day when it cometh no soul shall speak but by His leave, wretched some, and others blissful. As for the wretched, in the Fire shall they be, to sigh and to wail is their portion, abiding therein as long as heaven and earth endure, except as God will. Verily thy Lord is ever the doer of what He will. And as for the blissful, in the Garden shall they be, abiding therein as long as heaven and earth endure, except as God will – a gift that shall not be taken away.*[4]

The closing words show that it is not the Divine Will that the gift of Paradise to man after the Judgement shall be taken away from him as was his first Paradise. Other questions relating to this passage were answered by the Prophet himself, who continually spoke to his followers about the Resurrection, the Judgement, Hell and Paradise. On one occasion he said: "God, who bringeth whom He will into His Mercy, shall enter into Paradise the people of Paradise, and into Hell the people of Hell. Then will He say (to the Angels): 'Look for him in whose heart ye can find faith of the weight of a grain of mustard seed, and take him out of Hell' . . . Then they will take out a multitude of mankind and will say: 'Our Lord, we have left therein not one of those whereof Thou didst command us', and He will say: 'Return and take out him in whose heart ye find an atom's weight of good.' Then will they take out a multitude of mankind and will say: 'Our Lord, no goodness have we left therein.' Then will the Angels intercede, and the Prophets and the believers. Then will God say: 'The angels have interceded, and the prophets have interceded, and the believers have interceded. There remaineth only the intercession of the Most Merciful of the merciful.' And He will take out from the fire those who did no good and will cast them into a river at the entrance to Paradise which is called the River of Life."[5]

And of those in Paradise the Prophet said: "God will say to the people of Paradise: 'Are ye well pleased?' and they will say: 'How should we not be

1 B. LXIII, 26. 2 XXVIII, 88. 3 LV, 27.
4 XI, 105–8. 5 M. I, 79; B. XCVII, 24.

well pleased, O Lord, inasmuch Thou hast given us that which Thou hast not given to any of thy creatures else?' Then will He say: 'Shall I not give you better than that?', and they will say: 'What thing, O Lord, is better?' and He will say: 'I will let down upon you My *Riḍwān*.'"[1] The ultimate beatitude of *Riḍwān*, sometimes translated "Good Pleasure", is interpreted to mean God's final and absolute acceptance of a soul and His taking of that soul to Himself and His Eternal Good Pleasure therein. This supreme Paradise must not be taken as excluding what is known as Paradise in the usual sense, since the Koran promises that for each blessed soul there will be two Paradises,[2] and in speaking of his own state in the Hereafter the Prophet likewise spoke of it as a twofold blessing, "the meeting with my Lord, and Paradise".[3]

[1] M. LI, 2. [2] LV, 46. [3] I.I. 1000.

# XXXI

# *The Year of Sadness*

IN the year AD 619, not long after the annulment of the ban, the Prophet suffered a great loss in the death of his wife Khadījah. She was about sixty-five years old and he was nearing fifty. They had lived together in profound harmony for twenty-five years, and she had been not only his wife but also his intimate friend, his wise counsellor, and mother to his whole household including 'Alī and Zayd. His four daughters were overcome with grief, but he was able to comfort them by telling them that Gabriel had once come to him and told him to give Khadījah greetings of Peace from her Lord and to tell her that He had prepared for her an abode in Paradise.

Another loss followed closely upon the death of Khadījah, a loss less great and less penetrating in itself, but at the same time less consolable and more serious in its outward consequences. Abū Ṭālib fell ill, and it soon became clear that he was dying. On his deathbed he was visited by a group of the leaders of Quraysh – 'Utbah and Shaybah and Abū Sufyān of 'Abdu Shams, Umayyah of Jumaḥ, Abū Jahl of Makhzūm and others – and they said to him: "Abū Ṭālib, thou knowest the esteem we have for thee; and now this that thou seest hath come upon thee, and we fear for thee. Thou knowest what is between us and thy brother's son. So call him to thee, and take for him a gift from us, and take for us a gift from him, that he should let us be, and we will let him be. Let him leave us and our religion in peace." So Abū Ṭālib sent to him, and when he came he said to him: "Son of my brother, these nobles of thy people have come together on account of thee, to give and to take." "So be it," said the Prophet. "Give me one word – a word by which ye shall rule over the Arabs, and the Persians shall be your subjects." "Yea, by thy father," said Abū Jahl, "for that we will give thee one word, and ten words more." "Ye must say," said the Prophet, "*there is no god but God*, and ye must renounce what ye worship apart from Him." They clapped their hands and said: "Wouldst thou, O Muḥammad, make the gods one god? Thy bidding is strange indeed!" Then they said to each other: "This man will give you nothing of what ye ask, so go your ways and keep to the religion of your fathers until God judge between you and him."

When they had gone, Abū Ṭālib said to the Prophet: "Son of my brother, thou didst not, as I saw it, ask of them anything out of the way." These words filled the Prophet with longing that he should enter Islam. "Uncle," he said, "say thou the words, that through them I may intercede for thee on the day of the Resurrection." "Son of my brother," he said, "if I did not fear that Quraysh would think I had but said the words in dread of death, then would I say them. Yet would my saying them be but to please thee." Then, when death drew near to Abū Ṭālib, 'Abbās saw him moving his lips and he put his ear close to him and listened and then he said: "My brother hath spoken the words thou didst bid him speak." But the Prophet said: "I heard him not."

It was now becoming difficult in Mecca for almost all those who had no official protection. Before he joined the Prophet Abū Bakr had been a man of considerable influence, but unlike 'Umar and Ḥamzah, he was not a dangerous man in himself and therefore did not inspire fear except in those who had learned to esteem him for spiritual reasons; and when his Islam set a barrier between himself and the leaders of Quraysh his influence with them decreased almost to nothing, just as it increased within the community of the new religion. For Abū Bakr the situation was, moreover, aggravated by his being known to be responsible for many conversions; and it may have been partly in revenge for the Islam of Aswad the son of Nawfal that one day Nawfal himself, Khadījah's half-brother, organised an attack on Abū Bakr and Ṭalḥah, who were left lying in the public highway, bound hand and foot and roped together. Nor did any of the men of Taym intervene against the men of Asad, which suggests that they had disowned their two leading Muslim clansmen.

There may have been other incidents also. Abū Bakr was on increasingly bad terms with Bilāl's former master Umayyah, the chief of Jumaḥ, amongst whom he lived; and the time came when he felt he had no alternative but to emigrate. Having obtained permission of the Prophet, he set out to join those who had remained in Abyssinia. But before he had reached the Red Sea, he was met by Ibn ad-Dughunnah, at that time the head of a small group of confederate tribes not far from Mecca, allies of Quraysh. This Bedouin chief had known Abū Bakr well in his days of affluence and influence, yet now he had the appearance of a wandering hermit. Amazed at the change, he questioned him. "My people have ill-treated me," said Abū Bakr, "and driven me out, and all I seek is to travel over the face of the earth, worshipping God." "Why have they done this?" said Ibn ad-Dughunnah. "Thou art as an ornament to thy clan, a help in misfortune, a doer of right, ever fulfilling the needs of others. Return, for thou art beneath my protection." So he took him back to Mecca and spoke to the people, saying: "Men of Quraysh, I have given my protection to the son of Abū Quhāfah, so let no one treat him other than well." Quraysh confirmed the protection and promised that Abū Bakr should be safe, but at the instigation of the Bani Jumaḥ they said to his protector: "Tell him to worship his Lord within doors, and to pray and recite what he will there, but tell him not to cause us trouble by letting it be seen and heard, for his appearance is striking and he hath with him a way, so that we fear lest he seduce our sons and our women." Ibn ad-Dughunnah told this to Abū Bakr, and for a while he prayed only in his house and made there his recitations of the Koran; and for a while the tension was relaxed between him and the leaders of the Bani Jumaḥ. Abū Ṭālib was succeeded by Abū Lahab as chief of Hāshim; but the protection that Abū Lahab gave his nephew was merely nominal, and the Prophet was ill-treated as never before. On one occasion a passer-by leaned over his gate and tossed a piece of putrifying offal into his cooking pot; and once when he was praying in the courtyard of his house, a man threw over him a sheep's uterus filthy with blood and excrement. Before disposing of it, the Prophet picked up the object on the end of a stick and said, standing at his gate: "O sons of 'Abdu Manāf, what protection is this?" He had seen that the offender was the Shamsite 'Uqbah,[1] stepfather of 'Uthmān, Ruqayyah's husband. On another occasion, when the Prophet was coming from the Ka'bah, a man took a handful of dirt and threw it in his face and over his head. When he returned home one of his daughters washed him clean of it, weeping the while. "Weep not, little daughter," he said, "God will protect thy father."

It was then that he decided to seek help from Thaqīf, the people of Ṭā'if – a decision which eloquently reflected the apparent gravity of his situation in Mecca. For except that truth can conquer all things, what indeed could be hoped for from Thaqīf, the guardians of the temple of the goddess al-Lāt, whose shrine they liked to think of as comparable to the House of God? There must however be exceptions in Ṭā'if as there were in Mecca, and the Prophet was not without hope as he rode up from the desert towards the welcoming orchards and gardens and cornfields which were the outskirts of the walled city. On his arrival he went straight to the house of three brothers who were the leaders of Thaqīf at that time, the sons of 'Amr ibn Umayyah, the man whom Walīd looked on as his own counterpart in Ṭā'if, the second of "the two great men of the two townships". But when the Prophet asked them to accept Islam and help him against his opponents, one of them immediately said: "If God sent thee, I will tear down the hangings of the Ka'bah!", and another said: "Could God find none but thee to send?" As for the third, he said: "Let me never speak to thee! For if thou art a Messenger from God as thou sayest, then art thou too great a personage for me to address; and if thou liest, it is not fitting that I should speak to thee." So the Prophet rose to leave them, perhaps intending to try elsewhere in Ṭā'if; but when he had left them, they stirred up their slaves and retainers to insult him and shout at him, until a crowd of people were gathered together against him and he was forced to take refuge in a private orchard. Once he had entered it the crowd began to disperse, and, tethering his camel to a palm tree, he made for the shelter of a vine and sat in its shade.

When he felt himself to be in safety and at peace, he prayed: "O God, unto Thee do I complain of my weakness, of my helplessness, and of my lowliness before men. O Most Merciful of the merciful, Thou art Lord of the weak. And Thou art my Lord. Into whose hands wilt Thou entrust me? Unto some far off stranger who will ill-treat me? Or unto a foe whom Thou

[1] He was the second husband of 'Uthmān's mother Arwà, the Prophet's cousin, named after their aunt Arwà, the mother of Ṭulayb.

hast empowered against me? I care not, so Thou be not wroth with me. But Thy favouring help – that were for me the broader way and the wider scope! I take refuge in the Light of Thy Countenance whereby all darknesses are illuminated and the things of this world and the next are rightly ordered, lest Thou make descend Thine anger upon me, or lest Thy wrath beset me. Yet is it Thine to reproach until Thou art well pleased. There is no power and no might except through Thee."[1]

The place where the Prophet had found peace was not as empty as it had seemed. Every man of Quraysh hoped for riches enough to buy a garden and a house on the green hill of Ṭā'if to which he might escape when the heat of Mecca was at its fiercest, and this orchard was not owned by a man of Thaqīf but was part of a property that belonged to the Shamsite leaders 'Utbah and Shaybah, who were even now seated in a corner of their garden adjoining the vineyard. They had seen what had happened, nor were they without feelings of indignation at the way in which the rabble of Thaqīf had ventured to treat a man of Quraysh, who was, moreover, like themselves, of the sons of 'Abdu Manāf. As to the differences which had come between them, were not these now almost at an end? They had last seen Muḥammad at the deathbed of Abū Ṭālib; and now he was without a protector, and clearly in desperate straits. Feeling they could afford to be generous, they called a young Christian slave of theirs named 'Addās, and said to him: "Take a cluster of these grapes and put them on this platter. Then give it to that man, and bid him eat thereof." 'Addās did as they had ordered, and when the Prophet put his hand to the grapes he said: "In the name of God." 'Addās looked keenly into his face; then he said: "Those words are not what the people of this country say." "From what country art thou?" said the Prophet. "And what is thy religion?" "I am a Christian," he said, "of the people of Nineveh." "From the city of the righteous man Jonah, the son of Matta," said the Prophet. "How knowest thou aught of Jonah the son of Matta?" said 'Addās. "He is my brother," was the answer. "He was a Prophet, and I am a Prophet." Then 'Addās bent over him and kissed his head and his hands and his feet.

When they saw this, the two brothers exclaimed, each to the other, as if with one voice: "So much for thy slave! Already hath he been corrupted!" And when 'Addās came back to them, leaving the Prophet to eat in peace, they said: "Out upon thee, 'Addās! What made thee kiss that man's head and his hands and his feet?" He answered: "Master, there is nothing on earth better than this man. He hath told me of things that only a Prophet could know." "Out upon thee, 'Addās!" they said. "Let him not seduce thee from thy religion, for thy religion is better than his."

The Prophet left Ṭā'if and started on his way towards Mecca when he saw that no good was to be gained at this juncture from the tribe of Thaqīf. Late that night he reached the valley of Nakhlah, the half-way halt between the two townships which had rejected him. At the moment of his sharpest consciousness of this rejection, his prophethood had been acknowledged by a man from far-off Nineveh; and now, while he was standing in prayer at Nakhlah, a company of the jinn passed by – seven

[1] I.I. 280.

jinn from Naṣībīn – and they stopped spellbound by the words he was reciting from the Koran. The Prophet knew that he had not been sent to the world of men only. The Revelation had recently affirmed: *We sent thee not save as a mercy for the worlds*;[1] and one of the earlier *Sūrahs*[2] is addressed to the jinn as well as to men, warning them both of Hell as a punishment for evil and promising Paradise to both as a reward for piety. There now came the Revelation: *Say: it hath been revealed unto me that a company of the jinn gave ear, and then said: Verily we have heard a wondrous recitation which guideth unto rightness, and we believe in it.*[3] And another Revelation[4] told how the jinn thereupon returned to their community and urged them to respond to *God's summoner*, as they called the Prophet.

The Prophet was unwilling to return to the same conditions which only two days previously had impelled him to leave his home. But if he had a protector, he could continue to fulfil his mission. The Bani Hāshim had failed him, so his thoughts turned to his mother's clan. The situation there was abnormal, for by far the most outstanding and influential man of Zuhrah was Akhnas ibn Sharīq, who was not strictly speaking a member of the clan, nor even of Quraysh. He was in fact of Thaqīf, but he had long been a confederate of Zuhrah, and they had come to consider him as their chief. The Prophet had already decided to ask for his help, when he was overtaken by a horseman also on his way to Mecca but travelling faster than himself, so he asked him to do him the favour of going, on his arrival, to Akhnas and of saying to him: "Muḥammad saith: Wilt thou give me thy protection, that I may deliver the message of my Lord?" The horseman was well disposed, and even undertook to return with the answer, which proved to be negative, for Akhnas simply remarked that a confederate had no power to speak in the name of the clan with which he was federated and to grant a protection which would be binding upon them. The Prophet, who was by this time not far from Mecca, now sent the same request to Suhayl. His reply was equally disappointing, though the reason he advanced for his refusal had nothing to do with his opposition to Islam. It was once more a question of tribal principle. In the Hollow of Mecca his clan was distinct from all the rest as being descended from 'Āmir the son of Lu'ayy,[5] whereas the others were all descended from 'Amir's brother Ka'b. Suhayl simply replied that the sons of 'Āmir do not give protection against the sons of Ka'b. The Prophet now turned aside from the way that led to the city, and took refuge in the cave of Mount Ḥirā' where he had received the first Revelation. From there he sent his petition to a leader more closely related to himself, Muṭ'im, the chief of Nawfal, one of the five who had organised the annulment of the ban, and Muṭ'im immediately agreed. "Let him enter the city," he sent back word; and the next morning, fully armed, together with his sons and his nephews, he escorted the Prophet to the Ka'bah. Abū Jahl asked them if they had become followers of Muḥammad. "We are giving him protection," they replied; and the Makhzūmite could only say: "Whom ye protect, to him we give protection."

[1] XXI, 107. [2] LV. [3] LXXII, 1–2. [4] XLVI, 30–1.
[5] See the genealogical tree, p. 347.

# XXXII

# *"The Light of Thy Countenance"*

FĀṬIMAH, the widow of Abū Ṭālib, had entered Islam, either before or after her husband's death, and so had her daughter Umm Hāni', the sister of 'Alī and Ja'far; but Umm Hāni''s husband Hubayrah was altogether impervious to the message of God's Oneness. He none the less made the Prophet welcome when he came to their house, and if it was the time for a prayer during one of these visits the Muslims of the household would pray together. On one occasion, when they had all prayed the night prayer behind the Prophet, Umm Hāni' invited him to spend the night with them. He accepted her invitation; but after a brief sleep he rose and went to the Mosque, for he loved to visit the Ka'bah during the night hours. While he was there, the desire to sleep came over him again, and he lay down in the Ḥijr.

"Whilst I was sleeping in the Ḥijr," he said, "Gabriel came to me and spurred me with his foot whereupon I sat upright, yet I saw nothing and lay down once again. A second time he came; and a third time, and then he took me by the arm and I rose and stood beside him, and he led me out to the gate of the Mosque, and there was a white beast, between a mule and an ass, with wings at his sides wherewith he moved his legs; and his every stride was as far as his eye could see."[1]

The Prophet then told how he mounted Burāq, for so the beast was named; and with the Archangel at his side, pointing the way and measuring his pace to that of the heavenly steed, they sped northwards beyond Yathrib and beyond Khaybar, until they reached Jerusalem. Then they were met by a company of Prophets – Abraham, Moses, Jesus and others – and when he prayed on the site of the Temple, they gathered together behind him in prayer. Then two vessels were brought before him and offered him, one of wine the other of milk. He took the vessel of milk and drank from it, but left the vessel of wine, and Gabriel said: "Thou hast been guided unto the path primordial, and hast guided thereunto thy people, O Muḥammad, and wine is forbidden you."

Then, as had happened to others before him – to Enoch and Elijah and Jesus and Mary – Muḥammad was taken up out of this life to Heaven.

[1] I.I. 264.

From the rock in the centre of the site of the Temple he again mounted Burāq, who moved his wings in upward flight and became for his rider as the chariot of fire had been for Elijah. Led by the Archangel, who now revealed himself as a heavenly being, they ascended beyond the domain of earthly space and time and bodily forms, and as they passed through the seven Heavens he met again those Prophets with whom he had prayed in Jerusalem. But there they had appeared to him as they had been during their life on earth, whereas now he saw them in their celestial reality, even as they now saw him, and he marvelled at their transfiguration. Of Joseph he said that his face had the splendour of the moon at its full,[1] and that he had been endowed with no less than the half of all existing beauty.[2] Yet this did not diminish Muḥammad's wonderment at his other brethren, and he mentioned in particular the great beauty of Aaron.[3] Of the Gardens that he visited in the different Heavens he said afterwards: "A piece of Paradise the size of a bow is better than all beneath the sun, whereon it riseth and setteth; and if a woman of the people of Paradise appeared unto the people of earth, she would fill the space between Heaven and here below with light and with fragrance."[4] Everything he now saw, he saw with the eye of the Spirit; and of his spiritual nature, with reference to the beginnings of all earthly nature, he said: "I was a Prophet when Adam was yet between water and clay."[5]

The summit of his ascent was *the Lote Tree of the Uttermost End*. So it is named in the Koran, and, in one of the oldest commentaries, based on the sayings of the Prophet, it is said: "The Lote Tree is rooted in the Throne, and it marks the end of the knowledge of every knower, be he Archangel or Prophet-Messenger. All beyond it is a hidden mystery, unknown to any save God Alone."[6] At this summit of the universe Gabriel appeared to him in all his archangelic splendour, even as he was first created.[7] Then, in the words of the Revelation: *When there enshrouded the Lote Tree that which enshroudeth, the eye wavered not nor did it transgress. Verily he beheld, of all the signs of his Lord, the greatest.*[8] According to the commentary, the Divine Light descended upon the Lote Tree and enshrouded it and all else beside, and the eye of the Prophet beheld it without wavering and without turning aside from it.[9] Such was the answer – or one of the answers – to the supplication implicit in his words: "I take refuge in the Light of Thy Countenance."

At the Lote Tree the Prophet received for his people the command of fifty prayers a day; and it was then[10] that he received the Revelation which contains the creed of Islam: *The messenger believeth, and the faithful believe, in what hath been revealed unto him from his Lord. Each one believeth in God and His angels and His books and His messengers: we made no distinction between any of His messengers. And they say: we hear and we obey; grant us, Thou our Lord, Thy forgiveness; unto Thee is the ultimate becoming*[11]

They made their descent through the seven Heavens even as they had

[1] I.I. 270. [2] A.H. III, 286. [3] I.I. 270. [4] B. L.VI, 6.
[5] Tir. XLVI, 1; A.H. IV, 66. [6] Ṭab., *Tafsīr*, LIII.
[7] M. I, 280; B. LIX, 7. [8] LIII, 16–18.
[9] Ṭab., *Tafsīr*, LIII. [10] M. I, 280. [11] II, 285.

ascended. The Prophet said: "On my return, when I passed Moses – and what a good friend he was unto you! – he asked me: 'How many prayers have been laid upon thee?' I told him fifty prayers every day and he said: 'The congregational prayer is a weighty thing, and thy people are weak. Return unto thy Lord, and ask Him to lighten the load for thee and thy people.' So I returned and asked my Lord to make it lighter, and He took away ten. Then I passed Moses again, and he repeated what he had said before, so I returned again, and ten more prayers were taken from me. But every time I returned unto Moses he sent me back until finally all the prayers had been taken from me except five for each day and night. Then I returned unto Moses, but still he said the same as before; and I said: 'I have returned unto my Lord and asked Him until I am ashamed. I will not go again.' And so it is that he who performeth the five in good faith and in trust of God's bounty, unto him shall be given the meed of fifty prayers."[1]

When the Prophet and the Archangel had made their descent to the Rock at Jerusalem, they returned to Mecca the way they had come, overtaking many southbound caravans. It was still night when they reached the Ka'bah. From there the Prophet went again to the house of his cousin. In her words: "A little before dawn the Prophet woke us, and when we had prayed the dawn prayer, he said: 'O Umm Hāni', I prayed with you the last evening prayer in this valley as thou sawest. Then went I to Jerusalem and there prayed; and now have I prayed with you the morning prayer as thou seest.' He rose to go, and I seized his robe with such force that it came away, laying bare his belly, as if it had been but cotton cloth draped round him. 'O Prophet of God,' I said. 'Tell not the people this, for they will give thee the lie and insult thee.' 'By God, I will tell them,' he said."[2]

He went to the Mosque and told those whom he met there of his journey to Jerusalem. His enemies were immediately triumphant, for they now felt they had an irrefutable cause for mockery. Every child of Quraysh knew that a caravan takes a month to go from Mecca to Syria and a month to return. And now Muḥammad claimed to have gone there and back in one night. A group of men went to Abū Bakr and said: "What thinkest thou now of thy friend? He telleth us he went last night to Jerusalem and prayed there and then returned to Mecca." Abū Bakr accused them of lying, but they assured him that Muḥammad was in the Mosque at that moment, speaking about this journey. "If so he saith," said Abū Bakr, "then it is true. And where is the wonder of it? He telleth me that tidings come to him from Heaven to earth in one hour of the day or night, and I know him to be speaking the truth. And that is beyond what ye cavil at."[3] He then went to the Mosque to repeat his confirmation "If so he saith, then it is true," and it was for this that the Prophet gave him the name *aṣ-Ṣiddīq*, which means "the great witness of truth" or "the great confirmer of the truth". Moreover, some of those who had found the story incredible began to have second thoughts, for the Prophet described the caravans he had overtaken on the way home and said where they were and about when they might be expected to arrive in Mecca; and each arrived as predicted, and the details were as he had described. To those in the Mosque he spoke only of his

[1] I.I. 271. [2] I.I. 267. [3] I.I. 265.

journey to Jerusalem, but when he was alone with Abū Bakr and others of his Companions he told them of his ascent through the seven Heavens, telling them a part of what he had seen, with more to be recounted later over the years, often in answer to questions.

# XXXIII

# *After the Year of Sadness*

IN the year which followed the Year of Sadness, the Pilgrimage fell at the beginning of June; and on the Feast of the Sacrifices the Prophet went to the valley of Mina where the pilgrims camp for five days. It had been his practice now for several years to visit the various groups of tents and to declare his message to any who would listen, reciting for them such verses of the Revelations as he felt moved to recite. The nearest point of Mina to Mecca is 'Aqabah, where the road rises up steeply from the valley towards the hills in the direction of the holy city; and it was this year at 'Aqabah that he came upon six men of the tribe of Khazraj, from Yathrib. He did not know any of the six, but they had all heard of him and of his claim to prophethood, and as soon as he told them who he was their faces lit up with interest, and they listened to him attentively. Every man of them was familiar with the threat of their neighbours, the Yathrib Jews: "A Prophet is now about to be sent. We will follow him and we will slay you as 'Ād and Iram were slain"; and when the Prophet had finished speaking, they said to each other: "This is indeed the Prophet that the Jews promised us would come. Let them not be the first to reach him!" Then, after one or two questions had been asked and answered, each of the six men testified to the truth of the Prophet's message and promised to fulfil the conditions of Islam which he laid before them. "We have left our people," they said, "for there is no people so torn asunder by enmity and evil as they; and it may be that God will unite them through thee. We will now go to them and summon them to accept thy religion even as we have accepted it; and if God gather them together about thee, then no man will be mightier than thou."[1]

The Prophet continued to visit Abū Bakr regularly at his house amongst the dwellings of the Bani Jumaḥ. These visits were a memorable feature of the childhood of 'Ā'ishah, Abū Bakr's younger daughter. She could not remember a time when her father and mother were not Muslims, and when the Prophet was not a daily visitor to them.

During this same year that followed Khadījah's death, the Prophet

[1] I.I. 287.

dreamed that he saw a man who was carrying someone wrapped in a piece of silk. The man said to him: "This is thy wife, so uncover her." The Prophet lifted the silk and there was 'Ā'ishah. But 'Ā'ishah was only six years old, and he had passed his fiftieth year. Moreover Abū Bakr had promised her to Muṭ'im for his son Jubayr. The Prophet simply said to himself: "If this be from God, He will bring it to pass."[1] A few nights later he saw in his sleep an Angel carrying the same bundle of silk, and this time it was he who said to the Angel: "Show me." The Angel lifted the silk and there, again, was 'Ā'ishah, and again the Prophet said: "If this be from God, He will bring it to pass."[2]

As yet he mentioned these dreams to no one, not even to Abū Bakr. But now there came a third confirmation, of a different kind. Khawlah, the wife of 'Uthmān ibn Maẓ'ūn, had been very attentive to the various needs of the Prophet's household ever since Khadījah's death; and one day when she was in his house she suggested to him that he should take another wife. When he asked her whom he should marry, she said: "Either 'Ā'ishah the daughter of Abū Bakr or Sawdah the daughter of Zam'ah." Sawdah, the cousin and sister-in-law of Suhayl,[3] was now a widow, aged about thirty. Her first husband, Sakrān, Suhayl's brother, had taken her with him to Abyssinia, and they had been among the first to return to Mecca. Not long after their return Sakrān had died.

The Prophet told Khawlah to seek to arrange his marriages to both the brides she had suggested. Sawdah's answer was: "I am at thy service, O Messenger of God," and the Prophet sent back word saying: "Bid a man of thy people give thee in marriage." She chose her brother-in-law Ḥāṭib, who by this time had also returned from Abyssinia, and he gave her in marriage to the Prophet.

Meantime Abū Bakr approached Muṭ'im, who was persuaded without difficulty to forgo the marriage of 'Ā'ishah to his son; and, some months after the marriage of Sawdah, 'Ā'ishah also became the Prophet's wife, through a marriage contracted by him and her father, at which she herself was not present. She said afterwards that she had had her first inkling of her new status when one day she was playing with her friends outside, not far from their house, and her mother came and took her by the hand and led her indoors, telling her that henceforth she must not go out to play, and that her friends must come to her instead. 'Ā'ishah dimly guessed the reason, though her mother did not immediately tell her that she was married; and apart from having to play in their courtyard instead of in the road, her life continued as before.

About this time Abū Bakr decided to have a small mosque built in front of his house. It was surrounded by walls, but open to the sky, and there he would pray and recite the Koran. But the walls were not high enough to prevent passers-by from looking over them, and often a number of people would stand there and listen to his recitation, while at the same time they would see something of his reverence for the revealed Book, which moved him to the depth of his being. Umayyah now feared that the number of Abū Bakr's converts would be still further increased, and at his instance the

[1] B. XCI, 20. [2] ibid. [3] See p. 72 ff.

leaders of Quraysh sent a deputation to Ibn ad-Dughunnah, reminding him of what they had said at the outset of his protection, and pointing out that the walls of Abū Bakr's mosque were not sufficient to make it part of his house. "If he will worship his Lord within doors, then let him do so," they said, "yet if he must needs do it openly, then bid him absolve thee of thy protection of him." But Abū Bakr refused to give up his mosque, and he formally absolved Ibn ad-Dughunnah of his pact, saying: "I am content with the protection of God."

It was on that very day that the Prophet announced to him and to others of his Companions: "I have been shown the place of your emigration: I saw a well watered land, rich in date palms, between two tracts of black stones."[1]

[1] B. XXXVII 7.

# XXXIV

# *Yathrib Responsive*

"TORN asunder by enmity and evil." In so describing their people, the six recent converts of Yathrib had not exaggerated. The battle of Bu'āth, the fourth and most savage conflict of the civil war, had not been altogether decisive; nor had it been followed by any peace worthy of the name but merely by an agreement to stop fighting for the moment. The dangerously prolonged state of chronic bitterness fraught with an increasing number of incidents of violence had won over many of the more moderate men of both sides to the opinion that they needed an overall chief who would unite them as Quṣayy had united Quraysh, and that there was no other solution to their problem. One of the leading men of the oasis, 'Abd Allāh ibn Ubayy, was favoured by many as a possible king. He had not fought against Aws in the recent conflict but had withdrawn his men on the eve of the battle. He was none the less of Khazraj; and it was exceedingly doubtful whether Aws would be capable of accepting a king who was not of their tribe.

The six men of Khazraj delivered the message of Islam to as many of their people as would listen to them; and the next summer, that is, in AD 621, five of them repeated their Pilgrimage, bringing with them seven others, two of whom were of Aws. At 'Aqabah, these twelve men pledged themselves to the Prophet, and this pledge is known as the First 'Aqabah. In the words of one of them: "We pledged our allegiance to the Messenger of God on the night of the First 'Aqabah, that we would associate nothing with God, that we would neither steal, not commit fornication, nor slay our offspring[1] nor utter slanders; and that we would not disobey him in that which was right. And he said to us: 'If ye fulfil this pledge, then Paradise is yours; and if ye commit one of these sins and then receive punishment for it in this world, that shall serve as expiation. And if ye conceal it until the Day of the Resurrection, then it is for God to punish or forgive, even as He will.'"[2]

When they left for Yathrib the Prophet sent with them Muṣ'ab of 'Abd ad-Dār who had by that time returned from Abyssinia. He was to recite the Koran to them and give them religious instruction. He lodged with As'ad ibn Zurārah, one of the six who had entered Islam the previous year. Muṣ'ab had also to lead the prayer because, despite their Islam, neither Aws nor Khazraj could yet endure to give one another that precedence.

[1] In reference to the practice which had developed in Arabia among the indigent Bedouin, especially in time of famine, of burying unwanted female infants.

[2] I.I. 289.

The rivalry between the descendants of the two sons of Qaylah was of long standing. There had been none the less frequent intermarriages between the two tribes, and as a result of one of these, As'ad, the Khazrajite host of Muṣ'ab, was the first cousin of Sa'd ibn Mu'ādh, chief of one of the clans of Aws. Sa'd strongly disapproved of the new religion. He was therefore angry, yet at the same time embarrassed, to see his cousin As'ad together with Muṣ'ab and some newly converted Muslims sitting one day in a garden in the midst of his people's territory, in earnest conversation with members of his clan. Determined to put an end to such activities, yet not wishing to be involved in any unpleasantness himself, he went to Usayd who was next in authority to himself, and said: "Go thou to these two men who have come to our quarters to make fools of our weaker brethren" – he was no doubt thinking of his younger brother, the now dead Iyās, who had been the first man of Yathrib to enter Islam[1] – "and drive them out; and forbid them to come to our quarters again. If As'ad were not my kinsman I would save thee this trouble but he is my mother's sister's son, and I can do nothing against him." Usayd took his lance and went and stood over them and said, with as fierce an expression as he could muster: "What bringeth the two of you here, to make fools of our weaker brethren? Leave us, if ye have any care for your lives." Muṣ'ab looked at him and said gently: "Why not be seated and hear what I have to say? Then, if it please thee, accept it; and if not, keep thyself clear of it." "That is fairly spoken," said Usayd, who liked both the appearance and the manner of the Prophet's envoy; and striking his lance in the ground he sat down beside them. Muṣ'ab spoke to him about Islam and recited the Koran to him; and Usayd's expression changed, so that those who were present could see Islam in his face from the light that shone in it and the repose that softened it even before he spoke. "How excellent are these words and how beautiful!" he said, when Muṣ'ab had finished. "What do ye do, if ye wish to enter this religion?" They told him that he must wash himself from head to foot in order to be purified, and that he must also purify his garments and then perform the prayer. There was a well in the garden where they were sitting, so he washed himself and purified his garments and testified *There is no god but God and Muḥammad is the Messenger of God.* They showed him how to pray, and he prayed. Then he said: "There is a man behind me who, if he follow you, will be followed without fail by every man of his people, and I will send him to you now."

So he went back to his clansmen, and even before he reached them they could see that he was a changed man. "What hast thou done?" said Sa'd. "I spake unto the two men," said Usayd, "and by God I saw no harm in them. But I forbade them to continue and they said: 'We will do as thou wilt.' "I see thou hast been of no avail," said Sa'd, taking the lance from his hand and setting off to where the believers were still sitting peacefully in the garden. He remonstrated with his cousin As'ad and upraided him for taking advantage of their kinship. But Muṣ'ab intervened, speaking to him just as he had spoken to Usayd, whereupon Sa'd agreed to listen to him, and the result was finally the same.

[1] See p. 57.

When Sa'd had performed the prayer, he rejoined Usayd and those that were with him and together they went to the assembly of their people. Sa'd addressed them and said: "What know ye of my standing amongst you?" "Thou art our liege lord," they answered, "and the best of us in judgement, and the most auspicious in leadership." "Then I tell you," he said, "I swear I will speak neither to your men nor to your women until ye believe in God and His Messenger." And by nightfall there was no man or woman of his clan who had not entered Islam.

Muṣ'ab stayed with As'ad for about eleven months, and many were the people who embraced Islam during that time. Then, when the month of the next Pilgrimage drew near, he returned to Mecca to give tidings to the Prophet of how he had fared among the various clans of Aws and Khazraj.

The Prophet knew that the well watered land between two tracts of black stones which he had seen in a vision was Yathrib, and he knew that this time he too would be of the emigrants. Now there were few people in Mecca whom he trusted so much as his aunt by marriage, Umm al-Faḍl. He was also certain that his uncle 'Abbās, although he had not entered Islam, would never betray him and never divulge a secret confided to him. So he told them both that he hoped to go and live in Yathrib and that much depended on the delegation which was expected from the oasis for the coming Pilgrimage. On hearing this, 'Abbās said that he felt it his duty to go with his nephew to meet the delegates and speak with them, and the Prophet agreed.

Not long after Muṣ'ab's departure, some of the Muslims of Yathrib set out upon the Pilgrimage as had been arranged between him and them, in all seventy-three men and two women, hoping to make contact with the Prophet. One of their leaders was a Khazrajite chief named Barā', and during the first days of the journey a preoccupying thought came over him. They were on their way towards Mecca wherein was the House of God, the Ka'bah, the greatest centre of pilgrimage for the whole of Arabia; and therein was also the Prophet, to whom they were going, and it was there that the Koran had been revealed, and thither their souls were moving ahead of them in aspiration. Was it then right or reasonable, when the time came for prayer, that they should turn their backs on that direction and face towards the north, towards Syria? This may have been more than a mere thought, for Barā' had only a few more months to live, and men who are near to death are sometimes gifted with premonitions. However that may be, he told his companions what was in his mind, whereupon they said that as far as they knew the Prophet was wont to pray towards Syria, that is towards Jerusalem, and they did not wish to differ from him. "I shall pray towards the Ka'bah," said Barā', and he did so throughout the journey, while all the others continued to pray towards Jerusalem. They remonstrated with him to no avail, except that when they arrived in Mecca he had some misgivings and he said to Ka'b ibn Mālik, one of his younger clansmen – and one of the more gifted poets of Yathrib: "Son of my brother, let us go to the Messenger of God and ask him about what I did on this journey, for doubts have fallen into my soul through my seeing that ye were against me." So they asked a man in Mecca where they could find the Prophet, whom they did not even know by sight. "Know ye his uncle

'Abbās?" said the man, and they replied that they did, for 'Abbās was a frequent visitor to Yathrib and was well known there. "When ye enter the Mosque," said their informant, "he is the man sitting beside 'Abbās." So they went to the Prophet, who said, in answer to the question of Barā': "Thou hadst a direction, if thou hadst but kept to it." Barā' took to praying towards Jerusalem once more, in order to do as the Prophet did, though the answer he had received could have been taken in more than one sense.

Their journey to Mecca had been in a caravan together with the polytheist pilgrims of Yathrib, one of whom entered Islam in the valley of Mina, an eminent Khazrajite, Abū Jābir 'Abd Allāh ibn 'Amr, a leader of the Bani Salimah and a man of great influence. It was agreed that they should secretly meet the Prophet as before at 'Aqabah on the second of the nights immediately following the Pilgrimage. In the words of one of them: "We slept that night with our people in the caravan until when a third of the night had passed we crept out from amongst the sleepers to our appointed meeting with the Messenger of God, stealing as stealthily as sand-grouse, until we were all assembled in the gully near 'Aqabah. There we waited until the Messenger came, and with him came his uncle 'Abbās who was at that time still of the religion of his people, albeit that he wished to be present at his nephew's transaction and to make sure that the promises made to him were reliable. When the Prophet was seated, 'Abbās was the first to speak: 'People of Khazraj' – for so the Arabs were wont to address Khazraj and Aws – 'ye know the esteem in which we hold Muḥammad, and we have protected him from his people so that he is honoured in his clan and safe in his country. Yet hath he resolved to turn unto you and join himself with you. So if ye think that ye will keep to what ye promise him, and that ye will protect him against all that shall oppose him, yours be that burden which ye have taken upon yourselves. But if ye think ye will betray him and fail him after he hath gone out unto you, then leave him now.' 'We have heard what thou sayest,' they answered, 'but speak thou, O Messenger of God, and choose for thyself and for thy Lord what thou wilt.'"

After reciting from the Koran and pronouncing a summons to God and to Islam, the Prophet said: "I make with you this pact on condition that the allegiance ye pledge me shall bind you to protect me even as ye protect your women and your children." Barā' rose and took his hand and said: "By Him who sent thee with the truth, we will protect thee as we protect them. So accept the pledge of our allegiance, O Messenger of God, for we are men of war, possessed of arms that have been handed down from father to son." A man of Aws then broke in upon him and said: "O Messenger of God, there are ties between us and other men" – he meant the Jews – "and we are willing to sever them. But might it not be that if we do this, and if then God give thee victory, thou wilt return to thy people and leave us?" The Prophet smiled and said: "Nay, I am yours and ye are mine. Whom ye war against, him I war against. Whom ye make peace with, him I make peace with."

Then he said: "Bring out to me twelve of your men as leaders, that they may look to the affairs of their people." So they brought out to him twelve leaders, nine from Khazraj and three from Aws, since sixty-two of the men were of Khazraj and also the two women, whereas only eleven were from Aws. Amongst the nine leaders of Khazraj were As'ad and Barā'; amongst the three of Aws was Usayd whom Sa'd ibn Mu'ādh had sent to represent him.

When the people were about to pledge themselves, one by one, to the Prophet, a man of Khazraj, one of the twelve who had pledged himself the previous year, made a sign that they should wait, and he addressed them saying: "Men of Khazraj, know ye what it means to pledge yourselves to this man?" "We know," they said, but he disregarded them. "Ye pledge yourselves", he continued, "to war against all men, the red and the black.[1] So if ye think that when ye suffer the loss of possessions and when some of your nobles are slain ye will forsake him, forsake him now, for if ye forsake him then it will bring shame upon you in this world and the next. But if ye think ye will fulfil your pledge, then take him, for therein, by God, is the best of this world and the next." They said: "What though our possessions be lost and our nobles slain, yet do we take him. And what shall be ours thereby, O Messenger of God, if we fulfil to thee our pledge?" "Paradise," he said, and they said: "Stretch forth thy hand," and he stretched out his hand and they pledged their oaths.

And Satan was watching and listening from the top of 'Aqabah; and when he could contain himself no longer he cried out in the loudest voice possible and spoke the name Mudhammam, Reprobate; and the Prophet knew who it was who had thus cried, and he answered him, saying: "O enemy of God, I will give thee no respite."

[1] That is, all men whatsoever. After this second pledge at 'Aqabah, that of the First 'Aqabah came to be called "the pledge of the women". It continued to be used, but for women only, because it contained no mention of the duties of war.

# XXXV

# *Many Emigrations*

THE Prophet now encouraged his followers in Mecca to emigrate to Yathrib. But one of them had already done so. The death of Abū Ṭālib had deprived his nephew Abū Salamah of a protector, and he felt compelled to take refuge from his own clan. So he set off for the north, mounting his wife on a camel with their young son Salamah in her arms and himself leading the camel. But Umm Salamah was of the other branch of Makhzūm, the Bani l-Mughīrah, and first cousin to Abū Jahl; and some of her family went after them and snatched the camel's rope from Abū Salamah's hand. He was far outnumbered and knew it would be useless to resist so he told her to return with them. He would find a way for her to join him. But when his branch of Makhzūm heard of it they were angry with the Bani l-Mughīrah and made matters worse by claiming custody of the boy. So the three of them were cruelly separated until the whole clan took pity on her and allowed her to take her son and join her husband. She set off on a camel entirely alone except for Salamah, but after almost six miles she met a man of 'Abd ad-Dār, 'Uthmān ibn Ṭalḥah, not yet a believer, who insisted on escorting her to the end of her journey. They had heard that Abū Salamah was in Qubā', a village at the most southerly point of Yathrib where the oasis juts out into the lava tract which is one of "the two tracts of black stones"; so when they came within sight of the palm groves 'Uthmān said to her: "Thy husband is in this village, so enter it with God's blessing," and he himself turned back again towards Mecca. Umm Salamah never forgot his kindness, and never ceased to praise him for his nobility.

After the pledge of the Second 'Aqabah, the Muslims of Quraysh began to emigrate in considerable numbers. Amongst the first to go were some others of the Prophet's cousins, sons and daughters of Jaḥsh and Umaymah, 'Abd Allāh and his blind brother Abū Aḥmad, and their two sisters Zaynab and Ḥamnah. With them went many others of the Bani Asad who had long been confederates of 'Abdu Shams. Ḥamzah and Zayd went, leaving their wives in Mecca for the moment, but 'Uthmān took Ruqayyah with him, and 'Umar took his wife Zaynab, their daughter Ḥafṣah and their young son 'Abd Allāh. Ḥafṣah's husband, Khunays of Sahm, was also with them. Abū Salamah's half-brother, Abū Ṣabrah, took with him his wife Umm Kulthūm, Suhayl's daughter; and other young cousins of the Prophet who now went were Zubayr and Ṭulayb.

It was not long before all his closest Companions had left Mecca except

Abū Bakr and 'Alī. Abū Bakr had asked the Prophet's permission to emigrate, but he had said: "Hasten not away, for it may be that God will give thee a companion." So Abū Bakr understood that he must wait for the Prophet, and he gave orders for two of his camels to be fed on gum acacia leaves in preparation for their journey to Yathrib.

Quraysh did what they could to stop the emigrations. Suhayl's other daughter had now gone with her husband Abū Hudhayfah, just as they had previously gone to Abyssinia, but Suhayl was determined that this time his son 'Abd Allāh should not escape him, so he kept a close watch on him. Much the same happened to the son of the Sahmite leader 'Āṣ, Hishām, who likewise had been among the emigrants to Abyssinia. It was his half-brother 'Amr who had been sent by Quraysh to turn the Negus against the Muslim refugees, and Hishām had witnessed his failure and discomforture. 'Umar, who was Hishām's cousin – their mothers were sisters – had arranged that they should now travel to Yathrib together, leaving Mecca separately and meeting at the thorn-trees of Aḍāt about ten miles north of the city. 'Ayyāsh of Makhzum was also to travel with them; but at the appointed hour and place there was no sign of Hishām, so 'Umar and his family went on their way with 'Ayyāsh, for they had agreed that they would not wait for each other. Hishām's father and brother had heard of his plan and held him back by force; and they put so much pressure on him that after some days they even persuaded him to renounce Islam.

As to 'Ayyāsh, he reached Yathrib with 'Umar, but his two half-brothers, Abū Jahl and Ḥārith, followed him and told him that their mother, who was also his mother, had sworn not to comb her hair or take shelter from the sun until she set eyes on him again. 'Ayyāsh was very troubled by this, but 'Umar said to him: "They want nothing better than to seduce thee from thy religion; for by God, if lice troubled thy mother, she would use her comb; and if the heat of Mecca oppressed her, she would take shelter." But 'Ayyāsh would not listen: he insisted on returning to Mecca in order to release his mother from her oath. He also intended to retrieve some money he had left behind. But when they were half-way there Abū Jahl and Ḥārith fell upon him, bound him hand and foot, brought him home as a prisoner, saying as they entered the city: "O people of Mecca, do with your fools as we have done with this fool of ours." Like Hishām, 'Ayyāsh was prevailed upon to renounce Islam, but in neither case was this final. After a while they were conscience-stricken to the point of supposing that no atonement was possible for so great a sin, and that was 'Umar's opinion also. But later there came the Revelation: *O My slaves who have acted unwisely against yourselves, despair not of God's Mercy. Verily God forgiveth sins in their entirety. He is the All-Forgiving, the All-Merciful. And turn unto your Lord in repentance and surrender unto Him before there come unto you the punishment, when ye shall not be helped.*[1] 'Umar wrote down these words and found a way of sending the inscription to Hishām, who said: "When it came to me I raised it close to my eyes and lowered it away from them, but I could not understand it, until I said: 'O God, make me understand it.' Then God put it into my heart that it had

[1] XXXIX, 53–4.

been revealed for our very sakes with regard to what we were saying of ourselves and what was being said of us." Hishām showed it to 'Ayyāsh and they renewed their Islam and waited for their opportunity to escape.

# XXXVI

# *A Conspiracy*

THE apparent apostasies of Hishām and 'Ayyāsh were but small triumphs for Quraysh, heavily outweighed by the steady stream of emigrants which they were unable to control. Some of the larger houses in Mecca were now tenantless; others, which had been full, were now empty save for one or two old people. In the city which had seemed so prosperous and harmonious only ten years ago everything had changed, thanks to this one man. But while these feelings of sadness and melancholy came and went, there was the persistent consciousness of a growing danger from that city to the north where so many potential enemies were now gathering together – men who cared nothing for the ties of kinship if they came into conflict with their religion. Those who had heard the Prophet say "Quraysh, I bring you slaughter" had never forgotten it, though at the time there seemed to be nothing to fear. But if he now eluded them, despite the perpetual watch they kept upon his movements, and made his way to Yathrib, those words might prove to be more than a mere threat.

The death of Muṭ'im, the Prophet's protector, seemed to clear the way for action; and to clear it still further, Abū Lahab deliberately absented himself from the meeting which the leaders of Quraysh now held in the Assembly. After a long discussion, when various suggestions had been made and rejected, they agreed – some of them with reluctance – to the plan put forward by Abū Jahl as being the only effective solution to their problem. Every clan was to nominate a strong, reliable and well-connected young man, and at a given moment all these chosen men together should fall upon Muḥammad, each striking him a mortal blow, so that his blood would be on all the clans. The Bani Hāshim would not be able to fight the whole tribe of Quraysh; they would have to accept blood money – which would be offered them – in place of revenge; and so at last the community would be rid of a man who, as long as he lived, would give them no peace.

Gabriel now came to the Prophet and told him what he should do. It was noon, an unusual time for visiting, but the Prophet went straight to the house of Abū Bakr who knew at once, as soon as he saw him at that hour, that something important had happened. 'Ā'ishah and her elder sister Asmā' were with their father when the Prophet came in. "God hath allowed me to leave the city and to emigrate," he said. "Together with me?" said Abū Bakr. "Together with thee," said the Prophet. 'Ā'ishah was at that time in her seventh year. She used to say afterwards: "I knew not before that day that one could weep for joy until I saw Abū Bakr weep at those words."

When they had made their plans, the Prophet returned to his house and told 'Alī that he was about to leave for Yathrib, bidding him stay behind in Mecca until he had given back to their owners all the goods which had been deposited in their house for safe keeping. The Prophet had never ceased to be known as al-Amīn, and there were still many disbelievers who would trust him with their property as they would trust no one else. He also told 'Alī what Gabriel had told him about the plot Quraysh had made against him.

The young men chosen to kill him had agreed to meet outside his gate after nightfall. But while they were waiting until their numbers were complete, they heard the sound of women's voices coming from the house, the voices of Sawdah, Umm Kulthūm, Fāṭimah and Umm Ayman. That gave them cause to think; and one of the men said that if they climbed over the wall and broke into the house their names would be for ever held in dishonour among the Arabs because they had violated the privacy of women. So they decided to wait until their intended victim came out, as it was his wont to do in the early morning, if he came not out before.

The Prophet and 'Alī were soon aware of their presence; and the Prophet took up a cloak in which he used to sleep and gave it to 'Alī, saying: "Sleep thou on my bed, and wrap thyself in this green Ḥaḍramī cloak of mine. Sleep in it, and no harm shall come to thee from them." Then he began to recite the *Sūrah* that is named after its opening letters, *Yā-Sīn*; and, when he came to the words: *And We have enshrouded them, so that they see not,*[1] he went out of the house; and God took away their sight so that they did not see him, and he passed through their midst and went on his way.

A man was coming in the opposite direction, and their paths crossed, and he recognised the Prophet. A little later his path took him not far from the Prophet's house, and seeing men at its gate, he called out to them that if it was Muḥammad they wanted he was not there but had gone out not long since. "How could that be?" they thought. One of the conspirators had been watching the house and had seen the Prophet enter it before the others had arrived; and they were certain that no one had left it while they had been there. But now they began to be uneasy, until one of them who knew where the Prophet slept went to a point from which he could see through the window, just enough to make sure that someone was sleeping on the Prophet's bed, wrapped in a cloak, so he reassured his fellows that their man was still there. But when it was dawn 'Alī rose and went to the door of the house, still wrapped in the cloak; and they saw who it was, and began to think they had been somehow outwitted. They waited a little longer; the thinnest of crescents, all that was left of the waning moon of the month of Ṣafar, had risen over the eastern hills, and now it began to pale as the light increased. There was still no sign of the Prophet, and with a sudden impulse they decided to go, each one to his chief of clan, to give the alarm.

1 XXXVI, 9.

# XXXVII
# *The Hijrah*

MEANTIME the Prophet had returned to Abū Bakr, and losing no time they went out through a window at the back of his house where two camels, already saddled, were waiting for them. The Prophet mounted one of them, and Abū Bakr the other, with his son 'Abd Allah behind him. As they had planned, they made for a cave in the Mount of Thawr a little to the south, on the way to the Yemen, for they knew that as soon as the Prophet's absence was discovered search parties would be sent out to cover all the northern outskirts of the city. When they had gone a little way beyond the precincts of Mecca, the Prophet halted his camel, and looking back he said: "Of all God's earth, thou art the dearest place unto me and the dearest unto God, and had not my people driven me out from thee I would not have left thee."

'Āmir ibn Fuhayrah, the shepherd whom Abū Bakr had bought as a slave and then set free and put in charge of his sheep, had followed behind them with his flock to cover up their tracks. When they reached the cave, Abū Bakr sent his son home with the camels, telling him to listen to what was said in Mecca the next day when the Prophet's absence was discovered, and to bring them word of it the following night. 'Āmir was to pasture his sheep as usual with the other shepherds during the day and to bring them to the cave at night, always covering up the tracks of 'Abd Allāh between Thawr and Mecca.

The next night 'Abd Allāh returned to the cave and his sister Asma' came with him, bringing food. Their news was that Quraysh had offered a reward of a hundred camels to anyone who could find Muḥammad and bring him back to Mecca. Horsemen were already following every normal route from Mecca to Yathrib, hoping to overtake them both – for it was assumed that Abū Bakr was with the Prophet, since he also had disappeared.

But others, perhaps unknown to 'Abd Allāh, thought they must be in hiding, in one of the numerous caves in the hills round Mecca. Moreover, the Arabs of the desert are good trackers: even when a flock of sheep had followed in the wake of two or three camels, the average Bedouin would see at a glance the remains of the larger prints of the camel-hooves which the multitude of smaller prints had all but obliterated. It seemed unlikely that the fugitives would be to the south of the city; but for such a generous reward every possibility should be tried; and camels had certainly preceded the sheep on those tracks which led in the direction of Thawr.

On the third day the silence of their mountain sanctuary was broken by the sound of birds – a pair of rock doves they thought – cooing and fluttering their wings outside the cave. Then after a while they heard the faint sound of men's voices, at some distance below them but gradually growing louder as if the men were climbing up the side of the mount. They were not expecting 'Abd Allāh until after nightfall, and there were still some hours to go before sunset, although in fact there was strangely little light in the cave for the time of day they supposed it to be. The voices were now not far off – five or six men at least – and they were still approaching. The Prophet looked at Abū Bakr, and said: *Grieve not, for verily God is with us.*[1] And then he said: "What thinkest thou of two when God is their third?"[2] They could now hear the sound of steps, which drew nearer and then stopped: the men were standing outside the cave. They spoke decisively, all in agreement that there was no need to enter the cave, since no one could possibly be there. Then they turned back the way they had come.

When the sound of their retreating steps and voices had died away, the Prophet and Abū Bakr went to the mouth of the cave. There in front of it, almost covering the entrance, was an acacia tree, about the height of a man, which had not been there that morning; and over the gap that was left between the tree and the wall of the cave a spider had woven its web. They looked through the web, and there in the hollow of a rock, even where a man might step as he entered the cave, a rock dove had made a nesting place and was sitting close as if she had eggs, with her mate perched on a ledge not far above.

When they heard 'Abd Allāh and his sister approaching at the expected hour, they gently drew aside the web that had been their safeguard, and taking care not to disturb the dove, they went to meet them. 'Āmir had also come, this time without his flock. He had brought the Bedouin to whom Abū Bakr had entrusted the two camels he had chosen for their journey. The man was not yet a believer, but he could be relied on to keep their secret and also to guide them to their destination by such out-of-the-way paths as only a true son of the desert would know. He was waiting in the valley below with the two mounts, and had brought a third camel for himself. Abū Bakr was to take 'Āmir behind him on his, to look after their needs. They left the cave, and descended the slope. Asmā' had brought a bag of provisions, but had forgotten to bring a rope. So she took off her girdle and divided it into two lengths, using one to tie the bag securely to her father's saddle and keeping the other for herself. Thus it was that she earned the title "She of the two girdles".

When Abū Bakr offered the Prophet the better of the two camels he said: "I will not ride a camel that is not mine own." "But she is thine, O messenger of God." said Abū Bakr. "Nay," said the Prophet; "but what price didst thou pay for her?" Abū Bakr told him, and he said: "I take her at that price." Nor did Abū Bakr insist further on making it a gift, although the Prophet had accepted many gifts from him in the past, for this occasion was a solemn one. It was the Prophet's *Hijrah*, his cutting off of all ties of home and homeland for the sake of God. His offering, the act of emigra-

[1] IX, 40. [2] B. LVII, 5.

tion, must be entirely his, not shared by another in any respect. The mount on which the act was accomplished must therefore be his own, since it was part of his offering. The camel's name was Qaṣwā', and she remained his favourite camel.

Their guide took them away from Mecca to the *west* and a little to the *south* until they came to the shore of the Red Sea. Yathrib is due north of Mecca, but it was only at this point that any north came into their direction. The coastal road runs north-west and for a few days they kept to this. On one of their first evenings, looking across the water towards the Nubian desert, they saw the new moon of the month of Rabī'al-Awwal. "O crescent of good and of guidance, my faith is in Him who created thee."[1] This the Prophet would say when he saw the new moon.

One morning they were somewhat dismayed to see a small caravan approaching from the opposite direction. But their feelings changed to joy when they saw that it was Abū Bakr's cousin Ṭalḥah who was on his way from Syria where he had bought the cloth and other merchandise with which his camels were laden. He had stopped in Yathrib on his way, and intended to return there as soon as he had disposed of his wares in Mecca. The Prophet's arrival in the oasis, he said, was awaited with the greatest eagerness; and before bidding them farewell he gave them each a change of clothes from out of the fine white Syrian garments which he had intended to sell to some of the richer men of Quraysh.

Not long after their meeting with Ṭalḥah they turned due north, going slightly inland from the coast, and then north-east, now at last making directly for Yathrib. At one point of their journey the Prophet received a Revelation which told him: *Verily He who hath made binding upon thee the Koran will bring thee home once more.*[2]

Shortly before dawn on the twelfth day after leaving the cave they reached the valley of 'Aqīq, and crossing the valley, they climbed up the rugged black slopes on the other side. Before they reached the top the sun was well up and the heat was intense. On other days they would have stopped for rest until the great heat of the day had passed; but they now decided to climb the final ridge of the ascent, and when at last they came within sight of the plain below there could be no question of holding back. The place that the Prophet had dreamed of, "the well watered land between two tracts of black stones," was lying before them, and the grey-green of the palm groves and the lighter green of orchards and gardens stretched at one point to within three miles of the foot of the slope they had to descend.

The nearest point of greenery was Qubā', where most of the emigrants from Mecca had first stayed, and where many of them still were. The Prophet told their guide: "Lead us straight to the Bani 'Amr at Qubā', and draw not yet nigh unto the city" – for so the most densely inhabited part of the oasis was called. That city was soon to be known throughout Arabia, and thence elsewhere, as "the City", in Arabic *al-Madīnah*, in English Medina.

Several days previously news from Mecca of the Prophet's disappear-

[1] A.H. V, 329. [2] XXVIII, 85.

ance, and of the reward offered for him, had reached the oasis. The people of Qubā' were expecting him daily, for the time of his arrival was now overdue; so every morning, after the dawn prayer, some of the Bani 'Amr would go out to look for him, and with them went men of other clans who lived in that village, and also those of the emigrant Quraysh who were still there and had not yet moved to Medina. They would go out beyond the fields and palm groves onto the lava tract, and after they had gone some distance they would stop and wait until the heat of the sun became fierce; then they would return to their homes. They had gone out that morning, but had already returned by the time the four travellers had begun their descent of the rocky slope. Eyes were no longer staring expectantly in that direction; but the sun shone on the new white garments of the Prophet and Abū Bakr which were set off all the more against the background of bluish-black volcanic stones, and a Jew who happened to be on the roof of his house caught sight of them. He knew at once who they must be, for the Jews of Qubā' had asked and been told why so many of their neighbours had taken to going out in a body into the wilderness every morning without fail. So he called out at the top of his voice: "Sons of Qaylah, he is come, he is come!" The call was immediately taken up, and men, women and children hurried from their houses and streamed out once more onto the strip of greenery which led to the stone tract. But they had not far to go, for the travellers had by now reached the most outlying palm-grove. It was a noon of great joy on all sides, and the Prophet addressed them, saying: "O people, give unto one another greetings of Peace; feed food unto the hungry; honour the ties of kinship; pray in the hours when men sleep. Even so shall ye enter Paradise in Peace."[1]

It was decided that he should lodge with Kulthūm, an old man of Qubā' who had previously welcomed both Ḥamzah and Zayd in his house on their arrival from Mecca. The Bani 'Amr, Kulthūm's clan, were of Aws, and it was no doubt partly in order that both the Yathrib tribes might share in the hospitality that Abū Bakr lodged with a man of Khazraj in the village of Sunh which was a little nearer to Medina. After a day or two, 'Alī arrived from Mecca, and stayed in the same house as the Prophet. It had taken him three days to return all the property which had been deposited with them to its various owners.

Many were those who now came to greet the Prophet, and amongst them were some Jews of Medina who were drawn more by curiosity than good will. But on the second or third evening there came a man who was different in appearance from any of the others, clearly neither an Arab nor a Jew. Salmān, for so he was named, had been born of Persian Zoroastrian parents in the village of Jayy near Isfahan, but he had become a Christian and gone to Syria as a very young man. There he had attached himself to a saintly bishop who, on his deathbed, recommended him to go to the Bishop of Mosul, who was old like himself but the best man he knew. Salmān set off for the north of Iraq, and this was for him the beginning of a series of attachments to elderly Christian sages until the last of these, also on his deathbed, told him that the time was now at hand when a Prophet

[1] I.S. I/1, 159.

would appear: "He will be sent with the religion of Abraham and will come forth in Arabia where he will emigrate from his home to a place between two lava tracts, a country of palms. His signs are manifest: he will eat of a gift but not if it be given as alms; and between his shoulders is the seal of prophecy." Salmān made up his mind to join the Prophet and paid a party of merchants of the tribe of Kalb to take him with them to Arabia. But when they reached Wādi l-Qurà near the Gulf of 'Aqabah at the north of the Red Sea they sold him as a slave to a Jew. The sight of the palms in Wādi l-Qurà made him wonder whether this could be the township he was seeking, but he had his doubts. It was not long however before the Jew sold him to a cousin of his of the Bani Qurayẓah in Medina; and as soon as he saw the lie of the land, he knew beyond doubt that here was the place to which the Prophet would migrate.

Salmān's new owner had another cousin who lived in Qubā'; and on the arrival of the Prophet this Jew of Qubā' set off for Medina with the news. He found his cousin sitting beneath one of his palms; and Salmān, who was working in the top of the tree, heard him say: "God curse the sons of Qaylah! They are even now gathered together at Qubā' about a man who hath come to them this day from Mecca. They claim him to be a Prophet." Those last words filled Salmān with certainty that his hopes had been realised, and the impact was so great that his whole body was seized with trembling. He was afraid that he would fall out of the tree, so he climbed down; and once on the ground he eagerly began to question the Jew from Qubā', but his master was angry and ordered him back to his work in the tree. That evening however he slipped away, taking with him some of his food which he had saved, and went to Qubā', where he found the Prophet sitting with many companions, new and old. Salmān was already convinced, but he none the less approached him and offered him the food, specifying that he gave it as alms. The Prophet told his companions to eat of it, but did not eat of it himself. Salmān hoped that he would one day see the seal of prophecy, but to have been in the presence of the Prophet and to have heard him speak was enough for that first encounter, and he returned to Medina elated and thankful.

# XXXVIII

# *The Entry into Medina*

THE Prophet had reached the oasis on Monday 27 September AD 622. Various messages soon made it clear that the people of Medina were impatient for his arrival there, so he only stayed three full days in Qubā', during which he laid the foundations of a mosque, the first to be built in Islam. On the Friday morning he set out from Qubā', and at noon he and his companions stopped in the valley of Rānūnā' to pray the prayer with the Khazrajite clan of the Bani Sālim who were expecting him. This was the first Friday Prayer that he prayed in the country that from now on was to be his home. Some of his kinsmen of the Bani an-Najjār had come to meet him, and some of the Bani 'Amr had escorted him from Qūba', which brought the whole congregation up to about a hundred men. After the prayer the Prophet mounted Qaṣwā', and Abū Bakr and others of Quraysh also mounted their camels and set off with him for the city. To the right and to the left of them, dressed in armour with their swords drawn, rode men of Aws and Khazraj, as a guard of honour and by way of demonstration that the oath they had taken to protect him was no empty word, though they knew well that then and there he would need no protection. Never was a day of greater rejoicing. "Come is the Prophet of God! Come is the Prophet of God!" was the joyous cry that went up from more and more voices of men and women and children who had lined the route. Qaṣwā' set the slow and stately pace of the procession as it passed amid the gardens and palm groves to the south of Medina. The houses were still few and far between, but gradually they entered more closely built districts, and many were the eager invitations which were offered. "Alight here, O Messenger of God, for we have strength and protection for thee, and abundance." More than once a man or a group of clansmen took hold of Qaṣwā's halter. But each time the Prophet blessed them and then said: "Let her go her way, for she is under the command of God."

At one point it seemed as if she were making for the houses of the Prophet's nearest kinsmen of the 'Adī branch of the great Khazrajite clan of Najjār, for she turned into the eastern part of the city where most of the clan lived. But she passed by the place where he had stayed with his mother as a child and by all the other houses of those nearest to him, despite their earnest entreaties that he should make his home there. The Prophet gave them the same reply that he had given to the others, and they could only submit. He had now reached the houses of the Bani Malik branch of Najjār. To this subclan belonged two of those six men who had pledged allegiance to him the year before the First 'Aqabah, As'ad and 'Awf; and here Qaṣwā' turned from the road into a large walled courtyard which had in it a few date palms and the ruins of a building. One end had been used at some time as a burial ground. There was also a place set apart for drying dates. Slowly she made her way towards a rough enclosure which As'ad had set up as a place of prayer, and there at the entrance she knelt. The Prophet let go her rein, but did not alight; and after a moment she rose to her feet and began to walk leisurely away. But she had not gone far when she stopped, turned in her tracks and walked back to where she had first knelt. Then she knelt again; and this time she flattened her chest against the ground. The Prophet alighted and said: "This, if God will, is the dwelling."[1]

He then asked who owned the courtyard, and Mu'ādh, the brother of 'Awf, told him it belonged to two orphan boys, Sahl and Suhayl. They were under the guardianship of As'ad, and the Prophet asked him to bring them to him, but they were already at hand and came and stood before him. He asked them if they would sell him the courtyard, and told them to name their price, but they said: "Nay, we give it thee, O Messenger of God." He would not, however, take it as a gift, and the price was fixed with the help of As'ad. Meanwhile Abū Ayyūb Khālid, who lived nearby, had untied the baggage and carried it into his house. Others of the clan now came and begged the Prophet to be their guest, but he said: "A man must be with his baggage." Abū Ayyūb had been the first of the clan to pledge himself at the Second 'Aqabah. He and his wife now withdrew to the upper part of his house, leaving the ground floor for the Prophet; and As'ad led Qaswā' to the courtyard of his own house which was close by.

[1] B. LXIII.

# XXXIX

# *Harmony and Discord*

THE Prophet gave orders that his newly acquired courtyard should be made into a mosque, and as in Qubā' they began work on it immediately. Most of the building was done with bricks, but in the middle of the northern wall, that is, the Jerusalem wall, they put stones on either side of the prayer niche. The palms in the courtyard were cut down and their trunks were used as pillars to support the roof of palm branches, but the greater part of the courtyard was left open.

The Muslims of Medina had been given by the Prophet the title of *Anṣār* which means Helpers, whereas the Muslims of Quraysh and other tribes who had left their homes and emigrated to the oasis he called *Muhājirah*, that is, Emigrants. All took part in the work, including the Prophet himself, and as they worked they chanted two verses which one of them had made up for the occasion:

> "O God, no good is but the good hereafter,
> So help the Helpers and the Emigrants."

And sometimes they chanted:

> "No life there is but life of the Hereafter.
> Mercy, O God, on Emigrants and Helpers."

It was to be hoped that these two parties would be strengthened by a third, and the Prophet now made a covenant of mutual obligation between his followers and the Jews of the oasis, forming them into a single community of believers but allowing for the differences between the two religions. Muslims and Jews were to have equal status. If a Jew were wronged, then he must be helped to his rights by both Muslim and Jew, and so also if a Muslim were wronged. In case of war against the polytheists they must fight as one people, and neither Jews nor Muslims were to make a separate peace, but peace was to be indivisible. In case of differences of opinion or dispute or controversy, the matter was to be referred to God through His Messenger. There was, however, no express stipulation that the Jews should formally recognise Muḥammad as the

Messenger and Prophet of God, though he was referred to as such throughout the document.

The Jews accepted this covenant for political reasons. The Prophet was already by far the most powerful man in Medina, and his power seemed likely to increase. They had no choice but to accept; yet very few of them were capable of believing that God would send a Prophet who was not a Jew. At first they were outwardly cordial, whatever they may have said amongst themselves and however set they were in the consciousness of their own superiority, the immense and incomparable superiority of the chosen people over all others. But though their scepticism with regard to the new religion was normally veiled, they were always ready to share it with any Arab who might have doubts about the Divine origin of the Revelation.

Islam continued to spread rapidly throughout the clans of Aws and Khazraj, and some believers looked forward to the day when, thanks to the covenant with the Jews, the oasis would be one harmonious whole. But the Revelation now gave warning of hidden elements of discord. It was about this time that the longest surah of the Koran began to be revealed, *al-Baqarah* (the Heifer), which is placed at the beginning of the Book, immediately after the seven verses of al-Fātiḥah, the Opening. It starts with a definiton of the rightly guided: *Alif – Lām – Mīm. This beyond doubt is the Book, a guidance unto the God-fearing, who believe in the Unseen and perform the prayer and give of that which We have bestowed upon them; and who believe in that which is revealed unto thee and in that which was revealed before thee, and who are certain of the Hereafter. These are they who follow guidance from their Lord and these are they who shall prosper.*[1]

Then after mention of the disbelievers who are blind and deaf to the truth, a third body of people is mentioned: *And of men there are some who say: We believe in God and in the last day, yet they are not believers . . . When they meet those who believe they say: we believe. And when they go apart unto their satans, they say: Verily we are with you; we did but mock.*[2] These were the waverers and doubters and hypocrites of Aws and Khazraj in all their varying degrees of insincerity; and their satans, that is their inspirers of evil, were the men and women of the disbelievers who did all they could to sow the seeds of doubt. The Prophet was here warned of a problem by which he had been altogether untroubled in Mecca. There the sincerity of those who embraced Islam was never to be doubted. The reasons for conversion could only be spiritual, since as regards the things of this world a convert had nothing to gain and in many cases much to lose. But now there were certain worldly reasons for entering the new religion, and these were steadily on the increase. The days of the total absence of hypocrites from the ranks of the Muslims were gone for ever.

Some of the satans referred to were of the Jews. The same Revelation said: *Many of the people of the Book*[3] *long to bring you back into disbelief after your belief through envy that is in their souls.*[4] Eagerly the Jews had looked forward to the coming of the predicted Prophet, not for the sake of

[1] II, 2–5. [2] II, 8, 14. [3] The Bible. [4] II, 109.

the spiritual enlightenment it would bring but so that they might regain their former supremacy in Yathrib; and now to their dismay they saw that it was a descendant of Ishmael, not of Isaac, who was proclaiming the truth of the One God, with a success which was truly suggestive of Divine support. They feared that he was indeed the promised Prophet, whence their envy of the people to whom he was sent. Yet they hoped that he was not, and they sought continually to persuade themselves and others that he had not the true requisites of a Heaven-sent Messenger. "Muḥammad claimeth that tidings come to him from Heaven, yet he knoweth not where his camel is," said a man of the Jews on a day when one of the Prophet's camels had strayed. "I only know what God giveth me to know," said the Prophet when he heard of it, "and this He hath shown me: she is in the glen that I will tell you of, caught to a tree by her halter."[1] And some of the Helpers went and found her where he had said she was.

Many of the Jews welcomed at first what seemed to be the end of all danger of a further outbreak of civil war in the oasis. There had none the less been advantages in that danger, for the division between the Arabs had greatly enhanced the status of the non-Arabs, who were much in demand as allies. But the union of Aws and Khazraj made the old alliances unnecessary, while at the same time it gave the Arabs of Yathrib a formidable strength. The covenant of the Jews with the Prophet made it possible for them to share in that strength. But it also meant incurring obligations for a possible war against the far greater Arab strength which lay beyond the oasis; there might be other grave disadvantages for them in the new order of things, which was as yet untried, whereas the old order they knew and they were so well versed in its ways that many of them soon longed to return to it. One elderly Jewish politician of the Bani Qaynuqā', a master in the art of exploiting the discord between the Arab tribes, felt particularly frustrated by the new friendship between Aws and Khazraj. He therefore instructed a youth of his tribe who had a beautiful voice to go and sit amongst the Helpers when they were assembled together and to recite to them some of the poetry which had been composed by men of both tribes immediately before and after Bu'āth, the most recent battle of the civil war – poems in revilement of enemies, glorying in deeds of prowess, elegies for the dead, threats of revenge. The youth did as he was told, and he quickly held the attention of all who were there, transporting them from the present into the past. The men of Aws vehemently applauded the poetry of Aws and those of Khazraj the poetry of Khazraj; and then the two sides began to argue with each other, and to boast, and to shout abuse and threats, until, finally the cry burst forth: "To arms! To arms!" and they went out into the lava tract, bent on fighting the fight once again. When the news reached the Prophet he gathered together all the Emigrants who were at hand and hastened out to where the two hosts were already drawn up in battle order. "O Muslims," he said, and then he twice pronounced the Divine Name, *Allāh*, *Allāh*. "Will ye act," he went on, "as in the days of Ignorance, what though I am with you, and God hath guided you unto Islam, and honoured you with it, and thereby enabled you to

[1] I.I. 361.

break with pagan ways, and thereby saved you from disbelief, and thereby united your hearts?" At once they realised that they had been led astray, and they wept, and embraced each other, and returned with the Prophet to the city, attentive and obedient to his words.[1]

In order to unite the community of believers still further, the Prophet now instituted a pact of brotherhood between the Helpers and the Emigrants, so that each of the Helpers would have an Emigrant brother who was nearer to him than any of the Helpers, and each Emigrant would have a Helper brother who was nearer to him than any Emigrant. But he made himself and his family an exception, for it would have been too invidious for him to choose as his brother one of the Helpers rather than another, so he took 'Alī by the hand and said: "This is my brother"; and he made Ḥamzah the brother of Zayd.

Among the chief adversaries to Islam were two cousins, the sons of two sisters, but of Aws and of Khazraj through their fathers, each being of great influence in his tribe. The man of Aws, Abū 'Āmir, was sometimes called "the Monk" because he had long been an ascetic and had been known to wear a garment of hair. He claimed to be of the religion of Abraham, and had acquired a certain religious authority amongst the people of Yathrib. He came to the Prophet soon after his arrival, ostensibly to ask him about the new religion. He was answered in the words of the Revelation which had more than once defined it as *the religion of Abraham*.[2] "But I am of it," said Abū 'Āmir, and persisting in the face of denial he accused the Prophet of having falsified the Abrahamic faith. "I have not," said the Prophet, "but I have brought it white and pure." "May God let the liar die a lonely outcast exile!" said Abū 'Āmir. "So be it!" said the Prophet. "May God do that unto him who is lying!"[3]

Abū 'Āmir soon saw that his authority was rapidly losing weight; and he was still further embittered by his son Ḥanẓalah's devotion to the Prophet. It was not long before he decided to take his remaining followers, about ten in all, to Mecca, seemingly unaware that this was the beginning of his own self-imprecated exile.

His cousin of Khazraj was 'Abd Allāh ibn Ubayy, who also felt himself to have been frustrated by the coming of the Prophet and robbed not of spiritual authority but of the chief temporal power in the Yathrib oasis. He likewise had the bitterness of seeing his own son 'Abd Allāh altogether won over by the Prophet, as well as his daughter Jamīlah. But unlike Abū 'Āmir, Ibn Ubayy was prepared to wait, thinking that sooner or later the newcomer's overwhelming influence would begin to ebb. Meantime it was his policy to be as non-committal as possible, but he sometimes betrayed his feelings despite himself.

One such occasion was when another chief of Khazraj, Sa'd ibn 'Ubādah, was ill and the Prophet went to visit him. All the rich men of the oasis had their houses built as fortresses, and on his way he passed by Muzāḥam, the fortress of Ibn Ubayy, who was sitting in the shadow of its walls surrounded by some of his clansmen and other men of Khazraj. Out of courtesy to this chieftain, the Prophet dismounted from his ass and

[1] I.I. 386. [2] II, 135. [3] I.I. 411–12.

going to greet him sat for a while in his company, reciting the Koran and inviting him to Islam. When he had said all that he felt moved to say, Ibn Ubayy turned to him and said: "Naught could be better than this discourse of thine, were it but true. Sit then at home, in thine own house, and whoso cometh unto thee, preach unto him thus, but whoso cometh not, burden him not with thy talk, nor enter into his gathering with that which he liketh not." "Nay," said a voice, "come unto us with it, and visit us in our gatherings and our quarters and our houses, for that do we love, and that hath God given us of His Bounty, and thereunto hath He guided us." The speaker was 'Abd Allāh ibn Rawāḥah, a man whom Ibn Ubayy had thought he could count on for support at every turn. The disappointed chieftain now sullenly uttered a verse to the effect that when one is deserted by one's friends one is bound to be overcome. He had learned more clearly than ever that it was useless to resist. As to the Prophet, he went away deeply saddened, despite 'Abd Allāh's glowing tribute; and when he entered the sick man's house the rebuff he had received was still as it were written on his face. Sa'd immediately asked what was troubling him, and when he was told about Ibn Ubayy's impenetrable disbelief he said: "Deal gently with him, O Messenger of God, for when God brought thee unto us, even then were we fashioning for him a diadem wherewith to crown him; and he seeth that thou hast robbed him of a kingdom."

The Prophet never forgot these words; and as to Ibn Ubayy, he soon saw that his influence, once so great, was rapidly dwindling and that if he did not enter Islam it would vanish altogether. On the other hand he knew that a nominal acceptance of Islam would confirm him in his authority, for the Arabs were averse to breaking their old ties of allegiance unless there was a great reason for doing so. It was therefore not long before he decided to enter Islam; but although he formally pledged himself to the Prophet and regularly thereafter attended the prayers, the believers never came to feel sure of him. There were others about whom they were equally doubtful, but Ibn Ubayy was different from the majority of lukewarm or insincere converts by reason of his far-reaching influence, which made him all the more dangerous.

During the first months, while the Mosque was still being built, the community suffered a great loss in the death of As'ad, the first man in the oasis to pledge himself to the Prophet. It was he who had been the host of Muṣ'ab, and who had worked so closely with him during the year between the two 'Aqabahs. The Prophet said: "The Jews and the Arab hypocrites will surely say of me: 'If he were a Prophet, his companion would not have died.' And indeed my will availeth nothing for myself or for my companion against the Will of God."[1]

It was perhaps at the funeral of As'ad that the second meeting of Salmān the Persian with the Prophet took place, for Salmān himself described this meeting in later years to the son of 'Abbās, saying: "I went to the Messenger of God when he was in the Baqī' al-Gharqad,[2] whither he had followed the bier of one of his Companions." Salmān had known he would

[1] I.I. 346. [2] The cemetery at the south-east end of Medina.

be there, and he contrived to absent himself from his work in time to reach the cemetery after the burial, while the Prophet was still sitting there with some of the Emigrants and the Helpers. "I greeted him," said Salmān, "and then I circled round behind him in the hope that I might be able to look upon the Seal. And he knew what I desired, so he grasped his cloak and threw it off his back, and I beheld the Seal of Prophecy even as my Master had described it unto me. I stooped over it and kissed it and wept. Then the Messenger of God bade me come round and I went and sat in front of him and told him my story, and he was glad that his Companions should hear it. Then I entered Islam."[1] But Salmān was kept hard at work as a slave among the Bani Qurayẓah, and for the next four years he was able to have little contact with his fellow Muslims.

Another man of *the people of the Book* who embraced Islam at this time was a rabbi of the Bani Qaynuqā', Ḥuṣayn ibn Sallām. He came to the Prophet in secret and pledged allegiance to him. The Prophet thereupon gave him the name 'Abd Allāh, and the new convert suggested that before his Islam became known his people should be questioned about his standing amongst them. The Prophet concealed him in his house and sent for some of the leading men of Qaynuqā'. "He is our chief," they said in answer to his question, "and the son of our chief; he is our rabbi and our man of learning." Then 'Abd Allāh came out to them and said: "O Jews, fear God, and accept that which He hath sent unto you, for ye know that this man is the Messenger of God." Then he affirmed his own Islam and that of his household; and his people reviled him, and denied his good standing amongst them which they had previously affirmed.

Islam was now firmly established in the oasis. The Revelation prescribed the giving of alms and the fast of the month of Ramaḍān, and laid down in general what was forbidden and what was allowed. The five daily ritual prayers were regularly performed in congregation, and when the time for each prayer came the people would assemble at the site where the Mosque was being built. Everyone judged of the time by the position of the sun in the sky, or by the first signs of its light on the eastern horizon or by the dimming of its glow in the west after sunset; but opinions could differ, and the Prophet felt the need for a means of summoning the people to prayer when the right time had come. At first he thought of appointing a man to blow a horn like that of the Jews, but later he decided on a wooden clapper, *nāqūs*, such as the Oriental Christians used at that time, and two pieces of wood were fashioned together for that purpose. But they were never destined to be used; for one night a man of Khazraj, 'Abd Allāh ibn Zayd, who had been at the Second 'Aqabah, had a dream which the next day he recounted to the Prophet: "There passed by me a man wearing two green garments and he carried in his hand a *nāqūs*, so I said unto him: "O slave of God, wilt thou sell me that *nāqūs*?" "What wilt thou do with it?" he said. "We will summon the people to prayer with it," I answered. "Shall I not show thee a better way?" he said. "What way is that?" I asked, and he answered: "That thou shouldst say: *God is most Great, Allāhu Akbar.*" The man in green repeated this magnification four times, then each of the

[1] I.I. 141; I.S. IV, 56.

following twice: *I testify that there is no god but God; I testify that Muḥammad is the messenger of God; come unto the prayer; come unto salvation; God is most Great*; and then once again *there is no god but God.*

The Prophet said that this was a true vision, and he told him to go to Bilāl, who had an excellent voice, and teach him the words exactly as he had heard them in his sleep. The highest house in the neighbourhood of the Mosque belonged to a woman of the clan of Najjār, and Bilāl would come there before every dawn and would sit on the roof waiting for the daybreak. When he saw the first faint light in the east he would stretch out his arms and say in supplication: "O God I praise Thee, and I ask Thy Help for Quraysh, that they may accept Thy religion." Then he would stand and utter the call to prayer.

# XL

# *The New Household*

WHEN the Mosque was nearly finished the Prophet gave orders for two small dwellings to be attached to its eastern wall, one for his wife Sawdah and the other for his bethrothed, 'Ā'ishah. The building had taken altogether seven months, and during that time he lodged with Abū Ayyūb. But when Sawdah's house was nearly ready he sent Zayd to bring her to Medina, and with her Umm Kulthūm and Fāṭimah; and Abū Bakr sent word to his son 'Abd Allāh to bring Umm Rūmān, Asmā' and 'Ā'ishah. At the same time Zayd brought his own wife Umm Ayman and their small son Usāmah. Ṭalḥah also travelled with them, having disposed of all his immovable property, and making now his *Hijrah*. Not long after the arrival of the party, Abū Bakr gave Asmā' in marriage to Zubayr, who with his mother Ṣafiyyah had already been some months in Medina. Abū Bakr's sister Quraybah remained in Mecca to take care of their father, Abū Quḥāfah, who was old and blind. Unlike Quraybah, he had not yet entered Islam.

The Prophet now decided that in addition to Umm Ayman Zayd should have a second wife, one nearer his own age, and he asked his cousin 'Abd Allāh, the son of Jaḥsh, for the hand of his beautiful sister Zaynab. At first Zaynab was unwilling, and she had reason to be so, as events were to disclose. The reason she gave, namely that she was a woman of Quraysh, was not convincing. Her mother, Umaymah, of pure Quraysh stock on both sides, had married a man of Asad; and quite apart from Zayd's adoption into Quraysh, it could not be said that the tribes of his parents, the Bani Kalb and the Bani Ṭayy, were inferior to the Bani Asad. When she saw that it was the Prophet's desire that she should marry Zayd, she consented, and the marriage took place. About the same time her sister Ḥamnah was given in marriage to Muṣ'ab. Not long afterwards Umaymah came to Medina and pledged allegiance to the Prophet.

The Prophet and his daughters now went to live with Sawdah in her new house; and after a month or two it was decided that 'Ā'ishah's wedding should take place. She was then only nine years old, a child of remarkable beauty, as might have been expected from her parentage. Quraysh had given her father the name of 'Atīq, and some said that this was on account of his fine face.[1] Of her mother the Prophet had said: "Whoso would

[1] I.H. 161.

behold a woman of the wide-eyed Ḥūrīs of Paradise, let him look on Umm Rūmān."[1] To 'A'ishah the Prophet had long been very near and very dear, and she had been accustomed to see him every day, except during those few months when he and her father had already emigrated and she and her mother were still in Mecca. From her earliest years she had seen her father and mother treat him with such love and reverence as they gave to no one else. Nor had they failed to impress upon her the reasons for this: she knew well that he was the Messenger of God, that he had regular converse with the Angel Gabriel, and that he was unique amongst living men in that he had ascended to Heaven and returned from thence to earth. His very presence told of that ascent, and communicated something of the joy of Paradise. In his miraculous touch this joy was even tangible. When others were overcome by the heat, his hand would be "cooler than snow and more fragrant than musk".[2] He seemed, moreover, ageless, like an immortal. His eyes had lost nothing of their lustre, his black hair and beard had still the sheen of youth and his body had the grace of a man whose age was only the half of those fifty-three years which had passed since the Year of the Elephant.

Small preparations were made for the wedding – not enough, at any rate for 'Ā'ishah to have had the sense of a great and solemn occasion, and shortly before they were due to leave the house she had slipped out into the courtyard to play with a passing friend. In her own words: "I was playing on a see-saw and my long streaming hair was dishevelled. They came and took me from my play and made me ready."[3]

Abū Bakr had bought some fine red-striped cloth from Bahrain and it had been made into a wedding-dress for her. In this they now clothed her. Then her mother took her to the newly built house where some women of the Helpers were waiting for her outside the door. They greeted her with the words "For good and for happiness – may all be well!" and led her into the presence of the Prophet. He stood there smiling while they combed her hair and decked her with ornaments. Unlike his other marriages, at this there was no wedding feast. The occasion was as simple as possible. A bowl of milk was brought and having drunk from it himself, he offered it to her. She shyly declined it, but when he pressed her to drink she did so, and offered the bowl to her sister Asmā' who was sitting beside her. Others also drank of it; then they all went their ways, and the bridegroom and bride were left together.

For the last three years scarcely a day had passed without one or more of 'Ā'ishah's friends coming to play with her in the courtyard adjoining her father's house. Her removal to the Prophet's house changed nothing in this respect. Friends now came every day to visit her in her own appartment – new friends made since her arrival in Medina and also some of the old ones whose parents, like hers, had emigrated. "I would be playing with my dolls," she said, "with the girls who were my friends, and the Prophet would come in and they would steal out of the house and he would go out after them and bring them back, for he was pleased for my sake to have them there."[4] Sometimes he would say "Stay where ye are"[5] before they

[1] I.S. VII, 202. [2] B. LXI, 22. [3] I.S. VIII, 40–1.
[4] I.S. VIII, 42. [5] ibid., 41.

had time to move. He would also join in their games sometimes, for he loved children and had often played with his own daughters. The dolls or puppets had many different roles. "One day," said 'Ā'ishah, "the Prophet came in when I was playing with the dolls and he said: 'O 'Ā'ishah, whatever game is this?' I said: 'It is Solomon's horses', and he laughed."[1] But sometimes as he came in he would simply screen himself with his cloak so as not to disturb them.

'Ā'ishah's life had also its more serious side. Yathrib was well known throughout Arabia as a place where at certain seasons there was a great danger of fever, especially for those who were not native to the oasis. The Prophet himself escaped the fever, but it severely attacked many of his Companions including Abū Bakr and his two freedmen 'Āmir and Bilāl, who were at that time living with him. One morning 'Ā'ishah went to visit her father, and was dismayed to find the three men lying prostrate in an extremity of weakness. "How dost thou, my father?" she said, but he was too ill to adjust his reply to a girl of nine, and he answered her with two lines of poetry:

> "Each man each morn his kindred greet good day,
> And death is nearer than his sandal's thong."

She thought he did not know what he was saying and turned to 'Āmir, who also answered her in verse, to the effect that without actually dying he had been near enough to death to know what it was like. Meantime the fever had left Bilāl, though he was still too weak to do anything but lie in the courtyard of the house. But his voice had enough strength in it for him to chant:

> "Ah, shall I ever sleep the night again
> Midst thyme and nard that outside Mecca grow,
> And shall I drink the waters of Majannah,[2]
> And see before me Shāmah and Ṭafīl?"[3]

'Ā'ishah returned home deeply troubled. "They are raving," she said, "out of their minds, through the heat of the fever." But the Prophet was somewhat reassured when with the retentive memory of a child she repeated almost word for word the lines which they had uttered and which she had not fully understood. It was on that occasion that he prayed: "O God, make Medina as dear unto us as thou hast made Mecca, or even dearer. And bless for us its waters and its grain, and carry away from it its fever as far as Mahya'ah.[4]"[5] And God answered his prayer.

[1] ibid., 42. [2] A place near Mecca. [3] Two hills of Mecca.
[4] A place about seven camel days south of Medina. [5] I.I. 414.

# XLI

# *The Threshold of War*

UNTO *those who are attacked permission to fight*[1] *is given unto those who fight because they have been wronged; and God is Able to give them victory. Those who have been driven from their homes unjustly, for no cause other than for their saying: Our Lord is God.*[2] The Prophet had received this Revelation not long after his arrival in Medina. He knew moreover that permission was here a command, and the obligations of war had been stressed in the covenant with the Jews. An early Revelation had said: *Deal gently with the disbelievers, give them respite for a while,*[3] but the last three words were portentous; and now God had declared war on Quraysh. His Messenger was therefore obliged to attack them by every means in his power and to make it clear to them that Arabia would never be safe for them until they submitted to the Divine Will. Nor was he unaware that to give Quraysh no peace meant giving himself and his Companions no peace. This premonition was soon to be confirmed by another Revelation: *Fight them until persecution is no more, and religion is all for God.*[4] But for the moment there could be no question of anything but raids. Quraysh were vulnerable in their caravans, and it was especially in the spring and early summer months, when their trade with Syria was most active, that they lay open to attack from Medina. In the autumn and winter they sent most of their caravans to the south, mainly to the Yemen and to Abyssinia.

The information received in Medina about the caravans was seldom very precise, and there were liable to be last-minute changes of plan. The Meccan caravans altogether eluded some of the first raids from Medina, but the Muslims succeeded none the less in making treaties with Bedouin tribes at strategic points along the coast of the Red Sea.

When the Prophet went out himself he appointed one of his Companions to be in charge of Medina during his absence, and the first to have this honour was the Khazrajite chief, Sa'd ibn 'Ubādah. That was eleven months after the Hijrah; until then the Prophet himself took no part in the expeditions, and on each occasion when he remained behind he gave the

[1] According to some authorities this verb is passive, i.e. "those who are fought against", in which case "because" must be taken as referring back to "is given".
[2] XXII, 39–40. [3] LXXXVI, 17. [4] VIII, 39.

leader a white banner mounted on a lance. For the first year he sent out only those of his Companions who were Emigrants; but in September 623 news came that a rich Meccan caravan was returning from the north under the escort of Umayyah, the chief of Jumaḥ, with a hundred armed men. Umayyah had always been one of the fiercest enemies of Islam; and another reason for attack was the prize itself. The merchandise at stake was said to have been loaded on to as many as 2,500 camels. But the Emigrants alone would have been no match for a hundred Quraysh, so on this occasion the Prophet set out with two hundred men, over half of whom were Helpers. Once again, however, the information had been inadequate and there was no encounter. They also missed, some three months after that, another rich caravan, less heavily guarded, which the Shamsite Abū Sufyān was conducting to Syria. News of it had come too late, and when the Prophet and his men reached 'Ushayrah in the valley of Yanbū', which opens out on to the Red Sea south-west of Medina, the caravan had already passed. But Abū Sufyān would soon be returning from Syria, perhaps with an even richer load, and then, if God willed, they would not fail to waylay him.

Although no fighting had taken place as yet, Quraysh were already alert to the danger of having an enemy established in Yathrib. But it seemed to them that this would in no way affect their trade with the south. They were soon to be disillusioned, for the Prophet now received word of a caravan that was on its way from the Yemen, and he sent his cousin 'Abd Allāh ibn Jaḥsh with eight other Emigrants to lie in wait for it near Nakhlah, between Ṭā'if and Mecca. It was Rajab, one of the four sacred months of the year, and the Prophet gave 'Abd Allāh no instructions to attack the caravan but simply to bring him news of it. No doubt he wished to see how well the southern caravans were guarded, for future activity against them.

Soon after the Emigrants reached their destination and had camped at a point of vantage not far from the main route, a small caravan of Quraysh passed by them and then stopped and camped nearby, unaware of their presence. The camels were laden with raisins and leather and other merchandise. 'Abd Allāh and his companions were in a dilemma: the Prophet's only definite instructions had been to bring him news; but he had not forbidden them to fight, nor had he made mention of the sacred month. Were these pre-Islamic conventions still binding, they asked themselves. They thought also of the Revelation: *Permission to fight is given unto those who fight because they have been wronged . . . those who have been unjustly driven from their homes.*[1] They were at war with Quraysh, and they had recognised at least two of the merchants in the caravan as men of Makhzūm, which of all the clans of Mecca had shown itself most hostile to Islam. It was the morning of the last day of Rajab; sunset would bring in Sha'bān, which was not a sacred month, but by that time, though no longer protected by the calendar, their enemies would be protected by distance, for they would have reached the sacred precinct; and after much hesitation they decided to attack. Their first arrow killed a man of Kindah, a confederate of the clan of 'Abdu Shams, wereupon 'Uthmān, one of the

[1] XXII, 39.

men of Makhzūm, and Ḥakam, a freedman, surrendered, though 'Uthmān's brother Nawfal escaped to Mecca.

'Abd Allāh and his men took their prisoners and the camels and the merchandise back to Medina. He set aside a fifth part of the spoils for the Prophet, dividing the rest among his companions and himself. But the Prophet refused to accept anything and said: "I did not bid you fight in the sacred month," whereupon those who had done so thought they were doomed. Their brethren in Medina blamed them for their violation of Rajab, while the Jews said it was a bad omen for the Prophet, and Quraysh set about spreading far and wide the news that Muḥammad was guilty of sacrilege. Then came the Revelation: *They question thee about the sacred month and fighting therein. Say: to fight therein is a grave offence; but barring men from God's path and sacrilege against Him and the holy mosque and driving out His people therefrom are graver with God. And torturing is graver than killing.*[1]

The Prophet interpreted this as confirming the traditional ban on warfare in the sacred month but as making an exception in this particular case, so he relieved 'Abd Allah and his companions of the fear that lay so heavily upon them and accepted a fifth of the spoils for the general benefit of the community. The clan of Makhzūm sent ransoms for the two prisoners, but Ḥakam their freedman chose to enter Islam and remain in Medina, so 'Uthmān returned alone.

It was in this same moon of Sha'bān that there came a Revelation of great ritual importance. Its opening words refer to the Prophet's extreme care to face in the right direction for prayer. In the Mosque the direction was set by the Miḥrāb, the prayer-niche in the Jerusalem wall; but when he was outside the town he would check his direction by the sun if it were day and by the stars at night.

> *We have seen the turning of thy face unto the sky; and now We shall turn thee a way that shall well please thee. So turn thou thy face towards the Inviolable Mosque; and wheresoever ye may be, turn ye your faces toward it.*[2]

A Miḥrāb was forthwith made in the south wall of the Mosque, facing towards Mecca, and the change was accepted with joy by the Prophet and his Companions. From that day Muslims have turned in the direction of the Ka'bah for the performance of the ritual prayer, and by extension for other rites.

[1] II, 217. [2] II, 144.

# XLII
# *The March to Badr*

THE time was now at hand for Abū Sufyān to return with all the wares that he and his fellows had acquired in Syria. The Prophet sent Ṭalḥah and 'Umar's cousin Sa'īd – the son of Zayd the Ḥanīf – to Ḥawrā' on the sea-shore due west of Medina to bring him news as soon as the caravan arrived. This would enable him, by a quick march to the south-west, to overtake it further down the coast. His two scouts were hospitably received by a chief of Juhaynah who hid them in his house until the caravan had passed. But he and they might have spared themselves their pains, for someone in Medina, no doubt one of the hypocrites or one of the Jews, had already sent word of the Prophet's plans to Abū Sufyān, who immediately hired a man of the Ghifārī tribe, Damdam by name, to go with all speed to Mecca and urge Quraysh to march out at once with an army to their rescue, while he himself pressed forward along the coastal route, travelling by both day and night.

But his was not the only sense of urgency. The Prophet had his reasons for wishing to remain in Medina as long as possible, for his beloved daughter Ruqayyah had fallen seriously ill. But personal considerations could not be taken into account, and rather than risk being too late he decided not even to wait for the return of his scouts. By the time they reached Medina he had already set out with an army of Emigrants and Helpers, three hundred and five men altogether. At that time there were seventy-seven able-bodied Emigrants in Medina and all these were present on this occasion except three: the Prophet had told his son-in-law 'Uthmān to stay at home and tend his sick wife; the other two were Ṭalḥah and Sa'īd, who arrived back from the coast too late to set out.

At the first halt, which was still in the oasis, the Prophet's cousin Sa'd of Zuhrah noticed his fifteen-year-old brother 'Umayr looking troubled and furtive and he asked him what was the matter. "I am afraid," said 'Umayr, "that the Messenger of God will see me and say I am too young and send me back. And I long to go forth. It might be that God would grant me martyrdom." As he feared, the Prophet noticed him when he lined up the troops and said he was too young and told him to go home. But 'Umayr wept and the Prophet let him stay and take part in the expedition. "He was so young", said Sa'd, "that I had to fasten the straps of his sword-belt for him."

There were seventy camels which the men rode by turns, three or four men to one camel, and three horses, one of which belonged to Zubayr. The white banner was given to Muṣ'ab, no doubt because he was of the clan of 'Abd ad-Dār, whose ancestral right it was to carry the banner of Quraysh in war. After the vanguard came the Prophet himself, preceded by two black pennants, one for the Emigrants and one for the Helpers. These were borne respectively by 'Alī and Sa'd ibn Mu'ādh of Aws. During the Prophet's absence from Medina, the prayers were to be led by Ibn Umm Maktūm, the blind man referred to in the Revelation *He frowned and turned away when the blind man came unto him.*[1]

In Mecca, shortly before the arrival of Damdam, the Prophet's aunt 'Ātikah had a dream which terrified her and left her with a conviction of impending disaster for Quraysh. She sent for her brother 'Abbās and told him what she had seen: "I saw a man riding a camel and he halted in the valley and cried at the top of his voice: 'Haste ye forth, O men of perfidy, unto a disaster that in three days shall lay you prostrate.' I saw the people gather round him. Then he entered the Mosque with the people following him, and from out of their midst his camel carried him up to the roof of the Ka'bah, and again he cried out the same words. Then his camel bore him to the top of Mount Abū Qubays, and yet again he cried out to the people as before. Then he wrenched free a rock and sent it hurtling down the slope, and when it reached the foot of the mount it split into fragments, nor was there any house or any dwelling in Mecca but was smitten with a piece of it."

'Abbās recounted his sister's dream to 'Utbah's son, Walīd, who was his friend, and Walīd told his father, and the news spread throughout the city. The next day Abū Jahl exclaimed in the presence of 'Abbās, with gleeful mockery: "O sons of 'Abd al-Muṭṭalib, since when hath this prophetess been uttering her prophecies amongst you? Is it not enough for you that your men should play the prophet? And must your women do the same?" 'Abbās could not find a rejoinder, but Abū Jahl had his answer the next day, when the crags of Abū Qubays resounded with the powerful voice of Damdam. The people streamed out of their houses and out of the Mosque to where he had halted in the valley. Abū Sufyān had paid him handsomely, and he was determined to play his part well. He had turned round his saddle and was seated with his back to his camel's head; and in further sign of calamity he had slit his camel's nose, so that the blood poured forth from it, and he had rent his own shirt to ribbons. "Men of Quraysh," he shouted, "the transport camels, the transport camels! Your goods which are with Abū Sufyān! Muḥammad and his companions are upon them! Help! Help!"

The town was immediately in an uproar. The caravan now in danger was one of the richest of the year, and many were those who had reason to fear the loss of it. An army of about a thousand men was quickly mustered. "Do Muḥammad and his fellows think that this will be as the caravan of Ibn al-Ḥaḍramī?" they said, referring to 'Amr, the confederate of 'Abdu Shams who had been killed by an arrow in the sacred month at Nakhlah. The clan of 'Adī were alone in not taking part in the expedition. Every other chief of clan led out a contingent except Abū Lahab, who sent in his own stead a man of Makhzūm who owed him money. But the Bani Hāshim

[1] See p. 64.

and the Bani l-Muṭṭalib had none the less their interests in the caravan and felt in honour bound to defend it, so Ṭālib led out a body of men from both clans, and 'Abbās went with them, perhaps intending to act as peacemaker. Ḥakīm of Asad, Khadījah's nephew, went out with the same purpose. Like Abū Lahab, Umayyah of Jumaḥ had also decided to stay at home, for he was an elderly man of excessive corpulence; but while he was sitting in the Mosque 'Uqbah came to him with a censer of incense which he placed before him, saying: "Scent thyself with that, Abū 'Alī, for thou art of the women." "God curse thee," said Umayyah, and made ready to set out with the others.

The Prophet had by now left the direct route from Medina to the south and was making for Badr, which lay on the coastal route from Syria to Mecca, to his west. It was at Badr that he hoped to waylay Abū Sufyān, and he sent ahead two of their allies of Juhaynah, who knew the district well, to scout for news of the caravan. At Badr they halted on a hill above the well, and when they went to draw water they overheard a conversation between two girls from the village about a debt. "The caravan will come tomorrow or the next day," said one to the other, "and I will work for them and pay thee what I owe thee." When they heard these words they made haste back to the Prophet with the news. But if they had stayed a little longer they would have seen a solitary rider approaching the well from the west. It was Abū Sufyān himself, who had hastened ahead of the caravan in order to see whether it was safe to proceed to Mecca by the nearest route, that is by Badr. On reaching the water he found a villager there and asked him if he had seen any strangers. He answered that he had seen two riders who had made a halt on the hill above and who had then drawn some water and taken it away with them. Abū Sufyān went to their halting-place and took up some of the camel dung which he broke into pieces. There were some date stones in it. "By God," he said, "this is the fodder of Yathrib." He hastened back to his followers, and turning the caravan away from the road they pressed on at full speed along the shore by the sea, leaving Badr on their left.

Meantime the two scouts returned to the Prophet with the news that the caravan was expected to reach Badr on the following day or the day after. They would certainly stop at Badr, which had long been one of the great halts on the road between Mecca and Syria, and there was ample time for the Muslims to surprise them and overpower them.

Then came the news that Quraysh had set out with an army to rescue their caravan. This had always been considered as a possibility, but now that it had become a fact the Prophet felt bound to consult his men and to let theirs be the choice between advancing and retreating. Abū Bakr and 'Umar spoke for the Emigrants in favour of advancing and then, by way of confirmation of all that they had said, an ally of the Bani Zuhrah who had only recently come to Medina, Miqdād by name, rose to his feet and added: "O Messenger of God, do what God hath shown thee to do. We will not say unto thee as the children of Israel said unto Moses: *Go thou and thy Lord and fight; we shall sit here*,[1] but we will say: 'Go thou and thy

[1] K. V, 24.

Lord and fight, and with you we also will fight, on the right and on the left, before thee and behind thee.'" 'Abd Allāh ibn Mas'ūd used to tell in after years of the great light that dawned on the Prophet's face when he heard those words and as he blessed their speaker. Not that he was surprised, for he knew that the Emigrants were unreservedly with him. But could the same be said of all the Helpers who were now present? The army had set out from Medina in hope of capturing the caravan. But now it seemed that they might have to encounter something much more formidable. Moreover, when the Helpers had pledged allegiance to him in 'Aqabah, they had said that they were not responsible for his safety until he had entered their territory, but that when he was with them they would protect him as they protected their wives and their children. Would they be prepared to help him against an enemy now that he was no longer in Yathrib? "Men, give me your advice," he said, expressing himself in general but meaning the Helpers, some of whom had already divined his thoughts, though none of them had yet spoken. But now Sa'd ibn Mu'ādh rose to his feet. "It would seem," he said, "that we are the men thou meanest, O Messenger of God." And when the Prophet assented he went on: "We have faith in thee and we believe what thou hast told us, and we testify that what thou hast brought us is the truth, and we have given thee our binding oaths to hear and obey. So do what thou wilt, and we are with thee. By Him who hath sent thee with the truth, if thou shouldst bid us cross yonder sea and didst plunge into it thyself, we would plunge into it with thee. Not one man of us would stay behind. Neither are we averse from meeting our enemy tomorrow. We are well tried in war, trusty in combat. It may be that God will show thee prowess of ours such as shall bring coolness to thine eyes.[1] So lead us on with the blessing of God."

The Prophet rejoiced at his words; and the certainty came to him that they would indeed have to contend with either the army or the caravan but not with both. "Onwards," he said, "and be of good cheer, for God the All Highest hath promised me one of the two parties, and even now it is as if I saw the enemy lying prostrate."[2]

Although they were prepared for the worst, there was still hope that they would be able to attack the caravan and be well on their way back to Medina, enriched with plunder and prisoners, before the army of Quraysh arrived. But when they had reached a halt that was less than a day's march from Badr, the Prophet rode on with Abū Bakr and obtained some information from an old man from which he concluded that the Meccan army was already near. Returning to the camp he waited until nightfall and sent his three cousins 'Alī, Zubayr and Sa'd with some others of his companions to the well of Badr to see if either the army or the caravan or both had drawn water from it, or if anyone there had had any news of either party. At the well they chanced upon two men who were loading their camels with water for the army of Quraysh, and having overpowered them they brought them back to the Prophet, who was standing in prayer when they arrived. Without waiting until he had finished they began to

[1] "Coolness of the eyes" is a favourite term of the Arabs for expressing joy, delight, etc.

[2] I.I. 435.

question the two men, who said that they were the army's water-carriers. But some of their interrogators preferred to think that they were lying, for they fervently hoped that it was Abū Sufyān who had sent them to get water for the caravan, and they set about beating them, until they said "We are Abū Sufyān's men," and they let them be. The Prophet made the concluding prostrations to his prayer and gave the greetings of peace, and said: "When they told you the truth, ye beat them, and when they lied ye let them be. They are indeed of the army of Quraysh." Then he turned to the two prisoners. "Tell me, ye two," he said, "of Quraysh, of their whereabouts." "They are behind this hill," they said, pointing to 'Aqanqal, "on the further slope of the valley beyond it." "How many men are they?" he asked. "Many," they said, nor could they answer anything more precise, so he asked how many beasts they slaughtered. "Some days nine, some days ten" was the answer. "Then they are between nine hundred and a thousand," he said. "And what leaders of Quraysh are amongst them?" They named fifteen and these included, of 'Abdu Shams, the brothers 'Utbah and Shaybah; of Nawfal, Ḥārith and Ṭu'aymah; of 'Abd ad-Dār, Naḍr, who had pitted his tales of Persia against the Koran; of Asad, Khadījah's half brother Nawfal; of Makhzūm, Abū Jahl; of Jumaḥ, Umayyah; of 'Āmir, Suhayl. Hearing these eminent names, the Prophet remarked when he rejoined his men: "This Mecca hath thrown unto you the best morsels of her liver."

It was not long before news of the thousand-strong army reached Abū Sufyān, and by that time he had reached a point from which his rescuers were between him and the enemy. Realising that the caravan was now safe, he sent a messenger to Quraysh, saying: "Ye came out to defend your camels and your men and your goods; and God hath rescued them, therefore return." This message reached them when they were already encamped at Juḥfah, a little to the south of Badr. There was yet another reason why they should advance no further. Gloom had been cast over the whole camp on account of a dream – almost a vision – that Juhaym, a man of Muṭṭalib, had had. "Between sleeping and waking," he said, "I saw a man approach on horseback, leading a camel. Then he halted and said 'Slain are 'Utbah and Shaybah and Abū 'l-Ḥakam and Umayyah'" – and he went on to mention other chiefs of Quraysh that the horseman had named. "Then," said Juhaym, "I saw him stab his camel in the chest and let it run loose through the camp, and there was no tent that was not bespattered with its blood." When Abū Jahl was told of this he said in a tone of triumphant derision: "Here is yet another prophet from the sons of Muṭṭalib." He said "yet another" because the two clans of Muṭṭalib and Hāshim were often thought of as one. Then, seeking to dispel the gloom, he addressed them all: "By God, we will not return until we have been at Badr. Three days will we stay there; we will slaughter camels and feast and make flow the wine and the songstresses shall play and sing for us; and the Arabs will hear how we marched forth and of our mighty gathering, and they will stand in awe of us for ever. Onwards to Badr!"

Akhnas ibn Sharīq had come out with Zuhrah, whose confederate he was, and he now urged them to pay no attention to Abū Jahl, so they returned from Juḥfah to Mecca, every man of them. Ṭālib also returned with some of his fellow clansmen, for words had passed between him and others of Quraysh who had said: "O sons of Hāshim, we know that even though ye have come out with us, your hearts are with Muḥammad." But 'Abbās decided to go on to Badr with the rest of the army, and he took with him his three nephews, Abū Sufyān and Nawfal, the sons of Ḥārith, and 'Aqīl, the son of Abū Ṭālib.

Beyond the hill, a little to the north-east, the Muslims were breaking camp. The Prophet knew that it was imperative for them to reach the waters of Badr before the enemy, so he ordered an immediate advance. Not long after they had started rain began to fall, and he rejoiced in it as a sign of favour from God, a blessing and an assurance. It refreshed the men and laid the dust and made firm the soft sand of the valley of Yalyal where now they were marching; but it would impede the enemy, who had yet to climb the slopes of 'Aqanqal, which lay over to the left of the Muslims, on the opposite side of the valley from Badr. The wells were all on the gentler slopes of the near side, and the Prophet ordered a halt at the first well they came to. But a man of Khazraj, Ḥubāb ibn al-Mundhir, came to him and said: "O Messenger of God, this place where now we are – hath God revealed it unto thee, that we should neither advance nor retreat from it, or is it a matter of opinion and strategy of war?" He said that it was merely a matter of opinion, whereupon Ḥubāb said: "This is not the place to halt, but take us on, O Messenger of God, until we come unto that one of the large wells which is nearest the enemy. Let us halt there and stop up the wells that lie beyond it and make for ourselves a cistern. Then will we fight the enemy, and all the water will be ours to drink, and they will have none." The Prophet at once agreed, and Ḥubāb's plan was carried out in every detail. The further wells were stopped and the cistern was built, and every man filled his drinking vessel.

Then Sa'd ibn Mu'ādh came to the Prophet and said: "O Prophet of God, let us build for thee a shelter and put thy riding camels in readiness beside it. Then will we meet our enemy, and if God strengthen us and make us victorious over them, that is what we fervently desire. But, if not, then thou canst mount and ride to join those whom we left behind us. For as to some of those who came not out with thee, O Prophet of God, even our love for thee is not greater than theirs, nor had they stayed behind, if they had known thou wouldst meet with war. Through them God will protect thee, and they will give thee good counsel and fight at thy side." The Prophet praised him and invoked blessings upon him, and the shelter was fashioned with branches of palms.

That night God sent down a peaceful sleep upon the believers, and they awoke refreshed.[1] It was Friday 17 March AD 623 which was 17 Ramadan in the year AH 2.[2] As soon as it was dawn Quraysh marched forth and climbed the hill of 'Aqanqal. The sun was already up when they reached the top, and when the Prophet saw them on their richly caparisoned horses and camels descending the slope into the valley of Yalyal towards Badr, he prayed: "O God, here are Quraysh: they have come in their arrogance and their vanity, opposing Thee and belying Thy messenger. O

[1] See K. VIII, 11. [2] *Anno Hegirae*. The Islamic era begins at the Hijrah.

Lord, grant us Thy help which Thou didst promise us! O Lord, this morn destroy them!"

They made their camp at the foot of the slope; and since it appeared to them that the Muslims were fewer than they had anticipated they sent out 'Umayr of Jumaḥ on horseback to estimate their numbers and to see if they had any reinforcements in their rear. He reported that there was no sign of any further troops other than those who were now facing them on the opposite side of the valley. "But O ye men of Quraysh," he added, "I do not think that any man of them will be slain but he shall first have slain a man of you; and if they slay of you a number that is equal to their number, what good will be left in life thereafter?" 'Umayr had something of the reputation of a diviner throughout Mecca, and this added weight to his words. No sooner had he spoken than Ḥakīm of Asad, Khadījah's nephew, seized his opportunity and went on foot through the camp until he came to the men of 'Abdu Shams. "Father of Walīd," he said to 'Utbah, "thou art the greatest man of Quraysh, and their lord and the one whom they obey. Wouldst thou be remembered with praise amongst them until the end of time?" "How shall that be?" said 'Utbah. "Lead the men back," said Ḥakīm, "and take upon thyself the cause of thy slain confederate 'Amr." He meant that 'Utbah should eliminate one of the strong reasons for fighting and pay the blood-wite to the kinsmen of the man who had been killed at Nakhlah, whose brother 'Amir had in fact come to take his revenge on the field of battle. 'Utbah agreed to do all that he said, but urged him to go and speak to Abū Jahl, the man most likely to insist on war. Meantime he addressed the troops, saying: "Men of Quraysh, ye will gain naught by fighting Muḥammad and his companions. If ye lay them low, each man of you will for ever look with loathing on the face of another who hath slain his uncle or his cousin or some yet nearer kinsman. Therefore turn back and leave Muḥammad to the rest of the Arabs. If they slay him, that is what ye desire; and if not, he will find that ye have shown self-restraint towards him."

He no doubt intended to approach 'Āmir al-Ḥaḍramī at once with a view of paying the blood-wite for his brother, but Abū Jahl was too quick for him. He taunted 'Utbah with cowardice, with being afraid of death for himself and also for his son Abū Hudhayfah, who was in the ranks of the enemy. Then he turned to 'Āmir and urged him not to let slip his opportunity of revenge for his brother. "Arise," he said, "and remind them of thy covenant and of the slaying of thy brother." 'Āmir leapt to his feet, and frantically stripping off his clothes, he began to utter cries of lamentation at the top of his voice. "Alas for 'Amr! Alas for 'Amr!" So the fire of war was kindled and men's souls were filled with violence and it was in vain for 'Utbah or anyone else to seek to turn them back.

The now general absorbedness in final preparations for battle gave one man the chance he had been waiting for. Fearing that he might escape in his absence, Suhayl had brought his son 'Abd Allāh with him to Badr. Umayyah, chief of Jumaḥ, had done the same with his son 'Alī, whom he had coerced into forsaking Islam. But unlike 'Alī, who was a waverer, 'Abd Allāh was unshakeable in his faith; and going out of sight of the camp behind a nearby hillock, he quickly made his way across the uneven sands to the Muslim camp, where he went straight to the Prophet, and joy was on both their faces. Then he joyfully greeted his two brothers-in-law, Abū Ṣabrah and Abū Hudhayfah.

# XLIII

# *The Battle of Badr*

THE Prophet now drew up his army, and he passed in front of each man to give them good heart and to straighten the ranks, bearing an arrow in his hand. "Stand in line, O Sawād," he said to one of the Helpers who was too far forward, and he gave him a slight prick in the belly with his arrow. "O Messenger of God, thou hast hurt me," said Sawād, "and God hath sent thee with truth and justice, so give me my requital." "Take it," said the Prophet, laying bare his own belly and handing him the arrow whereupon Sawād stooped and imprinted a kiss where it was his due to place the point of the shaft. "What made thee do this?" said the Prophet. And he answered: "O Messenger of God, we are now faced with what thou seest; and I desired that at my last moment with thee – if so it be – my skin should touch thy skin;" and the Prophet prayed for him and blessed him.

Quraysh had now begun to advance. Seen across the undulating dunes, the Meccan army appeared to be much smaller than it was. But the Prophet was fully aware of their true numbers and of the great disparity between the two hosts, and he now returned to the shelter with Abū Bakr and prayed for the help which God had promised him.

A light slumber came upon him, and when he woke he said: "Be of good cheer, Abū Bakr; the help of God hath come to thee. Here is Gabriel and in his hand is the rein of a horse which he is leading, and he is armed for war."[1]

In the history of the Arabs many a battle had been averted at the last minute, even when two forces were drawn up face to face. But the Prophet was now certain that the battle would take place, and that this formidable array was the *one of the two parties* that he had been promised. The vultures also knew that carnage was now imminent and they were already in wait to feed on the carcasses of the slain, some wheeling overhead and others perched on the rocky slopes in the rear of either army. It was, moreover, clear from the movements of Quraysh that they were preparing to attack. They were already near and had now halted within easy reach of the cistern which the Muslims had made. It seemed likely that their first move would be to take possession of it.

Aswad of Makhzūm strode ahead of the others, clearly intending to drink. Ḥamzah went out to meet him and struck him a blow which severed one of his legs below the knee, and a second blow which killed him. Then

[1] B. LXIV, 10; I.I. 444.

'Utbah, still smarting from the taunts of Abū Jahl, stepped from the ranks and gave the challenge for single combat; and for the further honour of the family his brother Shaybah and his son Walīd stepped forward on either side of him. The challenge was immediately accepted by 'Awf of the Najjār clan of Khazraj, who had been one of the first six of the Helpers to pledge themselves to the Prophet; and with 'Awf stepped forward his brother Mu'awwidh. It was their quarter in Medina that Qaswā' had chosen as the ultimate halt of the Hijrah. The third to accept the challenge was 'Abd Allāh ibn Rawāḥah, who had defied his leader Ibn Ubayy in speaking words of welcome and comfort to the Prophet.

"Who are ye?" said the challengers. When the men answered, 'Utbah said: "Ye are noble and our peers, yet have we naught to do with you. Our challenge is against none but men of our own tribe." Then the herald of Quraysh shouted: "O Muḥammad, send forth against us our peers from our own tribe." The Prophet had not intended anything else, but the eagerness of the Helpers had forestalled him. Now he turned to his own family, since it was above all for them to initiate the battle. The challengers were two men of mature age and one youth. "Arise, O 'Ubaydah," he said. "Arise, O Ḥamzah. Arise, O 'Alī." 'Ubaydah was the oldest and most experienced man in the army, a grandson of Muṭṭalib, and he faced 'Utbah while Ḥamzah faced Shaybah and 'Alī faced Walīd. The combats were not long: Shaybah and Walīd were soon lying dead on the ground, while Ḥamzah and 'Alī were unhurt: but at the moment when 'Ubaydah struck 'Utbah to the ground he received from him a sweep of the sword that severed one of his legs. It was a triple contest, three against three, so Ḥamzah and 'Alī turned their swords on 'Utbah, and Ḥamzah gave him the death blow. Then they carried their wounded cousin back to their camp. He had lost a mortal quantity of blood, and the marrow was oozing from the stump of his leg. He had only one thought. "Am I not a martyr, O Messenger of God?" he said as the Prophet approached him. "Indeed thou art," he answered.

The tense stillness between the two hosts was now broken by the sound of an arrow from Quraysh, and a freedman of 'Umar fell to the ground, fatally wounded. A second arrow pierced the throat of Hārithah, a youth of Khazraj, as he was drinking at the cistern. The Prophet now exhorted his men saying: "By Him in whose hand is the soul of Muḥammad, no man will be slain this day, fighting against them in steadfast hope of his reward, advancing not retreating, but God shall straightway enter him into Paradise."[1] His words were passed on by those who heard them to those who were out of earshot. 'Umayr of the Salimah clan of Khazraj had a handful of dates which he was eating. "Wonder of wonders!" he exclaimed. "Is there naught between me and my entering Paradise, but that these men should slay me?", and he flung away the dates and put his hand to his sword, in eager readiness for the word of command.

'Awf was standing near to the Prophet, disappointed at having lost the honour of the challenge he had been the first to accept, and he now turned to him and said: "O Messenger of God, what is it that maketh the Lord

[1] I.I. 445.

laugh with joy at His slave?" At once came the answer: "When he plungeth without mail into the midst of the foe"; and 'Awf began to strip off the coat of mail he was wearing, while the Prophet took up a handful of pebbles and shouting at Quraysh "Defaced be those faces!", he hurled the pebbles at them, conscious that he was hurling disaster. Then he gave the order to charge. The battle cry he had devised for them, *Yā manṣūr amit,*[1] resounded from every throat as the men surged forward. 'Awf without his mail and 'Umayr were among the first to meet the enemy and both fought until they were slain. Their deaths and those of 'Ubaydah and the two killed by arrows brought the number of martyrs up to five. Only nine more of the faithful were to die that day, amongst them that other 'Umayr, Sa'd's younger brother, whom the Prophet had wanted to send home.

*Thou threwest not when thou threwest, but it was God that threw.*[2] These words were part of the Revelation which came immediately after the battle. Nor were the pebbles the only manifestation of Divine strength which flowed from the hand of the Prophet on that day. At one point where the resistance of Quraysh was at its strongest a sword broke in the hands of a believer, whose first thought was to go and ask the Prophet for another weapon. It was 'Ukkāshah, a kinsman of the family of Jaḥsh. The Prophet gave him a wooden club saying: "Fight with this, 'Ukkāshah." He took it and brandished it and it became in his hand a long, strong, gleaming sword. He fought with it for the rest of Badr and in all the Prophet's other battles, and it was named *al-'Awn* which means the Divine Help.

When the believers were ordered to charge, they did not charge alone, as well the Prophet knew, for he had been promised: *I will help you with a thousand of the angels, troop on troop.*[3] And the Angels also had received a Divine message: *When thy Lord revealed unto the angels: Lo, I am with you, so make firm the believers. I shall cast terror into the hearts of the disbelievers. It is for you to strike off their heads, and to smite their every finger.*[4]

The presence of the Angels was felt by all, as a strength by the faithful and as a terror by the infidels, but that presence was only visible or audible to a few, and in varying degrees. Two men of a neighbouring Arab tribe had gone to the top of a hill to see the issue and to take part – so they hoped – in the looting after the battle. A cloud swept by them, a cloud filled with the neighing of stallions, and one of the men dropped instantly dead. "His heart burst with fright," said the one who lived to tell of it, judging from what his own heart had felt.

One of the believers was pursuing a man of the enemy, and the man's head flew from his body before he could reach him, struck off by an unseen hand. Others had brief glimpses of the Angels riding on horses whose hooves never touched the ground, led by Gabriel wearing a yellow turban, whereas the turbans of the other Angels were white, with one end left streaming behind them. Quraysh were soon utterly routed and put to flight, except in small groups where the Angels had not passed. In one of these Abū Jahl fought on with unabated ferocity until Mu'ādh, the brother of 'Awf, smote him to the ground. 'Ikrimah, the son of Abū Jahl, then

[1] Concise in Arabic but not in English: "O thou whom God hath made victorious, slay!"
[2] VIII, 17. [3] VIII, 9. [4] VIII, 12.

struck Mu'ādh and all but severed his arm at the shoulder. Mu'ādh went on fighting with his good arm, while the other hung limply by its skin at his side; but when it became too painful he stooped, and putting his foot on his dead hand jerked himself up, tore off the encumbrant limb, and continued in pursuit of the enemy. Abū Jahl was still full of life, but Mu'awwidh, Awf's second brother, recognised him as he lay there and struck him a blow which left him dying. Then Mu'awwidh passed on and like 'Awf he fought until he was slain.

Most of Quraysh escaped, but some fifty were mortally wounded or killed outright in the battle or overtaken and cut down as they fled. About the same number were taken captive. The Prophet had said to his Companions: "I know that men of the sons of Hāshim and others have been brought out despite themselves, without any will to fight us." And he mentioned by name some of those whose lives should be spared if they were caught. But most of his army were in any case bent on holding their captives to ransom rather than putting them to the sword.

Since Quraysh so greatly outnumbered the believers, the possibility of their rallying and returning to the fight had still to be considered, and the Prophet was persuaded to withdraw to his shelter with Abū Bakr while some of the Helpers kept watch. Sa'd ibn Mu'ādh was standing on guard at the entrance with drawn sword, and when his fellow warriors started to bring their captives into the camp the Prophet was struck by the expression of strong disapproval on his face. "O Sa'd," he said, "it would seem that what they are doing is hateful in thine eyes." Sa'd vigorously assented; then he added: "This is the first defeat God hath inflicted on the idolaters; and I had rather see their men slaughtered than left alive." 'Umar was of the same opinion, but Abū Bakr was in favour of letting the captives live, in the hope that sooner or later they might become believers, and the Prophet inclined to his view. But later in the day, when 'Umar returned to the shelter, he found the Prophet and Abū Bakr in tears on account of a Revelation which had come: *It is not for a prophet to hold captives until he hath made great slaughter in the land.*[1] *Ye would have for yourselves the gains of this world and God would have for you the Hereafter, and God is Mighty, Wise.* But the Revelation then made it clear that the decision to spare the captives had been accepted by God and should not now be revoked; and the Prophet was given a message for the captives themselves: *O Prophet, say unto those captives who are in your hands: If God knoweth any good in your hearts, He will give you better than that which hath been taken from you, and He will forgive you. Verily God is Forgiving, Merciful.*[2]

There was, however, one man, Abū Jahl, who clearly could not be allowed to live. The general opinion was that he had been killed and the Prophet gave orders that his body should be searched for. 'Abd Allāh ibn Mas'ūd went out again to the battlefield and searched until he found the man who had done more than any other to stir up hatred of Islam amongst the people of Mecca. Abū Jahl still had enough life in him to recognise the enemy who now stood over him. 'Abd Allāh had been the first man to

[1] It was for wrongfully sparing a captive that Saul was deprived of his kingship (1 Samuel 15). [2] VIII, 70.

recite the Koran aloud in front of the Ka'bah, and Abū Jahl had struck him a severe blow and wounded him in the face, for he was merely a confederate of Zuhrah and a poor one at that, his mother having been a slave. 'Abd Allāh now placed his foot on the neck of Abū Jahl, who said: "Thou hast climbed high indeed, little shepherd." Then he asked him which way the fortunes of war had swung that day, his implication being that next time they would swing in the opposite direction. "God and His messenger have won," he answered. Then he cut off his head and took it to the Prophet.

Abū Jahl was not the only chief of Quraysh to be killed after the fighting had finished. 'Abd ar-Raḥmān ibn 'Awf was carrying coats of mail which he had taken as booty, and he passed by the corpulent Umayyah, who had lost his mount and was unable to escape. With him was his son 'Alī, whose hand he was holding. Umayyah called out to his one-time friend: "Take me prisoner, for I am worth more than coats of mail." 'Abd ar-Raḥmān agreed, and throwing down the mail he took him and his son each by a hand. But as he was leading them towards the camp Bilāl saw them and recognised his former master and torturer. "Umayyah," he exclaimed, "the head of disbelief! May I not live if he survive!" 'Abd ar-Raḥmān indignantly protested that they were his prisoners, but Bilāl repeated his cry: "May I not live if he survive!" "Wilt thou not hear me, thou son of a black mother?" said the outraged captor, whereupon Bilāl shouted with all the power of the voice that had won him the function of muezzin: "O Helpers of God, the head of disbelief, Umayyah! May I not live if he survive!" Men came running from all sides and narrowly encircled 'Abd ar-Raḥmān and his two captives. Then a sword was drawn and 'Alī was struck to the ground but not killed. 'Abd ar-Raḥmān let go the father's hand. "Make thine own escape," he said, "yet no escape there is, for by God I can avail thee nothing!" Pushing him aside the men closed in upon the prisoners with their swords and quickly made an end of them both. 'Abd ar-Raḥmān used to say in after years: "God have mercy on Bilāl! My coats of mail were lost to me, and he robbed me of my two prisoners."[1]

The Prophet gave orders that the bodies of all the infidels slain in the battle should be thrown into a pit; and when the body of 'Utbah was being dragged towards it the face of his son Abū Hudhayfah turned pale, and was filled with sorrow. The Prophet felt for him, and gave him a look of compassion, whereupon Abū Hudhayfah said: "O Messenger of God, it is not that I question thy command as to my father and the place where they have thrown him. But I used to know him as a man of wise counsel, forbearance and virtue, and I had hoped that these qualities would lead him unto Islam; and when I saw what had befallen him, and when I remembered what state of disbelief he died in after my hopes for him, it saddened me." Then the Prophet blessed Abū Hudhayfah and spoke to him words of kindness.

The peace and quiet of the camp was soon broken by voices raised in anger, for those who had stayed behind to guard the Prophet demanded a share of the booty, and those who had pursued the enemy and captured

[1] I.I. 448–9.

men and armour and weapons were unwilling to give up what their own hands had taken. But before the Prophet had time to restore harmony by ordering an equitable distribution of all that had been captured, the desired effect was achieved more simply and more immediately by a Revelation: *They will question thee concerning the spoils of war. Say: The spoils of war are for God and the messenger.*[1] So the Prophet ordered that everything that had been taken, including the captives, should be brought together and no longer be considered as the private property of any individual. The order was at once obeyed without question.

The most eminent of the captives was the chief of 'Āmir, Suhayl, cousin of Sawdah and brother of her first husband. Others more closely connected with the Prophet were his uncle 'Abbās, his son-in-law, Zaynab's husband Abū l-'Āṣ, and his cousins 'Aqīl and Nawfal. He gave a general order that all the captives should be well treated, though clearly they had to be bound. But the thoughts of his uncle suffering such duress prevented the Prophet from sleeping that night, and he gave orders that his bonds should be loosed. Other captives received less indulgent treatment from their nearest of kin. Muṣ'ab passed by his brother Abū 'Azīz as he was being bound by the Helper who had captured him, and he said: "Bind him fast for his mother is rich, and it may be that she will ransom him from thee." "Brother," said Abū 'Azīz, "is this how thou dost commend me to others?" "He is now my brother in thy stead," said Muṣ'ab. None the less, Abū 'Azīz used to tell in after years of the good treatment he received from the Helpers, who took him to Medina whence his mother ransomed him for 4,000 dirhems.

As soon as it became clear that the eight hundred or more Meccan troops still at large had been routed beyond possibility of rallying, the Prophet sent 'Abd Allāh ibn Rawāḥah to take the good tidings of victory to the people of Upper Medina, that is, the more southerly part of the city, and he sent Zayd to the people of Lower Medina. He himself remained with the army at Badr; and that night he went and stood by the pit into which the bodies of the enemies of Islam had been thrown. "O men of the pit," he said, "kinsmen of your Prophet, ill was the kinship ye showed him. Liar ye called me, when others took me in; against me ye fought, when others helped me to victory. Have ye found it to be true, what your Lord promised you? I have found it to be true, what my Lord promised me." Some of his Companions overheard him and wondered at his speaking to dead bodies. "Your hearing of what I say is not better than theirs," he said, "but they cannot answer me."[2]

Early next morning he set off for Medina with his army and the spoils. Two of the most valuable captives, that is those whose families could be relied upon to pay the full ransom of 4,000 dirhems, were Naḍr of 'Abd ad-Dār and 'Uqbah[3] of 'Abdu Shams. But these were two of the worst enemies of Islam, and if they were allowed to return they would immediately resume their evil activities, unless the Muslims' victory at Badr against such odds had made them reflect. The Prophet's eye was now constantly upon them; but there was no sign of any change of heart in

[1] VIII, 1. [2] I.I. 454. [3] See p. 98.

either man, and during the march it became clear to him that it was not in accordance with the Will of God that they should be left alive. At one of the first halts he gave orders that Naḍr should be put to death, and it was 'Alī who beheaded him. At a subsequent halt 'Uqbah suffered the same fate at the hands of a man of Aws. The Prophet divided the remainder of the captives and the rest of the spoils at a halt within three days' march of Medina, giving insofar as was possible an equal share to every man who had taken part in the expedition.

By that time Zayd and 'Abd Allāh ibn Rawāḥah had reached Medina, and there was great rejoicing amongst all except the Jews and the hypocrites. But Zayd was given sad news in exchange for his good news: Ruqayyah was dead; 'Uthmān and Usāmah had just returned from burying her. The lamentations in that part of the city were still further increased when Zayd told 'Afrā' of the death of her two sons 'Awf and Mu'awwidh. Sawdah went between her own house and theirs to join the mourning in both. For 'Afrā' there was joy mingled with sorrow on account of the glorious manner of her sons' deaths. But Zayd had also to tell Rubayyi' of the death of her youthful son Ḥārithah ibn Surāqah, whose neck had been pierced by an arrow as he was drinking at the cistern; and as soon as the Prophet himself returned a few days later she came to him and asked him about her son; for she was troubled by the thought that the youth had been slain before the battle had started and before he had had time to strike a blow for Islam. "O Messenger of God," she said, "wilt thou not tell me of Ḥārithah, so that if he be in Paradise I may bear my loss with patience, and if not I may do penance for him with weeping." The Prophet had already answered such questions in general, for he had promised that a believer is rewarded for what he purposes, even if he should not achieve it: "Deeds are counted according to the intention."[1] But he now answered her in particular, saying: "Mother of Ḥārithah, in Paradise are many Gardens, and verily thy son hath attained unto the all-highest, Firdaws."[2]

[1] B. I, 1. [2] B. LVI, 14.

# XLIV
# *The Return of the Vanquished*

THE army of Quraysh made its way back to Mecca in small groups, preceded or followed by single individuals. One of the first to arrive with the news was the Hāshimite Abū Sufyān whose brother Nawfal had been captured. Abū Sufyān's hostility towards the new religion had spurred him to write verses against it and against his cousin and foster-brother, the Prophet. But the experience of Badr had greatly shaken him. His first thought was to visit the Ka'bah, and it happened that his uncle Abū Lahab was sitting in the large tent that was known as the tent of Zamzam. Seeing his nephew, Abū Lahab called out to him to come and sit with him and tell him what had happened. "There is no more to it than this," said Abū Sufyān. "We met the enemy and turned our backs, and they drove us in flight or took captives even as they pleased. Nor can I blame any of our folk, for we had to face not only them but also men in white on piebald horses between heaven and earth who spared nothing and nothing could stand up against them."

Now Umm al-Faḍl was sitting in a corner of the tent, and with her was Abū Rāfi', one of 'Abbās's slaves, who was making arrows. Like her he was a Muslim, and they had both kept their Islam secret from all save a few. But Abū Rāfi' could not contain himself for joy at the news of the Prophet's victory; and when he heard speak of the "men in white between heaven and earth" he exclaimed in wonder and in triumph: "Those were the Angels." Immediately Abū Lahab was overcome by a paroxysm of rage and he struck Abū Rāfi' a wounding blow in the face. The slave tried to retaliate, but he was slight and weak, and the thickset ponderous Abū Lahab bore him to the ground, knelt on him and struck him again and again. Then Umm al-Faḍl took up a wooden post which was sometimes used to reinforce the tent poles, and she brought it down with all her strength on the head of her brother-in-law, splitting the skin and flesh away from his skull in a long gash that was never to heal. "Wilt thou treat him as of no account," she cried, "now that his master is away and cannot protect him?" The wound putrefied, and within a week his whole body was covered with festering pustules from which he died.

When further news of the battle was brought, and when the bereaved began to bewail their dead, a decision was quickly made in the Assembly that they should be told to restrain themselves. "Muḥammad and his companions," it was said to them, "will have news of this and rejoice." As to the kinsmen of the captives, they were urged to delay sending any offers of ransom to Yathrib. Through the deaths of so many eminent men, the Umayyad Abū Sufyān had become, in the eyes of many, the leading man of Quraysh; and as if to set an example he said with regard to his two sons, Ḥanzalah and 'Amr, the one killed and the other made captive: "Must I suffer the twofold loss of my blood and my wealth? They have slain Ḥanzalah, and must I now ransom 'Amr? Leave him with them. Let them keep him as long as they please!"

Abū Sufyān's fiery wife Hind was not the mother of either Ḥanzalah or 'Amr; but at the outset of the battle she had lost her father, 'Utbah, her uncle Shaybah, and her brother Walīd; and, though she held back her lamentations, she vowed that when Quraysh took their revenge on the Muslim army – as take it they must – she would eat raw the liver of Ḥamzah who had slain her uncle and given her father the death-blow.

As to the rich caravan load which Abū Sufyān had brought safely to Mecca, it was unanimously agreed in the Assembly that all the profits should be devoted to raising an army so large and so powerfully equipped that it could not fail to crush any resistance that Yathrib might be able to put up against it; and this time women would march out with the men, to urge them on and spur them to excel themselves in deeds of valour. It was also agreed, to the same purpose, to send messengers to all their many allies throughout Arabia, summoning them to join in their attack, and giving them what they thought to be powerful reasons why the followers of the new religion should be considered as a common enemy.

While respecting the precept of the Assembly about lamentation, most of Quraysh disregarded what had been said about ransoming, and men from almost every clan were soon on their way to Medina in order to make terms with the captors and set free one or more of their kinsmen or allies. Abu Sufyān kept his word; but at the next Pilgrimage he detained one of the pilgrims from the oasis, an old man of Aws, and said he would not release him until his son 'Amr had been returned to him; and the pilgrim's family persuaded the Prophet to agree to this exchange.

# XLV
# *The Captives*

THE captives arrived in Medina with their guards a day after the arrival of the Prophet. Sawdah, who had gone once more to visit 'Afrā', was astonished on her return to see her cousin and brother-in-law Suhayl, the chief of her clan, sitting in a corner of the room with his hands tied to his neck. The sight aroused long-forgotten sentiments and made her forget for the moment all that had replaced them. "O Abū Yazīd," she expostulated, "all too readily didst thou surrender. Thou shouldst have died a noble death." "Sawdah!" exclaimed the Prophet, whose presence she had not noticed. The reproof in his voice immediately brought her back, not without a sense of shame, from her pre-Islamic past to her Islamic present. There were still hopes that Suhayl would enter Islam, and surely the impact of the now flourishing and already powerful theocracy could not fail to impress him and the other captives. But the Prophet relied on his followers to put Islamic and not pagan ideas into their heads. Again he turned to the now repentant Sawdah: "Wouldst thou foment trouble against God and His Messenger?"

The eminence of Suhayl, like that of Abū Sufyān, had been greatly enhanced by the deaths of so many leaders. His influence could have been expected to bring many waverers to Islam from his own clan and also from others; but his stay in Medina was cut short, for the Bani 'Āmir quickly sent one of their clan to ransom him, and the man consented to remain as hostage while his chief went back to Mecca to arrange the payment of the sum agreed upon.

Each of the captives had been shared between three or more of the combatants, and the group of Helpers who owned 'Abbās now brought him to the Prophet and said: "O Messenger of God, allow us to forgo the ransom due to us for our sister's son." By "sister" they meant the captive's grandmother, Salmà. But the Prophet said: "Ye shall not remit a single dirhem." Then he turned to his uncle, saying: "Ransom thyself 'Abbās and thy two nephews, 'Aqīl and Nawfal, and thine ally 'Utbah, for thou art a rich man." 'Abbās protested: "I was already a Muslim, but the people made me march out with them." The Prophet answered: "As to thine Islam, God knoweth best. If what thou sayest is true, He will reward thee. But outwardly thou hast been against us, so pay us thy ransom." 'Abbās replied that he had no money, but the Prophet said: "Where then is the money thou didst leave with Umm al-Faḍl? Ye two were alone when thou didst say to her: 'If I should be slain, so much is for Faḍl, for 'Abd Allāh, for Qitham and for 'Ubayd Allāh.'" It was then only that faith truly entered the heart of 'Abbās. "By Him who sent thee with the truth," he said, "none knew of this but she and I. Now I know that thou art the Messenger of God."[1] And he agreed to ransom his two nephews and his confederate as well as himself.

One of the prisoners who was quartered with the Prophet was his son-in-law Abū l-'Āṣ, whose brother 'Amr came from Mecca with a sum of money sent by Zaynab to ransom him; and with the money she sent a necklace of onyx which her mother had given her on her wedding day. When the Prophet saw the necklace he turned pale, recognising it at once as Khadījah's. Deeply moved, he said to those who had a share in the prisoner: "If ye should see fit to release her captive husband and return to her the ransom, it is for you to do so." They at once agreed, and both the money and the necklace were returned together with Abū l-'Āṣ himself. It had been hoped that he would enter Islam while he was in Medina, but he did not, and when he left for Mecca the Prophet told him that on his return he should send Zaynab to Medina, and this he sadly promised to do. The Revelation had made it clear that a Muslim woman could not be the wife of a pagan man.

'Abd Allāh ibn Jaḥsh had a share in Walīd, the youngest son of the now dead Walīd, the former chief of Makhzūm. The youth's two brothers Khālid and Hishām came to ransom him. 'Abd Allāh would take no less than four thousand dirhems, and Khālid, the captive's half-brother, was unwilling to give so much, but the full brother Hishām reproached him saying: "True, he is not thy mother's son," whereupon Khālid consented. The Prophet, however, was against the transaction and told 'Abd Allāh that he should ask them for nothing less than their father's famous arms and armour. Khālid once more refused, but again Hishām won him over; and when they had brought the heirloom to Medina they set off with their brother again for Mecca. But at one of the first halts he slipped away from them and returned to Medina, where he went to the Prophet and made his formal entry into Islam, pledging allegiance to him. His brothers followed hard after him, and, when they saw what had happened, the outraged Khālid said to him: "Why was this not done before thou wert ransomed, and before our father's treasured legacy had left our hands? Why didst thou not become a follower of Muḥammad then, if that was thy purpose?" Walīd answered that he was not the man to let Quraysh say of him: "He did but follow Muḥammad to escape from having to pay ransom." Then he went back with his brothers to Mecca to fetch some of his possessions, not suspecting that they would do anything against him. But once there they imprisoned him with 'Ayyāsh and Salamah, the two Muslim half brothers of Abū Jahl, whom 'Ikrimah the son of Abū Jahl still kept under guard after his father's death. The Prophet used often to pray for the escape of all three of them and of Hishām of Sahm and others who were forcibly detained in Mecca.

Jubayr the son of Muṭ'im came to ransom his cousin and two of their confederates, and the Prophet received him graciously. He told him that if Muṭ'im had been alive and had come to him on behalf of the prisoners he

[1] Ṭab. 1344.

would have surrendered them to him free of ransom. Jubayr was impressed by everything he saw in Medina; and one evening, at sunset, he stayed outside the Mosque and listened to the prayer. The Prophet recited the Sūrah named *aṭ-Ṭūr*, The Mount, which warns of the Judgement and of Hell, and then speaks of the wonders of Paradise. It ends with the words: *Wait patiently for the fulfilment of thy Lord's decree, for verily thou art in Our sight; and glorify thy Lord with praise when thou uprisest, and glorify Him in the night, and at the dimming of the stars.*[1]

"It was then," said Jubayr, "that faith took root in my heart."[2] But he would not yet listen to its promptings for he was too engrossed with thoughts of his beloved uncle's recent death at Badr. Ṭu'aymah, Muṭ'im's brother, was one of those whom Ḥamzah had killed, and Jubayr felt bound in honour to avenge his death; and fearing lest he should weaken in his purpose, he left for Mecca as soon as he had reached an agreement about the ransoms.

Most of the ransomers were at least courteous to the Prophet. An exception was Ubayy of Jumaḥ, the brother of Umayyah and bosom friend of 'Uqbah, both of whom had been killed after the battle. As he was leaving with his ransomed son he said: "O Muḥammad, I have a horse named 'Awd that I feed every day on many measures of corn. I shall slay thee when I am riding him." "Nay," said the Prophet, "it is I who shall slay thee, if God will."[3]

Meantime in Mecca Ubayy's two nephews, Ṣafwān and 'Umayr, were speaking with savage bitterness about the irretrievable loss caused to Quraysh by the death of those leaders who had been thrown into the pit at Badr. Ṣafwān was the son of Umayyah and likely to become chief of Jumaḥ now that his father was dead. His cousin 'Umayr was the man who had ridden round the Muslim army at Badr and estimated its strength. "By God, there is no good in life, now that they are gone," said Ṣafwān. 'Umayr agreed, and he was nearer to sincerity than the other. His son was one of the captives, but he was too heavily in debt to ransom him, and he felt so oppressed with his life that he was prepared to sacrifice it to the common cause. "But for a debt I cannot pay," he said, "and a family I fear to leave destitute, I would ride out to Muḥammad and kill him." "On me be thy debt," said Ṣafwān, "and thy family be as mine! I will care for them as long as they live. They shall not want for aught that is mine to give them." 'Umayr immediately accepted his offer, and they swore to keep it a secret between the two of them until their end had been achieved. Then he sharpened his sword, smeared it with poison, and set off for Yathrib on the pretext of ransoming his son.

When he reached Lower Medina, the Prophet was sitting in the Mosque. On seeing 'Umayr girt with his sword, 'Umar stopped him from entering, but the Prophet called to him to let the Jumaḥite approach. So 'Umar said to some Helpers who were with him: "Go ye in unto the Messenger of God and sit with him and be on your guard for him against this villain, for he is in no wise to be trusted." 'Umayr wished them good day – a salutation of paganism – and the Prophet said: "God hath given us a better greeting than

[1] LII, 48–9. [2] B. LII, 25. [3] W. 251.

thine, O 'Umayr. It is Peace, the greeting of the people of Paradise." Then he asked him why he had come, and 'Umayr mentioned his son as the reason. "Why then that sword?" said the Prophet. "God damn swords!" said 'Umayr. "Have they done us any good service?" "Tell me the truth," said the Prophet. "To what end hast thou come?" And when 'Umayr reiterated the pretext of his son, the Prophet repeated to him word for word the conversation he had had in the Ḥijr with Ṣafwān. "So Ṣafwān took upon himself thy debt and thy family," he concluded, "that thou shouldst slay me; but God hath come between thee and that." "Who told thee this," cried 'Umayr, "for by God there was no third man with us?" "Gabriel told me," said the Prophet. "We called thee liar," said 'Umayr, "when thou didst bring us tidings from Heaven. But praise be to God who hath guided me unto Islam. I testify that there is no god but God, and that Muḥammad is the messenger of God." The Prophet turned to some of those who were present and said. "Instruct your brother in his religion, and recite unto him the Koran; and release for him his captive son."[1]

'Umayr was eager to return to Mecca that he might try to bring others to Islam, Ṣafwān amongst them. The Prophet gave him permission to go and he made many converts; but Ṣafwān considered him to be a traitor, and resolutely refused to speak to him or have anything to do with him. After some months 'Umayr returned to Medina as an Emigrant.

When Abū l-'Āṣ returned to Mecca, he told Zaynab that he had promised her father that he would send her to Medina. They agreed that their little daughter Umāmah should go with her. Their son 'Alī had died in infancy, and Zaynab was now expecting a third child. When all the preparations had been made for the journey, Abū l-'Āṣ sent with them his brother Kinānah as escort. They had kept their plans secret, but they none the less set off in daylight, and there was much talk about it in Mecca, until finally some of Quraysh decided to follow them and to bring Zaynab back into the bosom of the clan of 'Abdu Shams to which she belonged by marriage. When they were close upon them, a man of Fihr, Habbār by name, galloped on ahead and circled closely round them, brandishing his spear at Zaynab as she sat in her howdah with Umāmah, and then rejoining the others who were now close upon them. Kinānah dismounted, took his bow, knelt facing them, and emptied his quiver onto the sand in front of him. "Let one of you come near me," he said, "and by God, I will put an arrow into him." The men drew back as he bent his bow. Then, after a brief consultation, his chief, Abū Sufyān, and one or two others dismounted and walked forward, asking him to unbend his bow and discuss the matter with them. Kinānah agreed, and Abū Sufyān said to him: "It was a grave mistake to bring the woman out publicly over the heads of the people, when thou knowest the disaster that hath befallen us, and all that Muḥammad hath done against us. It will be taken as a sign that we have been humbled, and men will say that it is nothing but impotence on our part. By my life, it is not that we want to keep her from her father, nor would that serve us for revenge. But take the woman back to Mecca, and

[1] I.S. IV, 147; I.I. 472–3.

when tongues have stopped wagging about our meekness, and when the news hath spread that we went out after her and brought her back, then steal her out secretly to join her father." Kinānah accepted this proposal, and they all returned to Mecca together. Shortly afterwards Zaynab had a miscarriage which was attributed to the fright caused her by Habbār. When she had recovered, and when time enough had elapsed, Kinānah took her out with Umāmah under cover of the night, and escorted them as far as the valley of Yajaj, some eight miles from Mecca. There they were met by Zayd, as had previously been arranged, and he brought them safely to Medina.

# XLVI

# *Bani Qaynuqāʿ*

IT had long been clear that the Jews did not consider the Prophet's covenant as binding upon them, and that most of them preferred the pagan idolaters to the Muslim worshippers of the One God. While affirming the piety and trustworthiness of individuals amongst the Jews, the Revelations were now full of warnings against the majority. The Prophet and his followers were urged to beware of them: *They will do all they can to ruin you, and they love to cause you trouble. Their hatred is clear from what their mouths utter, and what their breasts conceal is greater.*[1]

There could be no doubt that the hopes of the Jews were turning more and more to the Prophet's own tribe as the chief means of obliterating the new religion and thus of restoring the oasis of Yathrib to what it had been in the past. His movements were regularly reported to Mecca; and if Quraysh marched out against him as far as the Jewish fortresses to the South of Medina, that is to within about half a day's journey from his Mosque, it seemed certain that the Meccan army would be reinforced at the crucial moment by powerful Jewish contingents.

*If good befall you, it is evil in their eyes, and if evil befall you they rejoice thereat.*[2] This was plainly demonstrated by the Jews' reaction to the victory at Badr. When the news came, the tribes of Qaynuqāʿ, Naḍīr and Qurayẓah were unable to conceal their dismay. Particularly striking was the case of Kaʿb the son of Ashraf. His father was an Arab of the tribe of Ṭayy, but Kaʿb counted himself as being, through his mother, of the Bani Naḍīr, who accepted him as one of themselves because his mother was a Jewess. He had become in fact a prominent member of the tribe, partly owing to his wealth and his strong personality, and also because he was a poet of some fame. When he heard the tidings that Zayd and ʿAbd Allāh brought, with the names of all the outstanding men of Quraysh who had been killed, he exclaimed: "By God, if Muḥammad have slain these men, then is the inside of the earth better than its outside"; and when he had made certain that the tidings were true he immediately left the oasis before the return of the Prophet, and went to Mecca where he composed a lament for Abū Jahl, ʿUtbah, Shaybah and others of the dead. At the same time he urged Quraysh to redeem their honour and take their revenge by mustering an invincible quantity of troops and leading them against Yathrib.

News of Kaʿb's activities came to Medina; but Kaʿb was out of reach for

[1] III, 118. [2] III, 120.

the moment, and more immediate action was called for against a Jewish tribe other than his. The Prophet was especially well informed of the treachery and hatred of the Bani Qaynuqāʿ, because ʿAbd Allāh ibn Sallām had been one of their leading men, and was well versed in their ways. Moreover it was they who were the allies of the Khazrajite Ibn Ubayy, leader of the hypocrites; and their presence was more felt than that of the other Jewish tribes because their settlements were close to the city itself, whereas the Bani Naḍīr and Qurayẓah, the allies of Aws, lived at some distance outside it.

The Prophet had recently received the command: *If thou fearest treachery from any folk, then throw back unto them their covenant. Verily God loveth not the treacherous.*[1] But the Revelation also said: *If they incline unto peace, incline thou also unto it, and trust in God.*[2] He was therefore unwilling to take irrevocable action if anything could be gained by gentler means, and on one of the first days after his return from Badr he went to meet the Bani Qaynuqāʿ in their market place in the south of Medina. Reflecting on the miracle of Badr might lead them to a change of heart, so he warned them not to call down upon themselves the anger of God which had just now fallen upon Quraysh. "O Muḥammad," they answered "be not deluded by that encounter, for it was against men who had no knowledge of war, and so thou didst get the better of them. But by God, if we make war on thee, thou shalt know that we are the men to be feared." The Prophet turned and left them, and they imagined for the moment that they had triumphed.

A few days later, in the same market-place, an incident occurred which brought things to a climax: a Muslim woman who had come to sell or exchange some goods was grossly insulted by one of the Jewish goldsmiths. A Helper who happened to be present came to her rescue and the offender was killed in the fight which ensued, whereupon the Jews fell upon the Muslim and killed him. His family then demanded vengeance and proceeded to rouse up the Helpers against the Qaynuqāʿ. But blood had been shed on both sides, and the affair could easily have been settled and reduced to its true proportions if the Jews had demanded the arbitration of the Prophet according to the covenant. But this they scorned to do; and, deciding that the time had come to teach the intruders a lesson, they sent for reinforcements to their two former allies of Khazraj, Ibn Ubayy and ʿUbādah ibn Ṣāmit, while they themselves withdrew – for the moment, as they thought – into their own powerfully fortified and well provisioned strongholds. They could muster an army of seven hundred men, which was more than double the Muslim army at Badr; and they relied on at least as many men again from Ibn Ubayy and ʿUbādah. When these appeared they no doubt intended to issue from their fortresses and show the Prophet that their recent threats had not been empty words.

But in fact those threats had been their own self-condemnation; and within a few hours they were astonished and dismayed to find themselves blockaded on all sides by an army which outnumbered their own and which demanded their unconditional surrender.

[1] VIII, 58. [2] VIII, 61.

Ibn Ubayy went to consult with 'Ubādah, but 'Ubādah was obdurate that no former treaty could stand in opposition to the covenant, and he renounced all responsibility for Qaynuqā'. As for Ibn Ubayy, it was not in his nature to cut in one moment the links which he had so deliberately forged over the years between himself and such powerful allies. But it was impossible for him to be blind, as the Jews were blind, to the present devotion of most of his fellow townsmen to the Prophet. He had too often tasted the bitterness of being clearly shown by his once devoted followers that their allegiance to him was far outweighed by another allegiance. Two years previously, with the help of the besieged from within, he could have broken the blockade of a larger army. But now he knew that once the Prophet had taken action he himself could do nothing against him. So the Bani Qaynuqā' waited in vain behind their battlements, and their hopes dwindled to despair as day after day passed without any sign of help. For two weeks they held out; and then they surrendered unconditionally.

Ibn Ubayy now came to the camp and approaching the Prophet he said: "O Muḥammad, treat my confederates well." The Prophet put him off, and then when the demand was repeated he turned away from him, whereupon Ibn Ubayy clutched him by his coat of mail, thrusting his hand into the neck of it. The Prophet's face grew dark with anger. "Let go thy hold," he said. "By God. I will not," said Ibn Ubayy, "until thou dost promise to treat them well. Four hundred men without mail and three hundred mailed – they protected me from the red and from the black.[1] Wilt thou cut them down in one morning?" "I grant thee their lives," said the Prophet. But the Revelation had commanded, with regard to those who broke treaties with him: *If thou overcomest them in war, then make of them an example, to strike fear into those that are behind them, that they may take heed*;[2] and, having decided that the Bani Qaynuqā' should forfeit all their possessions and be exiled, he told 'Ubādah to escort them out of the oasis. They took refuge with a kindred Jewish settlement to the north-west in Wādi l-Qurà, and with their help they eventually settled on the borders of Syria.

They were metalworkers by trade, and the Emigrants and Helpers were greatly enriched by the weapons and armour that were divided amongst them after the Prophet had taken his legal fifth for himself and his theocratic state.

[1] See p. 112, note. [2] VIII, 57.

# XLVII

# *Deaths and Marriages*

ONE of the immediate acts of the Prophet on his return from Badr had been to visit the grave of his daughter Ruqayyah, and Fāṭimah went with him. This was the first bereavement they had suffered within their closest family circle since the death of Khadījah, and Fāṭimah was greatly distressed by the loss of her sister. The tears poured from her eyes as she sat beside her father at the edge of the grave, and he comforted her and sought to dry her tears with the corner of his cloak. He had previously spoken against lamentations for the dead, but this had led to a misunderstanding, and when they returned from the cemetery the voice of 'Umar was heard raised in anger against the women who were weeping for the martyrs of Badr and for Ruqayyah. "'Umar, let them weep," he said. And then he added: "What cometh from the heart and from the eye, that is from God and His Mercy, but what cometh from the hand and from the tongue, that is from Satan."[1] By the hand he meant the beating of the breast and the lacerating of the cheeks, and by the tongue he meant the vociferous clamour in which all the women joined as a social gesture.

Fāṭimah was the youngest of his daughters, and she was at this time about twenty years old. To his family he had already spoken of 'Alī as the most fitting husband for her, but there had been no formal contract. Abū Bakr and 'Umar had both asked for her hand, but the Prophet had put them off, not by saying that she was already promised to another but by telling them that he must wait for the time appointed by Heaven. It was only in the weeks which followed his return from Badr that he became certain that the time had come and he then spoke words of encouragement to 'Alī in the wish that he should formally ask for her hand. 'Alī was at first hesitant on account of his extreme poverty. He had inherited nothing from his father, for the law of the new religion forbade a believer to inherit from a disbeliever. But he had acquired a humble dwelling not far from the Mosque and, since there was no doubt about the Prophet's wishes, he allowed himself to be persuaded. After the formal contract had been made, the Prophet insisted on a wedding feast. A ram was sacrificed and some of the Helpers brought offerings of grain. Abū Salamah, cousin to both

[1] I.S. VIII, 24.

bridegroom and bride, was anxious to help, the more so since he owed so much to 'Alī's father, who had given him protection against Abū Jahl and other hostile members of his clan. So Umm Salamah went together with 'Ā'ishah to make ready the house for the bridal couple and to prepare the food. Soft sand was brought from the river bed and they scattered it over the earthern floor of the house. The bridal bed was a sheepskin and there was a faded coverlet of striped cloth from the Yemen. For a pillow they stuffed a leather cushion with palm fibre. Then they laid out dates and figs for the guests to eat in addition to the main meal, and they filled the waterskin with water that they had perfumed. It was generally agreed that this wedding feast was one of the finest held in Medina at this time.

When the Prophet withdrew, as a sign for the guests to leave the bridal pair alone together, he told 'Alī not to approach his wife until he himself returned, which he did shortly after the last guest had departed. Umm Ayman was still there, helping to set the house in order after the celebrations. The Prophet had many special relationships in his life which were not shared by any except himself and the person in question. One of these was with Umm Ayman. When he asked permission to enter, it was she who now came to the entrance. "Where is my brother?" he said. "My father and my mother be thy ransom, O Messenger of God," she said, "who is thy brother?" "Abū Ṭālib's son 'Alī," he said. "How can he be thy brother," she said, "when thou hast even now married thy daughter to him?" "He is what I said," replied the Prophet, and asked her to bring him some water, which she did. Having taken a mouthful and rinsed his mouth, he spat it back into the vessel. Then, when 'Alī came, he bade him sit in front of him; and taking some of the water in his hand he sprinkled it over his shoulders and breast and arms. Then he called Fāṭimah to him and she came, tripping over her robe in the awe and reverence she had for her father. He did the same to her as to 'Alī, and invoked blessings upon them both and upon their offspring.[1]

In the year which followed the return from Badr the family of 'Umar suffered two losses. The first of these was the death of his son-in-law Khunays, the husband of his daughter Ḥafṣah. He had been one of the emigrants to Abyssinia, and it was on his return that the marriage had taken place. Ḥafṣah was only eighteen years old when she became a widow. She was both beautiful and accomplished, having learned like her father to read and write; and seeing that the death of Ruqayyah had left 'Uthmān so disconsolate, 'Umar offered him Ḥafṣah in marriage. 'Uthmān said that he would think about it, but after some days he came to 'Umar and said he thought it was better that he should not marry again for the moment. 'Umar was very disappointed and also somewhat hurt by 'Uthmān's refusal. But he was determined to find a good husband for his daughter so he went to Abū Bakr, whom he counted as his best friend, and proposed the match to him. Abū Bakr answered him evasively, which hurt 'Umar's feelings even more than 'Uthmān's definite refusal, though at the same time it was more understandable, for Abū Bakr already had one wife, to whom he was deeply attached, whereas 'Uthmān was now single.

[1] I.S. VIII, 12–15.

Perhaps he could be made to change his mind, and the next time 'Umar was with the Prophet he gave vent to his grievance. "Behold," said the Prophet, "I will show thee a better son-in-law than 'Uthmān, and I will show him a better father-in-law than thee." "So be it!" said 'Umar with a smile of happiness when, after a moment's reflection, he divined that the better man referred to in both cases was none other than the Prophet, who would himself take Ḥafṣah to wife and who would become, for the second time, the father-in-law of 'Uthmān by giving him in marriage Ruqayyah's sister Umm Kulthūm. It was after this that Abū Bakr explained the reason for his silence to 'Umar, namely that the Prophet had confided to him, as a secret not yet to be divulged, his intention to ask for the hand of Ḥafṣah.

The marriage of Umm Kulthūm and 'Uthmān took place first; and when the legally necessary four months had elapsed since the death of Khunays, and when an apartment had been added to those of Sawdah and 'Ā'ishah adjoining the Mosque, the Prophet's own marriage was celebrated, a little less than a year after the Battle of Badr. The arrival of Ḥafṣah did not mar the harmony of the household. 'Ā'ishah was pleased to have a companion nearer to her own age, and a lasting friendship was soon developed between the two younger wives, while Sawdah, who had been something of a mother to 'Ā'ishah, now extended a share of her maternal benevolence to the newcomer, who was nearly twenty years younger than herself.

It was about the time of this marriage that 'Umar's brother-in-law died, Ḥafṣah's maternal uncle, 'Uthmān ibn Maẓ'ūn. Both he and his wife Khawlah had always been very close to the Prophet, and 'Uthmān was the most ascetic of his Companions. He had been an ascetic before the Revelation of Islam, and since his emigration to Medina he had become so bent on suppressing earthly desires that he asked permission of the Prophet to make himself a eunuch and to spend the rest of his life as a wandering beggar. "Hast thou not in me a fair example?" said the Prophet. "And I go into women, and I eat meat, and I fast, and I break my fast. He is not of my people who maketh men eunuchs or maketh himself a eunuch." But the Prophet had reason to think that 'Uthmān had not fully understood him, so on another occasion he put the same question: "Hast thou not in me an example?" 'Uthmān fervently assented, then asked what was amiss. "Thou fastest every day," said the Prophet, "and keepest vigil every night in prayer." "Yea, that indeed I do," said 'Uthmān, for he had heard him speak again and again of the merits of fasting and of night prayer. "Do not so," said the Prophet, "for verily thine eyes have their rights over thee, and thy body hath its rights, and thy family have their rights. So pray, and sleep, and fast, and break fast."[1]

As an expression of the primordial religion, the Revelation continually stressed the importance of giving thanks to God for all the most elementary blessings of life. *He hath given you hearing and sight and heart-knowledge that ye may be thankful.*[2]

> *And of His signs is His creation for you of consorts from amongst yourselves, that ye may find rest in them, and His ordaining of love between you and mercy. Verily therein are signs for people who reflect.*[3]

[1] I.S. III/1, 289. [2] XVI, 78. [3] XXX, 21.

> *Say: Have ye thought, if God made night everlasting upon you till the Day of the Resurrection, who is a god beside God to bring you light? Will ye not then hear? Say: Have ye thought, if God made day everlasting upon you till the Day of the Resurrection, who is a god beside God to bring you a night wherein to rest? Will ye not then see? And of His mercy hath he made for you night and day, that therein ye may rest and that ye may go seek His favours, and that ye may be thankful.*[1]

For primordial man the natural enjoyments, consecrated by thankfulness to God, are modes of worship; and with reference to himself the Prophet spoke of the pleasures of the senses and of prayer in the same context: "It hath been given me to love perfume and women, and coolness hath been brought to mine eyes in the prayer."[2]

Immediately after the death of 'Uthmān, before his funeral, the Prophet went with 'Ā'ishah to visit Khawlah, and 'Ā'ishah said afterwards: "The Prophet kissed 'Uthmān when he was dead, and I saw his tears flowing over 'Uthmān's cheek." At his funeral the Prophet heard an old woman address the dead man with the words "Be glad, O father of Sā'ib, for Paradise is thine." The Prophet turned to her somewhat sharply and said: "What giveth thee to know that?" "O Messenger of God," she protested, "it is Abu s-Sā'ib!" "By God," he said, "we know naught but good of him." Then, to make it clear that his first remark had been in no sense directed against 'Uthmān but merely against her for saying more than she had right to say he turned to her again and added: "It would have been enough for thee to say: 'He loved God and His messenger.'"[3]

'Umar confessed to having been somewhat shaken in his high regard for his brother-in-law by the fact that he had not been blessed with a martyr's death. He said: "When 'Uthmān ibn Maẓ'ūn died without being slain he fell immeasurably from my esteem and I said: 'Behold this man who was severest of us all in abstaining from the things of this world, and now he hath died and was not slain.'" And so he remained in 'Umar's opinion until the Prophet and Abū Bakr had both died natural deaths, and he upbraided himself for having lacked a true sense of values, and said to himself: "Out upon thee, the best of us die!" – he meant "die naturally" – and 'Uthmān returned in his estimation to the place he had formally held.[4]

1 XXVIII, 71–3.
2 I.S. I/2, 112. See above, p. 141, note.
3 I.S. III/1, 289–90.
4 ibid.

# XLVIII
# *The People of the Bench*

PART of one of the long colonnades in the Mosque was now reserved for those newcomers who had nowhere to live and no means of sustenance. They were known as "the People of the Bench", *Ahl aṣ-Ṣuffah*, on account of a stone bench which had been placed there for their benefit; and since the Mosque was a prolongation of the Prophet's own dwelling, he and his household felt especially responsible for this growing number of impoverished refugees who lived at their very door, whose plight they witnessed daily and who came in ones and twos from all directions, drawn by the message of Islam and the reports of him and his community which had by now reached the tribes all over Arabia. The news of Badr was not without its effect in this way. Consequently it was seldom that those who lived in the dwellings adjoining the Mosque could eat their fill at any meal. The Prophet used to say: "The food of one is enough for two, the food of two enough for four, and the food of four enough for eight."[1]

Just as he loved sweet scents and fragrance in general, so also he was exceedingly sensitive to the slightest unpleasantness of odour, especially in the breath, in himself and in others. 'A'ishah said that the first thing he would do on entering the house was to take up his tooth-stick which was made of green palm wood. When he was on a journey, 'Abd Allāh ibn Mas'ūd could well be trusted to have one always in readiness for him. The Companions followed his example in the use of the tooth-stick, and also in the rinsing of the mouth after every meal.

Hunger made no difference to his extreme sensitivity, which he did not always expect others to share. There were certain kinds of food which the law allowed and which he encouraged his companions to eat but would not eat himself, such as the large lizards which were not to be found in Mecca but which were common in Yathrib and elsewhere. Sometimes he would refuse a dish more out of consideration for others than himself. Once a stew was brought to him as a gift from one of the Helpers but just as he was about to take some of it he noticed that it had a strong smell of garlic and withdrew his hand. Those who were with him immediately did

[1] M. XXXVI, 176.

the same. "What is amiss?" he said to them. "Thou withdrewest thy hand," they said, "so we have withdrawn ours." "Eat in the name of God," he said. "I hold intimate converse with one whom ye converse not with."[1] They knew he was referring to the Angel. On that occasion the dish had been prepared and must not be wasted. He none the less discouraged them in general from eating food that was overflavoured with garlic or onions, especially before going to the Mosque.[2]

Fāṭimah before her marriage had been as it were hostess to the People of the Bench. But despite the sacrifices that were part of the daily life of the Prophet's household, her life after her marriage seemed even more rigorous on account of a lack which she had not yet experienced. There had never been, for her, any shortage of helping hands. In addition to her sister, Umm Kulthūm, Umm Ayman had been there, always ready to do what she could. Umm Sulaym had given her ten-year-old son Anas as servant to the Prophet, and Anas was diligent and thoughtful far beyond his years, while his mother and Abū Ṭalḥah, her second husband, were always in the background, ready to help. Ibn Mas'ūd had attached himself to the Prophet so closely as to be almost one of the household; and recently, after his return to Mecca, 'Abbās had sent his slave Abū Rāfi' to the Prophet as a gift. The Prophet had set him free, but freedom had not diminished his readiness to serve. There was also Khawlah, the widow of 'Uthmān ibn Maẓ'ūn, who had long considered herself as their servant. But now Fāṭimah had no one in the house to help her. To relieve their extreme poverty, 'Alī earned some money as a drawer and carrier of water, and she as a grinder of corn. "I have ground until my hands are blistered," she said to 'Alī one day. "I have drawn water until I have pains in my chest," said 'Alī, "and God hath given thy father some captives, so go thou and ask him to give thee a servant." Not very readily she went to the Prophet, who said: "What hath brought thee here, little daughter?" "I came to give thee greetings of peace," she said, for in her awe of him she could not bring herself to ask what she had intended. "What didst thou do?" said 'Alī, when she returned empty-handed. "I was ashamed to ask him," she said, so the two of them went together, but the Prophet felt that they were less in need than others. "I will not give to you," he said, "and let the People of the Bench be tormented with hunger. I have not enough for their keep; but I will spend on them what may come from the selling of the captives."

They returned home in some disappointment but that night, after they had gone to bed, they heard the voice of the Prophet asking permission to enter. Giving him words of welcome they both rose to their feet, but he told them: "Stay where ye are," and sat down beside them. "Shall I not tell you of something better than that which ye asked of me?" he said, and when they said yes he said: "Words which Gabriel taught me, that ye should say *Glory be to God* ten times after every prayer, and ten times *Praise be to God*, and ten times *God is most great*. And that when ye go to bed ye should say them thirty-three times each." 'Alī used to say in after years: "I have never once failed to say them since the Messenger of God taught them to us."[3]

[1] I.S. I/2, 110. [2] B. XCVI, 24. [3] I.S. VIII, 16.

Their house was not very far from the Mosque, but the Prophet would have liked his daughter to be still nearer to him, and some months after the marriage Ḥārithah of Khazraj, a distant kinsman of the Prophet, came to him and said: "O Messenger of God, I have heard that thou wouldst fain bring Fāṭimah nearer to thee, and this my house is the nearest of all the dwellings of the sons of Najjār, and it is thine. I and my goods are all for God and for His Messenger, and I hold dearer what thou takest from me than what thou leavest with me." The Prophet blessed him and accepted his gift, and brought his daughter and son-in-law to live as his neighbours.

He greatly rejoiced in the generosity of Ḥārithah, and in the many other acts of generosity in Medina, both towards himself and towards others. One of these, however, which took place at this time, was fraught with some disappointment. The Prophet had a high opinion of Abū Lubābah of Aws, and on the way to Badr he had sent him back from Rawḥā' to take charge of Medina in his absence. Later that year an orphan under the guardianship of Abū Lubābah came to the Prophet and claimed the ownership of a certain lavishly fruiting palm-tree, which he said that his guardian had wrongly appropriated. They sent for Abū Lubābah who said that the palm belonged to him, as in fact it did. The Prophet heard the case and gave judgement in favour of the guardian and against the orphan, who was sadly grieved for the loss of the tree that he had always considered to be his. Seeing this, the Prophet asked for the palm as a gift to himself, intending to present it to the orphan, but Abū Lubābah refused. "O Abū Lubābah," he said, "give it then thou the orphan, and its like shall be thine in Paradise." But Abū Lubābah's sense of legal justice had been too much roused by the whole affair for him to agree, and again he refused, whereupon another of the Helpers, Thābit ibn ad-Daḥdāḥah, said to the Prophet: "O Messenger of God, if I should buy this palm and give it to this orphan, would mine be its like in Paradise?" "It would indeed," came the answer, so he went to Abū Lubābah and offered him an orchard of palms for the single tree. The offer was accepted, and Ibn ad-Daḥdāḥah gave the palm to the orphan.[1] The Prophet was exceedingly glad for his sake, but saddened on account of Abū Lubābah.

[1] W. 505.

# XLIX
# *Desultory Warfare*

AN important secondary result of Badr and of the expeditions which preceded it was that Juhaynah and the other neighbouring Red Sea tribes were now firmly allied with Medina. This meant that the coastal road to Syria was virtually barred to the Meccan caravans; and it raised the question: Would it not be possible to reduce the power of Quraysh still further by barring them from all access to the north, on the east as well as on the west? This latent danger had by no means escaped the notice of Quraysh themselves, and they had already taken some steps to strengthen their alliances with Sulaym and Ghaṭafān through whose territory the caravans had to pass if they took the north-easterly route to the head of the Persian Gulf and thence to Iraq. These tribes lived in the great plain of Najd to the east of Mecca and Medina. Caravans from Mecca would make their seventh halt in the middle of the fertile tract which was occupied by Sulaym; and this tribe in particular was now urged by Quraysh to let slip no opportunity of harrying the borders of Yathrib wherever they seemed to be most vulnerable.

During the next months the Prophet had warning of three projected raids on the eastern fringes of the oasis, two by Sulaym and one by Ghaṭafān. In every case he forestalled them by marching out at once into their territory, and in every case they had news of his approach and vanished before he reached their point of gathering. But one of these expeditions was none the less remarkably successful. It was against the Ghaṭafānī tribes of Tha'labah and Muḥārib, and this time the Prophet decided to follow the elusive Bedouin into their half hidden fastnesses in the hills to the north of Najd, with the help of a man of Tha'labah who entered Islam and offered his services as a guide. From the plain they ascended into the Muḥārib territory, and a sudden fall of rain drenched some of the men, including the Prophet, before they could take shelter. The Prophet withdrew a little from the others, removed his two wet garments and hung them on a tree to dry, while he himself lay down under the tree and was soon overcome by sleep. But all their movements and his in particular had been watched by many unseen eyes; and he woke to find a man standing over him with a drawn sword. It was none other than Du'thur, the chief of Muḥārib, who had himself been largely responsible for planning the projected raid of which the Prophet had had warning. "O Muḥammad," he said, "who will protect thee from me this day?" "God," said the Prophet, whereupon Gabriel, clothed all in white, appeared between them and, placing his hand on the man's chest, he thrust him backwards. The sword fell from his grasp, and the Prophet seized it. Gabriel vanished from Du'thur's sight and he realised that he had seen an Angel. "Who will protect thee from me?" said the Prophet. "Nobody," said Du'thur. "I testify that there is no god but God, and that Muḥammad is the messenger of God." The Prophet handed him back his sword, which touched the man deeply. They went together to the camp, and Du'thur was instructed in the religion. Then he returned to his people, and began to summon them to Islam.

By the time that the army had returned from Najd, Ka'b ibn al-Ashraf had left Mecca, and had returned to his fortress among the Bani Naḍīr, not far from the outskirts of Medina. In addition to his poems urging Quraysh to take revenge for Badr, he wrote others satirising the Prophet and his Companions; and among the Arabs a gifted poet was like a multitude of men, for his verses were repeated from mouth to mouth. If good, he was a power for good; if evil, a power for evil, to be suppressed at all costs. The Prophet prayed: "O Lord, deliver me from the son of al-Ashraf howsoever Thou wilt, for the evil he declareth and the poems he declaimeth." Then he said to those who were present: "Who is for me against the son of al-Ashraf, for he hath done me great injury?" The first to volunteer was a man of Aws, Muḥammad ibn Maslamah, of the clan of Sa'd ibn Mu'ādh. The Prophet told him to consult Sa'd, and four more volunteers were found. But they realised that nothing could be achieved without deception and lies, and they knew that lying was abhorrent to the Prophet; so they went to him and told him what was in their minds. He said that they were free to say whatever would serve their purpose, for deception was legitimate in warfare, being a part of its strategy, and Ka'b had declared war on them.[1]

Ka'b was lured out of his fortress under false pretences, and then killed. In indignation and in panic the Jews of Naḍīr went to the Prophet and complained that one of their chief men had been treacherously done to death, without any cause. The Prophet knew well that most of them were as hostile to Islam as Ka'b had been, and with great disappointment he had come to accept this. But it was vital to show them that if hostile thoughts were tolerable, hostile action was not. "If he had remained as others of like opinion remain," he said, "he would not have been killed by guile. But he did us injury and wrote poetry against us; and none of you shall do this but he shall be put to the sword."[2] He then invited them to make a special treaty with him in addition to the covenant, and this they did.

[1] I.I. 551; see also 369. [2] W. 192.

L

# *Preparations for Battle*

THE Meccans felt keenly the loss of their Red Sea caravan route. One of the disadvantages of the only alternative was that in the plain of Najd the wells were relatively far apart. But now that the summer months were drawing to a close the journey could easily be managed by adding to the number of water-carrying camels; and they decided to send a rich caravan to Iraq consisting mainly of bars of silver and silver vessels worth about a hundred thousand dirhems. It was to be under the leadership of Ṣafwān. Some of the Jews of Medina had secret information about the caravan and one of the Helpers happened to hear them discussing it. The Prophet knew that Zayd had gifts of leadership, and he now sent him at the head of a hundred horse to waylay the caravan near Qaradah, which was one of the chief watering places along the route. The relatively small and therefore more manageable force made it possible for Zayd to realise all the essentials of an effective ambush. Their sudden ferocious and unexpected onslaught put to flight Ṣafwān and his fellows, while Zayd and his men returned to Medina in triumph, having become themselves the escort of all the Meccan transport camels with their rich loads of silver and other merchandise, and a few captives.

In Mecca the disaster of Qaradah intensified and quickened the preparations which had been in progress ever since Badr for an irresistible attack on Medina. The sacred month of Rajab passed and with it midwinter and the New Year of AD 625. It was in the following month that Hafṣah's marriage took place. Then came Ramaḍān, and in this month of fasting, to the great joy of all the believers, Fāṭimah gave birth to a son. The Prophet spoke the words of the call to prayer into the ear of the new-born babe and named him al-Ḥasan, which means "the beautiful". The moon reached its full, after which, a day or two later, came the anniversary of Badr; and in the last days of the month a sealed letter was brought to the Prophet by a horseman who had ridden from Mecca to Medina in three days. It was from his uncle 'Abbās, warning him that an army of three thousand men was on the point of marching out against Medina. Seven hundred of the men were mailed, and there was a troop of horse two hundred strong. The camels were as many as the men, not counting the transport camels and those which carried howdahs for the women.

By the time the letter arrived Quraysh had already set out. Abū Sufyān, the commander-in-chief, took with him Hind and also a second wife. Ṣafwān likewise brought two wives, other chiefs one only. Jubayr the son of Muṭʻim remained in Mecca; but he sent out with the army an Abyssinian slave of his named Waḥshī who was, like many of his countrymen, an expert at throwing the javelin. Waḥshī had seldom been known to miss his mark; and Jubayr said to him: "If thou slayest Ḥamzah, Muḥammad's uncle, in revenge for mine, thou art a free man." Hind came to know of this, and during their halts, whenever she passed Waḥshī in the camp or saw him passing by, she would say to him: "Go to it, thou father of darkness, slake and then gloat!" She had already made it clear to him that she also, as well as his master, had a thirst to be slaked and a reward for the slaker.

The Emigrants and Helpers still had a week before the enemy could be upon them; but within that time room had to be made inside the walls of Medina for all those who lived in the outlying parts of the oasis, together with their animals. This was done and not one horse, camel, cow, sheep or goat was left outside the walls. It remained to be seen what the Meccan plan of action was. News came that they were taking the western route near the coast. In due course they turned inland, and made a brief halt about five miles west of Medina. Then they marched north-east for a few miles and camped on a strip of cultivated land in the plain below Mount Uḥud, which overlooks Medina from the north.

The Prophet sent out scouts, who returned the next morning with the information that the numbers of the enemy were indeed as the letter had stated. Quraysh had with them a hundred men of Thaqīf and also contingents from Kinānah and other allies. The three thousand and more camels and the two hundred horses were eating all the pasture and all the as yet unharvested crops to the north of the city, and soon not a blade of greenery would be left. The army showed no signs of being ready for any immediate action. None the less, the city was closely guarded that night, and the two Saʻds of Aws and Khazraj, that is Ibn Muʻādh and Ibn ʻUbādah, insisted on keeping watch outside the Prophet's door, and with them was Usayd and a strong bodyguard.

The Prophet himself was as yet unarmed. But he dreamed that he was wearing an impregnable coat of mail and that he was mounted on the back of a ram. His sword was in his hand and he noticed a dent in it; and he saw some kine which he knew to be his, and they were sacrificed before his eyes.

The next morning he told his Companions what he had seen, and he interpreted it, saying: "The impregnable coat of mail is Medina, and the dent in my sword is a blow that will be struck against myself; the sacrificed kine are some of my Companions who will be slain; and as to the ram which I rode upon, that is the leader of their squadron whom we shall slay if God will".[1]

His first thought was not to go out from the city, but to stand a siege within its walls. He none the less wished to have his opinion confirmed by others, for it was by no means a conviction, so he held a consultation as to

[1] W. 209.

whether they should march out or not. Ibn Ubayy was the first to speak: "Our city," he said, "is a virgin that hath never been violated against us. Never without severe losses have we gone out from her to attack an enemy; and none have entered her against us but it is they who have suffered the losses. Therefore let them be, O Messenger of God. Wretched will be their plight, so long as they stay; and when they return they will return dejected and frustrated in purpose, with no good gained."

A large number of the older Companions, of both the Emigrants and Helpers, inclined to the opinion of Ibn Ubayy. So the Prophet said: "Stay in Medina, and put the women and children in the fortresses." Only when he had spoken thus did it become apparent that most of the younger men were burning with eagerness to march out against the enemy. "O Messenger of God," said one of them, "lead us forth against the enemy. Let them not think we fear them or that we are too weak for them." These words were met with a murmur of approval from different parts of the assembly, and others said much the same, with the added argument that their inactivity and their failure to take reprisal for their devastated crops would only serve to embolden Quraysh against them in the future, not to speak of the tribes of Najd. Ḥamzah and Sa'd ibn 'Ubādah and others of the more experienced now began to incline towards this view. "At Badr," said one of them, "thou hadst but three hundred men, and God gave thee mastery over them. And now we are many and have been hoping for this occasion and praying God for it, and He hath sent it to our very door."[1] Then one of the oldest men present rose to speak, a man of Aws named Khaythamah. He repeated many of the arguments already given against remaining on the defensive. Then he spoke on a more personal note. His son Sa'd was one of the few Muslims who had been slain at Badr. "Last night in my sleep," he said, "I saw my son. Most beautiful was his appearance, and I witnessed how it was given to him to fulfil his every wish amid the fruits and the rivers of the Garden. And he said: 'Come unto us and be our companion in Paradise. All that my Lord promised me have I found to be true.' And I am old and I long to meet my Lord, so pray O messenger of God, that He will grant me martyrdom and the company of Sa'd in Paradise."[2] The Prophet made a prayer for Khaythamah, no doubt a silent one, for the words are not recorded. Then another of the Helpers rose to speak, this time a man of Khazraj, Mālik ibn Sinān. "O Messenger of God," he said, "we have before us one of two good things: either God will grant us the mastery over them, and that is what we would have; or else God will grant us martyrdom. I care not which it may be, for verily there is good in both."[3]

It was now clear, not only from the words that were spoken but from the general approval with which they were received, that the majority were against remaining behind the city walls, and the Prophet decided to attack. At noon they assembled for the Friday prayer, and the theme of his sermon was the Holy War and all that it demands of earnestness and effort; and he said that victory would be theirs if they remained steadfast. Then he bade them make ready to meet the enemy.

After the prayer two men waited behind to speak to the Prophet, each

[1] W. 210–11. [2] W. 212–13. [3] ibid.

having an urgent decision to make. One of them was Ḥanẓalah, the son of the self-styled Abrahamist Abū 'Āmir, who was even now, unknown to his son, in the enemy camp below Uḥud. It was Ḥanẓalah's wedding day – a day which had been chosen some weeks in advance. He was betrothed to his cousin Jamīlah, the daughter of Ibn Ubayy, and he was loth to postpone the marriage, yet determined to fight. The Prophet told him to celebrate his marriage and spend the night in Medina. There could be no fighting before sunrise, and Ḥanẓalah would have ample time to join him on the battlefield early the next morning. He could find out by inquiry which way the army had passed.

The other man was 'Abd Allāh ibn 'Amr of the Bani Salimah, one of the clans of Khazraj. It was he who nearly three years previously had gone out on the Pilgrimage as a pagan, and had entered Islam in the valley of Mina, where he had forthwith pledged allegiance to the Prophet at the Second 'Aqabah. And now, two or three nights previously, 'Abd Allāh had had a dream not unlike that which Khaythamah had recounted in the assembly. A man had come to him in his sleep and he recognised him as a Helper named Mubashshir, who said to him: "A few days, and thou shalt come unto us." "And where art thou?" said 'Abd Allāh. "In Paradise," said Mubashshir. "We do there all that it pleaseth us to do." "Wast thou not slain at Badr?" said 'Abd Allāh. "Even so," said Mubashshir, "but then was I brought to life." "Father of Jābir," said the Prophet to 'Abd Allāh when he told him the dream, "that is martyrdom."[1] 'Abd Allāh knew this in his heart, but he wished none the less to have it confirmed by the Prophet. Then he went home to make ready for war and to bid farewell to his children. His wife had died recently, leaving him with one son, Jābir, now just grown to manhood, and seven daughters much younger than their brother. Jābir had already returned from the Mosque, and was busy about his weapons and his armour. Not having been present at Badr, he was all the more eager to go out with the Prophet on this occasion. But his father had other thoughts. "My son," he said, "it is not meet that we should leave them" – he meant his daughters – "without a man. They are young and helpless, and I fear for them. But I shall go out with the Messenger of God, perchance to be martyred if God grant it me, so I leave them to thy care."

They all assembled again for the afternoon prayer, and by that time the men from Upper Medina had mustered and were present in the Mosque. After the prayer the Prophet took Abū Bakr and 'Umar with him into his house and they helped him to dress for battle. The men lined up outside; and Sa'd ibn Mu'ādh and his clansmen reproved them saying: "Ye have compelled the Messenger of God to go out against his will, albeit the command cometh down to him from Heaven. Put back the decision into his hands and let him decide afresh." When the Prophet came out, he had wound his turban about his helmet and donned his breastplate, under which he wore a coat of mail belted with a leather sword-belt. He had even girt on his sword and slung his shield across his back. Many of the men by that time had regretted the course they had taken, and as soon as he

[1] W. 266.

appeared they said: "O Messenger of God, it is not for us to oppose thee in aught, so do what seemeth best to thee." But he answered them saying: "It is not for a Prophet, when he hath put on his armour, to take it off until God hath judged between him and his enemies. So look to what I bade you do, and do it, and go forward in the Name of God. The victory is yours, if ye be steadfast."[1] Then he called for three lances and fastened upon them three banners. The banner of Aws he gave to Usayd, that of Khazraj to Ḥubāb, who had advised him about the wells at Badr, and that of the Emigrants to Muṣ'ab. Again he appointed the blind 'Abd Allāh ibn Umm Maktūm to lead the prayers in his absence. Then he mounted his horse Sakb,[2] and asked for his bow, which he hung over his shoulder, taking in his hand a spear. No other man was mounted. The two Sa'ds marched in front of him, and there were men on either side. In all they were about a thousand strong.

1 W. 214.
2 Running Water, so called because he could amble.

# LI

# *The Marḥch to Uḥud*

THE sun was already setting when they reached Shaykhayn, half-way between Medina and Uḥud. Bilāl made the call to prayer and they prayed, after which the Prophet reviewed his troops. It was then that he noticed the presence of eight boys who, despite their age, were hoping to take part in the battle. Amongst them were Zayd's son Usāmah and 'Umar's son 'Abd Allāh, both only thirteen years old. The Prophet ordered them and their six friends to return home immediately. They protested, and one of the Helpers assured the Prophet that the fifteen-year-old Rāfi', of the Awsite clan of Ḥārithah, was already a better archer than some of his elders. So Rāfi' was allowed to stay, whereupon Samurah, an orphan from one of the Najd tribes, whose mother had married a Helper of Rāfi''s clan, claimed that he could throw Rāfi' in wrestling. The Prophet told the two boys to show him what they could do, so they set about each other then and there; and Samurah proved his claim to be true, so he also was allowed to stay, while the others were sent back to their families.

The Meccans were hoping that the Muslims would come out against them and so enable them to use their greater strength, and in particular their cavalry, to the best possible advantage. The Prophet was aware of this and, having none the less decided to leave the city, he was determined to compensate for the disparity of numbers by taking up a position which would give his army an advantage and which would at the same time be unexpected and therefore disconcerting to the enemy. But for his purpose he would need a guide, so he made some inquiries, and since they would have to pass through the territory of the Bani Ḥārithah he accepted the offered services of a member of that clan who knew the lie of the land to perfection.

In Medina that night Ḥanẓalah and Jamīlah had consummated their marriage; and in her sleep, during the small hours, Jamīlah had a dream in which she saw her husband standing at the outside of Heaven; and a door opened for him and he entered through it, whereupon it closed behind him. When she woke, she said to herself: "This is martyrdom." They performed their ablutions and prayed the dawn prayer together, after which he bade her farewell. But she clung to him, and would not let him go, and again he lay with her. Then he tore himself from her embrace, and not even staying to repeat his ablution, he put on his coat of mail, seized his weapons, and hastened from the house.[1]

[1] W. 273.

The Prophet had given instructions that the army should be ready to move off from Shaykhayn shortly before dawn. But Ibn Ubayy had been in consultation with some of his nearest followers during the night, and when it was time to raise camp he turned back to Medina with three hundred of the hypocrites and doubters, to the great shame of his son ʻAbd Allāh, who remained with the army. Ibn Ubayy did not even speak to the Prophet, and when questioned by some of the Helpers he said: "He hath disobeyed me, and obeyed the striplings and men of no judgement. I see not why we should lose our lives in this ill chosen spot." Another Abd Allāh, the father of Jābir, went after them and called out: "I adjure you by God not to desert your people and your Prophet in the very presence of the enemy." But they only answered: "If we knew that ye would be fighting, we would not leave you. But we do not think there will be a battle." "Enemies of God", he retorted, "God will avail His Prophet beyond any need of you."

Reduced now to seven hundred, the army advanced for a short distance towards the enemy and then, still under cover of the darkness, they moved to their right and made their way across a volcanic tract until they came to the south-easterly end of the gorge of Uḥud. Turning again they advanced north-west up the gorge until in the half-light of dawn they saw the Meccan camp ahead of them, a little to their left and a little below them. They marched on until they were directly between the enemy and Uḥud. Having now reached his objective, which was to have the slope of the ground in his favour, the Prophet halted them and dismounted. Bilāl made the call to the morning prayer, and they moved into lines with their backs to the mountain. This was also their formation for battle, since the enemy were now between them and Mecca. Having led the prayer, the Prophet turned and exhorted them, saying: "Verily this day ye are at a station that is rich in reward and rich in treasure, for him who is mindful of what he is about and who devoteth his soul thereunto in patience and certainty and earnestness and effort."[1] When he had finished, Ḥanẓalah went forward to greet him, for he had just arrived from Medina.

The Prophet now chose out his best archers: of these he attached to himself Zayd, Saʻd his cousin of Zuhrah, and Sā'ib the son of ʻUthmān ibn Maẓʻūn amongst others; but he told fifty of them to take up their position on a rise a little to the left of his main force. He put over them ʻAbd Allāh ibn Jubayr, a man of Aws, and gave them their orders, saying: "Keep their cavalry from us with your arrows. Let them not come upon us from our rear. Be the tide of battle for us or against us, stay at this post! If ye see us plundering the enemy, seek not to have a share in it; and if ye see us being slain, come not to our aid."[2]

Having put on another coat of mail he took up a sword and brandished it, saying: "Who will take this sword, together with its right?" Immediately ʻUmar went to take it, but the Prophet turned away from him, saying again: "Who will take this sword, together with its right?" Zubayr said he would take it, but again the Prophet turned away, repeating his question a third time. "What is its right," O Messenger of God?" said Abū Dujanah, a man of Khazraj. "Its right," said the Prophet, "is that thou shouldst strike

[1] W. 221. [2] I.I. 560.

the foe with it until its blade be bent." "I will take it, together with its right," he said, and the Prophet gave it to him. He was a valiant man, who gloried in battle. His red turban was well known, and among the Khazraj it was called the turban of death. When he put it on, as now he did, winding it round his helmet, they knew that he meant to inflict great slaughter on the enemy; and none could doubt that this was his firm intention as sword in hand he strutted up and down between the lines. Seeing him, the Prophet said: "That is a gait which God detesteth, save at such a time and place as this."[1]

[1] I.I. 561.

# LII

# *The Battle of Uḥud*

THE sun was now up and Quraysh were already in line, with a hundred horse on either wing, commanded on the right by Khālid, son of Walīd, and on the left by ʻIkrimah, son of Abū Jahl. From the centre Abū Sufyān gave the order to advance. In front of him Ṭalḥah of ʻAbd ad-Dār carried the banner of Quraysh, and two of Ṭalḥah's brothers and four of his sons were in close attendance, each ready to take his turn if need be. Ṭalḥah and his brothers were determined to win glory for their clan that day. At Badr their two standard-bearers had ingloriously let themselves be taken prisoner, and Abū Sufyān had not failed to remind them of this on the way to Uḥud. Muṣʻab recognised his fellow clansmen from where he stood in front of the Prophet with the banner of the Emigrants.

As soon as the two hosts were within earshot of each other, Abū Sufyān halted his advance and stepped a little ahead of the standard. "Men of Aws and Khazraj," he said, "quit ye now the field, and leave to me my cousin. Then we will be gone from you, for we have no call to fight you." But the Helpers answered him with a roll of thunderous abuse. Then another man stepped forward from the Meccan ranks, and Ḥanẓalah was grieved to recognise his father, who now proclaimed his presence: "Men of Aws, I am Abū ʻĀmir!" He could not believe that his influence, once so considerable, had gone to nothing, and he had promised Quraysh that as soon as he made himself known many of the men of his clan would rally to his side. Instead, he received not only curses but a volley of stones which drove him back in dismay.

Again the order was given for the Meccans to advance, and not far from the front lines the women, led by Hind, also moved forward, beating their timbrels and their drums and chanting:

> On, ye sons of ʻAbd ad-Dār;
> Onwards, ye that guard the rear;
> Smite, with every sharp sword smite.

Then when the women felt they had reached their limit of nearness to the enemy they marked time to the beat of their drums, letting the men advance beyond them, and Hind started up a song which had been sung by another Hind in one of the wars of old:

Advance and we embrace you,
And soft carpets spread.
But turn your backs, we leave you,
Leave you and not love you.

When the two armies were almost joined the Prophet's archers shot a volley of arrows into Khālid's cavalry, and the neighing of horses drowned the women's voices and their drums. From the Meccan centre Ṭalḥah strode forward and shouted for a man to meet him in single combat. 'Alī went out to meet him, and finally felled him to the ground with a blow that cut through his helmet and split his skull. The Prophet knew at once that this was "the leader of the squadron" – the ram that had been subjected to him in his dream – and in a loud voice he magnified God, *Allāhu akbar*, and his magnification was echoed throughout the host. But the ram had signified not only one victim, for Ṭalḥah's brother now took his banner and he was cut down by Ḥamzah. Then Sa'd of Zuhrah put an arrow through the neck of Ṭalḥah's second brother, and his four sons were killed one after the other by 'Alī and Zubayr and 'Āṣim ibn Thābit of Aws. Two of them were carried dying to their mother Sulāfah, who was now in the rear; and when they told her who had dealt them their mortal wounds she vowed that one day she would drink wine out of 'Āṣim's skull.

No woman had been allowed to set out with the Muslims on the previous day. But Nusaybah, a woman of Khazraj, felt that her place was none the less with the army. Her husband Ghaziyyah and two of her sons were there, but that was not the reason. Other women had husbands and sons in the army and were content to stay at home. But Nusaybah had been one of the two women who had gone out with the seventy men of Medina to the Second 'Aqabah, nor could she find it in her nature to stay behind on this occasion. So she had risen early that morning, and having filled a skin with water she set off for the battlefield where she would at least be able to tend the wounded and give drink to the thirsty. She took with her none the less a sword and also a bow and a quiver of arrows. Following by inquiry the way that the army had taken, she reached without difficulty, not long after the battle had begun, the place at the foot of the mountain where the Prophet had now taken up his position on a piece of relatively high ground, with Abū Bakr, 'Umar and others of his closest Companions. The mother of Anas, Umm Sulaym, had had the same idea and arrived with her skin of water not long after Nusaybah. The group behind the lines was also joined by two men of Muzaynah, one of the Bedouin tribes to the west of the oasis. They were both recent converts to Islam, and not knowing of the Meccan attack they had gone to Medina that dawn to find the city more than half empty. On hearing why, they immediately set out for Uḥud, and having greeted the Prophet they drew their swords and went forward into the fray.

Abū Dujānah was being true to the promise of his red turban. Zubayr admitted afterwards: "I was hurt within my soul when I asked the Messenger of God for the sword and he kept it from me and gave it to Abū Dujānah and I said to myself: I am the son of Safiyyah, his father's sister, and I am of Quraysh; and I went to him and asked him for it before the other man, yet he gave it to him and set me aside. By God, I will go see what Abū Dujānah is about! And so I followed him." He then told how Abū Dujānah killed every man he encountered as easily as if he had been a reaper and his sword a scythe, and how he himself was reconciled to the Prophet's decision and told himself: "God and His Messenger know best."

Hind, a large woman of imposing appearance, was still in the midst of the men, urging them on to fight, and she narrowly escaped being cut down by Abū Dujānah, who thought she was a man. His sword was raised above her head when she shrieked, and, realising that she was a woman, he turned against the men at her side. She now joined the other wives and mothers in the rear, where the slaves had been put to guard the camp; and, as she retreated, Waḥshī, the Abyssinian, was making his way forward. Unlike the rest of those on the field, he was concerned with one man only, and unlike them his blood was cold. Ḥamzah was unmistakable for his unusually powerful stature, for his manner of fighting and for his ostrich plume. Waḥshī saw him from a distance and while keeping to the edge of the fray he was able to reach a point of relative safety that was none the less close enough for a javelineer to strike. Ḥamzah was now face to face with the last of the standard-bearers of 'Abd ad-Dār, and as he lifted his sword to strike he momentarily laid open a chink in his armour. Wahshī was quick to see his chance, and poising his javelin he launched it with perfect aim. Ḥamzah staggered a few paces forward, having already killed his man, and fell to the ground in the throes of death. Waḥshī waited until his body stopped moving, and then went and drew out his javelin and returned with all speed to the camp. As he himself said: "I had done all I had come to do, and I only killed him for the sake of my freedom."

The death of Ḥamzah made little difference to the sense of defeat which was beginning to spread through the Meccan army. Another Abyssinian, a slave of the family of the seven dead standard-bearers, now took up the standard himself, but he was soon killed and for a while it lay unheeded on the ground; and although Ḥamzah's ostrich feather was no longer to be seen, Abū Dujānah, Zubayr and others of the Emigrants and Helpers fought like incarnations of the Muslim battle-cry that day, *Amit*, *Amit*, which means "Kill, Kill". It seemed that none could resist them: 'Alī's white plume, Abū Dujānah's red turban, the bright yellow turban of Zubayr and the green turban of Ḥubāb were like flags of victory which gave strength to the ranks behind them. Abū Sufyān narrowly escaped the sword of Ḥanzalah, who was fighting valiantly near the centre and who was about to cut him down, when a man of Layth came in from the side and thrust Ḥanzalah through with his spear, felling him to the ground and killing him outright with a second thrust.

The battle had gradually moved down the slope away from the Prophet as the Meccans were driven back towards their camp. He could no longer discern in any detail what was happening, though he could see that so far his men were winning the day. But now his attention was drawn upwards from the battle and his eyes were raised as one who watches the flight of birds. After a moment he said to those beside him: "Your companion" – he meant Ḥanẓalah – "the Angels are washing him."[1] And afterwards he

[1] I.I. 568.

said to Jamīlah, as if seeking an explanation: "I saw the Angels washing Ḥanẓalah between heaven and earth with water from the clouds in vessels of silver."[1] Then she told him of her dream, and how through fear of being late for the battle, he had not made the ablution he would normally have made.

The Muslims continued to advance until at one point the enemy lines were broken altogether. The way to their camp was thus laid open, and there was a surge forward of would-be plunderers. Now the fifty chosen archers were at some distance to the left of the Prophet. Between him and them the ground sloped down to the plain and then rose up to the point of vantage at which he had placed them. They could see the first lines, and the sight of their fellows about to enrich themselves, as they thought, with enemy spoils, was too much for most of them. In vain their commander, 'Abd Allah ibn Jubayr, reminded them of the Prophet's order not to leave their post on any account. They replied that the Prophet had not meant them to stay there for ever. The battle was now finished, they said, and the disbelievers routed. About forty of them sped down the slope in the direction of the camp, leaving 'Abd Allāh at the head of a staunch but fatally depleted nucleus of bowmen.

So far the Meccan cavalry had been of no avail. In the centre the two armies were so interwoven that a charge of horse would have endangered their own men as well as their enemies; and they could not reach the rear of the Muslim army without first exposing themselves to the shafts of the archers over a long stretch of ground. But Khālid saw what now had happened, and realising that his moment had come, he led his men at full gallop for the post where the archers were stationed. 'Abd Allāh and his men vainly tried to head them off with their arrows; then they threw down their bows and fought to the death with sword and spear. Not one of the faithful ten was left alive; and wheeling round, Khālid led his men into the rear of their enemy's main force. 'Ikrimah followed his example, and the Meccan horsemen made much havoc in the unguarded ranks of the believers. 'Alī and his companions now turned to face the new danger, and some of the idolaters who had been put to flight rallied and came back into the fray. The tide of battle had suddenly changed, and the Quraysh war-cry "O 'Uzzah! O Hubal!" was taken up again all over the field. Many of the Muslims in the rear who had escaped being cut down by the horsemen now lost heart and fled towards the mountain, where they knew they could find refuge. The Prophet called to them to return, but their ears were closed to his voice, nor were their minds open to any thought but flight.[2] The majority of the Muslims fought on, but the initial impetus was now lost, and the weight of numbers told against them. They were driven back step by step, and the whole battle moved towards Uḥud in the direction of the Prophet.

He and his Companions, including the two women, shot volley after volley of arrows into the enemy, and their group was increased by others from the main force whose chief thought, when the day turned against them, had been the safety of the Prophet. Among the first to join them were the two men of Muzaynah, Wahb and Ḥārith. A small body of enemy

[1] W. 274. [2] KIII, 153.

horse now approached from the left. "Who is for this detachment?" said the Prophet. "I am, O Messenger of God," was the instant reply of Wahb, and he shot at them with such speed and dexterity that his arrows came upon them as from a group of archers and they withdrew. "Who is for this squadron?" said the Prophet as another body of horse made for them. "I am, O Messenger of God," said Wahb, and again he fought as if he were not one man but many, and again they withdrew. Then yet a third troop emerged from the lines. "Who will stand up to these?" said the Prophet. "I will," said Wahb. "Arise then," said the Prophet, "and rejoice, for Paradise is thine." And Wahb rose joyfully saying, as he drew his sword: "By God, I give no quarter and I seek no quarter." Then he plunged into their midst and fought his way through them and out at the other side while the Prophet and his Companions stopped their shooting to gaze at his prowess and his valour. "O God, have Mercy upon him!" said the Prophet, as Wahb returned into the midst of the troop, fighting on until they hemmed him in on all sides and killed him. He was found afterwards with twenty lance thrusts, any one of which would have sufficed, apart from what the swords had done to him. No one who saw his fighting ever forgot it. 'Umar would say in after years: "Of all deaths the one I would most fain have died was the Muzaynite's death."[1] And Sa'd of Zuhrah claimed ten years later that he still carried in his ears the sound of the Prophet's voice giving Wahb the good tidings of Paradise.

The main body of the fray had come gradually nearer as the Muslims were slowly driven backwards up the slope. Amid the battle-cries of both sides the individual shouts of the fighters could also be heard – challenges to single combat or the staking of claims in arrows shot or blows struck. "Take that: and I am the son of so-and-so." Abu Dujānah styled himself as the son of Kharashah, who was his grandfather. Not seldom the identity of the claimant was left uncertain. One of the Anṣār, that is the Helpers, was heard to shout: "Take that: and I am the Ansārī lad." The Prophet himself said that day, on at least one occasion: "I am Ibn al-'Awātik,"[2] which means "I am the son of the 'Atikahs," referring to his many ancestresses[3] of that name. But now there came a challenge of unmistakable identity as a single horseman emerged from the lines and said: 'Who will come forth against me? I am the son of 'Atīq." It was 'Abd al-Ka'bah, the eldest son of Abū Bakr, 'Ā'ishah's only full brother, the one member of their family who had not entered Islam. Abū Bakr threw down his bow and drawing his sword would have gone to the attack but the Prophet was too quick for him. "Sheathe thy sword," he said, "and go back to thy place, and give us the good of thy company."[4]

Another body of horse broke through the rear of the Muslims, and advanced in front of 'Abd al-Ka'bah, who now withdrew. "Which of you will sell himself for us?"[5] said the Prophet, and five of the Helpers drew their swords, threw themselves on the enemy, and fought till they were

1 W. 275. 2 W. 280.

3 I.S. I/1, 32–4, gives more than ten, including the mother of Hāshim and the mother of Lu'ayy. The name 'Ātikah is similar in meaning to Ṭāhirah, "the Pure".

4 W. 257. 5 I.I. 572.

killed, except for one, who was mortally wounded. But help was at hand to replace them, for ʿAlī, Zubayr, Ṭalḥah and Abū Dujānah and others who had been in the forefront of the battle had fought their way back through the host. They now reached the Prophet's side, but not before a sharp stone from the enemy had struck him in the mouth, gashing his lower lip and breaking one of his teeth. The blood flowed from his face, but doing what he could to staunch it, he reassured ʿAlī and the others that he was not seriously injured, and they returned to the fight, except for Ṭalḥah, who was too weak from loss of blood and who now fainted. "Look to thy cousin," said the Prophet to Abū Bakr, but Ṭalḥah almost immediately recovered consciousness, while Saʿd of Zuhrah and Ḥārith ibn Simmah of Khazraj went out instead of him, and together with the new reinforcements they made so great an onslaught against the enemy that for the moment their lines receded away from the bodies of the five Helpers who had even now sold their lives. The Prophet looked at them and invoked blessings upon them, and the one who was not yet dead began with an effort to work his way along the ground towards him. He sent two men to carry him, and as a pillow for the dying man's head he put out his foot, which he kept motionless until the man died with his cheek resting upon it.

"Know that Paradise is beneath the shadow of the swords,"[1] the Prophet said; and in after-years he would look back to this particular time and place as being so wondrously blessed that on one occasion he exclaimed: "Would I had been left abandoned with my Companions of the mountain's foot!"[2]

The enemy gradually began to gain the ground they had lost. In the little group round the Prophet the supply of arrows would soon be finished, and in any case it seemed that the time for archery was running out. If the enemy continued to advance every sword would soon have to be unsheathed for a final hand-to-hand conflict with an average of four pagans against every believer. Then suddenly a single horseman came in from the side and made straight for where the Prophet was standing. "Where is Muḥammad?" he shouted. "May I not survive if he survive!" It was Ibn Qami'ah, a man of one of the outskirt clans of Quraysh, who had already made much slaughter among the Muslims. With a quick glance at the group his sharp eye recognised his intended victim and urging on his horse, he brought down his sword in a blow which he was sure no helmet could resist. But Ṭalḥah, who was standing next to the Prophet, threw himself in the direction of the sword and was somehow able to deflect the blow a little, at the expense of losing the use of the fingers of one of his hands for the rest of his life. The blade narrowly missed the crown of the Prophet's helmet and glanced off the side of it, grazing his temple, driving two of the helmet rings into his cheek, and finally, with its force somewhat spent, striking his doubly mailed shoulder. The shock against the side of his head momentarily stunned him and he fell to the ground, whereupon his assailant withdrew as quickly as he had come. But others closed in to attack, and Shammās[3] of Makhzūm stationed himself in front of the Prophet and fought like a man inspired – the Prophet described him as a

[1] B. LII, 22. [2] W. 256. [3] See p. 82.

living shield – until he was cut down, and another man took his place, backed by Nusaybah, who had now drawn her sword.

A voice – perhaps that of Ibn Qami'ah himself – was heard to shout: "Muḥammad is slain!" The cry was taken up all over the field, interspersed with glorifications of al-'Uzzah and Hubal. The cliffs of Uḥud resounded and the Muslims who had fled were overcome with self-reproach and sorrow, while many of those who were still fighting in the plain lost heart and withdrew from the strife as best they might. But there were many exceptions, and one of these was Anas the son of Naḍr after whom his nephew, the Prophet's servant Anas, was named. It was his sister, the daughter of Naḍr, who had been told by the Prophet that her son, killed by an arrow at Badr, was in Firdaws, the highest Paradise. Anas came upon two of his fellows for whom life seemed to have lost its meaning, and who could bring themselves neither to continue fighting nor to climb the ascent to safety. "Why sit ye here?" he exclaimed. "The Messenger of God hath been slain," they said. "Then what will ye do with life after him?" said Anas. "Rise and die, even as he died."[1] And he set off for where the fight was thickest. There he found Sa'd ibn Mu'ādh, who told the Prophet afterwards that Anas had called to him: "Paradise! I scent its fragrance blowing from the other side of Uḥud." "O Messenger of God," said Sa'd, "I could not fight as he fought." Afterwards they found Anas lying dead with more than eighty wounds, so disfigured as to be unrecognisable to anyone save his sister, who knew him by his fingers.[2]

As to the believers who now sought refuge on the higher ground above the plain, withdrawal was made easier for them because most of the enemy felt that the battle was now over and they too slackened their efforts. The dead had not yet been counted, but it was evident that they had amply avenged those who had died at Badr; and now, by killing the man who had been the sole cause of all the strife, they had surely put an end to the new religion and virtually re-established the old order of things. *Yā lal-'Uzzah yā la-Hubal!*

The sudden relaxing of effort on the part of Quraysh was nowhere more apparent than amongst those who had half surrounded the little group of some twenty men who were acting as a bodyguard to the Prophet. It had become clear to the Meccans that these were men who would never be taken prisoner and who in fighting to the death would certainly deal death to others. So their better course, now that their main purpose had been achieved, was to live and let live, and to celebrate their victory.

The Prophet had almost immediately recovered consciousness, and when the enemy had withdrawn he rose to his feet and, motioning to his Companions to follow him, he led them towards the entrance of a glen which seemed to offer the easiest ascent to a point of safety from which they could watch over the movement of the enemy. But he was now in great pain from his cheek: the metal rings were deeply embedded in the flesh, so they halted for a moment and Abū 'Ubaydah caught one of them and then the other between his teeth and drew them out. The wound began to bleed again and Mālik of Khazraj put his mouth to it and sucked out the blood

[1] W. 280. [2] B. LVI, 12.

and swallowed it. It was he who had said in Medina: "We have before us one of two good things"; and except for Shammās, who appeared to be dead, he was the most severely wounded of those present. The Prophet said: "Whoso would look on a man whose blood is mingled with my blood, let him look on Mālik, the son of Sinān." Abū 'Ubaydah was also included, for in his effort to remove the rings he had pulled out two of his own teeth and his mouth was bleeding. The Prophet said to them: "Whose blood hath touched my blood, him the fire cannot reach."[1]

As the small party moved up the glen they were seen by some of those who had already taken refuge on Uhud, and they came down to meet them. Ka'b ibn Mālik was ahead of the others, and he was surprised to see a man whose stature and bearing were exactly like those of the Prophet, albeit that his gait was slower. Then, as he drew near, Ka'b saw the incomparable and unmistakable brightness of the eyes through the eyeholes of the visor, and he turned and shouted to those behind him: "O Muslims, be of good cheer! This is the Messenger of God!" The Prophet motioned him to be silent, and he did not shout the good news again, but it spread from mouth to mouth, and men came hurrying to reassure themselves that it was true. So great was the rejoicing that it was as if the defeat had suddenly been changed into victory.

But Ka'b's joyful shout was heard by a solitary horseman of Quraysh who had halted on the very site they had just vacated. It was Ubayy, the brother of Umayyah, who had sworn that from the back of his horse 'Awd, which he was now riding, he would kill the Prophet. Having learned that his intended victim was dead, he had no doubt come to look for the body to see if there was still life in it; and when he heard the shout of Ka'b he rode up the glen until he was hard on the heels of the Muslims. They turned to face him. "O Muḥammad," he called out, "if thou escape, then may not I escape!" Some of the Companions closed round the Prophet, and others were about to attack Ubayy when the Prophet ordered them to hold off their hands; and those who were round him said afterwards that he shook himself clear of them as if they had been no more than flies on a camel's back. Then he took a spear from Ḥārith ibn as-Simmah and stepped in front of them all. Not daring to move, they looked on in awe at his grim and deadly earnestness. As one of them said: "When the Messenger of God made a deliberate effort toward some end, there was no earnestness that could compare with his."[2] Ubayy approached with drawn sword, but before he could strike a blow the Prophet had thrust him in the neck. He bellowed like a bull, then swayed and almost fell from his horse but, recovering his balance, he turned and galloped down the slope and did not stop until he reached the Meccan camp where his nephew Ṣafwān and others of his clan were now assembled. "Muḥammad hath slain me," he said in a voice he could not control. They looked at his wound and made light of it, but he was convinced that it was mortal, as indeed it soon proved to be. "He told me he would kill me," he said, "and by God if he had spat upon me he would have killed me." Was Muḥammad not dead after all,

[1] W. 247. [2] W. 251.

they began to wonder. But Ubayy was clearly beside himself, and in any case it was easy to mistake one helmeted man for another.

When the Prophet and his Companions reached the top of the glen, 'Alī went to fill his shield with water from a cavity in the rocks. He held it out to the Prophet, but the odour of its stagnancy repelled him, and he could not bring himself to drink of it despite his thirst, though he used some of it to wash the blood from his face. Then, since they were still too easily accessible from the plain, he gave the word to move onwards to higher ground, and he tried to raise himself onto a ledge of rock from which further ascent could be made. But he was too weak for the effort, so Ṭalḥah crouched below the ledge with great violence to his wounds, and taking the Prophet on his back he raised him to the necessary height. The Prophet said of him that day: "He that would behold a martyr walking the face of the earth, let him look on Ṭalḥah the son of 'Ubayd Allāh."[1]

By the time they had found a place which could serve as a temporary camp the sun had reached its zenith and they prayed the noon prayer. The Prophet, who led it, remained seated throughout, and everyone followed his example. Then they lay down to rest and many of them slept a deep and refreshing sleep, while a relay of watchmen kept watch from a point of vantage overlooking the plain.

[1] I.H. 571.

# LIII

# *Revenge*

QURAYSH were now busy about their dead and their wounded. The losses had not been great: there were only twenty-two killed out of three thousand. Then they counted the losses of the enemy and found about sixty-five dead, many of whom they did not know. Only three were Emigrants: Ḥamzah of Hāshim, Muṣ'ab of 'Abd ad-Dār, and 'Abd Allāh ibn Jaḥsh. A few other bodies at some distance from the centre of the field, wounded as well as dead, escaped their notice. Amongst these was Shammās, still alive but unable to move. In vain they searched for the body of Muḥammad, and while they were doing so Waḥshī went back to the body of Ḥamzah, ripped open his belly, cut out his liver and brought it to Hind. "What shall be mine for slaying the slayer of thy father?" he said. "All my share of the spoils," was her answer. "This is Ḥamzah's liver," he said, and she took it from him and bit away a piece of it, chewed it, swallowed a morsel in fulfilment of her vow and spat out the rest. "Show me where he is," she said, and when they reached the body she cut off his nose and ears and other parts of his flesh. Then she took off her necklaces and pendants and anklets and gave them to Waḥshī, telling the women who were with her to mutilate others of the dead. They all made for themselves ornaments of vengeance with what they cut from the bodies of the Muslims, and Hind mounted upon a rock and uttered a chant of triumph. One or two men of Quraysh also sought to slake their thirst for revenge by mutilating the dead, but their Bedouin allies were outraged. Abu Sufyān was striking the side of Ḥamzah's mouth with the point of his spear and saying "Taste that, thou rebel" when Ḥulays passed by, the leader of one of the clans of Kinānah. In a loud voice, so that Abū Sufyān could hear, he said: "O sons of Kinānah, can this be the lord of Quraysh who is doing what ye see with the body of his dead cousin?" "Confound thee," said Abū Sufyān, "tell not of it. A slip it was, no more."[1]

Meantime Abū 'Āmir came upon the body of his son Ḥanẓalah, and grievously lamented over him saying: "Did I not warn thee against this man?" – he meant the Prophet. "But thou wast a dutiful son unto thy father, noble of character in thy life, and in thy death thou liest with the flower of thy companions. If God requite with good this slain one" – he pointed to Ḥamzah – "or any of the followers of Muḥammad, may he requite thee with good!"[2] Then he looked sternly at Hind and the other women and said in a loud voice: "O Quraysh, let not Ḥanẓalah be

[1] I.I. 582. [2] W. 274.

mutilated, what though he was mine adversary and yours!" And they respected his wishes.

It was now presumed that Ubayy had not been mistaken, and that the Prophet was with his army somewhere on the high ground above the plain. But the battle was over: there could be no question of attacking the mountain, and the slaves had already been told to strike camp. So when they had buried their own dead and taken their fill of revenge on the enemy dead, they loaded the armour and whatever else they had stripped from them onto their camels, and prepared to set off. But before they did so Abū Sufyān mounted his chestnut mare and rode to the foot of the mountain, to the point nearest where the Prophet and his Companions had been stationed, and shouted at the top of his voice: "War goeth by turns, and this is a day for a day. Exalt thyself, O Hubal! Make prevail thy religion!" The Prophet told 'Umar to go and answer him, saying: "God is All-Highest, Supreme in Majesty. We are not equal: our slain are in Paradise, yours are in the Fire." So 'Umar went to the edge of the precipice below which Abū Sufyān was standing and answered him as the Prophet had said, whereupon Abū Sufyān called up to 'Umar, having recognised his voice: "I adjure thee, 'Umar, by God, have we slain Muḥammad?" "No, by God," said 'Umar, "but he is even now listening to what thou sayest." "I take thy word for it as truer than the word of Ibn Qami'ah," said Abū Sufyān. He turned to go, but turning back once more he added: "Some of your dead have been mutilated. By God, I take no pleasure therein, neither am I wroth. I forbade it not, nor did I command it." Then he said: "Badr be your meeting-place with us next year!" Hearing this, the Prophet sent another of his Companions to the edge of the cliff, to shout his response: "That is a binding tryst between us."[1]

Abū Sufyān rode to where his army was waiting for him at the further side of the plain, and they set off towards the south. It was too far for 'Umar to discern clearly their formation, so the Prophet sent Sa'd of Zuhrah down to the plain to follow them and see what they were about. "If they are leading their horses", he said, "and riding their camels, they are for Mecca; but if they are riding their horses and leading their camels, they are for Medina; and by Him in whose hand is my soul, if that is their aim, I will overtake them and fight them." Sa'd went down to the gully where the Prophet's stallion Sakb had been tethered ever since their arrival in Uḥud, and having ridden after the Meccans until he had a clear sight of them, he then hastened back with the good tidings that their horsemen were on camelback leading their horses beside them. As one of them said in after-years, namely 'Amr[2], who had taken part with Khālid in the decisive cavalry charge: "We had heard that Ibn Ubayy had returned to Medina with a third of the army, and that some men of Aws and Khazraj had stayed in the city. Nor could we be certain that those who had retreated would not return to the attack; and many of us were wounded, and nearly all our horses had been pierced by arrows, so we went on our way."[3]

[1] I.I. 583. [2] See p. 81. [3] W. 299.

# LIV

# *The Burial of the Martyrs*

THE Prophet now led his Companions down into the plain. Ḥārith ibn as-Ṣimmah had been sent on ahead to look for the body of Ḥamzah, but when he found him he was so appalled at the sight and at having to tell the Prophet that he did not at once return, and 'Alī was sent after him. He found Ḥārith standing aghast by the mutilated body, and they both returned together. When the Prophet saw what had been done he said: "Never yet have I felt more anger than now I feel; and when next God giveth me a victory over Quraysh I will mutilate thirty of their dead."[1] But soon after this there came the Revelation: *If ye inflict punishment, then inflict only so much as ye have suffered; but if ye endure patiently, that is better for the patient.*[2] And not only did he not fulfil his threat, but he expressly forbade mutilation after every battle. Moreover, as regards the fighting itself, he told them to respect the human face as being the most godlike part of the body: "When one of you striketh a blow, let him avoid striking the face . . . for God created Adam in His image."[3]

'Abd Allāh ibn Jaḥsh had been struck down not far from Ḥamzah, and his body also had been mutilated. But when the Prophet turned away from them to look for others of the dead, a very different sight met his eyes. One of the nearest bodies to those of his two kinsmen was the body of Ḥanzalah. Neither man nor woman of Quraysh had ventured to touch him, and he lay there even as the Angels had laid him, with his hair still wet with water upon the noon-dry earth. None passed him by who did not give thanks, for in his beauty and his peace he was as a sign from Heaven, to inform the bereaved of the present state of their martyred kinsmen.

Not far away were the bodies of Khaythamah and Ibn ad-Daḥdāḥah – Khaythamah whose martyred son had appeared to him in his sleep, bidding him hasten to join him, and Thābit ibn ad-Daḥdāḥah who had made a gift of the palm-tree to the orphan. When the Prophet saw Thābit, he said: "Palms with low-hanging heavy-laden clusters, what a multitude of these hath the son of Daḥdāḥah in Paradise!"[4]

When one of the clans of Aws were looking for their dead, they found to

[1] I.I. 584. [2] XVI, 126. [3] A.H. I, 251; M. XLV, 32. [4] W. 505.

their surprise a man of theirs named Usayrim whom only the day before they had rebuked for not being a Muslim. Whenever they spoke to him about Islam he used to say: "If I knew it to be true, all that ye say, I would not hesitate." Yet there he was on the field of battle, mortally wounded but not yet dead. "What brought thee here?" they said. "Was it care for thy people, or was it for the sake of Islam?" "It was for Islam," he said. "Suddenly I believed in God and in his Messenger and I entered Islam. Then I took my sword and came out early this morning to be with the Messenger of God; and I fought until I was struck the blow that felled me here." He could say no more and they stayed with him until he died. Then they told the Prophet, who assured them that he was of the people of Paradise, and in after years Usayrim came to be known as the man who entered Paradise without ever having prayed one of the five daily prayers.

Amongst the dead they found a stranger, or so it seemed at first, until one of them recognised him as Mukhayrīq, a learned rabbi of the Jewish clan of Tha'labah. Early that morning, as they were afterwards informed, he had summoned his people to keep their pact with the Prophet and to join him in fighting the idolaters, and when they protested that it was the Sabbath he said: "Ye keep not the Sabbath truly." Then he adjured them to witness that Muḥammad was his sole heir. "If I am slain this day," he said, "my possessions are for Muḥammad, to use even as God shall show him." Then taking his sword and other weapons he set out for Uhud, where he fought till he was killed. Thereafter a large portion of the alms that were distributed in Medina came from the rich palm groves that the Prophet inherited from Mukhayrīq, "the best of the Jews", as he called him.

As soon as it was clear that the Meccans intended to return the way they had come, thus giving Medina a wide berth, women began to set out from the city to tend the wounded and to see for themselves how true or how false were the various rumours that ever since noon had been coming to their ears. Among the first women to come were Ṣafiyyah and 'Ā'ishah and Umm Ayman. The Prophet was distressed to see Ṣafiyyah approaching, and he called to Zubayr: "Help me with thy mother, and let Ḥamzah's grave be dug forthwith. Go thou to meet her and take her back, lest she see what hath befallen her brother." So Zubayr went to her and said: "Mother, the Messenger of God biddeth thee return." But Ṣafiyyah had already learned the news at the edge of the field. "Why should I return?" she said. "I have heard that my brother hath been mutilated, but it was for the sake of God, and that which is for His sake do we fully accept. I promise that I shall be calm and patient if God will." Zubayr returned to the Prophet, who told him to let her have her way. So she came and looked at her brother and prayed over him and recited the Verse of Return: *Verily we are for God, and verily unto Him are we returning*; and they all took comfort in remembering the context of this verse, from a Revelation which had been received after Badr: *O ye who believe, seek help of God in steadfastness and in prayer. Verily God is with the steadfast. And say not "dead" of those who have been slain in God's path, for they are living, only ye perceive not. And We shall surely try you with something of fear and of hunger, and loss of goods and lives and harvesting. But give good tidings unto the steadfast, who say when a blow befalleth them: Verily we are for*

*God, and verily unto Him are we returning. On these are blessings from their Lord and mercy; and these are the rightly guided.*[1]

Ṣafiyyah then stood and prayed over the body of her sister Umaymah's son, 'Abd Allāh ibn Jaḥsh, and she was soon joined by Fāṭimah. The two women wept over their dead, and it was a relief to the Prophet to weep with them. Fāṭimah then dressed her father's wounds. Their cousin Ḥamnah, 'Abd Allāh's sister, was now seen approaching, and their sorrow was increased by having to tell her of the death of her husband Muṣ'ab, as well as of the deaths of her brother and her uncle. When the battle was already well advanced the Prophet had seen Muṣ'ab, as he thought, still bearing the banner, and had called out to him. But the man had answered: "I am not Muṣ'ab", and the Prophet had known that it was an Angel and that Muṣ'ab must have been killed or disabled. He now stood by the dead man's body and recited the verse: *Of the believers are men who are true to their covenant with God. Some of them have made good their vow by death, and some are waiting, and they waver not nor change.*[2]

He ordered that all the dead should be brought and laid near the body of Ḥamzah, and that graves should be dug. Ḥamzah was wrapped in a mantle, and the Prophet prayed over him the funeral prayer, after which he prayed over each one of the dead, seventy-two prayers in all. As soon as a grave was ready, two or three were buried in it. Ḥamzah and his nephew 'Abd Allāh were laid together in one grave. The Prophet himself presided over every burial. "Look for 'Amr the son of Jamūḥ and 'Abd Allāh the son of Amr," he said. "In this world they were friends inseparable, so lay them in one grave." But Hind, wife of 'Amr and sister of 'Abd Allāh – the father of Jābir – had already brought the two bodies together, and with them the body of her son Khallād. She had tried to take them to Medina, but when her camel had reached the edge of the plain he had refused to go any further – by God's command, as the Prophet told her – and she had been obliged to bring the bodies once more to the battlefield. So the three were laid in one grave, and the Prophet stood beside them until they were buried. "O Hind," he said, "they are all of them together in Paradise, 'Amr and thy son Khallād and thy brother 'Abd Allāh." "O Messenger of God," said Hind, "pray God that He place me with them."

Unlike most of the dead, the man of Muzaynah who had fought so valiantly had none of his people present, for his nephew had also fought to the death. So the Prophet went to him and stood beside him saying: "May God be pleased with thee, even as I am pleased with thee."[3] They had wrapped his body in a green-striped cloak he was wearing, and when he was laid in the grave the Prophet drew it up to cover his face and his feet were uncovered. So he told them to gather some rue from the plain and to spread it over his feet. And this he bade them do with many of the dead, that both their faces and their feet might be covered before the earth was piled up over them.

When the last grave had been filled the Prophet called for his horse and mounted it, and they set off down the gorge, the way they had come at dawn. When they reached the beginning of the lava tract he told them to

[1] II, 153–7. [2] XXXIII, 23. [3] W. 277.

stand in line to give praise and thanksgiving to God, and the men formed two lines facing Mecca, with the women behind them, fourteen women in all. Then he glorified God, and prayed, saying: "O God, I ask of thee Thy blessing and Thy mercy and Thy grace and Thine indulgence. O God, I ask of Thee the eternal bliss that fadeth not nor passeth away. O God, I ask of Thee safety on the day of fear, and plenty on the day of destitution."[1]

[1] W. 315.

# LV

# *After Uḥud*

THE sun was setting as they approached the city and they prayed the sunset prayer as soon as they reached the Mosque. The Prophet then lay down to rest and fell into so deep a sleep that he did not hear Bilāl's call to the night prayer, but prayed it alone in his house when he woke. The two Sa'ds of the Helpers and other leaders of Aws and Khazraj spent the night at the door of the Mosque and took it in turns to stand on guard, for there was still always the possibility that Quraysh might return; and early the next morning, when the prayer had been prayed, the Prophet told Bilāl to announce to them and to others that the enemy must be pursued. "But none shall go out with us," he said, "save those who were present at the battle of yesterday."

When the chiefs returned to their various clans they found most of the men tending their wounds or having them tended by their women, for very few of the fighters at Uḥud were unscathed, and many of them were severely injured. But on hearing the Prophet's summons they bandaged their wounds as best they could and made themselves ready to set out once again, all except Mālik and Shammās. Mālik, now in an extremity of weakness, was being tended by his family. Shammās, none of whose nearest of kin were in Medina, had been carried unconscious from the battlefield to 'Ā'ishah's apartment. But Umm Salamah claimed the right to tend her fellow clansman, so he was put in her charge. Since his death seemed imminent, the Prophet left instructions that he should not be buried in Medina but with his fellow martyrs at Uḥud.

The Prophet himself was one of the first to be ready, although he could now scarcely move his right shoulder, which had taken the shock of the blow intended for his head. When Talḥah came to inquire about the time of departure, he was astonished to see him on horseback at the door of the mosque, with his visor down and nothing visible of him but his eyes. Disabled though he was, Ṭalḥah ran to his house to make himself ready.

Amongst those of the Bani Salimah who set out there were forty wounded men, some of them with more than ten gashes or thrusts or arrow wounds; and when they stood in line for the Prophet at the appointed place and he saw what plight they were in he rejoiced at the power of their souls over their bodies, and prayed: "O God, have mercy upon the Bani Salimah!" Of all the clans, only one man went out who had not fought at Uḥud, and that was Jābir. On hearing the summons that morning he had gone to the Prophet and said: "O Messenger of God, I was eager to be present at the battle, but my father left me in charge of my seven young sisters. And thus it was that for martyrdom God preferred him to me, though I had hoped for it. So let me go with thee now, O Messenger of God." And the Prophet gave him permission to march out with the others.

They made their first halt about eight miles from Medina. The enemy were by that time encamped at Rawḥā', which was not far ahead. On hearing this the Prophet ordered his men to spread themselves over a wide area of ground and to gather as much wood as they could find, piling it up each man for himself in a separate pile. By sunset they had prepared over five hundred beacons, and when night had fallen every man set fire to his. The flames were seen far and wide, as if a great army were encamped there. This impression was confirmed for Abū Sufyān by a man of Khuzā'ah who, though still an idolater, was friendly to the Muslims and who told him with deliberate untruth that the whole city of Medina had come out in pursuit of them, including all those who had stayed behind from Uḥud and all their confederates. "By God," he said, "ye will not have moved off before ye have seen the forelocks of their cavalry." Some of Quraysh had wanted to return and attack Medina, but they now unanimously decided to press on with all speed for Mecca. None the less Abū Sufyān sent back a parting message for the Prophet by some riders who were on their way to Medina for provisions. "Tell Muḥammad from me," he said, "that we are resolved to come against him and his companions and to root them out, those that yet remain, from the face of the earth. Tell him this, and when ye reach 'Ukāẓ on your return I will load your camel with raisins." When they delivered the message to the Prophet, he answered in the words of a recent Revelation: *God is our sufficiency, and supremely to be trusted is He.*[1]

He and his Companions spent the Monday, Tuesday and Wednesday at their camp, lighting beacons every night, and those were days of much-needed rest and plenty. There had been an excellent fruit harvest the previous summer, and Sa'd ibn 'Ubādah had loaded thirty camels with dates, and others had been brought to be sacrificed. On the Thursday they returned to Medina.

Shammās had died soon after they had set out and he had been buried at Uhud. Mālik had also died during their absence, but his family had buried him in Medina. The Prophet now gave orders that his body should be taken to Uhud and buried there.

On his return from fighting at Uhud, 'Abd Allāh the son of Ibn Ubayy had spent part of the night after the battle cauterising a wound, while his father enlarged on the folly of having gone out to attack the enemy. "By God, it was as if I had seen it all," he said. "What God did for His Messenger and the Muslims was good," said his son. But Ibn Ubayy was not to open to argument. "If the slain had been with us, they would not have been slain," he insisted. Nor had he been silent during his son's recent absence from Medina with the rest of the fighters, neither had the Jews refrained from affirming with more conviction than ever: "Muḥammad is nothing but a seeker of kingship. No Prophet hath ever met with such reverse. He was smitten in his own body, as well as in his companions."

Much of what had been said by both Jews and hypocrites was repeated

[1] III, 173.

to 'Umar on his return from the expedition of the beacons. He immediately went to the Prophet and asked his permission to kill those who were responsible, but the Prophet forbade him to do so. "God will make prevail His religion," he said, "and He will empower His prophet." Then he said: "O son of Khaṭṭāb, verily Quraysh shall not gain from us the like of that day again, and we shall greet the Corner."[1] – he meant that they would enter Mecca and kiss Black Stone.

Although 'Umar's hands were tied, Ibn Ubayy did not escape altogether unscathed. He had taken to occupying a place of honour in the Mosque at the Friday prayer, and no one had thought to deny him this on account of his standing in Medina. When the Prophet mounted the pulpit to preach, he would rise and say: "O people, this is the Messenger of God. May God through him be bountiful to you and give you strength! Help ye him therefore and honour him and hear him and obey him." Then he would be seated again. But when he rose to speak as usual on the day after their return, the first Friday since Uḥud, those of the Helpers who were nearest him seized him on both sides, saying "Sit, thou enemy of God. Thou art not worthy to hold forth, having done what thou didst," whereupon he left the congregation, threading his way through the densely seated men. One of the Helpers who met him at the door of the Mosque said to him: "Return and let the Messenger of God ask forgiveness for thee." But he said: "By God, I want not that he should ask forgiveness for me."

In the days which followed Uḥud, the Prophet received many Revelations concerning the battle, and it appeared from them that a considerable portion of two of the clans had seriously thought of deserting the army shortly before the fight was joined, and that God had strengthened them and given them resolution. One of the two were the Bani Salimah of Khazraj, whose bearing had so pleased the Prophet as they were setting out in pursuit of the enemy. When they and the Bani Ḥārithah of Aws heard the Revelation[2] they said that they were the ones referred to, but that they did not regret their moment of weakness because it had brought them strength from God, which was better than their own strength. Other verses were revealed with reference to those survivors of the sudden cavalry charge who had fled in panic to the mountain, and in particular to those of them who had previously urged the Prophet to go out to fight, so that they might attain to martyrdom. *Deemed ye that ye would enter Paradise ere God knoweth those of you that truly strive and ere He knoweth the steadfast? Ye wished for death until ye met it; now ye have seen it face to face!*[3]

But the Revelation made it none the less clear that those who had disobeyed orders had expiated their faults on the battlefield and had been forgiven. Part of their expiation had been their great sorrow at hearing that the Prophet was dead.[4] It was also affirmed, with reference to the visible ruins that remained from previous civilisations, that the established order of things in Arabia would pass away, and that Islam would triumph: *Ways of life have passed away before you. Travel in the land and see what was the end of those who belied God's messengers. This is a clear affirmation*

[1] W. 317. [2] III, 122. [3] III, 142–3. [4] III, 152–5.

*for mankind, and a guidance and an exhortation for the pious. Falter not nor grieve, for ye shall overcome them if ye are true believers.*[1]

There was also another reference to the future, of a different kind: *Muḥammad is but a messenger, and messengers have passed away before him. If he die or be slain, will ye then turn upon your heels? Whoso turneth upon his heels will thereby do no hurt unto God; and God will reward the thankful.*[2]

[1] III, 137–9. [2] III, 144.

# LVI

# *Victims of Revenge*

FOR two months and more there was nothing to disturb the peace. Then came news that the Bani Asad ibn Khuzaymah were planning a raid on the oasis. Notwithstanding the Islam of the Jaḥsh family and other Asadites who had previously lived in Mecca, the main body of this widespread and powerful tribe of Najd were still close allies of Quraysh, who had now encouraged them to take advantage of the disabling effect of Uḥud. It was therefore necessary to demonstrate to them and to all Arabia that the Muslims derived strength from Uḥud rather than weakness. So the Prophet sent out a body of a hundred and fifty well armed and well mounted men into their territory to the north of the central desert under the command of his cousin Abū Salamah with instructions to do all in his power to take their camp by surprise. This they succeeded in doing, but after a brief encounter, with little bloodshed on either side, the Bedouin withdrew and scattered in all directions, while the Muslims returned to Medina after eleven days with a large herd of camels and three herdsmen. The expedition had served its main purpose, which was to affirm the undiminished power of Islam.

About the same time news came of the danger of another projected raid from further south; but in this instance the Prophet divined that the hostility against Islam was all concentrated in one remarkably evil man, the chief of the Liḥyānite branch of Hudhayl. If they could be rid of him, the danger from that quarter would become negligible; so he sent 'Abd Allāh ibn Unays, a man of Khazraj, with instructions to kill him. "O Messenger of God," said 'Abd Allāh, "describe him to me that I may know him." "When thou seest him," said the Prophet, "he will remind thee of Satan. The certain sign for thee that he is indeed the man will be that when thou seest him thou wilt shudder at him." It was as he had said; and, having killed the man, 'Abd Allāh escaped with his life.

All idea of the projected raid against Medina was now abandoned, but it was no doubt in revenge for this death of one of their chiefs that in the following month some men of Hudhayl attacked six Muslims who were on their way to give religious instruction to two of the smaller neighbouring tribes. The encounter took place in Rajī', a watering place not far from Mecca. Three of the Prophet's men died fighting, and three were taken captive, one of whom was subsequently killed when he tried to escape. Amongst those who died fighting was 'Āṣim of Aws who had killed two of the standard bearers of Quraysh at Uḥud. Their mother had sworn to drink wine out of his skull, and the men of Hudhayl were bent on selling her his head for that purpose. But 'Aṣim's body was protected from them by a swarm of bees until nightfall, and during the night it was swept away by a flood, so that the mother's vow was never fulfilled. As for the two captives, Khubayb of Aws and Zayd of Khazraj, they were sold to Quraysh, who were still glad of any means of avenging those slain at Badr. Khubayb was bought by a confederate of the Bani Nawfal and presented to a member of that clan so that he might kill him in revenge for his father. Ṣafwān bought Zayd for a similar purpose, and the two men were imprisoned in Mecca until the sacred months were past.

After the sighting of the new moon of Ṣafar they were taken outside the hallowed precinct to Tan'īm. There they met for the first time since their imprisonment, and they embraced, and exhorted each other to patience. Then the Bani Nawfal and others who were with them took Khubayb a short distance away, and when he saw that they were about to bind him to a stake he asked to be allowed to pray first, and he prayed two cycles of the ritual prayer. It is said that he was the inaugurator of the wont that a condemned man should pray thus before his death. Then they bound him to the stake saying: "Revert from Islam, and we will let thee go free." "I would not revert from Islam," he said, "if by so doing I could have all that is on earth." "Dost thou not wish that Muḥammad were in thy place," they said, "and that thou wert sitting in thy home?" "I would not that Muḥammad should be pierced by a single thorn that I might thereby be sitting in my home," he answered. "Revert, O Khubayb," they persisted, "for if thou dost not we will surely slay thee." "My being slain for God is but a trifle, if I die in Him," he said, and then: "As to your turning my face away from the direction of holiness" – he meant from Mecca, for they had turned him another way – "verily God saith: *Wheresoever ye turn, there is the Face of God.*"[1] Then he said: "O God, no man is here who will take Thy Messenger my greeting of Peace, so take him Thou my greeting of Peace." Now the Prophet was sitting with Zayd and others of his Companions in Medina, and there came over him a state even as when the Revelation descended upon him, and they heard him say: "And on him be Peace and the Mercy of God!" Then he said: "This is Gabriel, who greeteth me with Peace from Khubayb."[2]

Quraysh had with them about forty boys whose fathers had been killed at Badr, and they gave each boy a spear and said: "This is he who slew your fathers." They speared him but did not kill him, so a man put his hand over the hand of one of the boys and gave Khubayb a mortal wound, and another did the same, yet he remained alive for an hour, continually repeating the two testifications of Islam: *There is no god but God, and Muḥammad is the messenger of God.*

His fellow captive Zayd was then put to death, and he also prayed two cycles of prayer before he was tied to the stake, and gave similar answers to the same questions. Akhnas ibn ash-Sharīq, the confederate of Zuhrah, who had gone out with the others to Tan'īm, was impelled to remark: "No father so loveth his son as the companions of Muḥammad love Muḥammad."

[1] II, 115. [2] W. 360.

When 'Ubaydah had died after his single combat with 'Utbah at the beginning of the battle of Badr, he had left a widow who was very much younger than himself, Zaynab, the daughter of Khuzaymah of the Bedouin tribe of 'Āmir. She was of a very generous nature, and already before the days of Islam she had been known as "the mother of the poor". A year after being widowed she was still unmarried, and when the Prophet asked her to marry him she gladly accepted. A fourth apartment was made for her in his house adjoining the Mosque, and it was doubtless in connection with this new alliance that the Prophet now received a visit from Abū Barā', the ageing chief of Zaynab's tribe. When Islam was put before him, the old man made it clear that he was not averse to it. He did not however embrace it then, but asked that some Muslims should be sent to instruct his whole tribe. The Prophet said that he was afraid they would be attacked by other tribes. The Bani 'Āmir were a branch of Hawāzin, and their territory lay to the south of Sulaym and other tribes of Ghaṭafān, against whom the oasis of Yathrib had to be continually on its guard. But Abū Barā' promised that no one would violate the protection which, as chief of 'Āmir, he would give them, so the Prophet chose forty of his Companions who were eminently representative of Islam both in piety and knowledge, and he placed in command of them a man of Khazraj, Mundhir ibn 'Amr. One of them was 'Āmir ibn Fuhayrah, the freedman whom Abū Bakr had chosen to accompany the Prophet and himself on the Hijrah.

It was not known in Medina that Abū Barā''s leadership was disputed within the tribe, and his nephew, who aspired to be chief in his place, killed one of the Companions who had been sent on ahead with a letter from the Prophet, and called upon his tribe to slaughter the others. When the tribe proved to be almost unanimous in upholding Abū Barā''s protection, the frustrated nephew sent a message of instigation to two clans of Sulaym who had recently been involved in hostilities with Medina. They immediately sent out a detachment of horse and massacred the whole delegation of unsuspecting Muslims in their camp by the well of Ma'ūnah, except for two men who had gone to pasture the camels. One of these two was Ḥārith ibn as-Simmah, who had fought so valiantly at Uḥud. The other was 'Amr, of the Ḍamrah clan of Kinānah. As they returned from pasturing, they were dismayed to see vultures in great numbers circling low above their camp, as over a battlefield when the fighting has been finished; and they found their companions lying dead in their own blood, with the horsemen of Sulaym standing near them, absorbed in so earnest a discussion amongst themselves that they did not appear to notice the newcomers. 'Amr was for escaping to Medina with the news, but Ḥārith said "I am not one to hold back from fighting on a field where Mundhir hath been slain," and he threw himself on the enemy, killing two of them before he and 'Amr were overpowered and taken captive. They were strangely unwilling to kill either of them, even Ḥārith, although two of their men had just died at his hands, and they asked him what they should do with him. He said he only wanted to be taken to where Mundhir's body lay and to be given weapons and set free to fight them all. They granted his request, and he killed another two men before he was finally killed himself. 'Amr they set free, and they asked him to tell them the names of all his dead companions. He went with them to each one, and told them his name and lineage. Then they asked him if any of them were missing. "I cannot find a freedman of Abū Bakr," he said, "named 'Āmir ibn Fuhayrah." "What was his position amongst you?" they asked. "He was one of the best of us," said 'Amr, "one of our Prophet's first Companions." "Shall I tell thee what befell him?" said his questioner. Then they called to one of their number, Jabbār, who had himself killed 'Āmir, and Jabbār recounted how he had come upon him from behind and thrust him between the shoulders with his spear. The point came out from 'Āmir's chest, and with his last breath the words "I have triumphed, by God" were ejaculated from his lips. "What could that mean?" thought Jabbār, feeling that he himself had more right to claim a triumph. In amazement he drew out his spear, to be still more amazed when unseen hands carried the body high up into the air until it was lost to sight. When it was explained to Jabbār that the "triumph" meant Paradise, he entered Islam. The Prophet said, when he heard of the event, that the Angels had taken 'Āmir to 'Illiyyūn,[1] which is one of the supreme Paradises.[2]

The men of Sulaym returned to their tribe, where the story of what had befallen was repeated again and again, and this was the beginning of their conversion. As to the liberated survivor, 'Amr, they told him that the massacre had been instigated by the Bani 'Āmir; and on his way back to Medina he killed two men of that tribe, thinking to avenge his dead companions. But both men were in fact entirely innocent, loyal to Abū Barā' and recognising his protection of the believers, so the Prophet insisted that blood-wite should be paid for them to their nearest of kin.

[1] W. 349. [2] K. LXXXIII, 18–19.

# LVII

# *Bani Naḍīr*

THE Jewish tribe of Naḍīr had long been confederates of the Bani 'Āmir, and the Prophet decided to ask them to help him pay the blood-wite. So he went to them with Abū Bakr and 'Umar and others of his Companions and laid the matter before them. They agreed to do what he requested, and invited them to stay until a meal could be prepared for them. The Prophet accepted their invitation, and some of the Jews withdrew, amongst them one of their chiefs, Ḥuyay, ostensibly to give instructions about the entertainment of their guests. While they were sitting there, in front of one of the fortresses, Gabriel came to the Prophet, unseen by any save him, and told him that the Jews were planning to kill him and that he must return to Medina at once. So he rose and left the company without a word, and everyone assumed that he would quickly rejoin them. But when some time had passed and he had not returned Abū Bakr suggested to the other Companions that they also should go, so they took their leave of the Jews and went to the Prophet's house. He explained to them what had happened and then he sent Muḥammad ibn Maslamah to the Bani Naḍīr, telling him what to say to them. He went with all speed to their fortresses and some of their leaders came out to meet him. "The Messenger of God," he told them, "hath sent me to you, and he saith: 'By your purposing to slay me, ye have broken the pact I made with you.'" Then, having recounted to them the exact details of their plot, as the Prophet had bidden him do, he delivered the gist of his message: "I give you ten days to depart from my country," saith the Prophet. "Whosoever of you is seen after that, his head shall be cut off." "O son of Maslamah," they said, "we never thought that a man of Aws would bring us such a message." "Hearts have changed," he replied.

Most of them had already started preparations to leave, but Ibn Ubayy sent word urging them to remain and promising his support, and Ḥuyay, not without difficulty, persuaded them to stand firm, for he felt sure that their Bedouin allies would not fail them in this crisis, let alone their powerful home allies, the Jews of Bani Qurayẓah; and having dispatched urgent appeals for help to all of these, he sent his brother to the Prophet with the message: "We shall not leave our dwellings and our possessions, so do what thou wilt." "*Allāhu Akbar*," said the Prophet, "God is most great," and his Companions who were sitting with him echoed his magnification. "The Jews have declared war," he informed them. Immediately he mustered an army and placing the banner in the hands of 'Alī he set off for the settlements of Naḍīr, a little to the south of the city. They prayed the afternoon prayer in a spacious courtyard which the Jews had now vacated since it was outside their defences. After the prayer the Prophet led his troops towards the fortresses.

The ramparts were manned by archers and slingers, who had also rocks at their disposal in case the walls came to be attacked. The two sides kept up an exchange of arrows and stones until dark. The Jews had been astonished by the speed of their attackers; but the next day – so they thought – help was bound to come from Qurayẓah and Ibn Ubayy; then, in two days or three, their allies of Ghaṭafān would be with them. Meantime the Muslim army was being increased by a continual stream of men from Medina who had been unable for some reason or another to set out with the Prophet. By the time of the night prayer the greatly increased army was large enough to surround the enemy on all sides. The Prophet prayed with them, and then returned with ten of his Companions to Medina, leaving ʿAlī in charge of the camp. They chanted a litany of magnification the whole night long, until it was time for the dawn prayer. The Prophet rejoined them in the course of the morning.

The days passed and the Bani Naḍīr began to despair of the help which many of them had thought to be certain. The Bani Qurayẓah refused to break their pact with the Prophet, the Bani Ghaṭafān maintained an enigmatic silence, and again Ibn Ubayy was forced to admit that he could do nothing. As the hopes of the besieged men dwindled, the mutual animosity amongst them increased. The tribe had long been rent with ill feeling and bitterness; and now that they were completely cut off from the outer world, with no sign of help from any direction, the situation was felt to be intolerable. It became altogether so when, after ten days or more, the Prophet gave orders to cut down some of the palm-trees which were in sight of the walls. This was a sacrifice, for he knew that the territory was virtually his own; but it was done by Divine permission,[1] which could be taken as a command, and it had the immediate effect of demolishing the enemy's resistance. They gloried in their palms, which were one of their chief sources of revenue; and if they were compelled to leave their land now they would still think of it as theirs, for they had reason to hope that in the near future they would have the opportunity of regaining it. Quraysh had promised to eradicate Islam from the oasis. But if the palms were destroyed it would take many years to replace them. Only a few had been cut down, but to what length would this destruction be carried? Ḥuyay sent word to the Prophet that they would leave their land, but the Prophet said he was no longer prepared to agree that they should take all their possessions into exile with them. "Leave your land," he said, "and take with you all that your camels can carry, except your arms and armour."

Ḥuyay at first refused, but his fellow tribesmen compelled him to accept; and they resumed the preparations that had been cut short two weeks previously. The doors of their houses and even the lintels were loaded on to their camels; and when all was ready they set off for the north upon the road to Syria. Never had a caravan of such magnificence been seen within living memory. As they made their way through the crowded market of

[1] K. LIX, 5.

Medina, the camels went into single file, and each one as it passed was an object of wonder, both for the richness of its trappings and the wealth of its load. The splendid curtains of the howdahs were drawn back to display the women in their garments of silk or brocade, or velvet, green or red, most of them laden with ornaments of the finest gold, set with rubies, emeralds and other precious stones. The Bani Naḍir were known to be opulent, but until now only a small portion of their riches had been seen by others than themselves. They went on their way to the music of timbrels and fifes, and proudly gave it out that if they had left their palms behind them, they had others equally good elsewhere, and to those they were now going. Many of them stopped and settled on land which they owned in Khaybar, but others went further north and settled in Jericho or in the south of Syria. According to the Revelation, the land of the Bani Naḍīr and all that they left behind them was the possession of the Prophet, to be given to the poor and needy, and in particular to *the poor emigrants who have been driven from their homes.*[1] Only two of the Helpers were given a share, and that was on account of their poverty. But by giving the main part to the Emigrants the Prophet made them independent, and thus relieved the Helpers of a heavy burden.

[1] LIX, 8.

# LVIII

# *Peace and War*

DURING the months which followed, soon after the New Year of AD 626, Fāṭimah gave birth to another son. The Prophet was so pleased with the name al-Ḥasan that he now named the younger brother al-Ḥusayn, which means "the little Ḥasan," that is "the little beautiful one." About the same time his new wife, Zaynab, "the mother of the poor," fell ill and died, less than eight months after he had married her. He led her funeral prayer and buried her in the Baqīʿ not far from the grave of his daughter Ruqayyah. The next month his cousin Abū Salamah died of a wound from Uḥud which had closed too soon and broken out afresh. The Prophet was with him at the end and prayed for him as he was breathing his last; and it was the Prophet who closed his eyes when he was dead.

Abū Salamah and his wife had been a most devoted couple, and she had wanted him to make a pact with her that if one of them died the other would not marry again, but he told her that if he died first she should marry again, and he prayed: "God grant Umm Salamah after me a man who is better than me, one who will cause her no sadness and no hurt." Four months after his death the Prophet came and asked for her hand in marriage. She replied that she feared she was not a suitable match for him. "I am a woman whose best time hath gone," she said, "and I am the mother of orphans. What is more, I have a nature of exceeding jealousy, and thou, O Messenger of God, hast already more than one wife." He answered: "As to age, I am older than thou; as to thy jealousy, I will pray God to take it from thee; as to thine orphan children, God and His Messenger will care for them." And so they were married, and he lodged her in the house which had belonged to Zaynab.

Despite what she had said of her age, Umm Salamah was still in her youth, no more than twenty-nine years old. She had been only eighteen when she had emigrated to Abyssinia with Abū Salamah. As regards her jealousy, she rightly feared that this marriage would put her to the test, nor was she alone in having such fears. ʿĀ'ishah had accepted Ḥafṣah without difficulty, and also Zaynab; but with this new wife it was different, partly no doubt because she herself was older, being almost in her fourteenth year. She had often met Umm Salamah, and it was together with her that she had made the preparations for Fāṭimah's wedding. But she had never looked on her as a possible rival. Now, however, when everyone in Medina was talking of the Prophet's new marriage and of the great beauty of his bride, she was troubled and apprehensive. "I was grievously sad," she said, "for what they told me of her beauty, so I made myself agreeable to her that

I might observe her closely, and I saw that she was many times more beautiful than they had said. I told Ḥafṣah of this and she said: 'Nay, this is naught but thy jealousy; she is not as they say.' Then she also made herself agreeable to Umm Salamah that she might let her own eyes judge, and she said: 'I have observed her, but she is not as thou sayst, nowhere near, yet she is indeed beautiful.' Then I went to see her again, and she was, by my life, as Ḥafṣah had said. Yet was I jealous."[1]

The time was drawing near for the second encounter at Badr, in accordance with Abū Sufyān's parting challenge after Uhud – a challenge which the Prophet had accepted. But it was a year of drought, and Abū Sufyān saw that there would be not a blade of greenery for their camels and horses to eat on the way. All the fodder for the expedition would have to be brought with them from Mecca, and their stores were already depleted. But he shrank from the dishonour of breaking the tryst which he had himself proposed. It was desirable that Muḥammad should be the one to break it, but reports had come from Yathrib that he was already making preparations to set out. Could he be induced to change his mind? Abū Sufyān went into consultation with Suhayl and one or two other leaders of Quraysh, and they formed a plan. There happened to be in Mecca at that time a friend of Suhayl's named Nu'aym, one of the leading men of the Bani Ashja', a clan of Ghaṭafān. They felt they could trust him, and since he was not of Quraysh he could pose as a neutral and objective onlooker. They offered him twenty camels if he could induce the Muslims to renounce their project of marching out to Badr. Nu'aym agreed and set out at once for the oasis, where he drew an alarming picture of the forces which Abū Sufyān was preparing to lead out to Badr. He spoke to all the different sections of the community, Emigrants, Helpers, Jews and hypocrites, and he would close his assessment of the danger with the urgent counsel: "Therefore stay here and go not out against them. By God, I do not think a single one of you will escape with his life." The Jews and the hypocrites were glad at the news of Meccan preparations for war, and they helped to spread the tidings throughout the city. Nor did Nu'aym fail to make an impression on the Muslims themselves, many of whom were inclined to think that it would indeed be most unwise to go out to Badr. News of this attitude reached the Prophet, and he began to fear that no one would go out with him. But Abū Bakr and 'Umar urged him on no account to break his tryst with Quraysh. "God will support His religion," they said "and He will give strength to His Messenger." "I will go forth," said the Prophet, "even if I go alone."

These few words cost Nu'aym his camels, making vain all his efforts just when he was beginning to think that he had succeeded. But despite himself, he was impressed by the total failure of his mission: some power was at work in Medina which was altogether beyond his influence and beyond his experience, and the seeds of Islam were sown in his heart. The Prophet set out as originally planned with fifteen hundred men on camels and ten horsemen. Many of them took merchandise with them, intending to trade at the fair of Badr.

[1] I.S. VIII, 66.

Meantime Abū Sufyān had said to Quraysh: "Let us go out and spend one night or two nights on the road, and then return. If Muḥammad go not out he will hear that we set forth and that we then returned because he came not out to meet us. This will be counted against him and in our favour." But as it happened, the Prophet and his Companions spent eight days at the fair of Badr, and those who attended it reported the news far and wide that Quraysh had broken their word but that Muḥammad and his followers had kept theirs and had come to fight Quraysh as they had promised. When the news reached Mecca of the great moral victory of their enemy and of their own moral defeat in the eyes of Arabia, Ṣafwān and others bitterly upbraided Abū Sufyān for ever having proposed the second encounter at Badr. But this mortification none the less served to intensify their preparations for the final and lasting revenge which they were planning to inflict on the founder and followers of the new religion.

After his return from Badr the Prophet had a month of peace in Medina, and then at the beginning of the fifth Islamic year, June 626, news came that some clans of Ghaṭafān were again planning to raid the oasis. He set out immediately into the plain of Najd with four hundred men, but the enemy vanished as before when they were almost upon them. It was on this expedition that when they were nearest to an encounter the Prophet received the Revelation instructing him how to pray "the Prayer of Fear", that is, how an army should abridge the ritual prayer and modify the movements of it at times of danger, and how some should keep watch while others pray.[1]

One of the Helpers who went out with this force was Jābir the son of 'Abd Allāh. In after years he would tell of an incident which took place at one of their encampments: "We were with the Prophet when a Companion brought in a fledgling which he had caught, and one of the parent birds came and threw itself into the hands of him who had taken its young. I saw men's faces full of wonderment, and the Prophet said: 'Do ye wonder at this bird? Ye have taken its young, and it hath thrown itself down in merciful tenderness unto its young. Yet I swear by God, your Lord is more merciful unto you than is this bird unto its fledgling.'[2] And he told the man to put back the young bird where he had found it."

He also said: "God hath a hundred mercies, and one of them hath He sent down amongst jinn and men and cattle and beasts of prey. Thereby they are kind and merciful unto one another, and thereby the wild creature inclineth in tenderness unto her offspring. And ninety-nine mercies hath God reserved unto Himself, that therewith He may show mercy unto His slaves on the day of the Resurrection."[3]

Jābir also recounted how on the way back to Medina most of the troops went on ahead, while the Prophet and a few others were riding in the rear. But Jābir's camel was old and weak, and could not keep up with the main force, so that it was not long before the Prophet overtook him and asked him why he was so far behind. "O Messenger of God," he said, "this camel of mine can go no faster." "Make him kneel," said the Prophet, making his own camel kneel also. Then he said: "Give me that stick," which I did, and

[1] IV, 101–2. [2] W. 487. [3] M. XLIX, 4.

he took it and gave him one or two prods with it. Then he told me to mount, and we went on our way, and, by Him who sent the Messenger with the truth, my camel outstripped his.

"On the way I conversed with the Messenger of God, and he said to me: "Wilt thou sell me this camel of thine?" I said: "I will give him to thee." "Nay," he said, "but sell him to me." Jābir knew from the tone of the Prophet's voice that he was expected to bargain. "I asked him," said Jābir, "to name me a price and he said: 'I will take him for a dirhem.' 'Not so,' I said, 'for then wouldst thou be giving me too little.' 'For two dirhems,' he said. 'Nay,' said I, and he went on raising his price until he reached forty dirhems, that is, an ounce of gold, to which I agreed. Then he said: 'Art thou yet married, Jābir?' And when I said that I was, he said: 'An already married woman or a virgin?' 'One already married,' I said 'Why not a girl,' he said, 'that thou mightst play with her and she with thee?' 'O Messenger of God,' I said, 'my father was struck down on the day of Uḥud and left me with his seven daughters, so I married a motherly woman who would gather them round her and comb their hair and look after their wants.' He agreed that I had made a good choice; and then he said that when we reached Ṣirār, which was only about three miles from Medina, he would sacrifice camels and spend the day there, and she would have news of our home-coming and would set about shaking the dust from her cushions. 'We have no cushions,' I said. 'They will come,' he said. 'So when thou returnest, do what is to be done.'

"The morning after we returned, I took my camel and knelt him outside the Prophet's door. The Prophet came out and told me to leave the camel and pray two prayer cycles in the Mosque, which I did. Then he bade Bilāl weigh me out an ounce of gold, and he gave me a little more than what tipped the scales. I took it and turned to go, but the Prophet called me back. 'Take thy camel,' he said, 'he is thine, and keep the price thou wast paid for him.'"[1]

It was during these months, between one campaign and another, that Salmān the Persian came to the Prophet to seek his counsel and his help. His master, a Jew of the Bani Qurayẓah, kept him so hard at work on his property to the south of Medina that he had never been able to have a close contact with the Muslim community. It had been out of the question for him to be at Badr or Uḥud or to take part in any of the lesser forays which the Prophet had led or sent out during the last four years. Was there no way of escape from his present situation? He had asked his master what it would cost to set him free, but the price was far beyond his means. He would have to pay forty ounces of gold and plant three hundred date palms. The Prophet told him to write his master an agreement to pay the gold and plant the trees. Then he called on his Companions to help Salmān with the palms, which they did, one contributing thirty palm-shoots, another twenty, and so on, until the full number had been reached. "Go dig the holes for them, Salmān," said the Prophet, "and tell me when thou hast done, and mine is the hand that shall put them in." The Companions helped Salmān to prepare the ground, and the Prophet planted each of the three hundred shoots, which all took root and thrived.

[1] I.I. 664.

As to the remainder of the price, a piece of gold the size of a hen's egg had been given to the Prophet from one of the mines, and he gave it to Salmān, telling him to buy himself free with it. "How far will this go towards what I have to pay?" said Salmān, thinking that the price had been greatly underestimated. The Prophet took the gold from him and putting it in his mouth he rolled his tongue round it. Then he gave it back to Salmān, saying: "Take it, and pay them the full price with it." Salmān weighed out to them forty ounces from it, and so he became a free man.[1]

There was another month of peace in Medina, and then at the head of a thousand men the Prophet made a rapid northward march of about five hundred miles to the edge of Dūmat al-Jandal, an oasis on the borders of Syria, which had become infested with marauders, mostly from the Bani Kalb. They had more than once plundered provisions of oil and flour and other goods which were on their way to Medina. There was also reason to suppose that they had entered into some agreement with Quraysh, which meant that they would close in from the north when the day came for a general onslaught upon Islam. The Prophet and his Companions had that day continually in mind; and though the immediate result of the expedition was no more than the scattering of the marauders and the capture of their flocks and herds which were grazing on the southern pastures of the oasis, it had also the desired effect of impressing the northern tribes in general with a sense of the presence of a new and rapidly increasing power in Arabia. Gone were the years of civil discord which had made Yathrib so vulnerable to outside attack. That discord had been replaced by a closely united expansive strength which could strike far and wide with amazing speed, and which was all the more to be feared because it knew that attack was the surest means of defence.

Such was the outward impression; but for those who were capable of approaching nearer the strength was seen to be even greater than it appeared, for it was based on a unity that was itself a miracle. The Revelation had told the Prophet: *If thou hadst spent all that is in the earth, thou couldst not have united their hearts. But God hath united their hearts.*[2] The presence of the Prophet was none the less one of the great means of realising this unitedness. Providentially, the attraction of that presence had been made so powerful that no man of normal good will could resist it. "Not one of you hath faith until I am dearer to him than his son and his father and all men together."[3] But this utterance of the Prophet was not so much a demand as a confirmation of the rightness of a love that had already been given – a love which found its expression so often in the words: "May my father and my mother be thy ransom."

A time of peace was not a time of rest for the Prophet. He put forward as an ideal that a third of each cycle of twenty-four hours should be for worship, a third for work and a third for the family. This last third included the time spent in sleep and at meals. As to worship, much of it was done during the night. In addition to the evening and dawn prayers they performed voluntary prayers after the same pattern. The Koran also

[1] I.I. 141–2. [2] VIII, 63. [3] M. I, 16.

enjoined long recitations of its own verses, and the Prophet recommended various litanies of repentance and praise. Lengthy night worship had been established as a norm by the first Revelations, but the community which had received these had been a spiritual elect. Medina had also had its own initial elect of believers. But the rapid spread of Islam within recent years had made the elect something of a minority; and they are referred to as *a group of those that are with thee* in a verse which was now revealed to lessen the sense of obligation attached to long vigils: *Verily thy Lord knoweth that thou keepest vigil wellnigh two thirds of the night, and some times half of it or a third of it, thou and a group of those that are with thee. God measureth the night and the day. He knoweth that ye will not be able to come up to the full measure of it, and therefore hath He relented unto you. Recite then even so much of the Koran as is easy for you.*[1]

The elect of the Companions none the less continued to pray much at night, of which the last third was mentioned by the Prophet as being especially blessed: "Each night, when a third of it hath yet to come, our Lord – blessed and exalted be He! – descendeth unto the nethermost heaven, and He saith: 'Who calleth unto Me, that I may answer him? Who prayeth unto Me a prayer, that I may grant him it? Who asketh My forgiveness, that I may forgive him?' "[2] It was also revealed about this time, in definition of the believers: *They turn aside from their beds to invoke their Lord in fear and in longing, and of what We have given them they give. And no soul knoweth the hidden bliss that lieth in store for them as meed for that which they were wont to do.*[3]

The equal distribution of the hours of the daily cycle between the three claims of worship, work and the family could only be approximate. As regards family, the Prophet had no room of his own, and every evening he would move to the apartment of the wife whose turn it was to give him a home for the next twenty-four hours. During the day he had frequent visits from his daughters and from his aunt Ṣafiyyah, or he would visit them. Fāṭimah would often bring her two sons to see him. Ḥasan was now nearly a year and a half old, and the eight-month-old Ḥusayn was already beginning to walk. The Prophet also loved his little granddaughter Umāmah, who nearly always accompanied her mother Zaynab. Once or twice he brought her with him to the Mosque perched on his shoulder and kept her there while he recited the verses of the Koran, putting her down before the inclination and prostrations and restoring her to his shoulder when he resumed his upright position.[4] Another loved one was the fifteen-year-old Usāmah, the son of Zayd and Umm Ayman, very dear to the Prophet for the sake of both his parents and also for his own sake. As a grandson of the house, he was often to be found inside it or about its doors.

Most afternoons the Prophet would visit Abū Bakr as he had done in Mecca. To some extent the claims of family and of work coincided, for he often wished to talk with Abū Bakr about affairs of state, as he likewise did with Zayd and with his two sons-in-law 'Alī and 'Uthmān. But work was in danger of invading the Prophet's whole life, because no voice in all Medina could compare with his for solving a problem or answering a

[1] LXXIII, 20. [2] B. XIX, 12. [3] XXXII, 16–17. [4] I.S. VIII, 26.

question or settling a dispute. Even those who did not believe him to be a Prophet would seek his help if need be, unless they were too proud. Quarrels between Muslims and Jews were not infrequent, and misplaced fervour was often to blame, as when, for example, one of the Helpers struck a Jew merely on account of an oath which he heard him utter. "Wilt thou swear," said the Muslim, "'by Him who chose Moses above all mankind' when the Prophet is present in our midst?" The Jew complained to the Prophet, whose face was full of anger when he rebuked the aggressor. In the Koran itself God is mentioned as saying: *O Moses, I have chosen thee above all mankind by My messages and My speaking unto thee.*[1] The Koran had also said: *Verily God chose Adam and Noah and the family of Abraham and the family of 'Imrān above all the worlds.*[2] But divining what was in the man's mind, the Prophet added: "Say not that I am better than Moses."[3] He also said, perhaps referring to another example of misplaced zeal: "Let none of you say that I am better than Jonah."[4] The Revelation had already given them the words, as part of the Islamic creed: *We make no distinction between any of His messengers.*[5]

In addition to what concerned the welfare of the community as a whole, both in its inward harmony and in its relations with the rest of Arabia and beyond, scarcely a day passed when his advice or help was not sought by one or more of the believers in connection with some purely personal problem, either material, as in the recent case of Salmān, or spiritual, as when on one occasion Abū Bakr brought to him a man of the Bani Tamīm, Ḥanẓalah by name, who had settled in Medina. Ḥanẓalah had first approached Abū Bakr with his problem, but Abū Bakr felt that in this case the answer should come from the highest authority. The man's face was full of woe, and when the Prophet questioned him he said: "Ḥanẓalah is a hypocrite, O Messenger of God." The Prophet asked him what he meant, and he answered: "O Messenger of God, we are with thee, and thou tellest us of the Fire and of Paradise until it is as if they were before our very eyes. Then go we out from thy presence, and our minds are engrossed with our wives and our children and our properties, and much do we forget." The Prophet's answer made it clear that the ideal was to seek to perpetuate their consciousness of spiritual realities without altering the tenor of their daily lives: "By Him in whose hand is my soul," he said, "if ye were to remain perpetually as ye are in my presence, or as ye are in your times of remembrance of God, then would the Angels come to take you by the hand as ye lie in your beds or as ye go your ways. But yet, O Ḥanẓalah, now this and now that, now this and now that, now this and now that!"[6]

Such demands as these upon the Prophet's time were not to be avoided; but there was a growing need that he should be protected in other ways, and the protection that now came was not unconnected with the following altogether unexpected event which served to emphasise his uniquely privileged position. It happened one day that he wanted to speak to Zayd about something and went to his house. Zayd was out, and Zaynab, not expecting any visitors at that time, was lightly clad. But when she was told

1 VII, 144. 2 III, 33. 3 B. LXV, Sūrah VII.
4 B. LXV, Sūrah XXXVII. 5 See p. 102 6 M. XLIX, 2.

that the Prophet had come, she was so eager to greet him that she leaped to her feet and ran to the door, to invite him to stay until Zayd returned. "He is not here, O Messenger of God", she said, "but come thou in, my father and my mother be thy ransom."[1] As she stood in the doorway, a radiant figure of joyous welcome, the Prophet was amazed at her beauty. Deeply moved, he turned aside, and murmured something which she could not grasp. All she heard clearly were his words of wonderment as he walked away: "Glory be to God the Infinite! Glory be to Him who disposeth men's hearts!" When Zayd returned she told him of the Prophet's visit and of the glorification she had heard him utter. Zayd immediately went to him and said: "I have been told thou camest unto my house. Why didst not enter, thou who art more to me than my father and my mother? Was it that Zaynab hath found favour with thee? If it be so, I will leave her."[2] "Keep thy wife and fear God," said the Prophet with some insistence. He had said on another occasion: "Of all things licit the most hateful unto God is divorce."[3] And when Zayd came again the next day with the same proposal, again the Prophet insisted that he should keep his wife. But the marriage between Zayd and Zaynab had not been a happy one, and Zayd found it no longer tolerable, so by mutual agreement with Zaynab he divorced her. This did not, however, make Zaynab eligible as a wife for the Prophet for although the Koran had only specified that men were forbidden to marry the wives of sons *sprung from their loins*, it was a strong social principle not to make a distinction between sons by birth and sons by adoption. Nor was the Prophet himself eligible, for he had already four wives, the most that the Islamic law allows.

Some months passed and then one day when the Prophet was talking with one of his wives the power of the Revelation overwhelmed him; and when he came to himself his first words were: "Who will go unto Zaynab and tell her the good tidings that God hath given her to me in marriage, even from Heaven?" Salmà was near at hand – Safiyyah's servant who had long considered herself a member of the Prophet's household – and she went in haste to Zaynab's house. When she heard the wonderful tidings, Zaynab magnified God and threw herself down in prostration towards Mecca. Then she took off her anklets and bracelets of silver, and gave them to Salmà.

Zaynab was no longer young, being almost in her fortieth year, but she had retained the appearance of youth. She was, moreover, a woman of great piety, who fasted much and kept long vigils and gave generously to the poor. As a skilled worker in leather she could make shoes and other objects, and all that she earned in this way was for her a means of charity. There could be no question in her case of any formal wedding, for the marriage was announced in the revealed verses as a bond already contracted: *We have married her to thee.*[4] It remained for the bride to be brought to the bridegroom, and this was done without delay.

The verses also said that in future adopted sons should be named after their fathers who begot them; and from that day Zayd was known as Zayd ibn Ḥārithah instead of Zayd ibn Muḥammad, as he had been called ever

[1] Ibn Sa'd, VIII, 71. [2] ibid., 72. See also Ṭab., *Tafsīr*, Bayḍāwī, Jalālayn, etc., on K.xxxiii, 37. [3] A.D. XIII, 3. [4] XXXIII, 40.

since his adoption some thirty-five years previously. But this change did not annul his adoption as such, nor did it affect in any way the love and the intimacy between the adopter and the adopted, who were now nearing their sixtieth and fiftieth years. It was merely a reminder that there was no blood relationship; and in this sense the Revelation continued: *Muḥammad is not the father of any man amongst you, but he is the Messenger of God and the Seal of the Prophets.*[1]

At the same time other Revelations stressed the great difference between the Prophet and his followers. They were not to address him ever by his name as they addressed each other. The permission which God had given him, in virtue of his new marriage, to have more than four wives, was for him alone, and not for the rest of the community. Moreover, his wives were given the title of *the mothers of the faithful*, and their status was such that it would be an enormity in the eyes of God if, having been married to the Prophet, they should ever be given in marriage to another man. If the believers wished to ask a favour of one of them – for their intercession with the Prophet was often sought – they must do so from behind a curtain. They were also told: *O ye who have faith, enter not the dwellings of the Prophet unto a meal without waiting for its time to come, except if leave be given you. But if ye are invited then enter, and when ye have fed then disperse. Linger not in hope of discourse. Verily that would be irksome unto the Prophet, and he would shrink from telling you, but God shrinketh not from the truth.*[2]

Such precepts were necessary on account of the great love they bore him, and their desire to be in his presence as long and as often as possible. Those who were with him were always loath to leave him. Nor could they have been blamed if they stayed, for when he spoke to anyone he would turn to him so fully and make him so amply the object of his attention that the man might well imagine himself to be privileged enough for liberties which others dared not take; and when he took a man's hand he was never the first to relinquish his hold. But while protecting the Prophet, the Revelation introduced at this time a new element into the liturgy, which made it possible for his people to give expression to their love and to benefit from his spiritual radiance without imposing unduly their presences upon him: *Verily God and His angels whelm in blessings the prophet. O ye who believe, invoke blessings upon him and give him greetings of Peace.*[3] And shortly afterwards the Prophet told one of his Companions: "An Angel came unto me and said: 'None invoketh blessings upon thee once, but God invoketh blessings upon him tenfold.'"[4]

[1] XXXIII, 40. [2] XXXIII, 53. [3] XXXIII, 56. [4] D. XX, 58.

# LIX

# *The Trench*

THE exiled Jews of Bani Naḍīr who had settled in Khaybar were determined to recover the land they had lost. Their hopes were centred on the preparations of Quraysh for a final attack on the Prophet; and towards the end of the fifth year of Islam – it was about the New Year of AD 627 – these preparations were brought to a head by a secret visit to Mecca of Ḥuyay and other Jewish leaders from Khaybar. "We are one with you," they said to Abū Sufyān, "that we may extirpate Muḥammad." "The dearest of men to us", he replied, "are those who help us against Muḥammad." So he and Ṣafwān and other chiefs of Quraysh took the Jews inside the Ka'bah, and together they swore a solemn oath to God that they would not fail one another until they had achieved their end and aim. Then it occurred to Quraysh that they should take this opportunity of asking the opinion of the Jews about the rights of their conflict with the founder of the new religion. "Men of the Jews," said Abū Sufyān, "ye are the people of the first scripture, and ye have knowledge. Tell us how we stand with regard unto Muḥammad. Is our religion the better or his?" They answered: "Your religion is better than his, and ye are nearer the truth than he is."

On this harmonious basis the two allies laid their plans. The Jews undertook to rouse up all the nomads in the plain of Najd who had grievances against Medina; and where desire for revenge was not sufficient the matter was to be clinched by bribery. The Bani Asad readily agreed to help them; as to the Bani Ghaṭafān, they were promised half the date harvest of Khaybar if they would join the confederacy, and their agreement to do so increased the army by nearly two thousand men, from the Ghaṭafānite clans of Fazārah, Murrah and Ashja'. The Jews also succeeded in securing a contingent from the Bani Sulaym seven hundred strong, which would no doubt have been larger but for the fact that ever since the massacre at the well of Ma'ūnah a small but increasing party within this tribe had been favourable to Islam. As to the southerly neighbour of Sulaym, the Bani 'Āmir, they remained altogether faithful to their pact with the Prophet.

Quraysh themselves and their closest allies were four thousand strong. Together with one or two other contingents from the south, they were to march out from Mecca along the west coastal route to Medina, the same route which they had taken to Uḥud. The second army, which was considerably less of a unity, was to close in on Medina from the east, that is, from the plain of Najd. Together the two armies were estimated at a total of more than three times the strength of Quraysh at Uḥud. There the Muslims had been defeated by a force of three thousand. What could they now hope to do against ten thousand? Moreover, instead of a troop of only two hundred horse, Quraysh had this time three hundred and could rely on Ghaṭafān for another troop of the same strength.

They marched forth from Mecca according to plan; and about the same time, possibly with the connivance of ʻAbbās, a number of horsemen from the Bani Khuzāʻah set out with all speed for Medina to warn the Prophet of the impending attack and to give him details of its strength. They reached him in four days, thus giving him only a week to make preparations. He at once alerted the whole oasis and spoke words of encouragement to his followers, promising them the victory if only they would have patience and fear God and obey orders. Then, as he had done at Uḥud, he summoned them to a consultation at which many opinions were expressed as to what would be the best plan of action; but finally Salmān rose to his feet and said: "O Messenger of God, in Persia when we feared an attack of horse, we would surround ourselves with a trench, so let us dig a trench about us now." Everyone agreed to this plan with enthusiasm, the more so as they were averse to repeating the strategy of Uḥud.

Time was short and all efforts would have to be strained to the utmost if no dangerous gap was to be left in the defences. But the trench did not need to be continuous; at many places a long stretch of fortress-like houses at the edge of the city was adequate protection; and to the north-west there were some masses of rock which in themselves were impregnable and merely needed to be connected to each other. The nearest of these, known as Mount Salʻ, was to be brought within the entrenchments, for the ground in front of it was an excellent site for the camp. The trench itself would bound the camp to the north in a wide sweep from one of the rocky eminences to a point on the eastern wall of the town. This was to be the longest single stretch of trench and also the most important.

As well as being the originator of the strategy, Salmān knew exactly how wide and how deep the trench would have to be; and having worked with the Bani Qurayẓah, he knew that they possessed all the implements that were needed. Nor were they averse to lending them in the face of the common danger; for although they had no love for the Prophet the majority of opinion amongst them had been that their pact with him was a political advantage, not to be thrown away. So mattocks, pickaxes and shovels were borrowed from them. They also supplied date-baskets which were strongly woven of palm-fibre and could thus be used for carrying the excavated earth.

The Prophet made each section of his community responsible for a part of the trench and he himself worked with them. They went out at dawn every day immediately after the prayers, and came home at twilight. As he led them out on one of the first mornings he chanted a reminder of their work at building the Mosque:

> "O God, no good is but the good hereafter.
> Forgive the Helpers and the Emigrants!"

It was immediately taken up by them all; and sometimes they chanted:

"O God, no life is but the life hereafter.
Have mercy on the Helpers and the Emigrants!"

They continually reminded each other that the time was short. The enemy would soon be upon them, and if any man showed signs of flagging he was at once an object of mockery. Salmān, on the other hand, was an object of admiration, for he was not only very strong and able-bodied but for years he had been used to digging and carrying for the Bani Qurayẓah. "He doth the work of ten men," they said, and a friendly rivalry started up between them. "Salmān is ours," the Emigrants claimed, in virtue of his having left many homes in search of guidance. "He is one of us," the Helpers retorted; "we have more right to him." But the Prophet said: "Salmān is one of us, the people of the House."[1]

Excavated rocks and stones that might serve as missiles were piled up along the Medina side of the trench; the earth they carried away in baskets on their heads, and having dumped it they filled the baskets with stones which they brought back to the trench. The best stones were to be found at the foot of Mount Sal'. The men were all stripped to the waist, and those who could not lay hands on baskets knotted into sacks the outer garments they had doffed and used them to shift the earth and also the stones. On the first morning they had been followed out to the camp by a number of boys, all eager to take part in the work. The youngest had been sent home forthwith, but the Prophet allowed many of the others to dig and carry on the understanding that they would have to leave the camp as soon as the enemy appeared. As to those who had been sent home from Uḥud, Usāmah and 'Umar's son 'Abd Allāh and their friends, they were now fifteen years old, and they and others of their age were allowed to join the ranks of the men not only for the work but also for the battle when it came. One of them, Barā' of the Ḥārithah clan of Aws, would tell in after years of the great beauty of the Prophet as he remembered him at the trench, girt with a red cloak, his breast sprinkled with dust and his black hair long enough to touch his shoulders. "More beautiful than him I have not seen," he would say. Nor was he alone conscious of this beauty, and of the general beauty of the scene. In particular the Prophet himself, as he looked about him, rejoiced at their simplicity and their nearness to nature – the nearness to man's primordial heritage – and he started a song in which everyone joined:

"This beauty not the beauty is of Khaybar.
More innocent it is, O Lord, and purer."[2]

He worked now with the Emigrants, and now with the Helpers, sometimes with a pickaxe, sometimes with a shovel and sometimes as a carrier. But wherever he might be, it was understood that he must be informed of any unusual difficulty. Despite the hardness of the work there

[1] The Prophet's family. [2] W. 446.

were moments of merriment. A convert from the Bani Ḍamrah, one of the People of the Bench who lived in the Mosque, was a man of considerable piety but in looks he was not well favoured and his parents had moreover given him the name Ju'ayl, which has the secondary meaning of "little beetle". The Prophet had recently changed this to the fine name of 'Amr, which means life, spiritual well-being, religion. The sight of the Ḍamrite digging at the trench prompted one of the Emigrants to a couplet:

"His name he changed, Ju'ayl to 'Amr,
Gave the poor man that day his help."

He repeated this to 'Amr, and those who overheard it took it up and made a song of it, not without laughter. The Prophet joined in this only at the words "'Amr" and "help", which he pronounced each time with considerable emphasis. Then he led them into another song:

"Lord but for Thee we never had been guided,
Never had given alms nor prayed Thy prayer.
Send then serenity upon us,
Make firm our feet for the encounter.
These foes oppressed us, sought to pervert us,
But we refused."[1]

The first cry for help came from Jābir, who had dug down to a rock which none of their implements could loosen. The Prophet called for some water and spat into it; then having prayed, he sprinkled the water over the rock, and they were able to shovel it out like a heap of sand.[2] Another day it was the Emigrants who needed help. After many vain attempts to split or dislodge a rock he had struck, 'Umar went to the Prophet, who took the pickaxe from him and gave the rock a blow at which a flare as of lightning flashed back over the city and towards the south. He gave it another blow and again there was a flash but in the direction of Uḥud and beyond it towards the north. A third blow split the rock into fragments, and this time the light flashed eastwards. Salmān saw the three flashes and knew they must have some significance, so he asked for an interpretation from the Prophet, who said: "Didst thou see them, Salmān? By the light of the first I saw the castles of the Yemen; by the light of the second I saw the castles of Syria; by the light of the third I saw the white palace of Kisra[3] at Madā'in. Through the first hath God opened unto me the Yemen; through the second hath He opened unto me Syria and the West; and through the third the East."[4]

Most of the diggers at the trench had not normally enough to eat, and the hard work increased the pangs of hunger. In particular, Jābir had been struck by the Prophet's exceeding leanness the day he had needed his help at the trench, and that evening he asked his wife if she could not cook him a meal. "We have naught but this ewe," she said "and a measure of barley." So he sacrificed the ewe, and the next day she roasted it and ground the

1 W. 448–9; I.S. II/1, 51. 2 I.I. 671.
3 Chrosroes, King of Persia. 4 W. 450.

barley and made some bread. Then, when it was too dark to continue working, Jābir went to the Prophet as he was leaving the trench and invited him to the meal of mutton and barley bread. "The Prophet put his palm against mine", said Jābir, "and knotted his fingers through my fingers. I wanted him to come alone, but he told a crier to call out: 'Go with the Messenger of God unto the house of Jābir. Respond, for Jābir inviteth you.'" Jābir uttered the verse which the faithful are recommended to utter at a moment of disaster: *Verily we are for God, and verily unto Him are we returning*, and he went on ahead to warn his wife. "Didst thou invite them or did he?" she said. "Nay, he invited them," said Jābir. "Then let them come," she said, "for he knoweth best." The meal was placed in front of the Prophet and he blessed it and uttered the Name of God over it and began to eat. There were ten sitting down with him, and when they had all eaten their fill they rose and went to their homes, making room for ten more, and so it went on until all the workers at the trench had satisfied their hunger, and there still remained some mutton and some bread.[1]

On another day the Prophet saw a girl enter the camp with something in her hand, and he called her to him. It was the niece of 'Abd Allāh ibn Rawāḥah. In her own words: "When I told the Messenger of God that I was taking some dates to my father and mine uncle, he bade me give them to him. So I poured them into his hands, but they did not fill them. He called for a garment, which was spread out for him, and he threw the dates upon it in such wise that they were scattered over its surface. Then he bade those who were with him invite the diggers to lunch, and when they came they began to eat, and the dates increased and they were still overflowing from the edges of the garment when the men turned away from them."[2]

[1] I.I. 672; W. 452. [2] I.I. 672.

# LX

# *The Siege*

SCARCELY had the trench been finished – it took them six days in all – when news came that the army of Quraysh were approaching down the valley of 'Aqīq and were now a little to the south-west of the town, while Ghaṭafān and the other tribes of Najd were moving towards Uḥud from the east. All the outlying houses of the oasis had already been evacuated and their tenants housed within the defences. The Prophet now gave orders for every woman and child to be allocated a place in one or other of the upper rooms of the fortresses. Then he encamped with his men, about three thousand in all, on the chosen site. His tent of red leather was pitched at the foot of Mount Sal'. 'Ā'ishah, Umm Salamah and Zaynab took turns to be with him there.

The Meccan army and their allies pitched separate camps not far from Uhud. Quraysh were dismayed to find that the crops of the oasis had already been harvested. Their camels would have to subsist on the acacias of the valley of 'Aqīq. Meantime the camels of Ghaṭafān were living on the two kinds of tamarisk which grow in the thicketed parts of the plain near Uhud. But there was nothing for the horses of either army except the fodder they had brought with them. It was therefore imperative to make an end of the enemy as quickly as possible, and with this intention the two armies joined together and advanced in the direction of the city. Abū Sufyān was commander-in-chief, but by turns each of the various leaders was to have his day of honour in which he would direct the actual fighting. Khālid and 'Ikrimah were again in command of the Meccan cavalry, and 'Amr was in Khālid's troop. As they approached they were heartened to see the enemy camp in front of them outside the town. They had been afraid that they would find them garrisoned behind their battlements; but out in the open they should be able to overwhelm them by sheer weight of numbers. When they drew nearer, however, they were amazed to see that a broad trench lay between them and the archers who were lined the whole way along it on its further side. Their horse would only be able to reach it with difficulty, and then would come the greater difficulty of crossing it. Even now a shower of arrows told them that they were already within range of the enemy, so they drew back to a safer distance.

The rest of the day was spent in consultation and finally they decided that their best hope lay in the possibility of forcing the enemy to withdraw their troops in large numbers from the north of the town in order to defend it elsewhere. If the trench were sufficiently unmanned, it should not be too difficult to cross it. Their thoughts turned towards the Bani Qurayẓah, whose fortresses blocked the approach to Medina from the south-east. According to agreement, Ḥuyay of the Bani Naḍīr had come from Khaybar to join the army, and he now pressed his services on Abū Sufyān as ambassador to his fellow Jews, assuring him that he could easily persuade them to break their pact with Muḥammad; and once their help had been secured the town could be attacked from two directions simultaneously. Abū Sufyān gladly accepted his offer, and urged him to lose no time.

The Bani Qurayẓah were afraid of Ḥuyay; they looked on him as a bearer of bad fortune, an inauspicious man who had brought disaster upon his own people, and who would do the same for them if they let him have his way. They feared him all the more because he had an overwhelming power of soul that was difficult to counter. If he wanted something, he would wear down all opposition and neither rest himself nor let others rest until he had gained his end. He now went to the fortress of Ka'b ibn Asad, the chief of Qurayẓah – it was he who had made their pact with the Prophet – and knocked on the gate, announcing who he was. Ka'b at first refused to unbolt it. "Confound thee, Ka'b," said Ḥuyay, "let me in." "Confound thee, Ḥuyay," said Ka'b, knowing well what he wanted. "I have made a pact with Muḥammad, and I will not break what is between me and him." "Let me in," said Ḥuyay, "and let us talk." "I will not," said Ka'b; but finally Ḥuyay accused him of not letting him in simply because he grudged sharing his food with him, and this so angered Ka'b that he opened the gate. "Confound thee, Ka'b," he said, "I have brought thee lasting glory for all time and power like that of a raging sea. I have brought thee Quraysh and Kinānah and Ghaṭafān with their leaders and chiefs, a full ten thousand of them, with their horse a thousand strong. They have sworn to me that they will not rest until they have rooted out Muḥammad and those with him. This time Muḥammad shall not escape." "By God," said Ka'b, "thou hast brought me shame for all time – a cloud without water, all thunder and lightning, and naught else in it. Confound thee, Ḥuyay. Leave me and let me be as I am." Ḥuyay saw that he was weakening, and his eloquent tongue enlarged on the great advantages that would come to them all if the new religion were blotted out. Finally, he swore by God the most solemn oath: "If Quraysh and Ghaṭafān return to their territories and have not smitten down Muḥammad, I will enter with thee into thy fortress, and my fate shall be as thine." This convinced Ka'b that there could be no possibility of survival for Islam, and he agreed to renounce the pact between his people and the Prophet. Ḥuyay asked to see the document, and when he had read it he tore it in two. Ka'b now went to tell his fellow tribesmen what had passed between them. "What advantage is it," they said, "if thou art slain, that Ḥuyay should be slain with thee?" and at first he met with considerable opposition. It was amongst the Bani Qurayẓah that Ibn al-Hayyabān had come to live, the old Jew from Syria who had hoped to meet the coming Prophet and who had described him and insisted that his advent was at hand, and many of them felt that Muḥammad must indeed be the man, though few of these were capable of being interested in a Prophet who was not a Jew, and still fewer were capable of drawing any practical conclusions about the gravity of opposing a Prophet, be he Jew or Gentile. As for the majority, they were simply averse to breaking a political pact; but when some of the hypocrites brought news which confirmed what Ḥuyay had said, and when some of their own men went singly and unobtrusively to see for themselves, the general opinion began to swing in favour of Quraysh and their allies. It was indeed a formidable sight, looking across the trench from the Medina side, to see the plain beyond it surging with men and horses as far and wide as the eye could reach.

Meantime Khālid and 'Ikrimah were examining the trench, albeit from a distance, to see where it might most easily be crossed. "This piece of trickery!" they exclaimed in exasperation. "Never have Arabs resorted to such a device. There must surely be with him a man of Persia." To their disappointment they saw that the work had been all too well done, except for a short section which was slightly narrower than the rest, and this was closely guarded. One or two attempts to storm it were a total failure. Their horses had never seen anything like the trench and manifested a strong aversion for it. This might change, but for the moment the fighting could be no more than an interchange of archery.

The Bani Qurayẓah's renunciation of their pact did not remain hidden. Many of the hypocrites were undetermined as to which side they belonged to, and they were ready to betray the secrets of either side to the other. 'Umar was the first of the Companions to hear that the Jews were now a potential enemy. He went to the Prophet, who was sitting in his tent with Abū Bakr. "O Messenger of God," he said, "I have been told that Bani Qurayẓah have broken their treaty and are at war with us." The Prophet was visibly troubled; and he sent Zubayr to find out the truth of the matter. Then, lest the Helpers should feel themselves to have been excluded, he called the two Sa'ds of Aws and Khazraj to him together with Usayd, and having told them the news he said: "Go and see if it be true. If it be false, then say so plainly. But if it be true, then tell me in some subtle way that I shall understand." They reached the fortresses of Qurayẓah soon after Zubayr and found that they had indeed renounced the pact. They adjured them by God to revert to it again before it was too late, but they only answered: "Who is the Messenger of God? There is no pact between us and Muḥammad nor any agreement." In vain they reminded them of the fates of the Bani Qaynuqā' and the Bani Naḍīr. Ka'b and the others were now too confident of the victory of Quraysh to listen to them; and when they saw that they were wasting their words they returned to the Prophet. " 'Aḍal and Qārah," they said to him, these being the two tribes who had betrayed Khubayb and his companions to the men of Hudhayl. The Prophet understood and magnified God: "*Allāhu Akbar!* Be of good cheer, O Muslims."

It was now necessary to reduce the strength of the forces at the trench and to keep a garrison within the town itself, so the Prophet sent back a hundred men. Then the warning came to him that Ḥuyay was urging Quraysh and Ghaṭafān to send by night each a thousand men to the fortresses of Qurayẓah and from there to raid the centre of the town and break into the fortresses of the Muslims and carry off their women and children. The appointed night, for various reasons, was put off more than once, and the project was never realised; but as soon as the Prophet heard of it he sent Zayd with a troop of three hundred horse to patrol the streets, magnifying God throughout each night, and it was as if the city was filled with a mighty host.

The horses were not needed at the camp, but the troops were sorely missed, for the trench had to be manned day and night, so that each man now kept watch for longer hours. The days passed and the strain was very great, with Khālid and ʻIkrimah and their men ever seeking to take advantage of a moment of slackness. But only once did they succeed in crossing the trench, and that was when ʻIkrimah suddenly noticed that the narrowest section happened for the moment to be badly guarded. He succeeded in making his horse leap the gap, and he was followed by three others. But by the time the fourth man had crossed, ʻAlī and those with him had remanned the narrow sector and made it once more impregnable, thereby also cutting off the retreat of the horsemen who were now on their side. One of these, ʻAmr, shouted a challenge to single combat. When ʻAlī offered himself he refused, saying: "I hate to kill the like of thee. Thy father was a boon companion of mine. Therefore go back, thou art but a stripling." But ʻAlī insisted, so ʻAmr dismounted and both men advanced. A cloud of dust soon hid them from view; then they heard ʻAlī's voice raised in magnification and they knew that ʻAmr was dead or dying. Meantime ʻIkrimah and his fellows took advantage of the distraction to regain the other side, but Nawfal of Makhzūm failed to clear the gap and his horse fell with him into the trench. They began to stone him but he called out: "O Arabs, death is better than this," so they went down and dispatched him.

The crossing of the trench, although abortive, had shown that it was a possibility; and the next day attacks had been made at various points even before sunrise. The Prophet exhorted the believers and promised them the victory if they were steadfast, and steadfast they remained, despite their initial weariness from the strain of overlong watches. The site of the camp had been well chosen, for the slope of the ground away from Mount Salʻ meant that the near bank was considerably higher than the far bank. Again and again throughout the day the enemy tried to force their way across, but they could achieve nothing, and the actual fighting was limited, as on previous days, to a discharge of archery. Nor was anyone killed on either side, but Saʻd ibn Muʻādh was struck in the arm by an arrow which severed a vein, and many of the horses of Quraysh and Ghaṭafān were wounded.

The time for the noon prayer came, but there was no question of any man relaxing his vigilance for a moment. When the time was running out, those who were nearest the Prophet called to him: "O Messenger of God, we have not prayed" – an obvious fact but greatly disturbing because such a thing had never happened before since the outset of Islam. His rejoinder reassured them somewhat: "Nor I, by God, I have not prayed." The time for the mid-afternoon prayer came, and went with the setting of the sun. But even so the enemy kept up their attacks, and it was only when the last light had faded from the west that they moved back to their two camps. As soon as they were out of sight the Prophet withdrew from the trench, leaving Usayd to continue on guard with a detachment of men, while he himself led the remainder in the four prayers which were now incumbent. Khālid suddenly reappeared later that evening with a body of horse in the hope that he would find the trench unguarded, but Usayd and his archers kept them at bay.

The Revelation referred to the strain of those days as the time *when eyes could no longer look with steadiness, and when men's hearts rose up into their throats, and ye were thinking strange thoughts about God. There the believers were tested and tried, and their souls were quaked with a mighty quaking.*[1]

The question arose in every mind as to how many more such days could be endured. Food was beginning to run short and the nights were exceptionally cold; and many of the weak in faith, unnerved by hunger and cold and lack of sleep, were almost ready to join the hypocrites, who were passing round the word that it was not possible to continue to resist such an enemy with only a trench between them, and that they should withdraw behind the city walls. But the faith of the true believers was confirmed by the hardship, and they received praise from the Revelation for having said, at the times of greatest stress, when they saw the clans massed together against them: *This is that which God and His Messenger did promise us. That which God and His Messenger foretold hath truly come to pass.* The Revelation added: *And it did but increase them in faith and in submission.*[2] They had spoken thus in recollection of a verse that had been revealed to the Prophet two or three years previously: *Think ye to enter Paradise, while yet there hath not come unto you the like of what came unto those who passed away before you? Affliction smote them and injuries and they were made to quake until the Messenger of God said, and with him those who believed: When cometh the help of God? Lo, verily the help of God is nigh.*[3]

The Prophet knew that in many souls amongst his people the powers of endurance were nearing their end. But he knew also that as each day passed the enemy likewise felt the grip of hardship tighten upon them. So he found a way of sending word by night to two of the chiefs of Ghaṭafān, offering them a third of the date harvest of Medina if they would withdraw from the field. They sent back word: "Give us half the dates of Medina." But he refused to increase his offer of a third, and they agreed to this, whereupon he sent for 'Uthmān and told him to draw up a peace treaty between the believers and the clans of Ghaṭafān. Then he sent for the two Sa'ds and they came to his tent – the chief of Aws with his wounded arm bound up – and he told them of his plan. They said: "O Messenger of God, is this something which thou wouldst have us do, or which God hath commanded and must be done? Or is it something which thou doest for our sakes?" He answered them: "It is something which I do for your sakes, and by God I would not do it but that I see the Arabs have shot at you from one bow and assailed you from every side, and I would break some of the sharpness of their assault against you." But the wounded Sa'd said to him: "O Messenger of God, we and these folk were believers in gods together with God, worshippers of idols, not truly worshipping God nor knowing Him.

[1] XXXIII, 10–11. [2] XXXIII, 22. [3] II, 214.

They then had no hope to eat one date of ours, save as guests or by barter. And now that God hath endowed us with Islam and guided us and strengthened us with thee and with it, shall we give them our goods? By God, we will give them naught but the sword, until He decide between us." "Be it as thou wilt," said the Prophet, and Sa'd took the pen and the vellum from 'Uthmān and struck through what had been written, saying: "Let them do their worst!"[1]

These negotiations which now came to nothing had been with the chiefs of the two clans of Fazārah and Murrah. The third Ghaṭafānite ally of Quraysh was the clan of Ashja' to which Nu'aym belonged, the man whom Abū Sufyān and Suhayl had bribed to intimidate, if he could, the Muslims from keeping their promise to meet the Meccans at the second Badr. His stay in Medina had profoundly affected him, and it was therefore with mixed feelings that he had now come out with the rest of his clan to support the Meccans on this occasion. His admiration for the men of the new religion had been confirmed and increased by their resistance to an army more than three times their strength. Then came the hour when, as he himself said, "God cast Islam into my heart"; and that night – it was almost immediately after the project of a separate truce with Ghaṭafān had been abandoned – he made his way into the city and thence to the camp, where he asked to see the Prophet. "What hath brought thee here, Nu'aym?" he said. "I have come," he answered, "to declare my belief in thy word and testify that thou hast brought the truth. So bid me do what thou wilt, O Messenger of God, for thou hast but to command me, and I will fulfil thy behest. My people and others know naught of my Islam." "To the utmost of thy power," replied the Prophet, "set them at odds with each other." Nu'aym asked permission to lie and the Prophet said. "Say what thou wilt to draw them off from us, for war is deception."[2]

Nu'aym went back through the town and made his way to the Bani Qurayẓah, who welcomed him as an old friend and offered him food and drink. "I came not for this," he said, "but to warn you of my fears for your safety and to give you my counsel." Then he proceeded to point out to them that if Quraysh and Ghaṭafān failed to inflict a decisive defeat on their enemy they would return home and leave the Jews at the mercy of Muḥammad and his followers. Therefore they should refuse to strike one blow for Quraysh until they had been given leading men as hostages, in guarantee that they would not withdraw until the enemy had been overwhelmed. His advice was accepted with enthusiasm by the Bani Qurayẓah, who had been increasingly beset by the very fears he had touched on. So they agreed to do what he had said, and promised not to tell his own people or Quraysh that it was he who had given them this counsel.

Then he went to his one-time friend Abū Sufyān and told him and the other chiefs of Quraysh who were with him that he had a very serious piece of information to impart, on the condition, which they agreed to, that they would swear to tell no one that he was their informer. "The Jews regret their treatment of Muḥammad," he said, "and they have sent to him saying: 'We regret what we have done, and will it satisfy thee if we take as

[1] I.I. 676. [2] I.I. 681; W. 480–1.

hostages some of the leading men of Quraysh and Ghaṭafān and give them to thee that thou mayst cut off their heads? Then will we fight with thee against those that be left.' Muḥammad hath sent them his agreement; so if the Jews ask you for some of your men as hostages, give them not one man of yours." Then he went to his own people and the other clans of Ghaṭafān and told them the same as he had told Quraysh.

After consultation, the leaders of the two invading armies decided to say nothing for the moment to Ḥuyay, but to put to the test what Nu'aym had said. So they sent 'Ikrimah to the Bani Qurayẓah with the message: "Make ye ready to fight on the morrow, that once and for all we may rid ourselves of Muḥammad." They answered: "Tomorrow is the Sabbath; nor in any case will we fight with you against Muḥammad unless ye give us hostages who shall be for us as a security until we have made an end of him. For we fear that if the battle go against you ye will withdraw to your own country, leaving us with that man in ours, and we cannot face him alone." When this message reached Quraysh and Ghaṭafān they said: "By God, what Nu'aym told us is indeed the truth." And they sent again to Bani Qurayẓah saying that they would not give them a single man, but bidding them fight none the less, which drew from them the answer that they would not strike one blow until they had received hostages.

Abū Sufyān now went to Ḥuyay and said: "Where is the help thou didst promise us from thy people? They have deserted us, and now they seek to betray us." "By the Torah, nay!" said Ḥuyay. "The Sabbath is here, and we cannot break the Sabbath. But on Sunday they will fight against Muḥammad and his companions like blazing fire." It was only then that Abū Sufyān told him about the demand for hostages. Ḥuyay was visibly taken aback, and interpreting his disconcertedness as a sign of guilt, Abū Sufyān said: "I swear by al-Lāt that this is naught but your treachery, theirs and thine, for I account thee as having entered into the treachery of thy people." "Nay," he protested, "by the Torah that was revealed unto Moses on the day of Mount Sinai, I am no traitor." But Abū Sufyān was unconvinced, and fearing for his life, Ḥuyay left the camp and made his way to the fortresses of the Bani Qurayẓah.

As to the relations between Quraysh and the tribes of Najd, there was little need for any action on the part of Nu'aym. Nearly two weeks had passed and nothing had been achieved. The provisions of both their armies were running out, while more and more of their horses were dying every day, of hunger or of arrow wounds or of both. Some camels had also died. Nor could Quraysh fail to perceive that Ghaṭafān and the other Bedouin were at the best reluctant allies. They had taken part in the campaign far more in hopes of plunder than out of hostility to the new religion; and those hopes by which they had been lured to the Yathrib oasis had proved totally vain. Recriminations were on many tongues, and mutual distrust spread throughout the two invading armies. The expedition had virtually failed; and now the final seal of failure was placed upon it by Heaven.

For three days, after the ritual prayer, the Prophet had uttered the supplication: "O God, Revealer of the Book, Swift Caller to account, turn the confederates to flight, turn them to flight and cause them to quake."[1]

[1] I.S. II/1, 53; W. 487.

And when all was over this verse was revealed: *O ye who believe, remember God's favour unto you when hosts came at you and We sent against them a wind and hosts ye saw not.*[1]

For days the weather had been exceptionally cold and wet; and now a piercing wind came from the east with torrents of rain which forced every man to take shelter. The night fell, and a tempest raged over the plain. The wind rose to hurricane force and what the wind did not accomplish was done by unseen hands. Throughout the two camps of the invaders there was soon not one tent left standing nor any fire left burning, and the men crouched shivering on the ground, huddled together for warmth.

The Muslims' camp was somewhat sheltered from the wind, which blew down none of their tents. But its bitterness filled the air, and together with the accumulated strain of the siege it reduced the believers to a weakness of soul that they would not have thought possible. The Prophet prayed late into the night; then he went among the men who happened to be nearest to his tent, and one of them, Ḥudhayfah the son of Yamān, told afterwards how they had heard him say: "Which of you will rise and go to see what the enemy are about and then return, and I will ask of God that he shall be my Companion in Paradise?" But there was no response. "We were so unnerved," said Ḥudhayfah, "so cold and so hungry that not one man rose to his feet." When it became clear that no one was intending to offer himself, the Prophet called to Ḥudhayfah, who rose and went to him, spurred into action by being singled out from the rest. "I could not but rise," he said, "when I heard my name upon his lips." "Go thou," said the Prophet, "and enter in amongst the men and see what they are about; but do naught else until thou hast returned unto us." "So I went," said Ḥudhayfah, "and entered amongst the people while the wind and the hosts of God were doing their work against them." He told how he made his way amongst the crouching figures of Quraysh – for it was to their camp that he had gone – until he came near to where their commander was seated. They spent the night benumbed with cold, and then towards dawn, when the wind began to abate, Abū Sufyān cried out in a loud voice: "Men of Quraysh, our horses and our camels are dying; the Bani Qurayẓah have failed us, and we have been informed that they seek to betray us; and now we have suffered from the wind what your eyes behold. Therefore begone from this place, for I am going." With these words he went to his camel and mounted it, so eager to set off that he forgot to untie its hobble, which he did only after he had forced it to rise on three legs. But 'Ikrimah said to him: "Thou art the head of the people and their leader. Wilt thou be clear of us so hastily, and leave the men behind?" whereupon Abū Sufyān was ashamed, and making his camel kneel once more, he dismounted. The army broke camp and moved off, and he waited until most of them were on the homeward march. Then he set off himself, having agreed with Khālid and 'Amr that they should bring up the rear with a detachment of two hundred horse. While they were waiting, Khālid said: "Every man of sense now knoweth that Muḥammad hath not lied," but Abū Sufyān cut him short saying: "Thou hast more right not to say so than any man else." "Wherefore?" said Khālid. And he answered: "Because Muḥammad

[1] XXXIII, 9.

belittled the honour of thy father, and slew the chief of thy clan, Abū Jahl."

As soon as Ḥudhayfah had heard the order to march he made his way to the camp of Ghaṭafān, but found the place deserted, for the wind had broken their resistance also and they were already on their way to Najd. So he returned to the Prophet, who was standing in prayer, cloaked against the cold in a wrapper belonging to one of his wives. "When he saw me," said Ḥudhayfah, "he motioned me to sit beside him at his feet, and threw the end of the wrapper over me. Then, with me still in it, he made the bowing and the prostrations. When he had uttered the final greeting of peace, I told him the news."[1]

Bilāl made the call to the dawn prayer; and when they had prayed it, the half-light of the approaching day revealed the total emptiness of the plain beyond the trench. The Prophet gave out that every man had permission to return home, whereupon most of them set off at great speed for the town. Then, fearing that the confederates might have left some spies, or that Bani Qurayẓah might be on the watch and that they might try to persuade the enemy to return, telling them that the trench was no longer guarded, he sent Jābir and 'Umar's son 'Abd Allāh in the wake of their departed comrades to call them back. They both went after them, shouting as hard as they could, but not one man so much as turned his head. Jābir followed the Bani Ḥārithah all the way, and stood for a while shouting outside their houses, but no one came out to him. When he and 'Abd Allāh finally returned to the Prophet to tell him of their complete failure, he laughed and set out for the town himself with those of his Companions who had waited to escort him.

[1] I.I. 683–4; W. 488–90.

# LXI

# *Bani Qurayẓah*

THEY had only a few hours to rest. When the noon prayer had been prayed Gabriel came to the Prophet. He was splendidly dressed, his turban rich with gold and silver brocade, and a cloth of brocaded velvet was thrown over the saddle of the mule he was riding. "Hast thou laid down thine arms, O Messenger of God?" he said. "The Angels have not laid down their arms, and I return this moment from pursuing the foe, naught else. Verily God in His might and His majesty commandeth thee, O Muḥammad, that thou shouldst go against the sons of Qurayẓah. I go to them even now, that I may cause their souls to quake."[1]

The Prophet gave orders that none should pray the afternoon prayer until he had reached the Qurayẓah territory. The banner was given to 'Alī, and before sunset all the fortresses had been invested by the same army, three thousand strong, which had opposed Quraysh and their allies at the trench.

For twenty-five nights they were besieged, and then they sent to the Prophet to ask him to let them consult Abū Lubābah. Like the Bani Naḍīr, they had long been allies of Aws, and Abū Lubābah had been one of their chief links with his tribe. The Prophet bade him go to them, and he was beset on his arrival by weeping women and children so that much of his sternness against the treacherous enemy was softened; and when the men asked him if they should submit to Muḥammad he said "Yea", but at the same time he pointed to his throat as much as to warn them that in his opinion submission meant slaughter. The gesture was in contradiction with his assent, and might have prolonged the siege still further; and no sooner had he made it than an overwhelming sense of guilt added itself to the guilt which he already felt in the depth of his soul on account of the palm-tree which he had refused to give to his orphan ward at the Prophet's request.[2] "My two feet had not moved from where they were," he said, "before I was aware that I had betrayed the Messenger for God." His face changed colour and he recited the verse: *Verily we are for God, and verily unto Him are we returning*. "What aileth thee?" said Ka'b. "I have betrayed God and His Messenger," said Abū Lubābah, and as he went down from the upper room he put his hand to his beard, and it was wet with his tears. He could not bring himself to go out the way he had entered and to face his fellow Awsites and others who, as he knew, were waiting eagerly to hear his news and to escort him to the Prophet. So he passed

[1] I.I. 684. [2] See p. 169.

through a gate at the back of the fortress and was soon on his way to the city. He went straight to the Mosque, and bound himself to one of the pillars, saying: "I will not stir from this place until God relent unto me for what I did."

The Prophet was waiting for his return, and when he finally heard what had happened he said: "If he had come to me I would have prayed God to forgive him; but seeing that he hath done what he hath done, it is not for me to free him until God shall relent unto him."[1]

He remained at the pillar for some ten or fifteen days. Before every prayer, or whenever it was necessary, his daughter would come to untie his bonds; then after he had prayed he would bid her bind him once more. Yet the grievousness of his plight was lessened on account of a dream he had had one night during the siege. He had felt himself to be embedded in a bog of foul slime out of which he could not pull himself until he almost died of the stench of it. Then he saw a flowing stream and he washed himself clean in it and the air about him was fragrant. When he woke he went to Abū Bakr to ask him what it could mean; and Abū Bakr told him that his body meant his soul and that he would enter into a state of soul which would oppress him sorely and that then he would be given relief from it; and during his days at the pillar he lived on the hope of that relief.

As to the Bani Qurayẓah, Ka'b suggested to them that since many of them believed Muḥammad to be a Prophet they should enter his religion and save their lives and their property. But they said that death was preferable, and that they would have nothing but the Torah and the law of Moses. So Ka'b made other suggestions, putting before them other possibilities of action, but these also were unacceptable. Now there were three young men of the Bani Hadl – descendants, that is, of Qurayẓah's brother Hadl – who had been in the fortresses of their kinsmen throughout the siege, and they reiterated the first proposal that Ka'b had made. In their boyhood they had known Ibn al-Hayyabān, the old Syrian Jew who had come to live amongst them, and they now repeated his words about the expected Prophet: "His hour is close upon you. Be ye the first to reach him, O Jews; for he will be sent to shed blood and to take captive the women and the children of those who oppose him. Let not that hold you back from him."[2] But the only answer they received was "We will not forsake the Torah", so the three youths went down from the fortress that night, and telling the Muslim guards of their intention to enter Islam, they pledged their allegiance to the Prophet. Of the Bani Qurayẓah themselves only two followed their example. One of these, 'Amr ibn Su'dā, had from the beginning refused to countenance the breaking of the pact with the Prophet and had formally dissociated himself from it. He now suggested that if they would not enter Islam they could offer to pay the Prophet tribute or a tax – "but by God, I know not if he would accept it". They replied, however, that it was preferable to be killed than to agree to pay tribute to the Arabs. So he himself left the fortress, and having passed through the guards as a Muslim, he spent that night in the Mosque in Medina. But he was never seen again, and to this day it is not known

[1] W. 507. [2] I.I. 136.

whither he went or where he died. The Prophet said of him: "That is a man whom God saved for his faithfulness." The other man, Rifā'ah ibn Samaw'al, eluded the guards and took refuge with Salmà bint Qays, the Prophet's maternal aunt, Āminah's half-sister, who had married a Khazrajite of the Bani an-Najjār. It was in her house that Rifā'ah entered Islam.

The next day, despite Abu Lubābah's warning, the Bani Qurayẓah opened the gates of their fortresses and submitted to the Prophet's judgement. The men were led out with their hands bound behind their backs and a space was allotted them on one side of the camp. On another side the women and children were assembled, and the Prophet put them in the charge of 'Abd Allāh ibn Sallām, the former chief rabbi of the Bani Qaynuqā'. The arms and armour, the garments and the household goods were collected from each fortress and all gathered together in one place. The jars of wine and fermented date juice were opened and their contents poured away.

The clans of Aws sent a deputation to the Prophet asking him to show their former allies the same leniency that he had shown the Bani Qaynuqā' who had been the allies of Khazraj. He answered them saying: "Will it satisfy you, men of Aws, if one of yourselves pronounce judgement upon them?" And they agreed. So he sent to Medina for their chief, Sa'd ibn Mu'ādh, whose wound had not healed and who was being cared for in a tent in the Mosque. The Prophet had placed him there so that he might visit him the more often, and Rufaydah, a woman of Aslam, was tending his wound. Some of his clansmen went to him, and mounting him on an ass they brought him to the camp. "Do well by thy confederates," they said to him on the way, "for the Messenger of God hath set thee in judgement upon them for no other purpose than that thou mayst treat them with indulgence." But Sa'd was a man of justice; like 'Umar he had been against sparing the prisoners at Badr, and their opinion had been confirmed by the Revelation. Many men of Quraysh who had been ransomed on that occasion had come out against them at Uḥud and again at the trench; and in this last campaign the strength of the invaders had been largely due to the hostile activities of the exiled Jews of Bani Naḍīr. If these had been put to death instead of being allowed to go into exile, the invading army might have been halved, and Bani Qurayẓah would no doubt have remained faithful to their pact with the Prophet. The arguments offered by past experience were not in favour of leniency, to say the least. Moreover, Sa'd had himself been one of the envoys to Qurayẓah at the moment of crisis and had seen the ugliness of their treachery when they had thought that the defeat of the Muslims was certain. It was true that if he gave a severe judgement most of the men and women of Aws would blame him, but that consideration would not have weighed much with Sa'd at any time and now it weighed not at all, for he was convinced that he was dying. He cut short the pleas of his clansmen with the words: "The time hath come for Sa'd, in the cause of God, to give no heed unto the blame of the blamer."

Sa'd was a man of mighty stature, of handsome and majestic appearance, and when he came to the camp the Prophet said "Rise in honour of your liege lord," and they rose to greet him saying: "Father of 'Amr, the Messenger of God hath appointed thee to judge the case of thy confederates." He said: "Do ye then swear by God and make by Him your covenant that my judgement shall be the verdict upon them?" "We do," they answered. "And is it binding upon him who is here?" he added, with a glance in the direction of the Prophet, but not mentioning him out of reverence. "It is," said the Prophet. "Then I judge," said Sa'd, "that the men shall be slain, the property divided, and the women and children made captive."[1] The Prophet said to him: "Thou hast judged with the judgement of God from above the seven heavens."

The women and children were taken away to the city where they were lodged, and the men spent the night in the camp where they recited the Torah and exhorted one another to firmness and patience. In the morning the Prophet ordered trenches, long and deep and narrow, to be dug in the market-place. The men, about seven hundred in all – according to some accounts more and to others less – were sent for in small groups, and every group was made to sit alongside the trench that was to be his grave. Then 'Alī and Zubayr and others of the younger Companions cut off their heads, each with a stroke of the sword.

When Ḥuyay was led into the market he turned to the Prophet, who was sitting apart with some of his older Companions, and said to him: "I blame not myself for having opposed thee, but whoso forsaketh God, the same shall be forsaken." Then he turned to his fellows and said: "The command of God cannot be wrong – a writ and a decree and a massacre which God hath set down in his book against the sons of Israel." Then he sat beside the trench and his head was cut off.

The last to die were beheaded by torchlight. Then one old man, Zabīr ibn Bāṭā, whose case was not yet decided, was taken to the house where the women were lodged. The next morning, when they were told of the death of their men, the city was filled with the sound of their lamentations. But the aged Zabīr quieted them, saying: "Be silent! Are ye the first women of the children of Israel to be made captive since the world began? Had there been any good in your men they would have saved you from this. But cleave ye to the religion of the Jews, for in that must we die, and in that must we live hereafter."

Zabīr had always been an enemy to Islam and had done much to stir up opposition to the Prophet. But in the civil wars of Yathrib he had spared the life of a man of Khazraj, Thābit ibn Qays, who wished to repay him for this, and who had gone to the Prophet to ask him to let Zabīr live. "He is thine," said the Prophet; but when Zabīr was told of his reprieve he said to Thābit: "An old man, without wife and without children, what will he do with life?" So Thābit went again to the Prophet, who gave him Zabīr's wife and children. But Zabīr said: "A household in the Hijāz without property, how can they survive?" Again Thābit went to the Prophet, who gave him all Zabīr's possessions except his arms and armour. But thoughts of the

[1] Sa'd's judgement was no doubt directed mainly against their treachery; but in fact it coincided exactly with Jewish law as regards the treatment of a besieged city, even if it were innocent of treachery: *When the Lord thy God hath delivered it unto thy hands, thou shalt smite every male therein with the edge of the sword: but the women, and the little ones, and the cattle, and all that is in the city, even all the spoil thereof, shalt thou take unto thyself.* Deuteronomy 20: 12.

death of all his fellow tribesmen now overwhelmed Zabīr and he said: "By God I ask thee, Thābit, by the claim I have on thee, that thou shouldst join me with my people, for now that they are gone, there is no good in life." At first Thābit refused, but when he saw that he was serious he took him to the place of execution and Zubayr was told to behead him. His wife and children were set free and their property was returned to them, under Thābit's guardianship.

As to the other women and children, they were divided, together with the property, amongst the men who had taken part in the siege. Many of these captives were ransomed by the Bani Naḍīr at Khaybar. As part of his share the Prophet had chosen Rayḥānah,[1] the daughter of Zayd, a Naḍīrite, who had married her to a man of Qurayẓah. She was a woman of great beauty and she remained the Prophet's slave until she died some five years later. At first he put her in the care of his aunt Salmà, in whose house Rifā'ah had already taken refuge. Rayḥānah herself was averse to entering Islam, but Rifā'ah, and his kinsmen of the Bani Hadl spoke to her about the new religion and it was not long before one of the three young converts, Tha'labah by name, came to the Prophet and told him that Rayḥānah had entered Islam, whereupon he greatly rejoiced. When it became clear that she was not pregnant, he went to her and offered to set her free and to make her his wife. But she said: "O Messenger of God, leave me in thy power; that will be easier for me and for thee."

[1] I.I. 693.

# LXII

# *After the Siege*

WHEN Sa'd had passed judgement on Bani Qurayẓah he returned to his sick-bed in the Mosque. He had already prayed that if God had any more fighting for him to accomplish against His enemies He would let him live, and if not that He would let him die; and now his condition grew rapidly worse. One night not long after the siege the Prophet found him apparently unconscious. He sat down at his head which he gently raised and laid against his breast, and then he prayed: "O Lord, verily Sa'd hath striven upon the path, with fullness of faith in Thy messenger, leaving naught undone that was his to do. Take then unto Thyself his spirit with the best acceptance wherewith Thou takest the spirits of Thy creatures." Sa'd heard the Prophet's voice, and opening his eyes he said: "Peace be on thee, O Messenger of God, I bear witness that thou hast delivered thy message." An hour or two later, after the Prophet had returned home, Gabriel came to him and told him that Sa'd was dead.

When they carried his bier to the cemetery, the bearers were amazed at the lightness of their load, for Sa'd was a heavy man, but when they mentioned this to the Prophet he said: "I saw the Angels carrying him." They set down the bier at the edge of the grave and he led the funeral prayer, with a multitude of men and women praying behind him. Then when they lowered the body unto the grave the Prophet's face turned suddenly pale and he said three times *Subḥān Allāh*, "Glory be to God!", this being an affirmation of the Absolute Transcendence of God, sometimes uttered, as now, with reference to a limit that needs to be transcended. All those who were present repeated it and the cemetery resounded with the glorifications. Then after a moment he gave utterance to the words of victory, *Allāhu Akbar*, "God is most Great", and the cemetery resounded again as the magnification was likewise taken up by those who were present. Afterwards, when asked why he had changed colour, the Prophet said: "The grave closed in upon your companion, and he felt a constriction which, if any man could escape it, Sa'd would have escaped. Then God gave him blissful relief."[1]

It was at the dawn of one of the days which followed, when the Prophet was in the apartment of Umm Salamah, that he announced to her: "Abū Lubābah is forgiven." "May I not give him the good tidings?" she said. "If thou wilt," he answered, so she stood at the door of her apartment which opened into the Mosque, not far from the pillar to which he had bound

[1] W. 529

himself, and called out: "O Abū Lubābah, be of good cheer, for God hath relented unto thee." The men who were in the Mosque surged upon him to set him free, but he stopped them saying: "Not until the Messenger of God set me free with his own hands." So the Prophet passed by him on his way to the prayer and loosed his bonds.

After the prayer Abū Lubābah came to the Prophet and said that he wished to make an offering in expiation of what he had done, and the Prophet accepted from him a third of his property, for the Revelation which had set him free had said: *Take alms of their wealth to purify them,*[1] the reference being not only to Abū Lubābah but also to other good men at fault who freely admitted that they were wrong.

About five months after the campaign of the Trench, the Prophet heard that a rich caravan of Quraysh was on its way from Syria, and Zayd was sent to waylay it with a troop of a hundred and seventy horse. They captured the entire merchandise, including much silver which was the property of Ṣafwān, and most of the men were taken captive. Amongst the few who escaped was Abū l'Āṣ, the Prophet's son-in-law; and as he approached Medina, near which he was bound to pass on his way to Mecca, he was filled with longing to see his wife and their little daughter Umāmah. Under cover of night he entered the city at considerable risk and was somehow able to find where Zaynab lived. He knocked at the door and she opened it and let him in. It was not far from daybreak, and when Bilāl made the call to the prayer Zaynab left him in the house with Umāmah and went to the Mosque to take her place as usual with her sisters and stepmothers in the front rank of the women, behind the ranks of the men. The Prophet made the initial magnification which the men repeated after him; and in the brief moment of silence which ensued Zaynab cried out with all the strength of her voice: "O people, I give protection to Abū l-'Āṣ the son of Rabī'." Then she entered the prayer herself with the magnification.

When the Prophet had pronounced the final greeting of Peace, he rose and turned to face the congregation saying "Did ye hear what I heard?", and there was a murmur of affirmation throughout the Mosque. "By him in whose hand is my soul," he said, "I knew naught of this until I heard what I heard. The meanest Muslim can grant protection which shall be binding on all other Muslims." Then he went to his daughter and said: "Receive him with all honour, but let him not come unto thee as a husband, for thou art not his by law." She told her father that Abū l-'Āṣ was troubled by the loss of the merchandise which he himself had acquired by barter in Syria on behalf of various men of Quraysh who had entrusted their goods to him, for he was one of the most trusted men of Mecca. So the Prophet sent word to those of the expedition who had taken the property of Abū l-'Āṣ: "This man is related to us as ye know, and ye have taken property of his. If ye should be so good as to return it unto him, that would please me; but if ye will not, it is booty which God hath given you, so that yours is the better right to it." They said they would give it back to him, and

[1] IX, 103.

they even went so far as to return old water-skins, small leather bottles and pieces of wood. Everything was returned to him without exception; and since there were signs that he had thoughts of entering Islam, one of the men said to him: "Why dost thou not enter Islam and take these goods unto thyself, for they are the property of idolaters?" But he answered: "It were a bad beginning to my Islam, that I should betray my trust." He took the goods to Mecca and gave them to their owners. Then he returned to Medina and entered Islam, pledging his allegiance. So Zaynab was united once more with her husband, and there was great rejoicing in the family of the Prophet and throughout the city.

# LXIII

# *The Hypocrites*

ZAYD'S successful ambush on the eastern caravan route turned the thoughts of Quraysh once more to the western route which they so much preferred; and they now stirred up their own Red Sea coast allies, the Bani l-Muṣṭaliq, a clan of Khuzā'ah, to make a raid on Medina, hoping no doubt that the raiders might gather support from other coastal tribes, and thus open up the way once more for themselves. But the other clans of Khuzā'ah were more favourably disposed to the Prophet than the Meccans realised, and news of this project reached him in good time. He was thus given the opportunity to demonstrate his undiminished and even increased power along the western route also, to within a few marches from Mecca itself. After eight days, considerably before the Bani l-Muṣṭaliq were prepared to set out, he was already encamped on their territory at one of their watering places. From there he advanced and by a quick manoeuvre was able to close in upon the tent-dwellers, who surrendered without much resistance. Only one Muslim was killed, and of the enemy no more than ten. About two hundred families were made captive, and the booty included some two thousand camels and five thousand sheep and goats.

The army camped there for a few more days, but its stay was cut short by an untoward incident. A quarrel broke out at one of the wells between two coastal tribesmen, from Ghifār and Juhaynah, as to which bucket belonged to which, and they fell to fighting. The Ghifārite, whom 'Umar had hired to lead his horse, shouted for help – "O Quraysh" – while the Juhaynite called on his traditional allies of Khazraj, and the more hotheaded of both Emigrants and Helpers rushed to the scene. Swords were drawn and blood might have been shed had not some of the closer Companions intervened on both sides. This would normally have been the end of the matter. But it so happened that more of the hypocrites than usual had taken part in this expedition; it was in familiar and well-watered territory, and from the outset there had been hope of an easy victory and spoils well worth the effort. They were not, however, prepared to change their point of view but still persisted in looking on the expeditions which set out from Yathrib as forays of Khazraj and Aws supplemented by auxiliaries. It was therefore to the sons of Qaylah that the camp belonged: the Quraysh refugees were there, as elsewhere, merely on sufferance. In this frame of mind Ibn Ubayy was sitting apart with a group of his intimates when the sound of the quarrel came to their ears, and one of them went to see what was the matter. He returned to report, quite truly, that 'Umar's man had been entirely to blame, and that it was he who had struck the first blow. This served to fan afresh the embers of bitterness which were still smouldering from the ordeal of the Trench. For the last five years the tension had gradually mounted until the presence of Muḥammad and the other Emigrants had brought the whole of Arabia against them. Added to this, the rich and hospitable Jewish tribes which had played so important a part in the community had been rooted out – two of them exiled and the third massacred. The civil wars of the oasis had indeed called for a solution, but Ibn Ubayy was convinced that if he had been made king he would have known how to put an end to the discord without involving his people in more dangerous hostilities. And now these impoverished refugees had had the effrontry to obstruct the passage of their benefactors to the well! "Have they gone so far as this?" said Ibn Ubayy. "They seek to take precedence over us, they crowd us out of our own country, and naught will fit us and these rags of Quraysh but the old saying 'Feed fat thy dog and it will feed on thee.' By God, when we return to Medina, the higher and the mightier of us will drive out the lower and the weaker." A boy of Khazraj named Zayd, who was sitting at the edge of the circle, went straight to the Prophet and told him what Ibn Ubayy had said. The Prophet changed colour, and 'Umar, who was with him, suggested that he should forthwith have the traitor beheaded, but he said: "What if men should say, O 'Umar, that Muḥammad slayeth his companions?" Meantime one of the Helpers had gone to Ibn Ubayy and asked him if he had in fact said what the boy had reported, and Ibn Ubayy came straight to the Prophet and swore that he had said no such thing. Some of the men of Khazraj who were present also spoke in his defence, anxious to avoid trouble. The Prophet let it seem as if the incident were closed; but a surer way of avoiding trouble was to busy men's minds with something else and he gave the order to break camp immediately.

Never before had he been known to move off at that hour: it was not long after midday; and with brief halts at the times of prayer they were kept on the march through the heat of the afternoon, then all through the night and from dawn until the heat of the next day became oppressive. When they were finally told to pitch camp, the men were too tired to do anything but sleep. During the march the Prophet confided to Sa'd ibn 'Ubādah, who for the Muslims had been gradually replacing Ibn Ubayy as the chief man of Khazraj, that he believed young Zayd to have spoken the truth. "O Messenger of God," said Sa'd, "thou, if thou wilt, shalt drive out him, for he is the lower and the weaker and thou art the higher and the mightier." He asked him none the less to deal gently with Ibn Ubayy, nor was the Prophet intending to mention the incident again; but soon after his talk with Sa'd the matter was taken out of his hands, for the Revelation descended upon him and that chapter was revealed which is named the Sūrah of the Hypocrites, one of whom it quotes, though not by name, as having said the very words spoken by Zayd. The Prophet did not however give out this chapter until they had returned to Medina. But he rode up to Zayd and leaning towards him took hold of his ear. "Boy," he said, "thine ear heard truly, and God hath confirmed thy speech."

Meantime 'Abd Allāh, the son of Ibn Ubayy, was deeply distressed for he knew that his father had spoken those words. He had also been told that ‘Umar had wanted the Prophet to put his father to death, and he was afraid that the sentence might be passed and the order given at any moment. So he went to the Prophet and said: "O Messenger of God, I am told that thou art minded to slay ‘Abd Allāh ibn Ubayy. If thou must needs do it, then give me the order, and I will bring thee his head. Khazraj know full well that there is no man amongst them of more filial piety unto his father than myself, and I fear that if thou shouldst give the order unto another my soul would not suffer me to look upon the slayer of my father walking amongst men, but I would slay him, and having thus slain a believer on behalf of a disbeliever I would enter the fire of Hell." But the Prophet said: "Nay, but let us deal gently with him and make the best of his companionship so long as he be with us."[1]

[1] I.I. 726–8.

# LXIV

# *The Necklace*

'Ā'ISHAH and Umm Salamah had accompanied the Prophet on this expedition; and at a sunset halt two or three days after the forced march, an onyx necklace which 'Ā'ishah was wearing came unclasped and slipped to the ground unobserved. When she noticed her loss, it was already too dark to make a search, and she was loath to go without it. Her mother had placed it round her neck on the day of her wedding, and it was one of her most treasured possessions. The place was without water and the Prophet had intended no more than a brief halt, but he now gave orders to camp there until daylight. The reason for the change of plan was passed from mouth to mouth, and much indignation was felt that a whole army should be kept waiting at such an inclement spot for the sake of a necklace. Some of the Companions went and complained to Abū Bakr, who was greatly embarrassed and scolded his daughter for her carelessness. There was not one well within reach, and the men had used up all the water they carried with them, intending to fill their skins and bottles at the well watered camp they had been aiming for. It would not be possible to pray at dawn, for they had no means of making their ablutions. But in the last hours of the night the verse of earth-purification was revealed to the Prophet – an event of untold importance for the practical life of the community: *If ye find not water then purify yourselves with clean earth, wiping therewith your faces and your hands.*[1] The feelings that had run so high throughout the host subsided, and Usayd exclaimed: "This is not the first blessing that ye have brought unto us, O family of Abū Bakr."

When daylight came, the necklace was still nowhere to be seen; but when all hopes of finding it were lost and they were preparing to set off without it, 'Ā'ishah's camel rose from where he had been kneeling all night, and there was the necklace on the ground beneath him.

One of the next camps was in a pleasant valley, with long stretches of level sand. The Prophet's two tents were pitched as usual somewhat apart from the others, and that day it was 'Ā'ishah's turn to be with him. She recounted afterwards how he had suggested that they should have a race. "I girded up my robe about me," she said, "and the Prophet did likewise. Then we raced, and he won the race. 'This is for that other race', he said, 'which thou didst win from me.'" He was referring to an incident which had taken place in Mecca, before the Hijrah. 'Ā'ishah added, by way of

[1] IV, 43.

explanation: "He had come to my father's house and I had something in my hand and he said: 'Bring it here to me', and I would not, and ran away from him, and he ran after me, but I was too quick for him."[1]

The clasp of 'Ā'ishah's necklace was insecure, and at one of the last halts before they reached Medina it slipped from her neck again. This was when the order to march had already been given and she had withdrawn from the camp to satisfy a call of nature. On her return, she and Umm Salamah seated themselves in their respective howdahs, closed the curtains and unveiled their faces. Only then did 'Ā'ishah realise her loss; and slipping out from under the curtain she went back to look for it. Meantime the men had saddled the camels, and led them to the howdahs which they strapped each upon its mount. They were accustomed to a considerable difference in weight between them – that of a thirty-year-old woman as compared with one of fourteen who was slight for her age – and they failed to notice that this time the lighter of the two howdahs was even lighter than usual, so they led away the camels to join the march without a second thought. "I found my necklace," said 'Ā'ishah, "and returned to the camp and not a soul was there. So I went to where my howdah had been, thinking that they would miss me and come back for me, and whilst I sat there mine eyes were overcome with heaviness and I fell asleep. I was lying there when Ṣafwān[2] the son of Mu'aṭṭal passed by. He had fallen behind the army for some reason and had not slept at the camp. Noticing me, he came and stood over me. He had been used to seeing me before the veil was imposed upon us, and when he recognised me he said: '*Verily we are for God, and verily unto Him we are returning*. This is the wife of the Messenger of God.'" His utterance of the verse of return woke her up; and she drew her veil over her face. Ṣafwān offered her his camel and escorted her himself on foot to the next halt.[3]

On the army's arrival there, 'Ā'ishah's howdah had been lifted from its mount and placed on the ground; and when she did not emerge from it they assumed that she was asleep. Great was the astonishment when, towards the end of the halt, after the men had rested, she rode into the camp led by Ṣafwān. That was the beginning of a scandal which was to shake Medina, and the tongues of the hypocrites were not slow in starting it, but for the moment the Prophet and 'Ā'ishah and most of the Companions were quite unaware of the impending trouble.

The spoils were divided as usual, and one of the captives was Juwayriyah, the daughter of Ḥārith, chief of the defeated clan. She fell to the lot of a Helper who fixed a high price for her ransom, and she came to the Prophet to ask for his intervention on her behalf. He was on that day in the apartment of 'Ā'ishah, who opened the door to her, and who said afterwards, recounting what had taken place: "She was a woman of great loveliness and beauty. No man looked on her but she captivated his soul, and when I saw her at the door of my room I was filled with misgivings, for

1 W. 427.

2 A young man of the Bani Sulaym who had come to live in Medina and was thus counted as one of the Emigrants.

3 I.I. 732; B. LII, 15; W. 426–8.

I knew that the Prophet would see in her what I saw. She entered unto him and said: 'O Messenger of God, I am Juwayriyyah, the daughter of Ḥārith, the lord of his people. Well thou knowest the distress that hath fallen upon me, and I have come to seek thy help in the matter of my ransom.' He answered: 'Wouldst thou have better than that?' 'What is better?' she asked, and he answered: 'That I should pay thy ransom and marry thee.' "[1]

Juwayriyah gladly accepted his offer, but the marriage had not yet taken place when her father arrived with some camels for her ransom. They were not the full number he had originally intended to offer, for in the valley of 'Aqīq, shortly before reaching the oasis, he had taken a last look at the fine animals and had been so smitten with admiration for two of them that he had separated them from the others and hidden them in one of the passes of the valley, unable to bring himself to part with them. The remainder he took to the Prophet and said: "O Muḥammad, thou hast captured my daughter and here is her ransom." "But where," said the Prophet, "are those two camels which thou didst hide in 'Aqīq?" And he went on to describe in exact detail the pass in which they were tethered. Then Ḥārith said: "I testify that there is no god but God, and that thou, Muḥammad, art the Messenger of God"; and two of his sons entered Islam with him. He sent for the two camels and gave them with the rest to the Prophet, who restored his daughter to him. Then she herself entered Islam, and the Prophet asked her father to give her to him in marriage, which he did;[2] and an apartment was built for her.

When it became known that the Bani Muṣṭaliq were now the Prophet's kinsmen by marriage, the Emigrants and Helpers set free their captives who had not yet been ransomed. About a hundred families were released. "I know of no woman," said 'Ā'ishah, referring to Juwayriyah, "who was a greater blessing to her people than she."[3]

[1] I.I. 729. [2] I.H. 729. [3] I.I. ibid.

# LXV

# *The Lie*

NOT long after her return to Medina, 'Ā'ishah fell ill. By that time the slander that the hypocrites had whispered against herself and Ṣafwān was being repeated throughout the city. Few took it seriously, though amongst those who did was her own cousin Misṭaḥ, of the clan of Muṭṭalib. But whether they believed it or not, everyone knew of it, except herself. She was none the less conscious of a certain reserve on the part of the Prophet, and she missed the loving attention which he had shown her in her other illnesses. He would come into the room and say to those who were nursing her "How are ye all today?", simply including her with the others. Deeply wounded, but too proud to complain, she asked his permission to go to her parents' house where her mother could nurse her. "As thou wilt," he said.

To recount what took place in 'Ā'ishah's own words: "I went to my mother without any knowledge of what was being said, and recovered from my illness some twenty days later. Then one evening I went out with the mother of Misṭaḥ – her mother was the sister of my father's mother – and as she was walking beside me she stumbled over her gown and exclaimed: 'May Misṭaḥ stumble!' 'God's Life,' I said, 'that was an ill thing to say of a man of the Emigrants who fought at Badr!' 'O daughter of Abū Bakr,' she said, 'can it be that the news hath not reached thee?' 'What news?' I said. Then she told me what the slanderers had said and how people were repeating it. 'Can this be so?' I said. 'By God, it is indeed!' was her answer, and I returned home in tears, and I wept and wept until I thought that my weeping would split my liver. 'God forgive thee!' I said to my mother. 'People talk their talk, and thou tellest me not one word of it!' 'My little daughter,' she said, 'take it not so heavily, for there is seldom a beautiful woman married to a man who loveth her but her fellow wives are full of gossip about her, and others repeat what they say.' So I lay awake the whole of that night, and my tears flowed without ceasing."[1]

But in fact, whatever jealousies there may have been between one and another, the wives of the Prophet were all women of piety, and not one of them took any part in spreading the slander. On the contrary, they defended 'Ā'ishah and spoke well of her. Of those chiefly to blame, the nearest to the Prophet's household was his cousin Ḥamnah, Zaynab's sister, who repeated the calumny, thinking thus to further her sister's interests: for it was generally thought that but for 'Ā'ishah Zaynab would

[1] B. LII, 15.

have been the Prophet's favourite wife; and Zaynab suffered much from her sister's ill conceived zeal on her behalf. Another of the slanderers, in addition to Misṭaḥ, was the poet Ḥassān ibn Thābit; and in the background were Ibn Ubayy and the other hypocrites who had started everything.

The Prophet clearly hoped for a Revelation, but when nothing came he questioned not only his wives but also other near ones. Usāmah, who was the same age as 'Ā'ishah, spoke vigorously in her defence. "This is all a lie," he said. "We know naught but good of her." His mother, Umm Ayman, was equally emphatic in praise of her. As for 'Alī, he said: "God hath not restricted thee, and there are many women besides her. But question her maidservant and she will tell thee the truth." So the Prophet sent for her and said: "O Burayrah, hast thou ever seen aught in 'Ā'ishah that might make thee suspect her?" She answered: "By Him that sent thee with the truth, I know only good of her; and if it were otherwise God would inform His Messenger. I have no fault to find with 'Ā'ishah but that she is a girl, young in years, and when I am kneeding dough and I bid her watch it she will fall asleep and her pet lamb will come and eat it. I have blamed her for that more than once."

When next the Prophet went to the Mosque he ascended the pulpit, and having praised God he said: "O people, what say ye of men who injure me with regard to my family, reporting of them what is not true? By God, I know naught but good of my household, and naught but good of the man they speak of, who never entereth a house of mine but I am with him." No sooner had he spoken than Usayd rose to his feet and said: "O Messenger of God, if they are of Aws we will deal with them; and if they be of our brethren of Khazraj then give us thy command, for they deserve that their heads should be cut off." Before he had finished Sa'd ibn 'Ubādah was already on his feet, for Ḥassān was of Khazraj, and so were the men who had subtly hatched the slander in the beginning. "God's Life, thou liest!" he said. "Ye shall not slay them, nor can ye. Neither wouldst thou have spoken thus, had they been of thy people." "God's Life, liar thyself!" said Usayd. "Slay them we shall, and thou art a hypocrite, striving on behalf of hypocrites." By this time the two tribes were about to come to grips with one another, but the Prophet motioned them to desist, and descending from the pulpit he quietened them and sent them away in peace.

If 'Ā'ishah had known that the Prophet had defended her in public from the pulpit, she would no doubt have been greatly comforted. But she knew nothing of it at the time. She was only aware of his questioning others about her, which suggested that he did not know what to think, and this greatly distressed her. She did not expect him, of himself, to look into her soul, for she knew that his knowledge of hidden things came to him from the next world. "I only know what God giveth me to know," he would say. He did not seek to read the thoughts of men; but she expected him to know that her devotion to him was such as to make the thing she was accused of impossible.

In any case, it was not enough that he should himself believe 'Ā'ishah and Ṣafwān to be innocent. The situation was a grave one, and it was imperative to have evidence which would convince the whole community.

To this end 'Ā'ishah herself had proved the least helpful of all concerned. It was now time that her silence should be broken. Not that anything she said could be enough to resolve the crisis. But the Koran promised that questions asked during the period of its revelation would be answered.[1] In the present case the Prophet had filled the air with questions – the same question, reiterated to different persons – but for the promised answer to be given by Heaven, it was perhaps necessary that the question should already have been put to the person most closely involved.

"I was with my parents," said 'Ā'ishah, "and I had wept for two nights and a day; and while they were sitting with me a woman from the Helpers asked if she could join us, and I bade her enter, and she sat and wept with me. Then the Prophet entered and took his seat, nor had he sat with me since people began to say what they said of me. A month had passed, and no tidings had come to him about me from Heaven. After uttering the testification *there is no god but God*, he said: 'O 'Ā'ishah, I have been told such and such a thing concerning thee, and if thou art innocent, surely God will declare thine innocence; and if thou hast done aught that is wrong, then ask forgiveness of God and repent unto Him; for verily if the slave confess his sin and then repent, God relenteth unto him.' No sooner had he spoken than my tears ceased to flow and I said to my father 'Answer the Messenger of God for me,' and he said: 'I know not what to say.' When I asked my mother she said the same, and I was no more than a girl, young in years, and there was not much of the Koran that I could recite. So I said: 'I know well that ye have heard what men are saying, and it hath settled in your souls and ye have believed it; and if I say unto you that I am innocent – and God knoweth that I am innocent – ye will not believe me, whereas if I confessed to that which God knoweth I am guiltless of, ye would believe me.' Then I groped in my mind for the name of Jacob, but I could not remember it, so I said: 'But I will say as the father of Joseph said: *Beautiful patience must be mine; and God is He of whom help is to be asked against what they say.*[2] Then I turned to my couch and lay on it, hoping that God would declare me innocent. Not that I thought He would send down a Revelation on my account, for it seemed to me that I was too paltry for my case to be spoken of in the Koran. But I was hoping that the Prophet would see in his sleep a vision that would exculpate me.

"He remained sitting in our company and all of us were still present when a Revelation came to him: he was seized with the pangs which seized him at such times, and as it were pearls of sweat dripped from him, although it was a wintry day. Then, when he was relieved of the pressure, he said in a voice that vibrated with gladness: 'O 'Ā'ishah, praise God, for He hath declared thee innocent.' Then my mother said 'Arise and go to the Messenger of God,' and I said: 'Nay by God, I will not rise and go to him, and I will praise none but God.'"[3]

The words of exculpation were: *Verily they who brought forth the lie are a party amongst you . . . When ye took it upon your tongues, uttering with your mouths that whereof ye had no knowledge, ye counted it but a trifle. Yet in the sight of God it is enormous. Why said ye not when ye heard*

[1] V, 101. [2] XII, 18. [3] B. LII, 15.

*it: To speak of this is not for us. Glory be to Thee! This is a monstrous calumny. God biddeth you beware of ever repeating the like thereof, if ye are believers.*[1]

The new Revelation also dwelt upon the whole question of adultery, and, while prescribing the penalty, it likewise prescribed, as the penalty for slandering honourable women, that the slanderers should be scourged. This sentence was carried out upon Misṭaḥ and Ḥassān and Ḥamnah, who had been most explicit in spreading the calumny and who confessed their guilt. But the hypocrites, who had been more insidious, had none the less been only implicit, nor did they confess to having had any part in it, so the Prophet preferred not to pursue the matter, but to leave them to God.

Abū Bakr had been in the habit of giving his kinsman Misṭaḥ an allowance of money on account of his poverty, but now he said: "Never again by God will I give unto Misṭaḥ, and never again will I show him favour, after what he hath said against 'Ā'ishah, and after the woe he hath brought upon us." But there now came the Revelation: *Let not the men of dignity and wealth amongst you swear that they will not give unto kinsmen and unto the needy and unto those who have migrated for the sake of God. Let them forgive and let them be indulgent. Do ye not long that God should forgive you? And God is Forgiving, Merciful.*[2] Then Abū Bakr said: "Indeed I long that God shall forgive me." And he returned to Misṭaḥ and gave him what he had been used to giving him and said: "I swear I will never withdraw it from him!" The Prophet likewise, after a certain time had elapsed, showed great generosity to Ḥassān; and he married his cousin Ḥamnah, Muṣ'ab's widow, to Ṭalḥah, by whom she had two sons.

[1] XXIV, 11, 15–17. [2] XXIV, 22.

# LXVI

# *The Dilemma of Quraysh*

THE Prophet fasted Ramaḍān in Medina and remained there also during the month which followed. One night towards its end he dreamed that with his head shaved he entered the Ka'bah, and its key was in his hand. The next day he told his Companions of this and invited them to perform the Lesser Pilgrimage with him, whereupon they hastily set about making preparations so that they could leave as soon as possible. Between them they purchased seventy camels to be sacrificed in the sacred precinct. Their meat would then be distributed among the poor of Mecca. The Prophet decided to take one of his wives with him, and when lots were cast the lot fell to Umm Salamah. Also amongst the pilgrims were the two women of Khazraj who had been present at the Second 'Aqabah, Nusaybah and Umm Manī'.

Each man took with him a sword, and what might be needed for hunting, but before they set off 'Umar and Sa'd ibn 'Ubādah suggested that they should go fully armed. Quraysh, they said, might well take the opportunity of attacking them, despite the sacred month. But the Prophet refused, saying: "I will not carry arms; I have come forth for no end other than to make the Pilgrimage." At the first halt he called for the sacrificial camels to be brought to him, and he himself consecrated one of them, turning it to face towards Mecca, making a mark on its right flank, and placing garlands round its neck, after which he ordered that the others should be consecrated in the same way. He then sent on ahead a man of Khuzā'ah, of the clan of Ka'b, to bring him back word of the reactions of Quraysh.

The Prophet was bareheaded and had already donned the age-old traditional pilgrim's dress of two pieces of unstitched cloth, one girt round the waist to cover the lower part of the body, and the other draped round the shoulders. He now consecrated himself for the Pilgrimage with two prayer cycles, after which he began to utter the pilgrim's cry *Labbayk Allāhumma Labbayk*, which means "Here I am at Thy service, O God." Most of the others followed his example, but a few preferred to wait until they had advanced somewhat further upon their journey, for the pilgrimal state carried with it certain restrictions about hunting.

When Quraysh heard of the departure of the pilgrims from Medina, they were filled with misgivings, as the Prophet had anticipated, and they immediately summoned a meeting in the Assembly. Never had they known a more serious dilemma. If they, the guardians of the sanctuary, were to hinder the approach of over a thousand Arab pilgrims to the Holy House, this would be a most flagrant violation of the laws on which all their own greatness was founded. On the other hand, if they allowed their enemies to enter Mecca in peace and comfort, it would be an immense moral triumph for Muḥammad. The tidings of it would spread throughout Arabia and be on everybody's lips; and it would serve to place the crown of defeat upon their own recent unsuccessful attack upon Medina. Perhaps worst of all, these pilgrims' performances of the ancient rites would serve to make the new faith more attractive and to confirm its claim to be the religion of Abraham. All things considered, it was out of the question to let them come. "By God, this shall not be," they said, "so long as there is a single eye amongst us with a glimmer of life left in it."

When the pilgrims reached 'Usfān, the scout who had been sent on ahead rejoined them with the news that Quraysh had sent Khālid with a troop of two hundred horse to bar their approach. So the Prophet asked for a guide who could take them on by another way, and a man of Aslam led them a little towards the coast and then by a devious and difficult path until they reached the pass which leads down to Ḥudaybiyah, an open tract of land below Mecca at the edge of the sacred territory. Their detour had kept them well out of sight of Khālid, but at one point, when it was too late for him to take up another position, they raised so much dust that he realised what had happened, and galloped back to Mecca with his troop to warn Quraysh of their approach.

The Prophet had chosen his favourite camel, Qaṣwā', for the Pilgrimage, and at the end of the pass she stopped and knelt. The rocks resounded as many of the men cried out *Hal! Hal!*, which is what they say to make a camel rise, but she remained as if rooted to the earth. "Qaṣwā' is stubborn," they said, but the Prophet knew well that it was a sign that they should go no further than Ḥudaybiyah, at any rate for the moment. "She is not stubborn," he said, "it is not in her nature; but He holdeth her who held the elephant." He added, referring to Quraysh: "They shall not ask of me this day any concession which honoureth the rights of God but I will grant it them."[1] Then he spoke to Qaṣwā', and she quickly rose to her feet and bore him down to the edge of Ḥudaybiyah, followed by the other pilgrims. Here he told them to camp; but there was almost no water, only the dregs of it at the bottom of one or two hollows, and the men were complaining of thirst. The Prophet called Nājiyah to him, the man of Aslam who was in charge of the sacrificial camels, and told him to bring him a pail of as much water as he could from the largest of the hollows, which he did. Having performed his ablution, the Prophet rinsed his mouth and spat back the water into the pail. Then, taking an arrow from his quiver, he said: "Go down with this water and pour it into the waters of the hollow; then stir them with this arrow." Nājiyah did as he was bid, and

[1] I.I. 741; W. 587.

water, clear and fresh, surged up so quickly and so plentifully at the touch of the arrow that he was almost overwhelmed before he could clamber out. The pilgrims gathered round the edge of the hollow and every man drank his fill, as did also the animals.

One or two of the hypocrites were amongst the pilgrims, including Ibn Ubayy; and, as he sat drinking his fill, one of his fellow clansmen addressed him saying: "Out upon thee, O father of Ḥubāb, hath not the time now come for thee to see how thou art placed? What more than this can there be?" "I have seen the like of this before," said Ibn Ubayy, whereupon the other man remonstrated with him so threateningly that Ibn Ubayy went with his son to the Prophet to forestall trouble and to say that he had been misunderstood. But before he had time to speak the Prophet said to him: "Where hast thou seen the like of that which thou hast seen this day?" He answered: "I have never seen the like of it." "Then why," said the Prophet, "didst say what thou saidst?" "I ask forgiveness of God," said Ibn Ubayy. "O Messenger of God," said his son, "ask forgiveness for him," and the Prophet did so.[1]

Having satisfied their thirst, the pilgrims were soon able also to eat their fill, thanks to a gift of camels and sheep from two Bedouin chiefs, whose tribe, the Bani Khuzā'ah, one-time guardians of the Sanctuary, included the clans of Aslam, Ka'b and Muṣṭaliq. To a man, these were now all well disposed towards the Prophet. For such of them as had not yet entered Islam, there was a political advantage in this alliance, which was needed to counterbalance the pact that their great enemies, the Bani Bakr, had long had with Quraysh. This situation was soon to give rise to events of the greatest importance. For the moment, however, there was no fighting between Khuzā'ah and Bakr, and Khuzā'ah were tolerated by Quraysh, but at the same time suspected. One of their leading men, Budayl ibn Warqā', was in Mecca when news came that the pilgrims were encamped at Ḥudaybiyah. He now went with some of his clansmen to the Prophet to inform him of the attitude of Quraysh. "They swear by God," he said, "that they will not leave the way open between thee and the House until the last of their fighting men hath perished." The Prophet said: "We came not here for battle; we came only to make our pilgrimal rounds about the House. He that standeth in our way, him we shall fight; but I will grant them time, if they so desire it, to take their precautions and to leave the way clear for us."

Budayl and his fellows returned to Mecca, and Quraysh received them in sullen silence. When they offered to tell them what Muḥammad had said to them, 'Ikrimah, the son of Abū Jahl, said they did not wish to hear it, whereupon 'Urwah, one of their allies of Thaqīf – his mother was a Meccan – protested that this attitude was absurd. So Ṣafwān said to Budayl: "Tell us what ye have seen and what ye have heard." And he told them of the peaceful intent of the pilgrims, and also that the Prophet had said he was ready to give Quraysh time to prepare for their coming. Then 'Urwah said: "Budayl hath brought you a goodly concession such as no man can refuse except to his own hurt. So accept his hearsay of it, but send

[1] W. 589.

me to bring confirmation direct from Muḥammad; and I will look on those who are with him, and I will be for you a scout, to bring you tidings of him."

Quraysh accepted his offer, but they had already sent, as scout and possible envoy, the man who commanded all their allies of the Bedouin tribes, known collectively as the Ahābīsh. This was Ḥulays of the Bani l-Ḥārith, one of the clans of Kinānah. It was he who had rebuked Abū Sufyān for the mutilations at Uhud. When the Prophet saw him coming, he knew – either from his gait and demeanour or from what he had heard of him – that he was a man of piety, with a great reverence for sacred things, so he gave orders that the animals they intended to sacrifice should be sent to meet him; and when the seventy camels solemnly filed past Ḥulays with their marks of consecration and their festive ornaments he was so impressed that without going to speak to the Prophet he went straight back to Quraysh and assured them that the pilgrims intentions were entirely peaceful. Exasperated, the Meccans told him that he was merely a man of the desert and that he had no knowledge of the situation. This was a great tactical error, as they soon realised, but too late. "Men of Quraysh," he said sternly, "not for this, by God, did we consent to be your allies, and not for this pledged we our pact with you. Shall one who cometh to honour the House of God be banned from it? By Him in whose hand is my soul, either ye let Muḥammad do what he hath come to do, or I lead away the Ahābīsh, every man of them." "Bear with us, Ḥulays," they said, "until we reach terms that we can accept."

Meantime 'Urwah of Thaqīf had arrived at the pilgrim's camp, and was already in converse with the Prophet. Seated in front of him, he began by treating him as an equal and took him by the beard when he addressed him; but Mughīrah, one of the Emigrants who was standing by, rapped his hand with the flat of his sword, and he took it away. A few moments later, when he ventured to take the Prophet's beard again, Mughīrah gave him a harder rap, saying: "From the beard of God's Messenger take thy hand while it is yet thine to take." 'Urwah refrained from any further familiarities with the Prophet; but after talking with him at some length, he stayed in the camp for several hours. He had promised Quraysh to be their scout as well as their envoy, and he was bent on taking note of everything. But what impressed him most were things which he had not come to see, things of which he had never seen the like; and when he returned to Mecca he said to Quraysh: "O people, I have been sent as envoy unto kings – unto Caesar and Chosroes and the Negus – and I have not seen a king whose men so honour him as the companions of Muḥammad honour Muḥammad. If he commandeth aught, they almost outstrip his word in fulfilling it; when he performeth his ablution, they wellnigh fight for the water thereof; when he speaketh, their voices are hushed in his presence; nor will they look him full in the face, but lower their eyes in reverence for him. He hath offered you a goodly concession; therefore accept it from him."[1]

While 'Urwah was still in the camp, the Prophet had mounted a man of Ka'b named Khirāsh on one of his camels and sent him as envoy to

[1] B. LIV, 15; W. 593–600.

Quraysh. When he arrived, 'Ikrimah hamstrung the camel; but Ḥulays and his men intervened and saved the envoy's life, compelling Quraysh to let him go back to the Prophet. "O Messenger of God," he said on his return, "send a man who is better protected than I am." The Prophet called 'Umar to him, but 'Umar said that Quraysh knew well of his great hostility to them, and that none of his own clan, the Bani 'Adī, were strong enough to defend him. "But I will show you," he said, "a man who is more powerful in Mecca than I am, richer in kinsmen and better protected – 'Uthmān ibn 'Affān." So the Prophet sent 'Uthmān and he was well received by his kinsmen of 'Abdu Shams and by others; and though they reiterated to him their refusal to allow any of those now in Ḥudaybiyah to approach the Ka'bah, they invited him personally to make his pilgrimal rounds, which he refused to do. Quraysh had already sent a message to Ibn Ubayy, offering the same concession to him also, but he replied: "I make not my rounds of the House until the Messenger of God maketh his." The Prophet was told of this and it pleased him.

# LXVII

# *"A Clear Victory"*

IT was during 'Uthmān's absence in Mecca that there came over the Prophet a state which was comparable to that of receiving a Revelation but which left him in full possession of his faculties. He gave instructions to one of his Companions, who thereupon went through the camp proclaiming: "The Holy Spirit hath descended upon the Messenger and commandeth allegiance. So go ye forth in the Name of God to make your pledge."[1] Meantime the Prophet had seated himself beneath an acacia tree that was green with its spring foliage breaking into leaf; and one by one the Companions came and pledged allegiance to him. The first man to reach him was Sinān, who was of the same tribe as the Jaḥsh family, that is the Bani Asad ibn Khuzaymah. The crier had specified nothing about the nature of the pledge, so Sinān said "O Messenger of God, I pledge thee mine allegiance unto that which is in thy soul," and the others pledged themselves accordingly. Then the Prophet said "I pledge the allegiance of 'Uthmān," whereupon he put out his left hand, as the hand of his son-in-law, and grasping it with his right hand, pledged the pact. Only one man present failed to respond to the crier, and that was the hypocrite Jadd ibn Qays who tried to hide behind his camel but was none the less seen.

Quraysh now sent Suhayl to conclude a treaty, and with him were his two clansmen Mikraz and Ḥuwayṭib. They conferred with the Prophet, and the Companions heard their voices rise and fall according to whether the point in question was hard to agree upon or easy. When they had finally reached an agreement the Prophet told 'Alī to write down the terms, beginning with the revealed words of consecration *Bismi Llāhi r-Raḥmāni r-Raḥīm, in the Name of God, the Good, the Merciful*, but Suhayl objected. "As to *Raḥmān*," he said, "I know not what he is. But write *Bismik Allāhumma*, In Thy Name, O God, as thou wert wont to write." Some of the Companions cried out "By God, we will write naught but *Bismi Llāhi r-Raḥmāni r-Raḥīm*," but the Prophet ignored them and said "Write *Bismik Allāhumma*," and he went on dictating: "These are the terms of the truce between Muḥammad the Messenger of God and Suhayl the son of 'Amr"; but again Suhayl protested. "If we knew thee to be the Messenger of God," he said, "we would not have barred thee from the House, neither would we have fought thee; but write Muḥammad the son of 'Abd Allāh." 'Alī had already written "the Messenger of God," and the Prophet told him to strike out those words, but he said he could not. So the Prophet told him

[1] W. 604.

to point with his finger to the words in question, and he himself struck them out. Then he told him to write in their place "the son of 'Abd Allāh," which he did.

The document continued: "They have agreed to lay down the burden of war for ten years, in which times men shall be safe and not lay violent hands the one upon the other; on condition that whoso cometh unto Muḥammad of Quraysh without the leave of his guardian, Muḥammad shall return him unto them; but whoso cometh unto Quraysh of those who are with Muḥammad, they shall not be returned. There shall be no subterfuge and no treachery. And whoso wisheth to enter into the bond and pact of Muḥammad may do so; and whoso wisheth to enter the bond and pact of Quraysh may do so." Now there were present in the camp some leading men of Khuzā'ah who had come to visit the pilgrims, whereas one or two representatives of Bakr had followed in the wake of Suhayl; and at this point the men of Khuzā'ah leaped to their feet and said: "We are one with Muḥammad in his bond and his pact." Whereupon the men of Bakr said: "We are one with Quraysh in their bond and their pact." And this agreement was subsequently ratified by the chiefs of both tribes. The treaty ended with the words: "Thou, Muḥammad, shalt depart from us this present year, and shalt not enter Mecca when we are present in despite of us. But in the year that is to come, we shall go out from Mecca and thou shalt enter it with thy companions, staying therein for three days, bearing no arms save the arms of the traveller, with swords in sheaths."[1]

In virtue of the Prophet's vision, the Companions had been certain of the success of their expedition; and when they heard the terms of the treaty and realised that having reached the very edge of the sacred precinct they must now return home with nothing accomplished, it was almost more than they could endure. But worse was to come: as they sat there in sullen and explosive silence, the clank of chains was heard and a youth staggered into the camp with his feet in fetters. It was Abū Jandal, one of the younger sons of Suhayl. His father had imprisoned him on account of his Islam, fearing that he would escape to Medina. His elder brother 'Abd Allāh was among the pilgrims and was about to welcome him when Suhayl caught hold of the chain that was round his prisoner's neck and struck him violently in the face. Then he turned to the Prophet and said: "Our agreement was concluded before this man came to thee." "That is true," said the Prophet. "Return him then unto us," said Suhayl. "O Muslims," shouted Abū Jandal at the top of his voice, "am I to be returned unto the idolaters, for them to persecute me on account of my religion?" The Prophet took Suhayl aside and asked him as a favour to let his son go free, but Suhayl implacably refused. His fellow envoys, Mikraz and Ḥuwayṭib, had been so far silent; but now, feeling that this incident was an inauspicious start for the truce, they intervened. "O Muḥammad," they said, "we give him our protection on thy behalf." This meant that they would lodge him with them, away from his father, and they held to their promise. "Be patient, Abū Jandal," said the Prophet. "God will surely give thee and those with thee relief and a way out. We have agreed on the terms of a truce

[1] I.I. 747–8.

with these people, and have given them our solemn pledge, even as they have done to us, and we will not now break our word."

At this point 'Umar could no longer contain himself. Rising to his feet, he went to the Prophet and said "Art thou not God's Prophet?" and he answered "Yea." "Are we not in the right and our enemies in the wrong?" he said, and again the Prophet assented. "Then why yield we in such lowly wise against the honour of our religion?" said 'Umar, whereupon the Prophet replied: "I am God's Messenger and I will not disobey Him. He will give me the victory." "But didst thou not tell us," persisted 'Umar, "that we should go unto the House and make our rounds about it?" "Even so," said the Prophet, "but did I tell thee we should go to it this year?" 'Umar conceded that he had not. "Verily thou shalt go unto the House," said the Prophet, "and shalt make thy rounds about it." But 'Umar was still seething with indignation, and went to Abū Bakr to work off his feelings still further. He put to him exactly the same questions he had put to the Prophet; but though Abū Bakr had not heard the answers, he gave him the same answer to each question in almost exactly the same words; and at the end he added: "So cleave unto his stirrup, for by God he is right." This impressed 'Umar, and though his feelings had not yet subsided, he gave no further vent to them, and when the Prophet summoned him to put his name to the treaty he signed it in silence. The Prophet also told Suhayl's son 'Abd Allāh to put his name to it. Others of the Muslims who signed it were 'Alī, Abū Bakr, 'Abd ar-Raḥmān ibn 'Awf and Maḥmūd ibn Maslamah.

Some of the general bitterness seemed to have been smoothed over; but when Suhayl and the others left the camp, taking with them the tearful Abū Jandal, men's souls were stirred up again. The Prophet was standing apart, with those who had signed the document. He now left them, and went towards the main body of the pilgrims. "Rise and sacrifice your animals," he said, "and shave your heads." Not a man moved, and he repeated it a second and a third time, but they simply looked at him in dazed and bewildered silence. It was not a rebellion on their part, but having had their expectations shattered by the turn of events they were now genuinely perplexed by the command to do something which they knew to be ritually incorrect; for according to the tradition of Abraham the sacrifices had to be performed within the sacred territory, and the same applied to the rite of shaving the head. None the less, their apparent disobedience dismayed the Prophet, who withdrew to his tent and told Umm Salamah what had happened. "Go forth," she said, "and say no word to any man until thou hast performed thy sacrifice." So the Prophet went to the camel which he himself had consecrated and sacrificed it, saying in a loud voice, so that the men could hear: *Bismi-Llāh, Allāhu Akbar*. At these words the men leaped to their feet and raced to make their sacrifices, falling over each other in their eagerness to obey; and when the Prophet called for Khirāsh – the man of Khuzā'ah he had sent to Mecca before 'Uthmān – to shave his head, many of the Companions set about shaving each other's heads so vigorously that Umm Salamah was afraid, as she afterwards remarked, that mortal wounds might be inflicted. But some of them merely cut locks of their hair, knowing that this was traditionally acceptable as a substitute. Meantime the Prophet had retired to his tent with Khirāsh; and when the rite had been accomplished he stood at the entrance with shaven scalp and said: "God have Mercy on the shavers of their heads!" Whereupon those who had cut their hair protested: "And on the cutters of their hair, O Messenger of God!" But the Prophet repeated what he had said at first, and the voices were raised in protest still louder. Then after another repetition and a third thunderous protest he added: "And upon the cutters of their hair!" When asked afterwards why he had first of all prayed only for the shavers of their heads, he answered: "Because they doubted not."

Returning to his tent, the Prophet gathered up his luxuriant black hair from the ground and threw it over a nearby mimosa tree, whereupon the men crowded round, each bent on taking what he could for its blessing. Nor was Nusaybah to be outdone by the men, and she also made her way to the tree, and was able to snatch some locks, which she treasured until her dying day.

The earth of the camp was strewn with the hair of the pilgrims. But suddenly there came a powerful gust of wind which lifted the hair from the ground and blew it towards Mecca, into the sacred territory; and everyone rejoiced, taking it as a sign that their pilgrimage had been accepted by God in virtue of their intentions, and they now understood why the Prophet had told them to perform their sacrifices.

After they had set off on the return journey to Medina, 'Umar's conscience began to trouble him; and his anxiety was greatly increased when he rode up to the Prophet, seeking to enter into conversation with him, and the Prophet, so it seemed to him, was markedly distant and reserved. 'Umar rode on ahead, saying to himself: "O 'Umar, let thy mother now mourn her son!" He said afterwards that he was so troubled for having questioned the wisdom of the Prophet that he feared there would be a special Revelation condemning him. His fears reached their height when he heard behind him the hooves of a galloping horse, and the rider summoned him back to the Prophet. But his troubles vanished in an instant when he saw the Prophet's face radiant with joy. "There hath descended upon me a *sūrah*," he said, "which is dearer to me than aught else beneath the sun."

The new Revelation left no doubt that the expedition from which they were now returning must be considered as a victorious one, for it opened with the words: *Verily We have given thee a clear victory.*[1] It also spoke of the recent pact of allegiance: *God was well pleased with the believers when they pledged allegiance unto thee beneath the tree. He knew what was in their hearts, and sent down the Spirit of Peace upon them, and hath given them the meed of a near victory.*[2] The Divine Good Pleasure referred to is no less than the promise of *Riḍwān*[3] for him who fulfilled his pledge, and so this beatific allegiance is known as the Pact of *Riḍwān*. The descent of the *Sakīnah*,[4] the Spirit of Peace, is mentioned also in another verse: *He it is who sent down the Spirit of Peace into the hearts of the believers that they might increase in faith upon their faith . . . that He may bring the believing men and the believing women into gardens that are watered by flowing rivers, gardens wherein they shall dwell immortal, and that He may take*

[1] XLVIII, 1. [2] XLVIII, 18. [3] See p. 95. [4] Hebrew *Shekinah*.

*from them all guilt of evil. Triumph immense for them is that in the sight of God.*[1]

The Prophet's vision, which had prompted the expedition, is referred to as follows: *God hath truly fulfilled for His Messenger the vision: God willing, ye shall enter the inviolable mosque in safety, not fearing, with the hair of your heads shaven or cut. But He knoweth what ye know not, and before that hath He given you a near victory.*[2]

[1] XLVIII, 4–5. [2] XLVIII, 27.

# LXVIII

# *After Ḥudaybiyah*

ABŪ BAṢĪR of the Bani Thaqīf was a young man whose family had come from Ṭā'if and settled in Mecca as confederates of the Bani Zuhrah. He had entered Islam and they had imprisoned him, but he escaped and made his way to Medina on foot, arriving there shortly after the Prophet's return from Ḥudaybiyah. He was soon followed by an envoy of Quraysh who demanded his return. While giving Abū Baṣīr the same words of comfort that he had given to Abū Jandal, the Prophet told him that he was bound by the treaty to deliver him into the hands of the envoy. The Companions, including 'Umar, were now more or less reconciled to the terms of the treaty, so when Abū Baṣīr was led off by the man of Quraysh and the freed slave he had brought with him for support, those Emigrants and Helpers who were present serenely echoed the words of the Prophet: "Be of good cheer! God will surely find thee a way out."

Their hopes were realised sooner than was expected. Despite his youth, Abū Baṣīr was a resourceful man and at the first halt he contrived to get the sword of the envoy and to kill him, whereupon the freedman, Kawthar by name, fled headlong back to Medina. He entered the Mosque unopposed and threw himself at the feet of the Prophet, who happened to be there and who said as he approached: "This man hath seen some terrible thing." Kawthar gasped out that his fellow had been killed and that he himself was all but killed, and it was not long before Abū Baṣīr himself appeared with the drawn sword in his hand. "O Prophet of God," he said, "thine obligation hath been fulfilled. Thou didst return me unto them, and God hath delivered me." "Alas for his mother!"[1] said the Prophet. "What a fine firebrand for war, had he but other men with him!" But if Quraysh sent further envoys to demand his return he would be bound to comply, as he had done in the first case. Such an idea however was far from the mind of Abū Baṣīr, who now suggested that the arms and the armour of the dead man together with the camels should be treated as booty, divided into five parts and distributed according to the law. "If I did that," said the Prophet, "they would hold that I had not fulfilled the terms I swore to keep." Then he turned to the terrified survivor of the two Meccans. "The spoil plundered from thy fellow is thy concern," he said. "And take thou back this man to those who sent thee," he added, indicating Abū Baṣīr. Kawthar turned pale: "O Muḥammad," he said, "I value my life. My strength is not

[1] An often used ellipsis meaning: "The man is such a hothead that his mother will soon have to mourn his death."

enough for him, nor have I the hands of two men." The Muslims had fulfilled their obligation, but the representative of Quraysh had refused to take custody of the prisoner. So the Prophet turned to Abū Baṣīr and said: "Go whither thou wilt."

He made his way to the shores of the Red Sea, with the words "had he but other men with him" still in his ears. Nor was he the only one who had taken note of this veiled authorisation and instruction. 'Umar had been intent on what had passed; and he contrived to pass the Prophet's words on to the Muslims in Mecca, together with information about Abū Baṣīr's whereabouts which he soon learned from friendly men of the coastal tribes who came to Medina. Now Suhayl's son, Abū Jandal, was no longer closely guarded by his protectors as he had been by his father; and in any case the treaty had made for a general slackening of vigilance in Mecca as to the watch kept on the young Muslim prisoners, for Muḥammad had shown that if they escaped to Medina he would keep to his word and return them. So Abū Jandal made his way to Abū Baṣīr, and other youths did the same, including Walīd, the brother of Khālid. Abū Baṣīr made with them a camp at a strategic point on the Meccan caravan route to Syria. They recognised him as their leader and he led them in prayer and advised them on questions concerning the rites and other aspects of the religion, for many of them were recent converts, and they greatly respected him and gladly obeyed him. Quraysh had been rejoicing in the re-established safety of their favourite road to the north. But no less than seventy young men joined Abū Baṣīr's camp, and they became the terror of the caravans. Finally, after they had suffered the loss of many lives and much merchandise, Quraysh sent a letter to the Prophet asking him to take these highwaymen into his community, and promising that they would not ask for them to be returned to Mecca. So the Prophet wrote to Abū Baṣīr that he could now come to Medina with his companions. But meantime the young leader had fallen seriously ill and when the letter arrived death was close upon him. He read it and died clasping it between his hands. His companions prayed over him and buried him, and made a mosque at the place of his burial; then they went to join the Prophet in Medina.[1]

When they reached the lava tract Walīd's camel stumbled and threw him, so that he cut his finger on a stone. As he bound it up, he addressed it in verse, saying:

> "What art thou but a finger shedding blood,
> With no wound else upon the path of God."

But the cut festered, and the wound proved to be mortal. He was able, none the less, before he died, to write a letter to his brother Khālid urging him to enter Islam.

Only one Muslim woman escaped from Mecca at this time and took refuge in Medina, and that was 'Uthmān's half-sister, Umm Kulthūm, the daughter of his mother Arwà and of 'Uqbah, who had been put to death on the way from Badr. But a Revelation now came forbidding the return of

[1] W. 624–9; B. LIV; I.I. 751–3.

any believing women to the disbelievers. So when Umm Kulthūm's two full brothers came to take her back, the Prophet refused to let them have her, and Quraysh accepted his refusal without protest. There had been no mention of women in the treaty. Then Zayd and Zubayr and 'Abd ar-Raḥmān ibn 'Awf asked for her hand in marriage, and the Prophet advised her to marry Zayd, which she did.

In the month which followed the treaty, 'Ā'ishah and her father suffered a great loss which was shortly to be followed by cause for great rejoicing. Umm Rūmān fell ill and died. She was buried in the Baqī', and the Prophet prayed over her and descended into her grave. Inevitably the news of her death was brought to Mecca and came to the ears of her son, 'Abd al-Ka'bah; and it is possible that his bereavement prompted him to take an action which he had no doubt been contemplating for some time. However that may be, it was not long after his mother's death that he came to Medina and entered Islam. When he pledged his allegiance, the Prophet changed his name to 'Abd ar-Raḥmān.

Nor was he the only new Muslim at this time. As the weeks and the months passed it became more and more apparent why the Koran had declared the truce to be *a clear victory*. The men of Mecca and Medina could now meet in peace and converse freely together; and during the next two years the community of Islam was more than doubled.

Soon after the return of the pilgrims a verse had been revealed at which everyone rejoiced: *It may be that God will establish love between you and those with whom ye are at enmity.*[1] These words seemed to refer in general to the many conversions which now took place. But they were also taken by some to refer in particular to an unexpected close relationship which was now to be established between the Prophet and one of the leaders of Quraysh.

A few months before Ḥudaybiyah news had come from Abyssinia of the death of 'Ubayd Allāh ibn Jaḥsh, the Prophet's cousin and brother-in-law. He had been a Christian before he entered Islam, and not long after his emigration to Abyssinia he had reverted to Christianity. This had greatly distressed his wife Umm Ḥabībah, Abū Sufyān's daughter, who remained a Muslim; and when four months had elapsed after the death of her husband the Prophet sent a message to the Negus, asking him to stand proxy for himself and to ratify a marriage between him and the widow, if she were willing. To her the Prophet sent no message directly; but she had a dream in which someone came to her and addressed her as "mother of the faithful", and she interpreted this as meaning that she would become the wife of the Prophet. The next day she received the message from the Negus which confirmed her dream, whereupon she chose her kinsman Khālid ibn Sa'īd[2] to give her in marriage, and he and the Negus solemnised the pact between them in the presence of Ja'far and others of the brethren. Then the Negus held a wedding feast in his palace, and all the Muslims were invited.

The Prophet had also sent word to Ja'far that it would please him if he and his community would now come to live in Medina. Ja'far forthwith set about making preparations for the journey, and the Negus gave them two

[1] LX, 7. [2] See p. 47.

boats. It was decided that Umm Ḥabībah should travel with them; and in Medina work was begun on the building of an apartment for her next to those of the other wives.

The Negus was not the only reigning prince to whom the Prophet sent a letter at this time. When he had split the seemingly invincible rock in the trench, he had seen the castles of the Yemen by the light which had flared from it at his first blow, whereas by the light which flared from his third and final blow he had seen the white palace of Chosroes at Madā'in. As to the certainty which had then been given him about the future spread of the empire of Islam, there was a connection between these two lights inasmuch as the Yemen was now under the rule of Persia; and the Prophet was moved to write to the Persian monarch, informing him of his Prophethood and summoning him to Islam. He may not have had much hopes of the success of his message, but it was necessary to offer him the possibility of making the right choice before any other action was taken.

As to the second of the three lights, it had revealed the castles of Syria, and the Prophet had received from it the certainty of the spread of Islam to those parts and also to the West. In due course he was to send a similar letter to Heraclius the Roman Emperor; and he now dictated another such letter which he sent to Alexandria, to the Muqawqis, the ruler of Egypt.

Meantime Chosroes had heard from other sources of the growing power of the Arab king of Yathrib who claimed to be a Prophet. So he dispatched an order to Bādhān, his viceroy in the Yemen, asking for further and clearer information about Muḥammad. Bādhān forthwith sent two envoys to Medina, so that they could see for themselves and bring him back news. Following a fashion that was prevalent at the Persian court, they had shaved their beards and grown long moustaches. Their appearance was abhorrent to the Prophet. "Who bade you do this?" he exclaimed. "Our lord," they said, meaning Chosroes. "My Lord," said the Prophet, "hath bidden me grow my beard and cut short my moustache." He sent them away, telling them to return to him the next day. That night Gabriel told him that on the same day there had been an uprising in Persia in which Chosroes had been killed, and his son now reigned in his stead. So when the envoys returned he told them of this, and bade them inform their master the viceroy. Then he said: "Tell him that my religion and mine empire will reach far beyond the kingdom of Chosroes; and say unto him from me: Enter Islam, and I will confirm thee in what thou hast, and I will appoint thee king over thy people in the Yemen."

They returned to Ṣan'ā', not knowing what to think, and delivered the message to Bādhān, who said: "We will see what befalleth. If what he said be true, then is he a Prophet whom God hath sent." But even before he had had time to send a man to Persia to find out the truth of the matter, a messenger arrived from Siroes, the new Shāh, announcing what had happened, and claiming their allegiance. Instead of replying, Bādhān entered Islam, and so did his two messengers and other Persians who were with him. He then sent word to Medina, and the Prophet confirmed his rule over the Yemen. That was the beginning of the fulfilment of what had been revealed in the first flash of light from the trench.

The Prophet's letter reached Madā'in after the death of Chosroes, so it was delivered to his successor, whose sole answer was to tear it in pieces. "Even so, O Lord, tear from him his kingdom," said the Prophet when he heard of this.

In these same weeks after the return of the pilgrims there was an attack on the Prophet's life by a means which had not yet been used against him. In every generation of the Jews in Arabia there could be found one or two adepts in the science of magic; and one of these was amongst the Jews still living in Medina, Labīd by name, an expert sorcerer who had also instructed his daughters in the subtle art lest his own knowledge should die with him. Labīd now received a heavy bribe to put as deadly a spell as he could upon the Prophet. For this purpose he needed some combings of his hair, which he or one of his daughters contrived to procure, possibly through the intermediary of an entirely innocent person. He tied eleven knots in the hair, and his daughters breathed imprecations upon each knot. Then he attached it to a sprig from a male date-palm which had on it the outer sheath of the pollen, and threw it into a deep well. The spell could only be undone by the untying of the knots.

The Prophet was soon aware that something was seriously wrong. On the one hand his memory began to fail him, while on the other hand he began to imagine that he had done things which in fact he had not done. He was also overcome with weakness, and when food was pressed upon him he could not bring himself to eat. He prayed God to cure him, and in his sleep he was conscious of two persons, one sitting at his head and the other at his feet. He heard one of them inform the other of the exact cause of his infirmity and of the name of the well.[1] When he woke Gabriel came to him, and confirming his dream he gave him two *sūrahs* of the Koran, one of which contains five verses and the other six. The Prophet sent 'Alī to the well, telling him to recite over it the two *sūrahs*. At each verse one of the knots untied itself until all were untied and the Prophet recovered his full strength of mind and body.[2]

The first of the two sūrahs is:

*Say: I take refuge in the Lord of daybreak*
*from the evil of that which He hath created,*
*and from the evil of dusk when it dimmeth into night,*
*and from the evil of the women who breathe upon knots,*
*and from the evil of the envier when he envieth.*[3]

The second is:

*Say: I take refuge in the Lord of men,*
*The King of men,*
*the God of men,*
*from the evil of the stealthy whisperer,*
*who whispereth in the breasts of men;*
*from jinn and from men.*[4]

[1] B. LIX, 10. [2] Bayḍāwī on K. CXIII, 4. [3] CXIII.

[4] CXIV. According to some authorities these two *sūrahs* which were recited on this occasion were not then newly revealed but had been given to the Prophet in Mecca before the Hijrah.

These *sūrahs* are placed last of all in the Koran. They are called "the two takings of refuge", and are recited continually for protection against all manner of evil.

The Prophet ordered the well to be filled up and another to be dug near at hand to replace it. He sent for Labīd, who confessed to having placed the spell upon him for the sake of a bribe, but he did not take any action against him.

# LXIX

# *Khaybar*

THE truce with Mecca made it possible to concentrate on the dangers which lay to the north. The greatest of these was the town of Khaybar, occupied by Jews who were for the most part implacably hostile to Islam. The sorcerer Labīd had almost certainly been bribed from there, though that could have been the work of an individual. But there were far more evident and general reasons for taking action against the exiled Bani Naḍīr and their Khaybarite kinsmen. Not that they were likely to invade Yathrib. Except for one or two men, they had not taken any direct part in the campaign of the Trench, but it was they who had given Quraysh every encouragement to attack, and it was their influence which had induced their allies of Ghaṭafān to side with Quraysh on that occasion. It was also largely through them that Ghaṭafān still remained virtually at war with the oasis. Medina could never know any fullness of peace while Khaybar remained as it was.

It had long been clear that something must be done, sooner or later, in that direction; and now the time had come, for the Prophet was certain that the *near victory* promised in the recent Revelation – a victory which would moreover be rich in spoils – could be nothing other than the conquest of Khaybar. But this was not to be shared by all who professed Islam. The Revelation made it clear that those Bedouin who had failed to respond to his summons to make the Lesser Pilgrimage had been largely prompted by mercenary motives. Since there was no hope of plunder on the Pilgrimage, it was not worth the effort. They were therefore not to be allowed to take part in the conquest of what was, without doubt, one of the richest communities in all Arabia.

This meant setting off with a smaller force, though it had the advantage that their plans could be kept secret until the last moment. But even when the project became known, it was passed from mouth to mouth as a pleasantry rather than a fact. The impregnable strength of Khaybar was almost proverbial. Quraysh and the other enemies of Islam hoped that the news was true because, if so, Muḥammad would at last receive a crushing defeat; but they feared it could not be true, for they knew he was not mad. As for the men of Khaybar themselves their confidence was such that they refused to believe it. They did not even trouble to ask their allies for help until certain news came from Medina that Muḥammad was about to set forth. Only then did Kinānah, their virtual chief, make a speedy visit to Ghaṭafān, offering them half the date harvest for that year if they would send them reinforcements. They agreed to do so and promised a force of four thousand men. The Jews of Khaybar were in the habit of donning their armour every day and lining up their full strength of fighting men, ten thousand in all. The help of Ghaṭafān would bring the number up to fourteen thousand; and according to the news from Medina, the invading army was of sixteen hundred men only.

Before the Prophet set out, one of the men of Aws known as Abū 'Abs came to him with a problem. He had a camel to ride, but his clothes were in rags and he had no means of procuring any provisions to take on the march and nothing to leave for the upkeep of his family, let alone buying himself a new garment. There were many others in similar circumstances, though this was an extreme case. But much had been spent on the Pilgrimage, and everything that had been gained so far in the way of spoil was outweighed by the increasing number of poverty-stricken converts who came to Medina from every direction. The Prophet gave Abū 'Abs a fine long cloak, all that was available for the moment; but on the march, a day or two later, he noticed that he had on a much poorer cloak and he asked him: "Where is the cloak I gave thee?" "I sold it for eight dirhams," said Abū 'Abs. "Then I bought two dirhams worth of dates as provision for myself, and I left two dirhams for my family to live on, and bought a cloak for four dirhams." The Prophet laughed and said: "O father of 'Abs, thou and thy companions are poor indeed. But by Him in whose hand is my soul, if ye keep safe and live yet a little while, ye shall have abundance of provisions and leave abundantly for your families. Ye shall abound in dirhams and in slaves; and it will not be good for you!"[1]

At one point on the march, between two camps, the Prophet halted his army and called to a man of Aslam known as Ibn al-Akwa', who had, as he knew, a beautiful voice. "Dismount," he said, "and sing us a song of thy camel-songs." The Bedouin would sing to their camels as they rode from place to place. They would chant poems to old melodies, monotonous, haunting and plaintive; and to the sadly serene cadences of one of these Ibn al-Akwa' now chanted some words which the Prophet had taught them while they were digging the trench:

> "God, but for Thee we never had been guided,
> Never had given alms, nor prayed Thy prayer."

So it began; and when he had finished the Prophet said to him: "God have Mercy on thee," at which 'Umar protested: "Thou hast made it inevitable, O Messenger of God. Would thou hadst let us enjoy him longer!" He meant, as they all knew, that the Prophet had foretold his early martyrdom, for they had come by experience to conclude that when he invoked Mercy upon anyone, that person had probably not long to live.

Within two and a half days they were only an evening's march from their goal. It was now important to take up a position that would put them as a barrier between Khaybar and her allies of Ghaṭafān. With this end in view the Prophet asked for a guide and during the night they reached an open

[1] W. 636.

space in front of the walls. It was very dark, for the young crescent moon had already set; and so quiet was their approach that no one stirred in the town, and no domestic bird or beast gave the alert. Only at cockcrow was the silence broken. The call to prayer was hushed that dawn in the Muslim camp; and having prayed, they looked ahead of them in silence at this "garden of the Ḥijāz" which the increasing light gradually revealed to them as the fortresses began to loom up above the rich palm groves and fields of corn. The sun rose, and when the land workers came out with their spades and mattocks and baskets they were astonished to find themselves face to face with a grimly silent army. "Muḥammad and his host," they cried, and fled back into their strongholds. "*Allāhu Akbar!*" said the Prophet, adding, in triumphant play upon the letters of the name: *Kharibat Khaybar!* (Khaybar is crushed!). Then he solemnly sealed its defeat by reciting the revealed verse which says of the punishment of God: *When it alighteth in front of their dwellings, bad morning then to those who have been warned!*[1] But instead of saying *it alighteth* he said, "we alight."

The Jews held a hurried council of war. But despite the warning of one of their chiefs they decided to trust to their battlements. There was no comparison, they said, between the fortresses of Yathrib and their own mountain citadels, as they liked to call them. This decision to fight in separate groups was largely based on their greatest weakness, which was lack of unity. What the Revelation had told the Prophet about the Jews of Yathrib was also true of the Khaybarites: *Ill feeling is rife amongst them. Thou countest them as one whole, but their hearts are divided.*[2] It was their misfortune to be now suddenly faced by an army which, though small, was penetrated with the discipline implied in the revealed verse: *Verily God loveth those who fight for His cause in ranks as if they were a close-built block*,[3] an army of men whose souls delighted in the promise of the words: *How many a little band hath overcome a multitude by God's leave! And God is with the steadfast.*[4]

On the first day when the Prophet attacked the nearest fortress, the garrisons of the others did not march out in a body to attack the besiegers but remained behind their own walls and busied themselves with strengthening their fortifications. These tactics reduced the disparity of numbers, but they put the steadfastness of the Muslims to the test of a long campaign on alien territory and many battles instead of one. The men of Khaybar were amongst the most expert marksmen of Arabia. Never before had the Muslims had such severe training in the use of their shields; and at the outset of the campaign the women in the camp were kept busy treating arrow wounds. Of the Prophet's wives the lot had fallen a second time in succession to Umm Salamah; and amongst the other women who accompanied the army to tend the wounded and keep up the supply of water behind the lines were the Prophet's aunt Ṣafiyyah, Umm Ayman, Nusaybah and Umm Sulaym, the mother of Anas.

For several days nothing was achieved; but on the sixth night, when 'Umar was in command of the watch, a spy was caught in the camp, and in return for his life he gave them valuable information about the various

[1] XXXVII, 177. [2] LIX, 14. [3] LXI, 4. [4] II, 249.

fortresses, telling them which they could capture most easily and suggesting that they should begin with one which was not well guarded and which had a quantity of weapons stored in its spacious cellars, including some engines of war that had been used in the past against other fortresses, for like Yathrib Khaybar had often been plagued with civil discord. The next day the fortress was taken and the engines brought out to be used in other assaults, a ballista for hurling rocks and two testudos for bringing men up to the walls beneath an impregnable roof so that they could breach an entrance. Partly thanks to these engines, the easier fortresses fell one by one. The first powerful resistance they encountered was at a stronghold named Na'īm. Here the garrison came out in great force, and on that day every attack made by the Muslims was repulsed. "Tomorrow," said the Prophet, "will I give the standard unto a man whom God and His messenger love. God will give us the victory by his hands; he is not one who turneth back in flight."

In his previous campaigns the Prophet had used relatively small flags as standards. But to Khaybar he had brought a great black standard made from a cloak of 'Ā'ishah's. They called it "the Eagle", and this he now gave to 'Alī. Then he prayed for him and his other Companions, that God should give them the victory. After another day of fierce fighting, in which Zubayr and the red-turbaned Abū Dujānah played an eminent part, 'Alī led his men in a final onslaught which drove back the garrison deep into their stronghold, leaving the Muslims in command of the doors. The fortress surrendered, but not before many of its men had escaped to other fortresses through a back outlet.

"Where are the Bani Ghaṭafān?" was a question that was being asked throughout Khaybar, but not answered. They had in fact set out with an army of four thousand men as promised. But after a day's march they had heard during the night a strange voice – they did not know whether it came from earth or heaven – and the voice cried out three times in succession: "Your people! Your people! Your people!", whereupon the men imagined that their families were in danger, and hastened back whence they had come, only to find everything in order. But having returned, they were unwilling to set out a second time, partly because many of them were convinced that they would now arrive too late to have a share in the defeat of the enemy.[1]

The most impregnable of the strongholds of Khaybar was known as the Citadel of Zubayr. It crowned a high mass of rock with a steep approach to the gates and sheer cliffs on all the other sides. Most of the fighting men who had escaped from the other fortresses had joined the citadel's garrison, which remained firmly within the walls. The Prophet besieged them for three days, and then a Jew from another stronghold came to him and told him that they had a hidden resource which would enable them to hold out almost indefinitely; and he offered to tell him the secret, on condition that his life and property and family should be safe. The Prophet agreed, and the man showed him where he could dig down to dam an underground rivulet which flowed beneath the rocks of the citadel. They had steps leading down to it from within, and since the stream was never dry they kept no stores of water. So when it was cut off they were soon

[1] W. 651–2; I.I. 757.

driven by thirst to come out and fight, and after a savage battle they were defeated.

The last of the strongholds to make any resistance was Qamūs. This belonged to the family of Kinānah, one of the richest and most powerful clans of the Bani Naḍīr. Some of them had long lived in Khaybar whereas others of the family, including Kinānah himself, had recently settled there after they had been exiled from Yathrib. It was they especially who had been counting on the help of Ghaṭafān, whose failure to keep their promise had been an unnerving disappointment for them; and they were still further demoralised by the bad news brought by all those fugitives who had now crowded into Qamūs. They none the less held out for fourteen days; then Kinānah sent word that he wished to come to terms with the Prophet, who said he was willing to negotiate. So the chieftain came down from the fortress with others of his family; and it was agreed that none of the garrison should be put to death or made captive – neither they nor their families – on condition that they should leave Khaybar and that all their possessions should become the property of the victors. The Prophet then added a further clause, namely that his obligation to spare their lives and let them go free should be annulled with regard to anyone who might try to conceal any of his possessions. Kinānah and the others agreed to this; and the Prophet called on Abū Bakr, 'Umar, 'Alī and Zubayr and ten of the Jews to witness the agreement.

But it soon became clear to both Jews and Muslims that much wealth was being hidden. Where was the famed treasure of the Bani Naḍīr which they had brought with them from Medina, and which they had so lavishly displayed in their procession through its streets? The Prophet questioned Kinānah about this, and he replied that since their arrival in Khaybar the treasure had all been sold to pay for more arms and armour and fortifications. The Jews knew that he was lying, and were all the more apprehensive because many of them now believed themselves to be in the presence of a Prophet. They held that they had no need to follow him, because he had not been sent to them; but it would be clearly vain to try to deceive him. One of them, who had Kinānah's welfare at heart, went to him and begged him to hide nothing, for if he did the Prophet would certainly be informed of it. Kinānah angrily rebuked him; but within less than a day the treasure was discovered, and Kinānah was put to death together with a cousin of his who was found to be privy to the concealment. Their families were made captive.

After the fall of Qamūs the two remaining fortresses surrendered on the same terms. Then the Jews of Khaybar consulted together, and sent a deputation to the Prophet, suggesting that since they were skilled in the management of their farms and their orchards he should allow them to remain in their homes, and they would pay him a yearly rent of half the produce. To this the Prophet agreed; but he stipulated that if in the future he decided to banish them they must go. It was then rumoured that the Muslims intended to extend their campaign to Fadak, a small but rich oasis to the north-east; and when the Jews of Fadak heard of the terms that had been imposed upon Khaybar they sent word offering to surrender on the same conditions. Fadak thus became the property of the Prophet, as did every other asset which had not been acquired by force of arms.

When all the terms had been agreed upon, and when the victorious army had rested, the widowed wife of Sallām ibn Mishkam roasted a lamb and poisoned every part of it with a deadly poison which she concentrated especially in the shoulders, having learnt on inquiry that the Prophet preferred the shoulder of lamb to the other joints. Then she brought it to the camp and set it before him, whereupon he thanked her and invited those of his Companions who were present to sup with him.

It happened on this occasion that seated next to the Prophet was a Khazrajite named Bishr, the son of that Barā' who had led the Muslims of Yathrib to the Second 'Aqabah and who had been the first ever to pray the ritual prayer in the direction of Mecca. When the Prophet took a mouthful of lamb, Bishr did the same and swallowed it, but the Prophet spat out what was in his mouth, saying to the others: "Hold off your hands! This shoulder proclaimeth unto me that it is poisoned." He sent for the woman and asked her if she had poisoned the joint. "Who told thee?" she asked. "The shoulder itself," said the Prophet. "What made thee do it?" "Well thou knowest," she said, "what thou hast done unto my people; and thou hast slain my father and mine uncle and my husband. So I told myself: 'If he be a king, I shall be well quit of him; and if he be a Prophet he will be informed of the poison.'" The face of Bishr was already ashen pale, and he died shortly afterwards. But the Prophet none the less pardoned the woman.[1]

She was not the only woman who had lost a father and a husband at the hands of the Muslims. Among the captives taken as a result of Kinānah's hiding the treasure was his widow Ṣafiyyah, the daughter of that Ḥuyayy who had persuaded the Bani Qurayẓah to break their treaty with the Prophet, and who had been put to death with them after the Battle of the Trench. She was seventeen years old and had only married Kinānah a month or two before the Prophet set out from Medina. The marriage, while it lasted, had not been a happy one. Unlike her father and her husband, Ṣafiyyah was of a deeply pious nature. From her earliest years she had heard her people talk of the Prophet who was soon to come, and this had filled her imagination. Then they had spoken of an Arab in Mecca, a man of Quraysh, who claimed to be that Prophet; and then came the news that he had arrived at Qubā'. That was seven years ago, when she was a child of ten; and she well remembered her father and her uncle setting confidently out for Qubā' in order to reassure themselves that the man was an impostor; but what had imprinted itself on her memory above all was their return late at night, both in a state of extreme dejection. It was clear from what they said that they believed the newcomer to be the promised Prophet, but that they intended to oppose him; and her young mind was puzzled.[2]

Soon after her marriage, and not long before the Prophet arrived in front of Khaybar, she had had a dream. She saw a brilliant moon hanging in the sky, and she knew that beneath it lay the city of Medina. Then the moon began to move towards Khaybar, where it fell into her lap. When she woke

1 B. LI, 28. 2 I.I. 354–5.

she told Kinānah what she had seen in her sleep, whereupon he struck her a blow in the face and said: "This can only mean that thou desirest the King of the Ḥijāz, Muḥammad." The mark of the blow was still visible when she was brought as captive to the Prophet. He asked her what had caused it, and she told him of her dream. Now Diḥyah[1] of the Bani Kalb, who had entered Islam shortly after Badr, had asked that Ṣafiyyah should be given him as his share of the booty of Khaybar, or as part of his share, and the Prophet had agreed; but on hearing her dream he sent to Diḥyah and told him he must take her cousin instead. He then told Ṣafiyyah that he was prepared to set her free, and he offered her the choice between remaining a Jewess and returning to her people or entering Islam and becoming his wife. "I choose God and His Messenger," she said; and they were married at the first halt on the homeward march.

The campaign was not yet finished, for instead of returning by the direct way they had come, the Prophet turned a little to the west and besieged the Jews of Wādi l-Qurà in their fortresses. They had been in league with Khaybar; and after three days they surrendered on the same terms.

Ibn al-Akwa', the Aslamite who had sung to them on their northward march, had been killed at Khaybar during the attack upon the Citadel. His own sword had somehow turned against him and given him a mortal wound, and one of the Helpers remarked that he could not be counted as a martyr. "He lieth who so sayeth," said the Prophet. "Verily he passeth through the Gardens of Paradise as freely as a swimmer passeth through water."[2] Another question about martyrdom arose at Wādi l-Qurà, where the Prophet's black slave Karkarah was killed by an arrow as he was unsaddling a camel. But the Prophet answered: "He is burning even now in Hell beneath a cloak which he stole at Khaybar and which hath become a cloak of flames."[3]

It was his wont to warn them continually that the privilege of living with him in his community brought with it a grave responsibility, for God was Just and would judge them more severely than those who lived in worse ages when it was more difficult to resist evil. He said: "Verily ye are in an age when whoso omitteth one tenth of the law shall be doomed. But there will come an age when whoso fulfilleth one tenth of the law shall be saved."[4]

[1] He was a man of great beauty, and the Prophet said of him: "The most like unto Gabriel of any man I have seen is Diḥyah al-Kalbī." I.S. IV, 184.

[2] W. 662. [3] I.I. 765. [4] Tir. XXXI, 79.

# LXX

# "Whom Lovest Thou Most?"

WHEN the victorious army reached Medina after their seven weeks' absence they found that Ja'far and his companions were already there. He had left for Abyssinia at the age of twenty-seven and was now a man of forty. He had not seen the Prophet for thirteen years, though they had been in constant communication. The Prophet clasped him to him and kissed him between the eyes. Then he said: "I know not for which of the two my rejoicing is greater, for the advent of Ja'far or for the victory of Khaybar." With Ja'far was his wife Asmā' and their three sons, 'Abd Allāh, Muḥammad and 'Awn, who had been born in Abyssinia.

With him also was Umm Ḥabībah, whose apartment was ready to receive her, and a second marriage feast was held to celebrate her union with the Prophet. She was now about thirty-five years old. The other wives, all except 'Ā'ishah, had known her in Mecca. She was, moreover, the sister-in-law of Zaynab, and Sawdah and Umm Salamah had been her close companions in their early days together in Abyssinia. Her coming had been expected, and caused little stir. An object of much greater concern to the wives was the unexpected addition to their household, the young and beautiful Ṣafiyyah. On their arrival in Medina the Prophet lodged her temporarily in one of the houses of the ever-hospitable Ḥārithah; and hearing of her beauty, 'A'ishah sent to Umm Salamah to ask her about their new companion. "She is beautiful indeed," said Umm Salamah, "and the Messenger of God loveth her much." 'Ā'ishah went to the house of Ḥārithah and entered with the throng of women who were visiting the new bride. She herself was veiled, and without revealing her identity she remained somewhat in the background, but close enough to see for herself that what Umm Salamah had said was true. Then she left the house, but the Prophet who was there had recognised her, and following her out he said: "O 'Ā'ishah, how didst thou find her?" "I saw in her," said 'Ā'ishah, "a Jewess like any other Jewess." "Say not so," said the Prophet, "for she hath entered Islam and made good her Islam."

None the less, Ṣafiyyah was particularly vulnerable amongst the wives on account of her father. "O daughter of Ḥuyayy", in itself a respectful address, could be changed by the tone of voice into an insult, and on one occasion she came to the Prophet in tears because one of her new companions had tried to make her feel inferior. He said: "Say unto them: my father is Aaron, and mine uncle is Moses."

Of all the wives Ṣafiyyah was the nearest in age to 'Ā'ishah, nearer even than Ḥafṣah, who was now twenty-two. This had increased 'Ā'ishah's fears at first; but as the weeks passed the two youngest wives found a certain sympathy for each other, and Ḥafṣah likewise befriended the newcomer. "We were two groups," said 'A'ishah in after years, "in one myself and Ḥafṣah and Ṣafiyyah and Sawdah, and in the other Umm Salamah and the rest of the wives."

'Ā'ishah was at that time in her sixteenth year, old for her age in some respects but not in others. Her feelings were always clear from her face, and nearly always from her tongue. On one occasion the Prophet said to her: "O 'Ā'ishah, it is not hidden from me when thou art angered against me, nor yet when thou art pleased." "O dearer than my father and my mother," she said, "how knowest thou that?" "When thou art pleased," he said, "thou sayst in swearing 'Nay, by the Lord of Muḥammad', but when thou art angered it is 'Nay, by the Lord of Abraham'."[1] On another occasion, when the Prophet came to her somewhat later than she had expected, she said to him: "Where hast thou been this day until now?" "O little fair one," he said, "I have been with Umm Salamah." "Hast thou not had thy fill of Umm Salamah?" she said; and when he smiled without answering, she added: "O Messenger of God, tell me of thyself. If thou wert between the two slopes of a valley, one of which had not been grazed whereas the other had been grazed, on which wouldst thou pasture thy flocks?" "On that which had not been grazed," said the Prophet. "Even so," she said; "and I am not as any other of thy wives. Every woman of them had a husband before thee, except myself." The Prophet smiled and said nothing.[2]

'Ā'ishah knew well that she could not have the Prophet for herself alone. She was one woman, and he was as twenty men. The Revelation had said of him: *Verily of an immense magnitude is thy nature.* It was as if he were a whole world in himself, comparable to the outer world and in some ways mysteriously one with it. She had often noticed that if there was a roll of thunder, even in the distance, his face would change colour; the sound of a powerful gust of wind would likewise visibly move him; and on at least one occasion when there was a downpour of rain he bared his head and shoulders and breast and went out into the open so that he might share the delight of the earth in receiving the bounty of heaven directly upon his skin.

'Ā'ishah was not any the less jealous by reason of his difference from other men; but she knew that jealousy, unlike love, was for this life only. Speaking of Paradise, the Revelation had promised more than once: *And we remove whatever there may be of rancour in their breasts.*[3] One day she said to the Prophet: "O Messenger of God, who are thy wives in Paradise?" "Thou art of them," he said, and she treasured these words for the rest of her life, as also his having said to her once: "Gabriel is here and he

[1] I.S. VIII, 47. [2] I.S. VIII, 55. [3] VII, 43; XV, 47.

giveth thee his greetings of Peace." "Peace be upon him, and the Mercy of God and His Blessings!" she had answered.[1]

Of her jealousy she would say in after-years: "I was not jealous of any other wife of the Prophet as I was jealous of Khadījah, for his constant mentioning of her and because God had bidden him give her good tidings of a mansion in Paradise of precious stones. And whensoever he sacrificed a sheep, he would send a goodly portion of it unto those who had been her intimate friends. Many a time said I unto him: It is as if there had never been any other woman in the world, save only Khadījah."[2]

'Ā'ishah's perceptions and reactions were exceedingly quick. Soon after Khaybar, or perhaps a little before it, Hālah the mother of Abū l-'Āṣ had come on a visit to Medina to see her son and daughter-in-law Zaynab and her little granddaughter Umāmah; and one day when the Prophet was in 'Ā'ishah's apartment there was a knock on the door, and a woman's voice was heard asking if she might enter. The Prophet turned pale and trembled; and immediately divining the cause, 'Ā'ishah was overwhelmed by a wave of jealousy and scolded him; for she knew that in the voice of Hālah he had heard the voice of her sister Khadījah. He confirmed this afterwards, and said that also her manner of asking to enter had been the same as that of his dead wife.[3]

Sawdah, now grown somewhat elderly, gave her day with the Prophet to 'A'ishah because she felt sure that this would greatly please him; and the rest of the community, including the other wives, had no doubt that of those wives now living it was 'Ā'ishah that the Prophet loved most. This was not mere conjecture, since from time to time, by one or another of his Companions, he would be asked the question: "O Messenger of God, whom lovest thou most in all the world?" And although he did not always give the same answer to this question, inasmuch as he felt great love in more than one direction – for his daughters and their children, for 'Alī, for Abū Bakr, for Zayd and Usāmah – the answer was sometimes 'Ā'ishah but never one of the other wives. For this reason it was becoming the custom in Medina that if a man had a favour to ask of the Prophet, and if he was offering him a gift with a view to his petition as the Koran recommended, he would postpone the offering until the Prophet was in 'Ā'ishah's apartment on the assumption that he was then at his happiest and therefore at his readiest to grant favour. This caused ill feeling in the household of the Prophet, and Umm Salamah went to him on behalf of herself and the others asking him to make an announcement that anyone wishing to give him a present should do so without waiting until it was his day to be in a particular house. The Prophet did not answer her, and she asked him a second time, and again he remained silent. Then she asked him a third time, and he said: "Trouble me not with regard unto 'Ā'ishah, for verily the Revelation cometh not unto me when I am beneath the coverlet of a wife, except that wife be 'Ā'ishah."[4] Umm Salamah said: "I repent unto God for my having troubled thee." But others of the wives were not content to stop there and they sent to Fāṭimah and asked her to intervene on their behalf and to say to him: "Thy wives adjure thee by God to give

[1] I.S. VII, 55. [2] B. LXIII, 20. [3] ibid. [4] B. LI, 8.

them justice in respect of the daughter of Abū Bakr." Fāṭimah reluctantly agreed to this, but put off doing it for some days until finally her cousin Zaynab, the daughter of Jaḥsh, came to her and insisted. So she went to her father and said what she had been asked to say. "My little daughter," said the Prophet, "lovest thou not what I love?" And when she assented he said: "Then love her" – meaning 'Ā'ishah. Then he said: "It was Zaynab who sent thee, was it not?" "Zaynab and the others," said Fāṭimah. "I swear," said the Prophet, "it was she who set this afoot." And when Fāṭimah admitted it, he smiled.

She returned to the wives and recounted what had happened. "O daughter of God's Messenger," they said, "thou hast availed us nothing!" They pressed her to go a second time, but she refused, so they said to Zaynab "Go thou," and she went to the Prophet, who finally told 'Ā'ishah to speak to her, and she produced arguments against which Zaynab could say nothing. The Prophet was bound to be just and equitable towards his wives, and to encourage others to follow his example; but he was not responsible for the equity of others towards his own wives. Nor would his sensitivity have allowed him to interfere; it was for him to receive a present with thanks, and to leave all else to the donor. When Zaynab had gone he said to 'Ā'ishah: "Thou art indeed the daughter of Abū Bakr."[1]

Jealousy was inevitable in the Prophet's household, and he did his best to make light of it. Once he came into a room where his wives and others of his family were assembled, and in his hand was an onyx necklace which had just been given him. Holding it out to them he said: "I shall give this unto her whom I love best of all." Some of the wives began to whisper wryly to each other: "He will give it to the daughter of Abū Bakr." But when he had kept them long enough in suspense, he called his little granddaughter Umāmah to him and clasped it round her neck.

He was no less fond of his grandsons, the sons of Alī and Fāṭimah. "The dearest unto me of the people of my house are Ḥasan and Ḥusayn," he would say. Usāmah was counted also as a grandson, and more than once the Prophet took him and Ḥasan each by a hand and prayed: "O God, I love them, love them Thou!"[2]

[1] B. LI, 8; I.S. VIII, 123. [2] I.S. IV/1, 43.

# LXXI

# *After Khaybar*

THE campaign of Khaybar was followed by six relatively small expeditions two of which, under ʿUmar and Abū Bakr respectively, were against hostile clans of the tribe of Hawāzin whose territory blocked the main approach to the Yemen. The others were to the east and the north, against clans of Ghaṭafān. Two of these were against the Bani Murrah, whose territory adjoined the oasis of Fadak, which now belonged to the Prophet. Reduced to being his tenants, the Jews of Fadak required protection against the Bedouin; but the strength of these marauders was underestimated in Medina, so that only thirty men were sent on the first expedition, and they were nearly all killed. The Prophet immediately sent out a second force of two hundred, and the enemy were put to flight with considerable loss of life. There were also some captives taken, as well as camels and sheep. The seventeen-year-old Usāmah was allowed to take part in this expedition. He had been with the army behind the Trench, but this was his first campaign in the fullest sense. During the encounter, a man of Murrah mocked at him on account of his youth. He soon had reason to regret it. Already bent on showing his mettle, Usāmah was now goaded to fury and pursued the man far into the desert despite the orders given before the battle that they should all keep together; He finally caught up with him and wounded him, whereupon the Murrite shouted *lā ilāha illā Llāh*, there is no god but God. But despite this testification of Islam, Usāmah dealt him the death-blow.

The commander of the expedition was Ghālib ibn ʿAbd Allāh;[1] and one of his first thoughts after the battle was: "Where is Usāmah?" He and every other man in the army knew of the Prophet's great love for the son of Zayd; and despite the victory it was to an exceedingly troubled camp that Usāmah returned, one hour after nightfall. Ghālib sternly rated him. "I went after a man who was scoffing at me," said the youth, "and when I had come up with him and had fleshed him, he said *lā ilāha illa Llāh*." "Whereupon thou didst sheathe thy sword?" said Ghālib. "Nay," said Usāmah, "not until I had made him drink the draught of death." At that the whole camp thundered abuse, and he buried his head in his hands, overcome with shame. Nor could he bring himself to eat any food during the march home. There had been a Revelation which the older men well knew in connection with one or two cases where a believer had been about

[1] Of the Bani Layth, a clan of Kinānah.

to kill a disbeliever, who had then professed Islam; and exasperated at the idea of losing the spoils of armour and weapons which he had thought were his, the victor had said "Thou art not a believer," and had killed him. In Usāmah's case the motive had been honour not spoils, but the principle was the same. The revealed verse was: *O ye who believe, when ye fight in the way of God, discriminate, nor say unto him who proffereth you peace: "Thou art not a believer," seeking the gains of this lower life, for with God are spoils in plenty. Thus were ye wont to be aforetime, but God hath sent down His Grace upon you. Therefore discriminate. Verily God is Informed of what ye do.*[1]

As soon as they reached Medina Usāmah went to the Prophet, who fondly embraced him. Then he said: "Now tell me of thy campaign." So Usāmah told him all that had happened since they had set out, and when he reached the point where he had killed the man, the Prophet said: "Didst thou, O Usāmah, slay him when he had said *lā ilāha illa Llāh*? "O Messenger of God," he answered, "he did but say it to escape from being slain." "And so," said the Prophet, "thou didst split open his heart to know if he spake the truth or if he lied!" "Never again will I slay any man who saith *lā ilāha illā Llāh*," said Usāmah. And he would say afterwards: "I wished that I had only entered Islam on that day."[2] For the Prophet had affirmed that the entry into the religion effaces the guilt of all past sins.

After his return from Khaybar the Prophet himself stayed in Medina for nine months. Despite the lesser campaigns, the truce to the south and the victory to the north made these months a time of relative peace and prosperity, though the wealth which had been won from the Garden of the Ḥijāz gave rise also to certain problems.

'Umar came one morning to the house of the Messenger, and as he approached he heard the sound of women's voices raised to a pitch which he considered to be unseemly in the prophetic presence. The women were moreover of Quraysh, that is, of the Emigrants, which confirmed his opinion that they were learning bad ways from the women of Medina who for generations had been less restrained and more self-assertive than the women of Mecca. The Prophet hated to refuse a request, as well they knew, and they were now asking him with some insistence to give them various garments which had come to him as part of his fifth in the spoils of war. There was a curtain spread across part of the room, and when 'Umar's voice was heard asking permission to enter there was a sudden total silence and the women hid themselves behind the curtain with such speed that he entered to find the Prophet speechless with laughter. "May God fill thy life with laughter, O Messenger of God," he said. "Wondrous it was," said the Prophet, "how these women who were with me even now – how speedily upon hearing thy voice they were gone behind that curtain!" "It is rather thy right, not mine, that they should stand in awe of thee, not of me," said 'Umar. Then, addressing the women, he said: "O enemies of yourselves, fear ye me, and fear ye not God's Messenger?" "It is even so," they said, "for thou art rougher and harsher than God's Messenger." "That is true, O son of Khaṭṭāb," said the Prophet. Then he added: "By Him in whose

[1] IV, 94. [2] W. 725.

hand is my soul, if Satan found that thou wert travelling upon a certain path, he would choose to go himself by any other path but thine."[1]

The newly won wealth and the consequent easing of the situation encouraged even Umm Ayman to ask the Prophet for a favour. She had long felt the need of a camel that she could call her own; and now she went to him and asked him to give her a mount. He looked at her seriously and said: "I will mount thee on the child of a camel." "O Messenger of God," she exclaimed, thinking that he meant a calf, "that is not meet for me. I want it not." "I will not mount thee," he said "save on the child of a camel."[2] And so the altercation continued until a smile on the Prophet's face made her realise that he was teasing her and that every camel is necessarily the child of a camel.

On another day, however, 'Umar found the Prophet in less good humour, with his head resting on his hand which was against his cheek. "O 'Umar," he said, "they ask of me that which I have not." He had said on his way to Khaybar, speaking of the increase of riches that the promised victory would bring to Medina: "It will not be good for you." It was as he had said, and this applied to his own household as well as to others. Until then the Prophet and his family had lived a life of the utmost frugality. 'Ā'ishah said that before Khaybar she had not known what it was to eat her fill of dates. Such was the poverty of their ever-increasing dependants that the Prophet's wives had only asked him for what they needed, and not always that. Things that could be dispensed with were given away, or else sold so that the money could be charitably spent. But the Prophet now had the pleasure of giving presents to his wives, and they for their part were not slow in learning to ask for more, which sometimes created problems, because equity demanded that what was given to one must be given to all.

At the same time they began to take advantage of his indulgence in other ways. One day 'Umar rebuked his wife for something and she sharply answered him back: and when he expostulated with her she replied that the wives of the Prophet were in the habit of answering him back so why should she not do the same. "And there is one of them," she added, meaning their daughter, "who speaketh unto him her mind unabashed from morn till night." Greatly troubled by this, 'Umar went to Ḥafṣah, who did not deny that what her mother had said was true. "Thou hast neither the grace of 'Ā'ishah nor the beauty of Zaynab," he said, hoping to shake her self-confidence; and when these words seemed to have no effect, he added: "Art thou so sure that if thou angerest the Prophet, God will not destroy thee in His anger?"[3] Then he went to his cousin Umm Salamah and said: "Is it true that ye speak your minds unto God's Messenger and answer him without respect?" "By all that is wonderful," said Umm Salamah, "what call hast thou to come between God's Messenger and his wives? Yea, by God, we speak unto him our minds, and if he suffer us to do so that is his affair, and if he forbid us he will find us more obedient unto him than we are unto thee."[4] 'Umar felt that he had gone too far, and that the reproof was just; but there could be no doubt that all was not well in the Prophet's household.

[1] B. LXII, 6. [2] I.S. VIII, 163. [3] I.S. VIII, 131. [4] I.S. VIII, 137.

The relatively sudden redress which now took place was partly due to an altogether unexpected event. The Prophet's letter to the Muqawqis, summoning him to Islam, was answered evasively; but with his answer the ruler of Egypt sent a rich present of a thousand measures of gold, twenty robes of fine cloth, a mule, a she-ass and, as the crown of the gift, two Coptic Christian slave girls escorted by an elderly eunuch. The girls were sisters, Māriyah and Sīrīn, and both were beautiful, but Māriyah was exceptionally so, and the Prophet marvelled at her beauty. He gave Sīrīn to Ḥassān ibn Thābit, and lodged Māriyah in the nearby house where Ṣafiyyah had lived before her apartment adjoining the Mosque was built. There he would visit her both by day and by night; but his wives became so openly jealous that she was unhappy, and he then lodged her in Upper Medina. 'Ā'ishah and the others were at first relieved, but they soon found that they had gained nothing. For the Prophet did not visit Māriyah any the less often, and the added distance meant that his absences were even longer than before.

They well knew that he was altogether within his rights – rights which had been recognised from the time of Abraham and before. Were they not all, except Ṣafiyyah, descended from the union of Abraham with the bondmaid Hagar? Moreover, the law revealed to Moses had corroborated such rights, and the Koran itself expressly allowed a master to take his bondmaid as concubine on condition of her free consent. But the wives also knew that the Prophet was exceedingly sensitive, and they saw to it that his whole domestic life was now penetrated by their deliberately undisguised reactions. In particular Ḥafṣah gave vent to such feeling that the Prophet was finally induced to swear that he would not see Māriyah again, and 'Ā'ishah was Ḥafṣah's accomplice on this occasion.

The Revelation which now came is known as the Sūrah of Banning[1] because it opens with a reproof to the Prophet for having banned Māriyah from his life: *O Prophet why bannest thou, to please thy wives, that which God hath made lawful unto thee?* Then, having formally absolved him from his oath, it addresses Ḥafṣah and 'Ā'ishah, though not by name: *If ye twain repent unto God ye have cause, for your hearts were set upon the ban; and if ye aid each the other against him, verily God, even He, is his Protecting Friend, and Gabriel, and the elect of the faithful; and beyond these, the angels are massed to help him.* The next verse is addressed to all the wives: *It may be, if he divorce you, that his Lord will give him wives in your stead who are better than you, submissive unto God, believing, devout, penitent, inclined unto worship and fasting, widows and virgin maids.*

The Sūrah ends with examples from sacred history of two evil women and two women who were perfect:

> *God citeth as example for those who disbelieve, the wife of Noah and the wife of Lot. They were under two righteous men from amongst Our slaves, men whom they betrayed and who thus availed them naught against God; and it was said unto both: Enter ye the fire with them who enter it.*

[1] LXVI.

*And God citeth as example for those who believe the wife of Pharaoh when she said: "My Lord, build for me a dwelling with Thee in Paradise, and save me from Pharaoh and his deeds, and save me from the people who transgress"; and Mary, the daughter of 'Imrān, who kept chaste her womb and We breathed therein of Our Spirit. And she testified to the truth of the words of her Lord and His scriptures, and was of those who are absorbed in prayer.*

When he had recited this Revelation to his wives, the Prophet left them to meditate upon it, and withdrew to a roofed verandah which was the only room he had but for their apartments. News spread throughout Medina that he had divorced his wives, and it came to the ears of 'Umar that night. At dawn he went as usual to the Mosque, but immediately after the prayer, before 'Umar could address him, the Prophet withdrew to his porch. 'Umar went to Ḥafṣah and found her in tears. "Why weepest thou?" he said, adding before she could answer: "Did I not tell thee this would happen? Hath God's Messenger divorced you?" "I know not," she said, "but he is there, secluded by himself in that porch." Its entrance was from the Mosque, to which 'Umar now returned. There were gathered a group of men, sitting round the pulpit. Some of them were in tears; 'Umar sat with them for a while and then unable to endure his feelings he went to the door of the porch where a black Abyssinian boy, a servant of the Prophet, was standing. "Ask permission for 'Umar to enter," he said to the boy, who went in and then came out after a moment saying: "I mentioned thee to him, but he was silent." 'Umar returned to where he had been sitting. Then he went again to ask if he might enter, and again he was told that the Prophet had made no response. This happened yet a third time; but just as 'Umar had turned away the boy called out to him that the Prophet had said he might enter. 'Umar went in and found him reclining on a rush mat. His back, which was partly bare, showed clearly the marks of the matting where it had pressed against his skin. A leather cushion, stuffed with palm fibre, was at his side, and on this he was leaning. His eyes were downcast, and he did not look at 'Umar as he entered. "O Messenger of God," said 'Umar, "hast thou divorced thy wives?" The Prophet raised his eyes to 'Umar's. "Nay, I have not," he said. "*Allāhu Akbar!*" exclaimed 'Umar, in a voice which could be heard in all the neighbouring houses. Umm Salamah said afterwards: "I was weeping, and when anyone came unto me they said 'Hath God's Messenger divorced thee?' and I said 'By God, I know not.' This continued until 'Umar came to the Prophet. We heard his magnification – we were all in our apartments – and we knew that the Messenger of God had answered 'Nay' to his question." There was in fact only one question in anybody's mind, and they were certain that 'Umar would be especially preoccupied with it on account of his daughter.

"I stood there," said 'Umar, "feeling my way with the Messenger of God as to what was his state, and I said: 'We were used to having, we men of Quraysh, the upper hand over our wives, but when we came to Medina we came unto a people whose wives have the upper hand over them.'" He saw a suggestion of a smile cross the Prophet's face, so he went on to tell him what he had previously said to Ḥafṣah by way of warning, and again the

Prophet smiled, whereupon he ventured to sit down. Once more he was struck by the bareness of the room – a mat on the floor, three leather cushions, and nothing else. He suggested that the Prophet should allow himself more luxury, and by way of contrast he mentioned the Greeks and the Persians, but he was cut short with the words: "Art thou in any doubt, O son of Khaṭṭāb? Their good things have been hastened on for them in this their earthly life."

It was now the time of the new moon, and the Prophet let it be known to his wives that he did not wish to see any of them until the month had passed. When the moon had altogether waned, he went first to 'Ā'ishah's apartment. Delighted to see him, yet surprised, she said to him: "It is but twenty-nine nights." "How dost thou know?" he asked, and she answered: "I have been counting them – how I have counted them!" "But this was a month of twenty-nine," he said. She had forgotten that a lunar month is sometimes only twenty-nine days instead of thirty. He then told her of another Revelation he had received, which made it necessary for him to put before her a choice between two possibilities. He said he had asked her father to help him by counselling her in this matter. "Nay," said 'Ā'ishah, "none shall help thee with regard to me. But tell me what it is, O Messenger of God." He answered saying: "God putteth before thee this choice," and then he recited the newly revealed verses: *O Prophet, say unto thy wives: If ye desire this lower life and its adornments, then come and I will bestow its goods upon you, and I will release you with a fair release. But if ye desire God and His messenger and the abode of the Hereafter, then verily God hath laid in store for you a meed immense, for such of you as do good.*[1] She said: "Verily I desire *God and His messenger and the abode of the Hereafter.*" And there was not one of his wives who did not say the same.

[1] XXXIII, 28-9.

# LXXII

# *The Lesser Pilgrimage and its Aftermath*

THE months drew on until almost a year had passed since the signing of the treaty of Ḥudaybiyah. It was now time to set off for Mecca in accordance with the promise of Quraysh that the Prophet and his Companions should have safe access to the Holy Precinct in order to perform the rite of the Lesser Pilgrimage. There were about two thousand pilgrims in all, including the would-be pilgrims of the previous year, except for a few who had died or been killed in battle. Amongst those who had not been at Ḥudaybiyah was Abū Hurayrah, a man of the Bani Ḍaws.[1] He had arrived in Medina with others of his tribe during the campaign of Khaybar, and being destitute he had joined the People of the Bench. On entering Islam his name had been changed to 'Abd ar-Raḥmān, but he was always known as Abū Hurayrah, "the kitten man", literally "the father of a kitten", because like the Prophet he was very fond of cats and often had a kitten to play with. He soon found favour with the Prophet, who on this occasion put him in charge of some of the sacrificial camels.

When they heard that the pilgrims had reached the edge of the sacred territory, Quraysh vacated the whole of the hollow of Mecca and withdrew to the tops of the surrounding hills. The chiefs of Quraysh were gathered together on Mount Abū Qubays, from which they could look down into the Mosque. They also had a wide view of the surrounding country; and now they saw the pilgrims emerge in a long file from the north-western pass which leads down into the valley just below the city. Their ears soon caught an indistinct murmur which quickly became distinguishable as the age-old pilgrim's cry: *Labbayk Allāhumma Labbayk*, Here I am, O God, at Thy service.

The long procession of bare-headed, white-robed men was led by the Prophet mounted on Qaṣwā', with 'Abd Allāh ibn Rawāḥah on foot, holding the bridle. Of the others some were on camelback and some on foot. They made straight for the Holy House by the nearest way. Each man

[1] See pp. 54–5.

was wearing his upper garment as a cloak, but at the entrance to the Mosque the Prophet adjusted his, passing it under his right arm, leaving the shoulder bare, and crossing the two ends over the left shoulder so that they hung down back and front. The others followed his example. Still mounted, he rode to the south-east corner of the Ka'bah and reverently touched the Black Stone with his staff. Then he made the seven circuits of the House, after which he withdrew to the foot of the little hill of Ṣafā, and passed to and fro between it and the hill of Marwah, seven courses in all, ending at Marwah, to which many of the sacrificial animals had now been led. There he sacrificed a camel, and his head was shaved by Khirāsh, who had done the same for him at Ḥudaybiyah. This completed the rite of the Lesser Pilgrimage.

He then returned to the Mosque, intending to enter the Holy House, cluttered with idols though it was. But the doors were locked, and the key was with a member of the clan of 'Abd ad-Dār. The Prophet sent a man to ask for it, but the chiefs of Quraysh replied that this was not in their agreement, the entry into the House not being part of the Pilgrimage rite. So none of the Muslims entered it that year; but when the sun had reached its zenith the Prophet told Bilāl to go up to the roof of the Ka'bah and make the call to prayer. His resonant voice filled the whole valley of Mecca and floated up to the tops of the hills, first with the magnification, then with the two testifications of Islam: "I bear witness that there is no god but God. I bear witness that Muḥammad is the Messenger of God." From Abū Qubays the chiefs of Quraysh could plainly distinguish Bilāl, and they were outraged at the sight of the black slave on the roof of the Holy House. But above all they were conscious that this was a triumph for the enemy which might have incalculable repercussions, and they bitterly regretted having signed the treaty, which a year ago had seemed to be in their favour.

The pilgrims spent three days in the evacuated city. The Prophet's tent was pitched in the Mosque. During the nights those of the Meccans who were Muslims in secret stole down from the hills, and there were many joyous encounters. 'Abbās, whose Islam was tolerated by Quraysh, openly spent most of the three days with the Prophet. It was then that he offered him in marriage his wife's sister Maymūnah, now a widow, and the Prophet accepted. Maymūnah and Umm al-Faḍl were full sisters, and with them, living in the household of 'Abbās, was their half-sister Salmà, the widow of Ḥamzah, and her daughter 'Umārah. 'Alī suggested that their cousin, Ḥamzah's daughter, should not be left amongst the idolaters, to which the Prophet and 'Abbās agreed; and since Fāṭimah was one of the pilgrims it was arranged that she should take 'Umārah with her in her howdah.

When the three days were at an end, Suhayl and Ḥuwayṭib came down from Abū Qubays and said to the Prophet who was sitting with Sa'd ibn 'Ubādah and others of the Helpers: "Thy time is finished, so begone from us." The Prophet answered: "How would it harm you to give me some respite, that I may celebrate my marriage amongst you and prepare for you a feast?" "We need not thy feast," they said. "Begone from us. We adjure thee by God, O Muḥammad, and by the pact which is between us, to leave our country. This was the third night, which now is passed." Sa'd was angry at their lack of courtesy, but the Prophet silenced him, saying: "O Sa'd, no ill words to those who have come to visit us in our camp!" Then he gave orders that by nightfall every pilgrim should have left the city. But he made an exception for his servant, Abū Rāfi', whom he told to stay behind and bring Maymūnah with him, which he did; and the marriage was consummated at Sarif, a few miles outside the Sacred Precinct.

This new alliance established another unforeseen relationship with the enemy. Maymūnah and Umm al-Faḍl and their half-sisters Salmà and Asmā' were all daughters of the same mother. But Maymūnah and Umm al-Faḍl had another half-sister on their father's side, by name 'Aṣmā',[1] widow of the great Walīd of Makhzūm. It was she who had borne him Khālid, who had now become the Prophet's nephew by marriage.

One day soon after the return to Medina, the Prophet was woken from an afternoon siesta by the sound of a somewhat heated discussion. He recognised the voices of 'Ali, Zayd and Ja'far, and it was evident that they were all three at odds with each other. It was also evident that the more they argued, the further they were from reaching an agreement. Opening the door of the room he was in, he called them to him and asked what was the cause of their dispute. They exclaimed that it was a question of honour, as to which of them had most right to be the guardian of Ḥamzah's daughter, who had been in 'Alī's house ever since her arrival from Mecca. "Come to me," said the Prophet, "and I will judge between you." When they were all seated he turned first to 'Ali and asked him what he had to say for himself. "She is mine uncle's daughter," he said, "and it was I who brought her out from Mecca, and I have most right to her." The Prophet then turned to Ja'far, who said: "She is mine uncle's daughter, and her mother's sister is in my house." His wife Asmā' was 'Umārah's maternal aunt. As to Zayd, he simply said "She is my brother's daughter," for the Prophet had made the pact of brotherhood between Ḥamzah and Zayd when they first came to Medina, and Ḥamzah had made a testament leaving Zayd in charge of his affairs. There was no doubt that each of the three was convinced that he had the best right to the honour in question. So before pronouncing his judgement the Prophet spoke words of praise to each one of them. It was then that he said to Ja'far: "Thou art like me in looks and in character."[2] Not until he saw that he had made each one of them happy did he voice his decision, which was in favour of Ja'far. "Thou hast most right to her," he said. "The mother's sister is as a mother." Ja'far said nothing, but rose to his feet and circled around the Prophet with the steps of a dancer. "Ja'far, what is this?" said the Prophet. He answered: "It is that which I have seen the Abyssinians do in honour of their kings. If ever the Negus gave a man a good reason to rejoice, that man would rise and dance about him."

It was not long before the Prophet arranged a marriage between 'Umārah and his own stepson, her cousin Salamah, whose father, Abū

[1] Although transcribed by the same Latin letters, apart from diacritics, this name, beginning with *'ayn* and *ṣād*, differs considerably in sound from Asmā', which begins with *alif* and *sīn*.

[2] I.S. IV/1, 24.

Salamah, was the son of Ḥamzah's sister Barrah. On that occasion the Prophet said: "Have I now requited Salamah enough?" He meant that he was indebted to Salamah for having given him his mother Umm Salamah in marriage, and now in return he had given Salamah a bride.

The Prophet's entry into Mecca had been witnessed by the most eminent men of Quraysh. But there had been two notable exceptions: Khālid and 'Amr were not on Abū Qubays, nor were they encamped on any of the other hills above Mecca. Both had withdrawn from the city well in advance of the Prophet's approach. Their decisions to absent themselves had been made independently, nor were their reasons for doing so the same. But on one point they were in complete agreement, namely that the treaty of Ḥudaybiyah had been a great moral victory for the Prophet, and that his entry into Mecca would prove to be the end of their resistance to him. But the hostility of 'Amr against Islam had not diminished, whereas Khālid had for some years now been a man who is in two minds. Outwardly this had not been evident: his military prowess had thrust him to the fore in every action that Quraysh had taken against the Prophet. But he confessed afterwards that he had come away from Uhud and from the Trench with the uneasy feeling that the battle had been pointless and that Muḥammad would triumph in the end; and when the Prophet had eluded his squadron on the way to Ḥudaybiyah, Khālid had exclaimed: "The man is inviolably protected!" That had been his last action against Islam. Then had come the amazing victory at Khaybar.

But there were also considerations of a different kind: almost despite himself he had a personal liking for the Prophet; and from the letter that his younger brother Walīd had written him before his death he had learned that the Prophet sometimes asked after him and that he had said: "If he would put his redoubtable vigour on the side of Islam against the idolaters it would be better for him; and we would give him preference over others." To this Walīd had added: "So see, my brother, what thou hast missed!"

There was, in addition, an even closer family influence at work. Khālid's mother, 'Aṣmā', who had long been favourable to the Prophet, had recently entered Islam; and now his aunt Maymūnah had become the Prophet's wife. Not long after this marriage Khālid had a dream in which he was aware of being in a country which was shut in on all sides and extremely barren. Then he went out from this confinement into a land which was green and fertile, with pastures which stretched far and wide. He knew that this was something of a vision; and having divined the essence of its meaning, he made up his mind to go to Medina. But he preferred to go with a companion. Was there no one else of like mind with himself? Next to 'Amr, who was not to be found, his nearest comrades in arms were 'Ikrimah and Ṣafwān. He sounded both of them, but Ṣafwān said: "Even if every other man of Quraysh were to follow Muḥammad, I would never follow him." 'Ikrimah said much the same; and Khālid remembered that both their fathers had been killed at Badr, where Ṣafwān had lost also a brother. Regretfully he set out alone, but no sooner had he left his house than he fell in with 'Uthmān the son of Ṭalhah of 'Abd ad-Dār – the man who, years ago, had gallantly escorted Umm Salamah from Mecca to Medina. 'Uthmān was a close friend to Khālid, closer than either Ṣafwān or 'Ikrimah; but Khālid's experience with the other two had made him reticent; and he remembered moreover that 'Uthmān had lost his father, two uncles and four brothers at Uhud. They rode on together in silence for a while. Then Khālid suddenly decided to speak, and with a searching look he said: "Our plight is no better than that of a fox in his earth. Pour in but a pail of water, and out he must come!" He immediately saw that 'Uthmān understood perfectly what he meant, so he told him where he was going and why; and 'Uthmān, who had been gradually coming to the same decision, now resolved to accompany him. Khālid gladly agreed to wait for him while he returned home for provisions and clothes; and early the next morning the two of them set off together for Medina.

As to 'Amr, he was of one mind with Ṣafwān and 'Ikrimah about Islam, but he saw more clearly than they did the precariousness of the situation; and gathering round him a few younger men, his clansmen of Sahm and others, who looked on him as a leader, he persuaded them to go with him to Abyssinia. He pointed out that if Muḥammad triumphed in the inevitably imminent struggle for power then they would have safe asylum; and if Quraysh should triumph after all they could return to Mecca. "We had rather be under the Negus than under Muḥammad," he said, and they agreed.

'Amr was an astute politician, and a man of great perseverance, not easily discouraged. Despite his total failure to undermine the powerful impression which Ja'far and his companions had made, he had none the less been at pains to appease the Negus as far as he was concerned, and had assiduously maintained relations with him throughout the years, always avoiding any mention of the Muslim refugees. But now they had left the country and gone to Medina; and with them would have gone, so 'Amr wrongly concluded, all the Negus's prejudice in favour of the new religion. At his first audience his rich gift of leather was graciously accepted, and the Negus seemed so well disposed that 'Amr decided to come at once to the point and to ask for asylum. But in doing so he spoke slightingly of the Prophet, and this provoked a sudden overwhelming outburst of royal anger. 'Amr was altogether taken aback: from what the Negus said it was clear that the best way for him to build a future for himself at his court – far better than gifts of leather – was to become a follower of Muḥammad. He had fled from Islam only to find that Islam had outstripped him to the very refuge he had hoped to take; and with the ruin of his plans his resistance began to crumble. "Dost thou testify unto this, O King?" he said, meaning to the prophethood of Muḥammad. "I bear witness to it before God," said the Negus. "Do what I tell thee, O 'Amr, and follow him. His is the truth, by God, and he will triumph over every persuasion that setteth itself against him, even as Moses triumphed over Pharaoh and his hosts."[1]

History has not recorded the names of the companions of 'Amr or what they decided to do. But 'Amr himself boarded a boat which took him to a port on the Yemeni coast, where he bought a camel and provisions and set

[1] W. 743.

off for the north; and when he reached Haddah, one of the first halts on the coastal route from Mecca to Medina, he came upon Khālid and 'Uthmān, and they travelled the rest of their way together.

They were joyfully received in Medina, and Khālid said of the Prophet: "His face shone with light as he returned my greeting of Peace." He was the first to pledge allegiance. "I bear witness that there is no god but God, and thou art the Messenger of God." "Praise be to God who hath guided thee," said the Prophet. "I ever saw in thee an intelligence which I hoped would not bring thee in the end to anything but good." "O Messenger of God," said Khālid, "thou didst see all those fields of battle whereon I took part against thee in obstinate resistance to the truth. Pray therefore unto God that He may forgive me them." "Islam cutteth away all that went before it," said the Prophet. "Even so much as that?" said Khālid, still visibly troubled in conscience; and the Prophet prayed: "O God forgive Khālid for all his obstructing of the way to Thy path."[1] Then 'Uthmān and 'Amr pledged their allegiance; and 'Amr said afterwards that he had been quite unable to raise his eyes to the Prophet's face, such was the reverence he felt for him at that moment.

'Umar's cousin Hishām,[2] the brother of 'Amr, had escaped from Mecca to Medina shortly after the battle of the Trench. Since then he had been joined by his nephew 'Abd Allāh, the son of 'Amr. 'Abd Allāh, now in his sixteenth year, was deeply devout and much given to fasting. He also showed promise of being one of the most learned of the Companions, and recorded many of the sayings of the Prophet, who gave him permission to write them down. Both 'Abd Allāh and Hishām had prayed for the Islam of 'Amr, and his reunion with them in Medina was a matter of great rejoicing both for them and for him.

Two other events of joy in these months were the Islam of 'Aqīl, the brother of Ja'far and 'Alī, and of Jubayr, the son of Muṭ'im. The faith which had taken root in Jubayr's heart when he had come to ransom some of the captives of Badr was now a growth which could not be set aside. To 'Aqīl, when he came to pledge his allegiance, the Prophet said: "I love thee with two loves, for thy near kinship unto me, and for the love which I ever saw for thee in mine uncle."[3]

The earlier half of this same year of rejoicing, the eighth year after the Hijrah, was also a time of bereavement. The first of the deaths in the household of the Prophet was that of his daughter Zaynab. He was with her at the end and spoke words of comfort to his son-in-law and little granddaughter. Then he gave instructions to Umm Ayman, together with Sawdah and Umm Salamah, to make ready the body for burial. When the ablutions had been performed, the Prophet took off an undergarment he was wearing, and told them to wrap her in it before they shrouded her. Then he led the funeral prayer, and prayed also beside her grave.

Khadījah was the only one of his wives who had borne him children. The people of Medina longed that a child should be born to the Prophet in their city. Only two of his present wives – Umm Salamah and Umm Habībah – had borne children to their first husbands. But at each new

[1] W. 741–9. [2] See pp. 114–15. [3] I.S. IV/2, 30.

marriage the citizens were filled with fresh hopes, which gradually faded, for not one of the later wives was destined to be the mother of a child to the Prophet. Yet now, shortly after the death of his eldest daughter, it appeared that he was again to become a father. Māriyah, his Coptic bondmaid, was expecting a child. She was already a centre of attention for the people of Medina who knew well the Prophet's affection for her, and who sought to please him by their kindness to her; and now their attentiveness was redoubled.

# LXXIII

# *Syria*

ABOUT three months after his return from the Lesser Pilgrimage the Prophet sent fifteen men to act as peaceful messengers of Islam to one of the tribes on the borders of Syria; but their friendly greetings were met by a shower of arrows, and having been obliged to fight they were all killed but one.

There was another setback, smaller in that it involved only a single death, but of greater political import. A messenger to Bostra was intercepted by a chief of the tribe of Ghassān and put to death. Such an act could not be allowed to go unpunished, despite the risk that the Ghassānids, who were mainly Christian, might be able to persuade Caesar's representative to send them help.

The Prophet mustered an army of three thousand men and put Zayd in command of them, with instructions that if Zayd should be killed Ja'far should take his place. 'Abd Allāh ibn Rawāḥah was named as third in order of precedence. If these three should all be incapacitated, the men were to follow a commander of their own choosing. The Prophet then gave Zayd a white standard, and with others of his Companions he accompanied the army to where the ground rises up towards the Pass of Farewell, an opening between the hills a little to the north of Uḥud.

'Abd Allāh had with him, on the back of his saddle, an orphan boy whose guardian he was. On the way the boy heard him reciting some verses he had composed, expressing the desire to be left behind in Syria when the army returned home. "When I heard these verses I wept," said the boy, "and he flicked me with his whip and said: 'What harm to thee, wretched fellow, if God grant me martyrdom and I have rest from this world and its toil and its cares and its sorrows and its accidents, and thou returnest safe in the saddle?' After that, during a halt in the night, he prayed two prayer cycles followed by a long supplication. Then he called me and I said: 'Here I am, at thy service.' 'If God will,' he said, 'it is martyrdom.'"[1]

When the army reached the Syrian border they heard that not only had the northern tribes come out in considerable strength, but that Caesar's representative had greatly reinforced them with imperial troops. Altogether the enemy were said to be a hundred thousand strong. Allowing for the probability of gross exaggeration, Zayd none the less decided to halt and to hold a council of war. Most of the men were in favour of sending immediately to inform the Prophet of this grave turn of events.

[1] W. 759.

Then he could either order them home or give them auxiliaries. But ʿAbd Allāh spoke vigorously against any such course. Using the same unanswerable argument which had been used before Uḥud, and which was to be used again and again in the future, he ended his speech with the words: "We have before us the certainty of one of two good things, either victory or martyrdom – to join our brethren and be their companions in the gardens of Paradise, On then to the attack!"

ʿAbd Allāh's resolution prevailed, and the army continued its northward advance. They were now not far from the southern end of the Dead Sea, separated from its long and deep valley by the range of hills which rises up from its eastern shores. A few hours' march brought them within sight of the enemy. Whatever the exact numbers of the combined Arab and Byzantine forces, the Muslims could see at a glance that they themselves were vastly outnumbered, on a scale which they had never yet experienced. Nor had any of them witnessed before such military splendour as that of the imperial squadrons which formed the centre of the host, with the Arabs on either flank. The pomp of Quraysh as they had descended the hill of ʿAqanqal at Badr had been as nothing to the wealth of arms and armour and the richly caparisoned horses which now met their eyes. Their approach moreover had been anticipated, and the legions were ready for them, drawn up in battle formation.

Wishing to avoid an immediate engagement, for the slope of the land was against them, Zayd gave orders to withdraw southwards to Mu'tah, where they would have the advantage, and there they consolidated their position. The enemy, conscious of the great superiority of their numbers and bent on making it an altogether decisive day, followed them to Mu'tah. As they drew near, instead of retreating further as they had expected, Zayd gave the order to attack.

At that moment the space between Mu'tah and Medina was folded up for the Prophet and he saw Zayd with the white standard leading his men into battle. He saw him many times mortally wounded until finally he fell to the ground, and Jaʿfar took the standard and fought until his life also flowed out from his wounds. Then ʿAbd Allāh took the standard and the attack which he led against the enemy was repulsed with a vigorous onslaught in which he too was killed and his men driven back in disarray. Another Helper, Thābit ibn Arqam, seized the standard and the Muslims rallied, whereupon he gave it to Khālid who at first refused the honour saying that Thābit had more right to it. "Take it man," said Thābit; "I did but take it to give it thee." So Khālid took command and knit the ranks together, and the enemy advance was so firmly checked that they drew back enough to enable the Muslims to beat an orderly retreat. It was a victory for the other side, but they gained no advantage from it; and of the Muslims, apart from their three leaders, only five were killed. It was thus something of a victory for Khālid; and when the Prophet told his Companions of the battle and of the deaths of Zayd and Jaʿfar and ʿAbd Allāh he said: "Then one of God's swords took the standard, and God opened up the way for them" – that is, for the Muslims to reach safety; and thus it was that Khālid came to be called "the Sword of God".

As the Prophet described the battle the tears were flowing down his cheeks, and when the time came for the prayer he led it and immediately withdrew from the Mosque instead of turning to face the congregation as was his wont. He did the same again at sunset, and yet again after the night prayer.

Meantime he had been to the house of Ja'far. "O Asmā'," he said, "bring me Ja'far's sons." With some misgivings at the gravity of his face she fetched the three boys. The Prophet kissed them, and then again his eyes filled with tears and he wept. "O Messenger of God," she said, "dearer than my father and my mother, what maketh thee weep? Hath news reached thee of Ja'far and his companions?" "Even so," he said. "They were struck down this day." She uttered a cry of lamentation, and women hastened to her side. The Prophet returned to his house, and ordered food to be prepared for the family of Ja'far during the next days. "Their grief doth busy them", he said, "beyond caring for their own needs."

Umm Ayman and Usāmah and the rest of Zayd's family were in his house. He had already condoled with them; and as he returned, Zayd's little daughter came out into the street in tears, and seeing him she ran into his arms. He now wept unrestrainedly, and as he clasped the child to him his body shook with sobs. Sa'd ibn 'Ubādah happened to pass by at that moment and searching in himself for words of comfort, he murmured: "O Messenger of God, what is this?" "This," said the Prophet, "is one who loveth yearning for his beloved."[1]

That night the Prophet had a vision of Paradise, and he saw that Zayd was there, and Ja'far and 'Abd Allāh and the other martyrs of the battle; and he saw Ja'far flying with wings like an Angel. At dawn he went to the Mosque; his Companions sensed that the weight of his sorrow had left him; and after the prayer he turned as usual to face the congregation. Then he went again to Asmā', to tell her of his vision; and she was greatly consoled.

When Khālid and his men returned to Medina the Prophet called for his white mule, Duldul, which the Muqawqis had given him, and putting Ja'far's eldest boy in front of him on the saddle he rode out to meet them. Many men and women had already lined the route, and as the troops passed they jeered at them and threw dust in their faces. "Runaways," they shouted. "Did ye flee from fighting in God's path?" "Nay," said the Prophet, "they are not runaways but returners again to the fight, if God will."[1]

The setback at Mu'tah was an encouragement to the northern Arabs to strengthen their resistance to the new Islamic state, and in the following month news came that the tribes of Balī and Quḍā'ah were massing in considerable numbers on the Syrian border, with intent to march south. But this time there appeared to be no question of reinforcements from Caesar. The Prophet sent 'Amr at the head of three hundred men, with instructions to fight where necessary and to win allies where possible. The choice of commander may have been partly determined by the close ties of kinship which 'Amr had with one of the tribes in question, for his mother was a woman of Balī. By dint of night marches and relatively secluded

[1] I.S. III/1, 32.  [1] W. 765.

camps he avoided attracting undue attention, and reached the Syrian border in ten days. Winter had set in early that year and unaccustomed to being so far north, the men of Mecca and Medina set about gathering firewood as soon as they had made their final halt. But 'Amr forbade the lighting of a single fire; and grumblers were silenced with the words: "Ye were ordered to hear me and obey me; therefore do so."

Quickly realising that the enemy were in greater numbers than had been anticipated, and that there was little hope, for the moment, of local assistance, he sent back a man of Juhaynah to the Prophet asking for reinforcements. Abū 'Ubaydah was immediately dispatched with an additional two hundred men. As one of the closest Companions, and one who moreover had fought in every campaign, he expected to take precedence; but 'Amr insisted that the newcomers were merely an auxiliary force and that he himself was commander-in-chief. The Prophet had told Abū 'Ubaydah to see that there was perfect co-operation and no division between the two forces, so the older man gave way, saying to 'Amr: "In case *thou* shouldst disobey *me*, by God *I* will obey *thee*." When the Prophet heard of this, he invoked blessings upon Abū 'Ubaydah.

'Amr now led his five hundred men across the Syrian border, and as they advanced the enemy dispersed. There was only one brief exchange of arrows; for the rest, it was a question of coming upon deserted camps whose very recent occupants had vanished; and in the absence of the hostile clans, friendly elements – individuals and groups – ventured to manifest themselves. So 'Amr was able to claim, in a letter to the Prophet, that he had re-established the influence of Islam upon the Syrian frontier.

That influence was now rapidly growing throughout the tribes on all sides of the Yathrib oasis. The reasons were not purely spiritual: the Prophet was now known as a dangerous and incalculable enemy and as a powerful, reliable and generous ally; by comparison, other alliances were beginning to seem less attractive and more hazardous. In many cases the political and religious motives were inextricably connected; but there was also a factor, slow-working yet powerful and profound, which had nothing whatsoever to do with politics, and which was also largely independent of the deliberate efforts made by the believers to spread the message of Islam. This was the remarkable serenity which characterised those who practised the new religion. The Koran, the Book of God's Oneness, was also the Book of Mercy and the Book of Paradise. The recitation of its verses, combined with the teaching of the Messenger, imbued the believers with the certainty that they had within easy reach, that is through the fulfilment of certain conditions well within their capacity, the eternal satisfaction of every possible desire. The resulting happiness was a criterion of faith. The Prophet insisted: "All is well with the faithful, whatever the circumstances."[1]

Meantime, in Syria itself, there had been an event which, it seems, had not yet come to the ears of the Prophet, though it was no doubt partially the cause of the success of 'Amr's campaign. At any rate, it could be said to explain why the hostile Arab tribes against whom he had marched had had to rely entirely on their own strength, without any imperial reinforcements.

[1] N. XXI, 13.

Heraclius had received the news of his army's final victory over the Persians and of the recapture of the Rood which they had taken from Jerusalem. He was at that time in Homs, from which he made a pilgrimage on foot to the Holy City in thanks to God for the recovery of all that had been lost. One night while he was there he had a dream of remarkable clarity from which he knew for certain that the years of Byzantine sovereignty over Syria and Palestine were numbered. The next morning those who were with him were struck by the troubled expression on his face, and in answer to their questions, he said: "In a vision of the night I beheld the victorious kingdom of a circumcised man." Then he questioned them about circumcision, as to who practised it. His generals and the other officials who were present told him that only the Jews were circumcised, and they were trying to persuade him to take action against the Jews, when in came a messenger from the Governor of Ghassan, leading with him a Beduin. "This man, O King," said the messenger, "is from the Arabs, a folk of sheep and camels. He speaketh of a wonder that hath befallen in his country, so bid him tell thee of it." Heraclius told his interpreter to question him, and he answered: "A man hath appeared amongst us and he allegeth that he is a prophet. Some have followed and believed him, others have opposed him. There have been fights between them in many places. I left them even so." Heraclius then told his attendants to see if the man was circumcised or not, and when the answer came that he was circumcised, he said: "This, by God, is the vision which I saw, not what ye say." Then he sent for his chief of police and told him to search the country for a man of the same tribe as the claimant to prophethood.

Now Abū Sufyān, the chief of 'Abdu Shams, had not been present in Mecca at the time of the Lesser Pilgrimage of the Muslims from Medina, for he had taken advantage of the armistice to go with one or two other merchants of Quraysh to Syria. It was in Gaza, where they happened to be trading, that the Emperor's men found them, and from there they were immediately taken to Jerusalem. As soon as they were ushered into the royal presence, they were asked which of them was nearest of kin to the one who claimed to be a prophet, and Abū Sufyān replied that he was the nearest, whereupon Heraclius summoned him forward and sat him in front of him, saying to the others: "I will question him, and if he lieth, do ye confute him." When asked a general question about his Hāshimite cousin, Abū Sufyān began to belittle him, and said: "Let him not cause thee any anxiety; his importance is less than thou hast heard it to be," but the Emperor impatiently cut him short with more particular questions, and having received a precise answer on every point, he summed up his conclusion as follows: "I asked thee about his lineage, and thou didst affirm that it was pure and of the best amongst you; and God chooseth no man for prophet save him who is of the noblest lineage. Then I asked if any of his kinsmen had made claims the like of his, and thou saidst nay. Then I asked them if he had been dispossessed of sovereignty and had made this claim for the sake of recovering it, and again thine answer was nay. Then I asked thee about his followers, and thou said they were the weak and the poor and young slaves and women, and such have been the followers of the prophets in all times. Then I asked if any of his followers left him and thou saidst none. Even so is the sweetness of faith: once it hath entered the heart, it departeth not away. Then I asked if he were treacherous, and thou didst answer nay; and verily if what thou hast told me of him be the truth, he will vanquish me here where now I stand, and I would I were with him, that I might wash his feet. Go ye now about your business."[1]

The Prophet had written a letter to Heraclius on the same lines as his letters to the rulers of Persia and of Egypt, summoning him to Islam; and this letter, which had been delivered by Dihyah al-Kalbī to the Governor of Bostra, was forwarded to Jerusalem soon after Abū Sufyān had, despite himself, convinced the Emperor that the Arab claimant to prophethood was indeed a true Prophet. The letter from Medina confirmed this; but for still further assurance, Heraclius set down on paper all that he had learned, including an account of his vision, and sent it to a man in Constantinople whose knowledge and judgement he relied on, and the man replied: "He is the Prophet whom we expect. There is no doubt of it, therefore follow him and believe in him." Meantime Heraclius had returned to Homs, and it was there that he received this answer. Having read it he invited all the chief men of the Byzantines who were in that city to assemble in a room in his palace, and he gave orders that the doors should be locked. Then he himself addressed them from an upper chamber, saying, "Romans, if success and right guidance be your aim, and if ye would that your sovereignty remain firm, then pledge your allegiance to this Prophet." They understood his words, for they knew of the Prophet's letter; and as one man they turned and fled to the doors which they tried in vain to open. Seeing their great aversion, Heraclius despaired of making them believe as he believed; so he called them back and reassured them: "I but said what I said that I might test the strength of your faith, which now I have seen". And they prostrated themselves before him, and were reconciled. He was none the less certain that Syria would inevitably be conquered by the followers of the Prophet; but for the moment he felt obliged to keep his convictions to himself.

[1] T 1564; see also B.I,6.

# LXXIV

# *A Breach of the Armistice*

DESPITE the treaty, some of the men of Bakr were still determined to prolong their feud with Khuzā'ah; and not long after the campaign of 'Amr to Syria, a clan of Bakr made a night raid against Khuzā'ah, one of whom was killed. In the fighting which ensued, some of which took place inside the sacred territory, Quraysh helped their allies with weapons; and one or two men of Quraysh took part in the fighting under cover of darkness. The Bani Ka'b of Khuzā'ah immediately sent a deputation to Medina to inform the Prophet of what had happened and to ask for his help. He told them they could rely on him, and sent them back to their territory. When they had gone, he went to 'Ā'ishah, who could see from his face that he was in great anger. He asked for some water to perform his ablution, and she heard him say as he poured it over himself: "May I not be helped if I help not the sons of Ka'b."[1]

Meantime the Meccans were exceedingly troubled as to the possible consequences of what had happened, and since Abū Sufyān had now returned from Syria, they sent him to pacify the Prophet, if need be. On his way, he met the men of Khuzā'ah returning home and he feared he was too late. His fears were increased by the inscrutable demeanour of the Prophet. "O Muḥammad," he said, "I was absent at the time of the truce of Ḥudaybiyah, so let us now strengthen the pact and prolong its duration." The Prophet parried his request with the query: "Hath aught befallen to break it on your side?" "God forbid!" said Abū Sufyān uneasily. "We likewise," said the Prophet, "are keeping to the truce for the period agreed upon at Ḥudaybiyah. We will not modify it, neither will we accept another in its place." He was clearly not prepared to say more, so Abū Sufyān went to see his daughter, Umm Ḥabībah, hoping she might agree to intervene on his behalf. They had not met for fifteen years. The best place to sit was the Prophet's rug, but as he was about to take his seat she hastily folded it up from beneath him. "Little daughter," he said, "is this rug too good for me, thinkest thou, or am I too good for it?" "It is the Prophet's rug," she said, "and thou art an idolator, a man unpurified." Then she added: "My father, thou art lord of Quraysh and their chief. How is it that thou hast failed to enter Islam, and that thou worshippest stones which neither hear nor see?" "Wonder of wonders,"

[1] W. 791.

he said, "am I to forsake what my fathers worshipped to follow the religion of Muḥammad?" And, feeling that no help was to be expected from her, he went to Abū Bakr and others of the Companions to ask them to intercede on his behalf for a renewal of the pact, for he was now sure, although the Prophet had not said so, that he considered the pact to have been abrogated by the recent fighting. But it would serve the same purpose as a renewal of the pact, that is, it would prevent bloodshed, if some man of influence would grant a general protection between man and man. Abū Sufyān suggested this alternative to Abū Bakr but he merely answered: "I grant protection only within the scope of protection granted by the Messenger of God."

Others replied much the same, and finally Abū Sufyān went to the house of 'Alī, making much of their kinship, for they were both great-grandsons of the two brothers Hāshim and 'Abdu Shams. But 'Alī said: "Alas for thee, Abū Sufyān! The Messenger of God hath resolved not to grant thy request; and none can speak to him in favour of a thing when he is averse to it." For the Companions knew well that the Revelation had said to the Prophet: *Consult them about affairs; and when thou art resolved, then trust in God*;[1] and they had come to know by experience that when the Prophet had reached the degree of resolution he had clearly reached on this occasion it was useless to seek to deter him. Abū Sufyān now turned to Fāṭimah, who was present, with Ḥasan sitting on the floor in front of her. "O daughter of Muḥammad," he said, "bid thy little son grant protection between man and man, that he may become for ever the lord of the Arabs." But Fāṭimah replied that boys do not grant protection, and Abū Sufyān turned again to 'Alī in desperation and begged him to suggest some course of action. "I see nothing for it", said 'Alī, "but that thou thyself shouldst rise and grant protection between man and man. Thou art lord of Kinānah." "Would that avail me aught?" said Abū Sufyān. "By God, I think not so," said 'Alī, "but I find naught else for thee to do." So Abū Sufyān went to the Mosque and said in a loud voice: "Behold, I grant protection between man and man, and I do not think that Muḥammad will fail to uphold me." Then he went to the Prophet and said: "O Muḥammad, I do not think thou wilt disavow my protection." But the Prophet merely answered: "That is what *thou* thinkest, O Abū Sufyān;"[2] and the Umayyad chief returned to Mecca with great misgivings.

The Prophet began to prepare for a campaign, and Abū Bakr asked if he also should make ready. The Prophet said he should and told him that they were going out against Quraysh. "Must we not wait for the time of the truce to run out?" said Abū Bakr. "They have betrayed us and broken the pact," said the Prophet, "and I shall attack them. But keep secret what I have told thee. Let one thinker think that God's Messenger is for Syria, and let another think he is for Thaqīf, and another for Hawāzin. O God, take from Quraysh all sight of us, and all tidings of us, what we are about, that we may come suddenly upon them in their land."

In answer to this prayer word came to him from Heaven that one of the Emigrants, Ḥāṭib by name, had somehow learned the secret and had sent a

1 III, 159. 2 I.I. 807–8; W. 794.

letter to Quraysh to warn them of the impending attack. He had given it to a woman of Muzaynah who was travelling to Mecca, and she had hidden it in her hair. The Prophet sent 'Alī and Zubayr after her, and having failed to find the letter in her baggage they threatened to search her if she did not produce it. So she gave them the letter and they took it to the Prophet, who sent for the writer of it. "What made thee do this, O Ḥāṭib?" he said. "O Messenger of God," he answered, "I am indeed a believer in God and His Messenger. I have not changed my belief, and naught else hath taken its place. But I am a man without standing amongst the people of Mecca, without kinsmen of influence; and for the sake of my son and my family who are there in their midst I sought to win their favour." "O Messenger of God," said 'Umar, "let me strike off his head. The man is a hypocrite." But the Prophet said to him: "How knowest thou, O 'Umar, that God hath not looked upon the men of Badr and said: 'Do what ye will, for I have forgiven you?'"[1]

The Prophet now sent messengers to those of the tribes whom he felt he could now rely on for help, with a general summons to be present in Medina at the beginning of the next month, which was Ramaḍān. The Bedouin faithfully responded; and when the appointed day came the army was the largest that had ever set out from Medina. No able-bodied Muslim stayed behind. The Emigrants were seven hundred, with three hundred horse; the Helpers were four thousand, with five hundred horse; and the tribes, including those who joined them on the way, brought the total numbers up to nearly ten thousand men. The cavalry rode on camelback, leading their horses; and except for a few of the closest Companions none of them knew who the enemy were.

When they were about half-way they were met by 'Abbās and Umm al-Faḍl and their sons. 'Abbās had decided that it was now time for them to leave Mecca and to live in Medina. The Prophet invited them to join his expedition, which they did, to the joy of Maymūnah, who had come with the Prophet.

Umm Salamah was also with the Prophet; and at one of the next halts she was told that two men of Quraysh were in the camp and wished to speak with her. One of them was her half-brother 'Abd Allāh, the son of her father and the Prophet's aunt 'Ātikah; the other was a son of the Prophet's eldest uncle Ḥārith, the poet Abū Sufyān, a one-time nurseling of Ḥalīmah. He had with him his small son Ja'far. Both men had been close to the Prophet until the Revelation came, when they turned against him. Now they had come to seek his forgiveness, and to ask Umm Salamah to intercede for them. She went to the Prophet and said: "Thy wife's brother, son of thine aunt, is here, and thine uncle's son who is thy foster-brother." But he said: "I have no call to see them. As to my brother – he meant her brother 'Abd Allāh – he said unto me what he said in Mecca;[2] and as to mine uncle's son, he hath brought dishonour upon me." Abū Sufyān had satirised him in his poems. She pleaded for them, but to no effect, and when she told them this, Abū Sufyān said: "Either he shall see me or I will take my son by the hand and go out into the desert until we die of thirst and

[1] I.I. 809–10. [2] See p. 62.

hunger. And thou" – he meant the Prophet – "art the most long-suffering of men, even apart from my kinship with thee." When she repeated this to the Prophet he relented[1] and agreed to receive them in his tent, where they both uttered their professions of faith; and both made good their Islam.

During the march on one of these days the Prophet saw a bitch lying by the side of the road with a litter of recently born pups which she was feeding, and he was afraid that she might be molested by one or another of the men. So he told Ju'ayl of Damrah to stand on guard beside her until every contingent had passed.[2] The name Ju'ayl still clung to him, despite the new name of 'Amr which the Prophet had given him.

In Qudayd the army was joined by the Bani Sulaym, a troop of cavalry nine hundred strong. "O Messenger of God," said one of their spokesmen, "thou thinkest we are dissemblers, and yet we are thy maternal uncles" – he was referring to Hāshim's mother, 'Ātikah, who was a woman of their tribe – "so we have come unto thee that thou mayest put us to the test. We are steadfast in war, gallant at the encounter, horsemen firm in the saddle."

Like those who had come with the main force from Medina, they had brought their standards and their pennants unmounted and furled. They now asked the Prophet to mount them and to give them to men of his own choice from amongst them; but the time had not yet come for the flying of flags. Nor did he yet tell them where they were going.

At the outset the Prophet had sent a man through the army to proclaim: "He that would keep his fast, let him keep it, and he that would break his fast, let him break it." In case of travel in Ramaḍān it was permissible to break the fast, provided that the full number of days missed were fasted later. The Prophet himself and many others fasted until they were within a certain distance of the sacred territory; then he gave orders to break the fast; and when they had encamped at Marr aẓ-Ẓahrān he let it be known that the reason for breaking the fast had been to gather up their strength for meeting the enemy. This aroused the curiosity of some of the men to breaking-point. From Marr aẓ-Ẓahrān, Mecca could be reached in one long day's march, and easily in two. But in view of the truce it was unlikely that they had come out against Quraysh. Their camp was also on the way to the territory of the hostile tribes of Hawāzin. Or could it be that having gained possession of the northern garden of the Hijāz, the Prophet was now bent on capturing its southern garden, the hitherto impregnable Ṭā'if, the centre of the worship of al-Lāt?

Seeing that the question "Who are the enemy?" was being passed from man to man throughout the host, Ka'b ibn Mālik volunteered to go to the Prophet and ask him. He did not however venture to put the question directly, but going to where the Prophet was seated outside his tent he knelt in front of him and recited four melodious verses he had just composed for the occasion. The gist of these was that the men had reached the point of drawing their swords and interrogating them as to what enemy their edges were destined for, and that if the swords could have spoken they too would have put the same question. But the Prophet's only answer was a smile, and

[1] W. 811. [2] W. 804.

Ka'b had to return to the men with nothing achieved.

Their desire to know their own destination was no more than idle curiosity as compared with the eagerness of Quraysh and Hawāzin to know the answer to the same question. The great tribe of Hawāzin were spread mainly over the slopes of the hill country which dominated the southern extremity of the plain of Najd. Ṭā'if was on one of these slopes, and it was Thaqīf, the inhabitants of Ṭā'if and guardians of its temple, who took the initiative of sending an urgent message to all their fellow clans of Hawāzin that an army of ten thousand was on its way south from Yathrib, and that they must be prepared for the worst. Most of the clans immediately responded, and troops began to assemble at a point of vantage to the north of Ṭā'if.

As to Quraysh, although they would have liked to think that Ṭā'if was in danger rather than Mecca, they were conscious of having broken the pact. This, together with the Prophet's refusal to renew it, made them apprehensive almost to the point of despair. The Prophet was aware of this, and in order to increase their fears he ordered his men to spread out and each man to light a fire after dark. From the outskirts of the sacred territory ten thousand camp-fires could now be seen burning, and news was quickly brought to Mecca that Muhammad's army was far larger than they had feared. After a hurried consultation Quraysh accepted the offer of Abū Sufyān to go out and speak to the Prophet again. With him went Ḥakīm, Khadījah's nephew, who had done his best to stop the battle of Badr, and Budayl of Khuzā'ah, who had helped the Prophet at Ḥudaybiyah and who had recently accompanied some of his clansmen to Medina in connection with the rupture of the pact. As they approached the camp, already within earshot of the grumbling of the camels, they saw a man on a white mule coming apparently to meet them. It was 'Abbās, who had slipped out of the camp, hoping to find someone on his way to the city who could take a message for him to Quraysh. It was imperative, he thought, that they should send a deputation to the Prophet before it was too late. When they had recognised and greeted each other, 'Abbās took them to the tent of the Prophet, and Abū Sufyān said: "O Muḥammad, thou hast come with a strange assortment of men – some known and some unknown – against thy kindred." But the Prophet cut him short. "It is thou who art the transgressor," he said. "Ye broke the pact of Ḥudaybiyah, and abetted the attack on the Bani Ka'b, thereby sinfully violating the holy precinct of God and His Sanctuary." Abū Sufyān sought to change the subject somewhat. "Alas," he said, "hadst thou but turned thine anger and thy strategy against Hawāzin! For they are further from thee in kinship, and fiercer in enmity against thee." "I hope", said the Prophet, "that my Lord will grant me all of that – by victory over Mecca, by the triumph therein of Islam, and by the rout of Hawāzin – and that He will enrich me with their goods as plunder and their families as captives." Then he said to the three men: "Bear witness that there is no god but God, and that I am the Messenger of God." Ḥakīm and Budayl thereupon made their professions of faith, but Abū Sufyān testified "there is no god but God" and then was silent. When told to pronounce the second testification he said: "O Muḥammad, there is still in my soul a scruple about this; give her a respite." So the Prophet told his uncle to take them to his tent for the night. At dawn the call to prayer was made throughout the camp, and Abū Sufyān was greatly shaken by the sound of it. "What are they about?" he said. "The prayer," said 'Abbās. "And how often do they pray each day and night?" said Abū Sufyān, and when told that the prayers were five he said: "By God, it is too much!" Then he saw the men eagerly crowding and jostling each other that they might be splashed with water from the Prophet's ablution, or have some drops of what was left from it, and he said: "O Abu l-Faḍl, I have never seen such sovereignty as this." "Out upon thee!" said 'Abbās. "Believe!" "Take me to him," said Abū Sufyān, and after the prayer 'Abbās took him again to the Prophet and he testified to his prophethood, that he was indeed the Messenger of God. 'Abbās took the Prophet aside and said: "O Messenger of God, well knowest thou the love of Abū Sufyān for honour and glory. Grant him therefore some favour." "I will," said the Prophet, and going to the Umayyad chief he told him to return to Quraysh and say to them: "Whoso entereth the house of Abū Sufyān shall be safe, and whoso locketh upon himself his door shall be safe, and whoso entereth the Mosque shall be safe."[1]

[1] W. 818.

# LXXV

# *The Conquest of Mecca*

THE tents had already been loaded on to the transport camels, and the Prophet had at last called for the standards and pennants to be brought to him. These he mounted one by one, placing each in the hand of the bearer he had chosen for it. He told 'Abbās to accompany Abū Sufyān as far as the narrow end of the valley, and keep him there, so that he could see for himself the size of the army as it passed. There would be time enough for him then to return to Quraysh and deliver his message, for a single man could reach Mecca by a more direct way than the army would take.

"Who is that?" said Abū Sufyān, pointing to the man at the head of the host which now came in sight. "Khālid the son of Walīd," said 'Abbās; and when he came level with them Khālid uttered three magnifications, *Allāhu Akbar*. With Khālid were the horse of Sulaym. They were followed by the yellow-turbaned Zubayr at the head of a troop of five hundred Emigrants and others. He likewise uttered three magnifications as he passed Abū Sufyān, and the whole valley resounded as with one voice his men echoed him. Troop after troop went by, and at the passing of each Abū Sufyān asked who they were, and each time he marvelled, either because the tribe in question had hitherto been far beyond the range of influence of Quraysh, or because it had recently been hostile to the Prophet, as was the case with the Ghaṭafānite clan of Ashja', one of whose ensigns was borne by Nu'aym, the former friend of himself and Suhayl.

"Of all the Arabs," said Abū Sufyān, "these were Muḥammad's bitterest foes." "God caused Islam to enter their hearts," said 'Abbās. "All this is by the grace of God."

The last of the squadrons was the Prophet's own, consisting entirely of Emigrants and Helpers. The glint of their steel gave them a greenish-black appearance, for they were fully armed and armoured, only their eyes being visible. The Prophet had given his standard to Sa'd ibn 'Ubādah, who led the van; and as he passed the two men at the side of the route he called out: "O Abū Sufyān, this is the day of slaughter! The day when the inviolable shall be violated! The day of God's abasement of Quraysh." The Prophet was in the midst of the troop, mounted on Qaṣwā', and on either side of him were Abū Bakr and Usayd, with whom he was conversing. "O

Messenger of God," cried Abū Sufyān when he came within earshot, "hast thou commanded the slaying of thy people?" – and he repeated to him what Sa'd had said. "I adjure thee by God," he added, "on behalf of thy people, for thou art of all men the greatest in filial piety, the most merciful, the most beneficent!" "This is the day of mercy," said the Prophet, "the day on which God hath exalted Quraysh." Then 'Abd ar-Raḥmān ibn 'Awf and 'Uthmān said to him, for they were close at hand: "O Messenger of God, we are not sure of Sa'd, that he will not make a sudden violent attack upon Quraysh." So the Prophet sent word to Sa'd to give the standard to his son Qays, a man of relatively mild temperament, and to let him lead the squadron. To honour the son was to honour the father, and in the hand of Qays the standard would still be with Sa'd. But Sa'd refused to hand it over without direct command from the Prophet, who thereupon unwound the red turban from his helmet and sent it to Sa'd as a token. The standard was immediately given to Qays.[1]

When the army had passed, Abū Sufyān went back to Mecca with all speed and standing outside his house he shouted at the top of his voice to a quickly gathering crowd: "O men of Quraysh, Muḥammad is here with a force ye cannot resist. Muḥammad is here with ten thousand men of steel. And he hath granted me that whoso entereth my house shall be safe." Hind now came out of the house and seized her husband by his moustaches. "Slay this greasy good-for-nothing bladder of a man," she cried. "Thou miserable protector of a people!" "Woe betide you," he shouted, "let not this woman deceive you against your better judgement, for there hath come unto you that which ye cannot resist. But whoso entereth the house of Abū Sufyān shall be safe." "God slay thee!" they said. "What good is thy house for all our numbers?" "And whoso locketh upon himself his door shall be safe," he answered, "and whoso entereth the Mosque shall be safe," whereupon the crowd that had gathered dispersed, some to their houses and some to the Mosque.

The army halted at Dhū Ṭuwā, which is not far from the city and within sight of it. This was the place where two years previously Khālid had been stationed to bar their approach. But now there was no sign of any resistance. It was as if the city were empty, as it had been at their visit the previous year. But this time there was no three-day limit to their stay; and when Qaṣwā' came to a halt the Prophet bowed his head until his beard almost touched the saddle, in gratitude to God. He then drew up his troops, putting Khālid in command of the right and Zubayr in command of the left. His own troop which was now in the centre he divided into two; half of it was to be led by Sa'd and his son, and the other half, in which he himself would ride, was to be led by Abū 'Ubaydah. When the order was given they were to divide and to enter the city from four directions, Khālid from below and the others from the hills through three different passes.

High above the gathered host, on the slopes of Mount Abū Qubays, were two figures which a keen sight could have distinguished as a somewhat bent old man with a staff, guided and helped by a woman. They were Abū Quḥāfah and Quraybah, the father and sister of Abū Bakr. That morning, when the news came of the Prophet's arrival in Dhū Ṭuwā, the blind old man had told his daughter to guide him up the mount and tell him

1 W. 819–22.

what she could see. As a young and vigorous man he had climbed the hills on the other side of Mecca to see the army of Abrahah and his elephant. Now he was old, and had been blind for many years; but he would at least have a sight, through the eyes of his daughter, of this host of ten thousand in which were his son and two grandsons. Quraybah described what she could see as a dense mass of black, and he told her that those were the horsemen drawn up in close formation, waiting for orders. Then she saw the black mass spreading out until it became four distinct divisions, and her father told her to take him home with all speed. They were still on their way when a troop of horse swept past them, and one man leaned over from his saddle and snatched the silver necklace that Quraybah was wearing. Otherwise they suffered no harm and reached home in safety.

They had not been alone on Abū Qubays. At another part of the mount 'Ikrimah, Ṣafwān and Suhayl had gathered a force of Quraysh together with some of their allies of Bakr and Hudhayl. They were determined to fight; and when they saw Khālid's troop making for the lower entrance to the city they came down and attacked them. But they were no match for Khālid and his men, who put them to flight, having killed some thirty of them with the loss of only two lives on their own side. 'Ikrimah and Ṣafwān escaped on horseback to the coast; Suhayl went to his house and locked the door.

The fight was almost at an end when the Prophet entered through the pass of Adhākhir into Upper Mecca. Looking down towards the market-place, he was dismayed to see the flash of drawn swords. "Did I not forbid fighting?" he said. But when it was explained to him what had happened he said that God had ordained it for the best.

He could see his red leather tent which Abū Rāfi' had now pitched for him not far from the Mosque. He pointed it out to Jābir who was at his side; and after a prayer of praise and thanksgiving he made his way down to the hollow. "I shall not enter any of the houses," he said.

Umm Salamah, Maymūnah and Fāṭimah were waiting for him in the tent; and just before his arrival they had been joined by Umm Hāni'. The law of Islam had made it clear that marriages between Muslim women and pagan men were dissolved, and this applied to her marriage with Hubayrah, who had foreseen the fall of Mecca and gone to live in Najrān. But two of her kinsmen by marriage, one of them the brother of Abū Jahl, had taken part in the fighting against Khālid and had afterwards fled to her house for refuge. Then 'Alī had come to greet her, and seeing the two Makhzūmites he drew his sword and would have killed them despite the formal protection she had given them; but she threw a cloak over them, and stepping between him and them she said: "By God, thou shalt slay me first!", whereupon he left the house. And now, having locked the door upon them, she had come to intercede with the Prophet. She found Fāṭimah no less stern than 'Alī. "Dost thou give protection to idolaters?" she said. But Fāṭimah's reproaches were cut short by the Prophet's arrival. He greeted his cousin with great affection, and when she told him what had happened he said: "It shall not be. Whom thou makest safe, him we make safe; whom thou protectest, him we protect."

He performed the rite of the greater ablution and prayed eight cycles of prayer, after which he rested for an hour or more. Then he called for Qaṣwā', and having put on his coat of mail and his helmet, he girt on his sword; but in his hand he carried a staff, and his visor was up. Some of those who had ridden with him that morning were already in line outside the tent, and they made an escort for him as he went to the Mosque, talking to Abū Bakr, who was at his side.

He rode straight to the south-east corner of the Ka'bah and reverently touched the Black Stone with his staff, uttering as he did so a magnification. Those who were near him repeated it, *Allāhu Akbar*, *Allāhu Akbar*, and it was taken up by all the Muslims in the Mosque and the whole of Mecca resounded with it, until the Prophet motioned them to silence with his hand. Then he made the seven rounds of the Holy House with Muḥammad ibn Maslamah holding his bridle. At the Lesser Pilgrimage that honour had been given to a man of Khazraj. It was therefore fitting that this time it should go to a man of Aws.

The Prophet now turned away from the Ka'bah towards the idols which surrounded it in a wide circle, three hundred and sixty in all. Between these and the House he now rode, repeating the verse of the Revelation: *The Truth hath come and the false hath vanished. Verily the false is ever a vanisher*,[1] and pointing at the idols, one by one, with his staff; and each idol, as he pointed at it, fell forward on its face. Having completed the circle he dismounted and prayed at the Station of Abraham, which was at that time adjoining the Ka'bah. Then he went to the Well of Zamzam where 'Abbās gave him to drink; and he confirmed for ever the traditional right of the sons of Hāshim to water the pilgrims. But when 'Alī brought him the key of the Ka'bah, and when 'Abbās asked him to give their family also the right of guarding it, he said: "I give you only that which ye have lost, not that which will be a loss for others." Then he called for the man of 'Abd ad-Dàr who earlier had come to him in Medina with Khālid and 'Amr, 'Uthmān ibn Ṭalḥah; and handing him the key he confirmed for ever his clan's traditional right of guardianship. 'Uthmān reverently took the key and went to open the door of the Holy House, followed by the Prophet. Usāmah and Bilāl were close behind, and bidding them enter after him the Prophet told 'Uthmān to lock the door behind them.

Apart from the icon of the Virgin Mary and the child Jesus, and a painting of an old man, said to be Abraham, the walls inside had been covered with pictures of pagan deities. Placing his hand protectively over the icon, the Prophet told 'Uthmān to see that all the other paintings, except that of Abraham, were effaced.[2]

He stayed awhile inside, and then, taking the key from 'Uthmān, he unlocked the door; and standing on the threshold with the key in his hand, he said: "Praise be to God, who hath fulfilled His promise and helped His slave and routed the clans, He alone." The Meccans who had taken refuge in the Mosque had since been joined by many of those who had at first taken refuge in their homes and they were sitting in groups, here and there, not far from the Ka'bah. The Prophet now addressed them, saying: "What say ye, and what think ye?" They answered: "We say well, and we think

[1] XVII, 81. [2] W. 834; A.I, 107. But other accounts say "all" without mention of these two exceptions.

well: a noble and generous brother, son of a noble and generous brother. It is thine to command." He then spoke to them in the words of forgiveness which, according to the Revelation, Joseph spoke to his brothers when they came to him in Egypt: "Verily I say as my brother Joseph said: *This day there shall be no upbraiding of you nor reproach. God forgiveth you, and He is the most Merciful of the merciful.*[1]

Abū Bakr had left the Mosque in order the visit his father, and he now returned leading Abū Quḥāfah by the hand, followed by his sister Quraybah. "Why didst thou not leave the old man in his house," said the Prophet, "for me to go to him there?" "O Messenger of God," said Abū Bakr, "it is more fitting that he should come unto thee than that thou shouldst go unto him." The Prophet gave him his hand and drawing him down to sit in front of him, he invited him to make the two testifications of Islam, which he readily did.

Having given orders that Hubal, the largest of the fallen idols, should be broken to pieces and that all of them should be burned, the Prophet had it proclaimed throughout the city that everyone who had an idol in his house must destroy it. He then withdrew to the nearby hill of Ṣafā, where he had first preached to his family. Here he received the homage of those of his enemies who now wished to enter Islam, both men and women. They came to him in hundreds. Amongst the women was Hind, the wife of Abū Sufyān. She came veiled, fearing that the Prophet might order her to be put to death before she had embraced Islam; and she said: "O Messenger of God, praise be to Him who hath made triumph the religion which I choose for myself." Then she unveiled her face and said: "Hind, the daughter of 'Utbah"; and the Prophet said: "Welcome." Another of the women who came to Ṣafā was Umm Ḥakīm, the wife of 'Ikrimah. When she had entered Islam she begged the Prophet to give her husband immunity. He did so, although 'Ikrimah was still at war with him; and Umm Ḥakīm found out where he was, and went after him to bring him back.

The Prophet looked round at the gathering in front of him, and turning to his uncle he said: "O 'Abbās, where are thy brother's two sons, 'Utbah and Mu'attib? I see them not." These were the two surviving sons of Abū Lahab. It was 'Utbah who had repudiated Ruqayyah under pressure from his father, and it seemed that they were afraid to appear. "Bring them to me," said the Prophet, so 'Abbās fetched his nephews, who entered Islam and pledged their allegiance. Then the Prophet took them each by the hand, and walking between them, he led them to the great place of supplication which is named al-Multazam and which is that part of the Ka'bah wall which lies between the Black Stone and the door. There he made a long prayer, and noticing the joy on his face, 'Abbās remarked on it. He was answered: "I asked my Lord to give me these two sons of mine uncle, and He hath given me them."[2]

The nearest to Mecca of the three most eminent shrines of paganism was the temple of al-'Uzzà at Nakhlah. The Prophet now sent Khālid to destroy this centre of idolatry. At the news of his approach the warden of the temple hung his sword on the statue of the goddess and called upon her to

[1] XII, 92. [2] I.S. IV/1, 41–2.

defend herself and slay Khālid or to become a monotheist. Khālid demolished the temple and its idol, and returned to Mecca. "Didst thou see nothing?" said the Prophet. "Nothing," said Khālid. "Then thou hast not destroyed her," said the Prophet. "Return and destroy her." So Khālid went again to Nakhlah, and out of the ruins of the temple there came a black woman, entirely naked, with long and wildly flowing hair. "My spine was seized with shivering," said Khālid afterwards. But he shouted "'Uzzà, denial is for thee, not worship," and drawing his sword he cut her down. On his return he said to the Prophet: "Praise be to God who hath saved us from perishing! I was wont to see my father set out for al-'Uzzà with an offering of a hundred camels and sheep. He would sacrifice them to her and stay three days at her shrine, and return unto us rejoicing at what he had accomplished!"[1]

Meantime most of the Meccans had pledged their allegiance. Suhayl was an exception; but having taken refuge in his house, he sent for his son 'Abd Allāh to ask him to intervene with the Prophet on his behalf. For despite the general amnesty he could scarcely believe that it would apply to him. But when 'Abd Allāh spoke to the Prophet he immediately answered: "He is safe, under the protection of God, so let him appear." Then he told those about him: "No harsh looks for Suhayl, if ye meet him! Let him come out freely, for by my life he is a man of intelligence and honour, not one to be blind to the truth of Islam." So Suhayl came and went as he pleased; but he did not yet enter Islam.

As to Ṣafwān, his cousin 'Umayr obtained for him a two months' respite from the Prophet, whereupon he set out after him and found him waiting for a boat at Shu'aybah, which was in those days the port of Mecca. Ṣafwān was suspicious and flatly refused to change his plans, whereupon 'Umayr went again to the Prophet, who gave him his turban of striped Yemeni cloth to take to his cousin as a token of his safety. This convinced Ṣafwān, who decided to return and seek further assurances for himself. "O Muḥammad," he said, "Umayr telleth me that if I agree to a certain thing" – he meant the entry into Islam – "well and good, but that if not, thou hast given me two months' respite." "Stay here," said the Prophet. "Not until thou givest me a clear answer," said Ṣafwān. "Thou shalt have four months' respite," said the Prophet; and Ṣafwān agreed to stay in Mecca.

'Ikrimah was the last of the three to come into the presence of the Prophet after the victory of Mecca. Yet he was the first of them to enter Islam. He had decided to take a boat from the coast of Tihāmah to Abyssinia, and as he was about to step on board the captain said to him: "Make good thy religion with God." "What shall I say?" said 'Ikrimah. "Say: there is no god but God" was the answer, and the man made it clear that for fear of shipwreck he would accept no passenger who did not so testify. The four words *lā ilāha illa Llāh* entered into the soul of 'Ikrimah, and he knew at that moment that he could have uttered them with sincerity. Yet he did not embark, for his sole reason for wishing to do so had been to escape from those words, that is from the message of Muḥammad which was summed up in *lā ilāha illa Llāh*. If he could accept

[1] W. 873–4.

that message on board boat, he could accept it on shore. "Our God at sea is our God on land," he said to himself. Then his wife joined him and told him that the Prophet had guaranteed his safety in Mecca, and they returned forthwith. The Prophet knew he was coming and said to his Companions: "'Ikrimah the son of Abū Jahl is on his way to you, as a believer. Therefore revile not his father, for the reviling of the dead giveth offence unto the living and reacheth not unto the dead."

On his arrival in Mecca 'Ikrimah went straight to the Prophet, who greeted him with a face full of gladness, saying to him, after he had formally entered Islam: "Thou shalt not ask of me any thing this day but I will give it thee." "I ask thee," said 'Ikrimah, "that thou shouldst pray God to forgive me for all mine enmity against thee," and the Prophet prayed as he had asked. Then 'Ikrimah spoke of the money he had spent and the battles he had fought to bar men from following the truth, and he said that he would henceforth spend the double of it and fight with doubled effort in the way of God; and he kept his promise.[1]

[1] W. 850–3.

# LXXVI

# *The Battle of Ḥunayn and the Siege of Ṭā'if*

THE Prophet's final definite move against Quraysh had not stopped Hawāzin from continuing to consolidate their forces. Nor were their apprehensions allayed by the news of his easy conquest of Mecca and his destruction of all its idols; and great was their alarm at the fate of the temple of al-'Uzzà, which had been the sister-shrine to their own temple of al-Lāt. By the time that the invaders had spent two weeks in Mecca, Hawāzin had assembled an army of some twenty thousand men in the valley of Awṭās, to the north of Ṭā'if.

Leaving a man of 'Abdu Shams in charge of Mecca, and appointing Mu'ādh ibn Jabal, a young but well informed man of Khazraj, to instruct converts in all matters that concerned the religion, the Prophet marched out with his whole army, now increased by an additional force of two thousand Quraysh. Most of these had recently pledged allegiance to him, but some, including Suhayl and Ṣafwān, had not yet entered Islam and were simply there to defend their city against Hawāzin. Before setting out, the Prophet had sent to Ṣafwān to borrow a hundred coats of mail which he was known to possess, and the weapons that went with them. "O Muḥammad," said Ṣafwān, "is it a question of 'Give or I will take?' " "It is a loan to be returned," said the Prophet, whereupon Ṣafwān agreed to provide the camels for the transport of the armour and arms which he handed over to the Prophet when they had reached their final camp.

The clans of Hawāzin which had come out against them were Thaqīf, Naṣr, Jusham, and Sa'd ibn Bakr. Their commander-in-chief was a thirty-year-old man of Naṣr named Mālik, who had already won for himself, despite his youth, a reputation for great valour and princely munificence. Against the advice of older men he had ordered them to bring with them all their women and children and cattle, on the grounds that with these in the rear of the army the men would fight more valiantly. He sent out three scouts to bring him information about the army now approaching from Mecca, but it was not long before they returned almost speechless, in a strangely shattered condition, their joints having been loosed by terror, some even to the point of dislocation. "We saw white men on piebald horses," said one, "and at once we were smitten with what thou seest." "We are not fighting people of earth," said another, "but people of Heaven. Take our advice and withdraw; for if our men see what we have seen they will suffer what we have suffered." "Shame upon you!" said Mālik. "Ye are the cowards of the camp." And so wretched was their plight of body and soul he gave orders for them to be put in detention away from the rest of the troops lest they should spread panic throughout the army. Then he said to those about him: "Show me a man of courage." But the man chosen came back in the same state as the others, having seen the same terrifying horsemen in the van of the opposing host. "The very sight of them is unbearable," he gasped. But Mālik refused to listen, and after dark he gave orders to advance to the valley of Ḥunayn, through which he knew the enemy were bound to pass. He called a halt at his end of Ḥunayn, where the road began to slope down into the valley bed. On either side were ravines, some of them capacious with wide entrances which could be seen from above but which were completely masked from below. In one or two of these he posted a large part of his horse, with orders to charge down upon the enemy when he gave the signal. The rest of the army was drawn up on the road itself near the top of the gorge.

The Prophet encamped that night not far from the other end of the valley; and, having prayed the dawn prayer with his men, he exhorted them, and gave them good tidings of victory if they were steadfast. The sky was overcast, so that it was still almost dark as they descended into the valley bed. Khālid was in the van as before, commanding Sulaym and others. Next came the Muslim part of the new Meccan contingent. The Prophet, mounted on Duldul, was this time in the midst of the army, with the same squadron of Emigrants and Helpers, but surrounded by more members of his own family than ever before, including his cousins Abū Sufyān and 'Abd Allāh, who had joined him on his way to Mecca, and the two eldest sons of 'Abbās, Faḍl and Qitham, and the two sons of Abū Lahab. In the rear of the army were those of the Meccans who had not yet entered Islam.

The van had almost finished its descent when in the half-light the stationary host of Hawāzin loomed into view above them on the opposite slope. It was a formidable spectacle, the more so because in the rear of the army itself there were thousands of camels, unmounted or mounted by woman, and in the dimness of dawn they appeared to be part of the army itself. The road was clearly barred in that direction; but before any new instructions could be sought or any new orders given, Mālik gave his signal. The squadrons of Hawāzin suddenly wheeled out of the ravines and swept down upon Khālid and his men. The onslaught was so fierce and so sudden that he could do nothing to rally the Bani Sulaym, who made little or no resistance, but turned and fled headlong, scattering the ranks of the Meccans who were behind them and who now followed them in flight up the slope that they had just descended. The terrible stampede of horses and camels choked the defile in its narrowest parts, but the Prophet was at a point where he could withdraw a little to his right, and he now made a firm stand at the side of the road with a small body of those who had been riding near him – Abū Bakr, 'Umar and others of the Emigrants, some of the

Helpers, and all the men of his family who were present. Ḥārith's son Abū Sufyān stood beside him and took hold of the ring of Duldul's bridle.

The Prophet called for others to join him, but his words were drowned by the din of battle. So he turned to 'Abbās, who had a voice of exceptional power, and told him to shout: "O Companions of the Tree! O Companions of the Acacia!" Immediately the summons was answered from all sides – *Labbayk!*, "Here at thy service" – as Helpers and Emigrants rallied to him. He soon had with him a hundred men, and spreading out across the defile they momentarily checked the onslaught of the enemy. 'Abbās continued to shout and many of those who had fled now returned to the fight. The Prophet stood up in his stirrups, the better to be seen and the better to see. The enemy were preparing a fresh onslaught, and he prayed: "O God, I ask of Thee Thy promise!" Then he told his foster-brother to give him some pebbles, and taking them in his hand he flung them in the face of the enemy as he had done at Badr. The tide of the battle suddenly turned for no apparent reason – or rather, it was not apparent to the believers, but it was apparent to the enemy, as it had been previously to their scouts; and afterwards there came the Revelation: *God hath helped you on many fields, and on the day of Ḥunayn, when ye exulted in your numbers and they availed you naught, and the earth for all its breadth was straitened for you, and ye turned back in flight. Then God sent down His Spirit of Peace upon His Messenger and upon the faithful, and sent down hosts that ye saw not, and punished those who disbelieved. Such is the wage of the disbelievers; and afterwards God relenteth unto whom He will, for God is Forgiving, Merciful.*[1]

The rout was tremendous: Mālik fought with great bravery, but finally retreated with the men of Thaqīf to their walled city of Ṭā'if. The main part of Hawāzin was pursued with much slaughter as far as Nakhlah. From there they returned to their camp at Awṭās; but the Prophet sent a force to dislodge them, and they took to the hills.

The Muslims had lost many men at the outset of the battle, in particular the Bani Sulaym who had borne the brunt of the initial ambush. But after the first onslaught relatively few had been killed. One of these few was Ayman, Usāmah's elder brother, who was struck down at the side of the Prophet.

The Hawāzin women and children who had been behind the lines were all made captive; and in addition to the camels, sheep and goats there were also 4,000 ounces of silver amongst the spoils. The Prophet put Budayl in charge, and gave orders that it should all be taken, including the captives, to the nearby valley of Ji'rānah, about ten miles from Mecca.

Among the divisions of Hawāzin was a contingent from the Bani Sa'd ibn Bakr, the clan with whom the Prophet had spent his infancy and early childhood; and one of the older captives rebuked her captors saying: "By God, I am the sister of your chief." They did not believe her, but none the less brought her to the Prophet. "O Muḥammad, I am thy sister," she said. The Prophet gazed at her wonderingly: she was an old woman, of seventy or more. "Hast thou any sign of that?" he said, and she at once showed him

[1] IX. 25–7.

the mark of a bite. "Thou didst bite me," she said, "when I was carrying thee in the valley of Sarar. We were there with the shepherds. Thy father was my father, and thy mother was my mother." The Prophet saw that she was speaking the truth: it was indeed Shaymā', one of his foster-sisters; and spreading out his rug for her, he bade her be seated. His eyes filled with tears as he asked her for news of Ḥalīmah and Ḥārith, his foster-parents, and she told him that they had both died in the fullness of years. After they had talked he offered her the possibility of staying with him or returning to the Bani Sa'd. She said she wished to enter Islam, but chose to return to her clan. The Prophet gave her a rich present, and intending to give her more he told her to remain with those of her people who were in the camp, saying that he would see her again on his return. He then set off with the army for Ṭā'if.

Thaqīf had enough provisions in their city to last them for a year. They had also ample means of resisting the engines of war which the Prophet ordered to be used against them when all else had failed; and they were expert archers. There were many fierce exchanges of arrows, but half a month passed and the Muslims were no nearer to capturing the town than they had been on the first day. All that had been achieved was the entry of some men into Islam, for the Prophet had one day announced by means of a crier that any slave of Thaqīf who joined the Muslims would be set free. About twenty slaves contrived to make their way out of the city, and coming to the camp, they pledged their allegiance. Almost another week had passed when the Prophet had a dream that he was given a bowl of butter, and a cock came and pecked at it, and spilt it. "I do not think thou wilt gain from them this day what thou desirest," said Abū Bakr, and the Prophet agreed. Perhaps he had already come to the conclusion that to besiege Thaqīf was not the best way to overcome them. However that may be, he now gave orders to raise the siege and to proceed to Ji'rānah. As they moved away from the city, some of the men asked the Prophet to curse its inhabitants. Without replying, he raised his hands in supplication and said: "O God, guide Thaqīf and bring them to us."

Amongst those killed beneath the walls of Ṭā'if was Umm Salamah's half-brother, the Prophet's cousin 'Abd Allāh, who had so recently entered Islam.

# LXXVII

# *Reconciliations*

WHEN the army reached Ji'rānah the captives were in a large enclosure, sheltering from the sun, about six thousand women and children. Most of them were very poorly clad, and the Prophet sent a man of Khuzā'ah to Mecca to buy a new garment for each one, to be paid for out of the silver which was part of the spoils. The camels were about twenty-four thousand in number; as for the sheep and goats, no one attempted to count them, but they judged them to be forty thousand, more or less.

Many of the men were impatient to receive their share of the spoils, but the Prophet was unwilling to commit himself for the moment to any irrevocable extent, for he anticipated that Hawāzin would send him a delegation begging for generous treatment. There was, however, one sector of distribution which he did not wish to delay. His fifth of the spoils served the same purposes as the money received by way of alms; and a recent Revelation had introduced a new category of persons entitled to benefit from such funds, namely *those whose hearts are to be reconciled.* The revealed verse said: *The alms are for the poor and the needy, and for those who collect them, and those whose hearts are to be reconciled, and to set free slaves and captives, and for the relief of debtors, and for the cause of God, and for the wayfarer – an obligation enjoined by God. And God is Knowing, Wise.*[1] An immediate example of men *whose hearts are to be reconciled* were those of Quraysh who had recently entered Islam through the force of circumstances when their world – the world of Arab paganism – had been shattered by the establishment of the new religion in Mecca. The Prophet now gave Abū Sufyān a hundred camels, and when he thereupon asked that his two sons Yazīd and Mu'āwiyah should not be forgotten they were each given a hundred, which meant in fact that Abū Sufyān received three hundred. This did not escape the notice of others, and when Khadījah's nephew Ḥakīm was given a hundred he asked for two hundred more, which the Prophet allotted him forthwith. As in the case of Abū Sufyān, any hesitation or reluctance would have defeated the purpose of the gift. But to Ḥakīm the Prophet none the less said: "This property is a fair green pasture. Whoso taketh it in munificence of soul shall be blessed therein; but whoso taketh it for the pride of his soul shall not be blessed therein; and he shall be as one that eateth and is not filled. The upper hand is better than the lower hand; and begin thy giving with

[1] IX, 60.

such of thy family as are dependent upon thee." "By Him who sent thee with the truth, I will not receive aught from any man after thee," said Ḥakīm determined that for the future his hand should never be the lower hand; and he took only a hundred camels, relinquishing his claim to the rest.[1]

Included in the same category of recipients were those who were on the brink, and had not yet made their decision to enter Islam. Some of these were also given a hundred camels. The most important of them were Ṣafwān and Suhayl. Both had fought at Ḥunayn and when one of the unconverted Meccans in the rear had expressed satisfaction at the initial flight of the Muslims he was sharply rebuked by Ṣafwān: "If an overlord I must have," he said, "let it be a man of Quraysh rather than Hawāzin!" After he had received his hundred camels, Ṣafwān accompanied the Prophet as he rode through the valley of Ji'rānah to look at the spoils. There were many side valleys opening out from the main valley, and in one of these the pasture was especially luxuriant so that it was full of camels and sheep and goats, with the men who herded them. Seeing that Ṣafwān was struck with wonder at the sight, the Prophet said to him: "Doth it please thee, this ravine?" And when Ṣafwān warmly assented, he added: "It is thine, with all that is in it." "I bear witness," said Ṣafwān, "that no soul could have such goodness as this, if it were not the soul of a Prophet. I bear witness that there is no god but God, and that thou art His Messenger."

As to Suhayl, it was also at Ji'rānah that his final doubts were overcome, either through his renewed acquaintance with his son 'Abd Allāh, or his witnessing of the miraculous victory of Ḥunayn, or his experience of the Prophet's presence and his magnanimity, or through all of these together; but once he entered Islam he entered it without reserve; and three years later, when 'Abd Allāh was killed in battle, and Abū Bakr spoke words of comfort to the bereaved father, he replied: "I have been told that God's Messenger said: 'The martyr shall intercede for seventy of his people.' And I have hopes that my son will not begin with anyone before me."

Amongst others who entered Islam at Ji'rānah were some leading men of Makhzūm: two brothers of Abū Jahl; Khālid's half-brother Hishām, the full brother of the young Walīd who had died; and a second son of the Prophet's aunt 'Ātikah, Zuhayr, whose brother had recently been martyred at Ṭā'if. It was Zuhayr who, some ten years previously, in defiance of Abū Jahl, had been the first to speak in the Assembly in favour of the annulment of the ban on the Bani Hāshim and the Bani l-Muṭṭalib. His mother, 'Ātikah, had already entered Islam before either of her sons.

The Muslim army had now spent several days in the valley, but still no delegation had come from Hawāzin, so the Prophet allocated each man his portion of the spoils. No sooner had he finished doing so than the delegation arrived, and in it was the brother of his foster-father Ḥārith. Fourteen of them were already Muslim. The remainder now entered Islam, and insisting that the whole tribe of Hawāzin must be considered as his foster-kinsmen, they asked for his generosity. "We nursed thee on our

[1] W. 945.

laps, and suckled thee at our breasts," they said. He told them that he had waited for them until he thought they were not coming, and that the spoils had already been distributed. Then, although knowing the answer, he asked them which were the dearer to them, their sons and their wives, or their possessions; and when they said "Give us back our sons and our wives" he said: "As for those which have fallen unto me and unto the sons of 'Abd al-Muṭṭalib, they are yours; and I will plead with other men on your behalf. When I have led the congregation in the noon prayer, then say: 'We ask the Messenger of God to intercede for us with the Muslims, and we ask the Muslims to intercede for us with the Messenger of God.'"[1]

They did as they were told, and the Prophet turned to the congregation and explained that they were asking for their children and their wives to be returned to them. The Emigrants and Helpers immediately presented their captives to the Prophet. As for the tribes, some of them did the same, and some refused; but those who refused were persuaded to let their captives go in return for future compensation; and so they were all returned to their people except one young woman who had fallen to the lot of the Prophet's maternal cousin, Sa'd of Zuhrah, and who wished to remain with him.

The Prophet gave his foster-sister some more camels and some sheep and goats, and bade her farewell. Then, as the delegation were leaving, he asked them for news of their leader, Mālik. They told him that he had joined Thaqīf in Ṭā'if. "Send him word," he said, "that if he come to me as a Muslim, I will return his family to him and his possessions, and I will give him a hundred camels." He had deliberately lodged Mālik's family with his aunt 'Ātikah in Mecca, and had withheld his property from being distributed.

When the message reached Mālik in Ṭā'if, he said nothing to Thaqīf for fear they would imprison him if they suspected his intention; and leaving the town by night, he made his way to the camp and entered Islam. The Prophet put him in command of the already large and increasing Muslim community of Hawāzin, with instructions to give Thaqīf no peace. The raising of the siege of Ṭā'if had thus been no more than the briefest of respites. Another kind of siege, less acute but more implacable, was now to take its place.

The Prophet knew well that though the religion had power in itself to work upon souls, this power depended on the religion's being accepted with some degree of commitment, and not just nominally. It was to remove barriers to that commitment, such as a sense of bitterness or frustration, that the principle of giving to those *whose hearts are to be reconciled* had been revealed; but this principle was not understood at first by many of the older Companions, let alone others. In addition to what has already been mentioned, rich gifts had also been given to some prominent Bedouin whose Islam was highly questionable, whereas more deserving men of the desert had been neglected. Sa'd of Zuhrah asked the Prophet why he had given a hundred camels each to 'Uyaynah of Ghaṭafān and Aqra' of Tamīm and nothing to the devout Ju'ayl of Damrah, who was moreover, unlike the other two, exceedingly poor. The Prophet replied: "By Him in

[1] I.I. 877.

whose hand is my soul, Ju'ayl is worth more than a worldful of men like 'Uyaynah and Aqra'; but their souls have I reconciled that they might better submit unto God, whereas I have entrusted Ju'ayl unto the submission[1] he hath already made."[2]

There were no further objections on the part of the Emigrants; but by the end of the Prophet's halt in Ji'rānah there was a growing disquietude of soul among the four thousand Helpers. Many of them were impoverished, and out of the exceptionally plentiful spoils each man had received only four camels or their equivalent in sheep and goats. They had hoped for good ransoms from the captives, but their share in these they had unhesitatingly sacrificed to please the Prophet. Meantime they had witnessed the bestowal of rich gifts upon sixteen influential men of Quraysh and four chiefs of other tribes. All these recipients were men of wealth. But not one of the Helpers had received a gift from the Prophet. The same was true of the Emigrants; but that was no consolation to the citizens of Medina, for most of the gifts had gone to men of Quraysh, that is to close kinsmen of the Emigrants. "The Messenger of God hath joined his people," the Helpers were saying amongst themselves. "In time of battle it is we who are his companions, but when the spoils are divided his companions are his own people and family. And we would fain know whence this cometh: if it be from God, then we accept it with patience; but if it be no more than a thought which hath occurred to God's Messenger, we would ask him to favour us also."

When feeling rose high amongst them, Sa'd ibn 'Ubādah went to the Prophet and told him what was in their minds and on their tongues. "And where standest thou in this, O Sa'd?" said the Prophet. "O Messenger of God," he answered, "I am as one of them. We would fain know whence this cometh." The Prophet told him to gather all the Helpers together in one of the enclosures that had been used to shelter the captives; and some of the Emigrants also joined them, with Sa'd's permission. Then the Prophet went to them, and, having given praise and thanks to God, he addressed them: "Men of the Helpers, word hath come to me that ye are deeply moved against me in your souls. Did I not find you erring, and God guided you, poor and God enriched you, enemies each of the other and God reconciled your hearts?" "Yea indeed," they answered. "God and His Messenger are most bountiful and most gracious." "Will ye not retort against me?" he said. "How should we retort?" they asked, in some perplexity. "If ye wished," he answered, "ye might say unto me, and say truthfully, and be believed: 'Thou didst come unto us discredited, and we credited thee, forlorn and we helped thee, an outcast and we took thee in, destitute and we comforted thee.' O Helpers, are ye stirred in your souls about the things of this world whereby I have reconciled men's hearts that they may submit unto God, when you yourselves I have entrusted unto your Islam? Are ye not well content, O Helpers, that the people take with them their sheep and their camels, and that ye take with you the Messenger of God unto your homes? If all men but the Helpers went one way, and the Helpers another, I would go the way of the Helpers. God have Mercy upon

[1] *islām*. [2] W. 948.

the Helpers, and on their sons, and on their sons' sons." They wept until their beards were wet with their tears, and with one voice they said: "We are well content with the Messenger of God as our portion and our lot."[1]

[1] I.I. 886.

# LXXVIII

# *After the Victory*

FROM Ji'rānah the Prophet made the Lesser Pilgrimage and then returned to Medina. Shortly before his arrival he was overtaken by 'Urwah of Thaqīf, the man who had been so impressed at Ḥudaybiyah by the reverence of the Muslims for their leader.[1] 'Urwah had been absent in the Yemen during the recent campaign; and the accounts which he had heard on his return of the miraculous victory of Ḥunayn had brought to fullness his already half-formed intention to pledge his allegiance to the Prophet. Having done so, he now asked his permission to return to Ṭā'if and summon the people of Thaqīf to Islam. "They will slay thee," said the Prophet. "O Messenger of God," said 'Urwah, "I am dearer to them than their first-born." "They will slay thee," reiterated the Prophet. But when 'Urwah asked his permission a third time he said: "Then go if thou wilt." It was as the Prophet had said: they surrounded his house with archers and it was not long before he was mortally wounded by an arrow. His family asked him, as he was dying, what he thought of his death, and he said: "It is a grace which God in His Bounty hath given me." Then he told them to bury him with the martyrs who had recently been killed while besieging Ṭā'if, and they did so. When the Prophet was told of his death, he said: " 'Urwah is even as the man of Yā-Sīn.[2] He summoned his people unto God and they slew him."[3] The man was Ḥabīb, a carpenter of Antioch, who summoned his people to accept the message of Jesus after they had driven away the Apostle Peter and others. They killed him; and in the words of the Koran: *It was said to him: Enter Paradise. He said: O that my people knew how God hath forgiven my sins and lavished upon me His bounty!*[4] After 'Urwah's death his son and his nephew left Ṭā'if, and came to the Prophet in Medina, where they entered Islam, and lived with their cousin Mughīrah, who was one of the Emigrants.

The death of 'Abd Allāh ibn Rawāḥah at Mu'tah had deprived the Prophet not only of one of his valued Companions but also of a valued poet, for he is said to have considered the verses of 'Abd Allāh as equal to those of Ḥassān and of Ka'b ibn Malik. But by general consent there were two Arab poets at that time who outshone all the others. One of these was Labīd;[5] the second was another Ka'b, the son of one of the chief poets of the previous generation, Zuhayr ibn Abī Salmà. Although he was a man of Muzaynah, Ka'b had spent most of his life with Ghaṭafān and had therefore not come

[1] See p. 250. [2] Sūrah XXXVI. [3] W. 961.
[4] XXXVI, 26–7. [5] See p. 93.

under the Islamic influence which was so powerful in his own tribe. His brother Bujayr had entered Islam after Ḥudaybiyah, but Ka'b vociferously rejected the new religion and wrote satirical verses against the Prophet, who let it be known that anyone who killed the offender would be doing a service to the cause of God. Bujayr had already – but in vain – urged his brother to go to the Prophet and ask his forgiveness. "He slayeth not him who cometh unto him in repentance," he had said; and now, after the victory of Mecca, he followed up his previous messages with a poem in which were the lines:

> Alone unto God, not to 'Uzzà nor Lāt,
> Can be thine escape, if escape thou canst,
> On a day when escape there is none, no fleeing from men,
> Save for him whose heart is pure in submission to God.

With new multitudinous entries into Islam on all sides, Ka'b felt as if the earth were closing in upon him, and in fear of his life he went to Medina, to the house of a man of Juhaynah, a friend of his, to whom he made his profession of Islam. The next day he joined the congregation in the Mosque for the dawn prayer, after which he went to the Prophet and put his hand in his, saying: "O Messenger of God, if Ka'b the son of Zuhayr came unto thee in repentance, a Muslim, asking thee to grant him immunity, wouldst thou receive him if I brought him unto thee?" And when the Prophet answered that he would, Ka'b said: "I, O Messenger of God, am Ka'b the son of Zuhayr." One of the Helpers leapt to his feet and asked to be allowed to cut off his head, but the Prophet said: "Let him be, for he hath come in repentance, and is no longer as he was." Then Ka'b recited an ode which he had composed for the occasion. It was in the traditional Bedouin style, splendid in diction and highly melodious, with many vivid descriptions of nature; but the gist of it was to beg forgiveness. It ended with a passage in praise of the Prophet and the Emigrants, which begins:

> The Messenger a light is, source of light;
> An Indian blade, a drawn sword of God's swords,
> Amid Quraysh companions. When they chose
> Islam in Mecca's vale, men said: "Be gone!"
> They went, not weaklings, not as men that flee,
> Swaying upon their mounts and poorly armed,
> But heroes, proud and noble of mien, bright-clad
> In mail of David's weave[1] for the encounter.

When he had finished, the Prophet drew off his striped Yemeni cloak and threw it over the shoulders of the poet in recognition of his mastery of language.[2] But he said afterwards to one of his Companions: "Had he but spoken well of the Helpers, for verily they deserve it!" and this was reported to Ka'b, who composed another poem in praise of the Helpers, dwelling on their prowess and bravery in battle, the surety of their protection, and their generosity as hosts.[3]

[1] According to the Koran (XXXIV, 10) David invented chain armour.
[2] I.I. 893. [3] I.H. 893.

It was now clear that they had not long to wait for the birth of Māriyah's child. Salmà, who had attended on Khadījah at the birth of all her children, was now an elderly woman. It was twenty five years since she had helped to bring Fāṭimah into the world; but she none the less insisted that she would do the same for this new child of the Prophet, so when the birth was thought to be imminent she moved to the quarter where Māriyah lived in Upper Medina.

The child was born at night, and that same night Gabriel had come to the Prophet and addressed him as never before: "O father of Ibrāhīm." Immediately after the birth Salmà sent her husband, Abū Rāfi', to tell the Prophet that he had a son; and the next morning at the Mosque, after the dawn prayer, the Prophet told his Companions of the birth. "And I have named him," he added "by the name of my father, Ibrāhīm." There was great rejoicing in Medina, and strong rivalry among the women of the Helpers as to who should be the foster-mother. The choice fell on the wife of a blacksmith in Upper Medina who lived near the babe's mother; and the Prophet would visit his son nearly every day, and would often take his siesta there.

Sometimes Ibrāhīm was brought to his father's house. 'Ā'ishah said that one day the Prophet brought him to her in his arms and said: "Behold his likeness unto me." "I see no likeness," she said. "Dost thou not see how fair of skin he is, and how fine of flesh?" said the Prophet. "All that are fed on the milk of ewes are plump and fair of skin," she answered. One of the shepherds had instructions to send milk every day to the child's foster-mother.

The Prophet stayed six months in Medina after his return from Mecca, and during that time he sent out several small expeditions. One of these, under the leadership of 'Alī, was against the tribe of Ṭayy whose territory lay to the north-east of Medina. 'Alī had previously been sent to destroy the shrine of Manāt at Qudayd on the Red Sea, so that of Arabia's three principal centres of idolatry only the shrine of al-Lāt at Ṭā'if now remained. But the temple of Fuls was a centre of idol worship for those of the people of Ṭayy who were not Christian; and the main object of this present raid was to destroy that temple. Ṭayy was the tribe of the poet Ḥātim.[1] His son 'Adī, a Christian like his father, had succeeded him on his death as chief of the tribe.

At the sudden approach of 'Alī and his men, 'Adī escaped with his immediate family except for one of his sisters, who was taken captive with many others of the tribe. When she was brought before the Prophet in Medina she threw herself at his feet and begged him to set her free. "My father would ever free the captive," she said, "lodge well the guest, feed full the hungry and comfort the distressed. Nor turned he ever away the seeker of a boon. I am the daughter of Ḥātim." The Prophet answered her with kind words, and turning to those about him he said: "Let her go, for her father loved noble ways, and God likewise loveth them."

Meantime a man of her tribe had come to ask for her release, and the Prophet put her in his charge, giving her a camel and fine raiment. She went

[1] See p. 37.

in search of her brother 'Adī and persuaded him to go to Medina. There he entered Islam, pledging his allegiance to the Prophet, who confirmed his chieftaincy of Ṭayy; and he proved thereafter to be a faithful and influential ally.

It was during these same months, at the beginning of Rajab, that word of the death of the Negus came to the Prophet. After the next ritual prayer to be prayed in the Mosque, he turned to the congregation and said: "This day a righteous man hath died. Therefore arise and pray for your brother Ashamah."[1] Then he led them in the funeral prayer. Reports came later from Abyssinia that a light was constantly seen shining over the king's grave.[2]

[1] B. LXIII, 37. [2] I.I. 223.

# LXXIX

# *Tabūk*

NOT long after the battle of Ḥunayn the Emperor Heraclius had restored the Holy Rood to Jerusalem, and this marked the final fulfilment of the victory of the Byzantines over the Persians – the victory which the Revelation had predicted and of which it had said *that day the believers will rejoice.*[1] There was indeed cause for rejoicing that the Persians had been forced to evacuate their troops from both Syria and Egypt. But as regards Syria, one danger seemed to have been replaced by another. It was from that direction alone that the new Islamic state appeared to be threatened. There were growing rumours in Medina that Heraclius had advanced a year's pay to his army in view of a lengthy campaign against Yathrib. It was said, moreover, that the Byzantines had already marched south as far as Balqā' and had mustered the Arab tribes of Lakhm, Judham, Ghassān and 'Āmilah. These reports were partially exaggerated and partially the reverse of the truth. The Arab tribes of Syria and its borders were not preparing to attack; and as for the Emperor, his movements towards the south, and ultimately his defence of Syria itself, had been inhibited by his vision of "the victorious kingdom of a circumcised man" and his belief that this man was truly a Messenger of God. He had made no further attempts to win over his people to accept this belief; but when his return to Constantinople became imminent, his sense of royal responsibility impelled him to propose to his generals that a treaty should be made with the Prophet, giving him the province of Syria on condition that there should be no further northward advance. Their amazement at this idea and their extreme aversion to it caused him to abandon it, but in no way modified his conviction; and when, on his journey home, he reached the pass which is known as the Cilician Gates, he looked back to the south and said: "O land of Syria, for the last time, I bid thee farewell."[2]

The Prophet likewise was certain that God would open up Syria to his armies of Islam; and whether because he thought the time had come or whether because he wished to give his troops some training for the inevitable northern campaign, he now announced an expedition against the Byzantines, and set about mustering by far the largest and best equipped army which he had led. Hitherto it had been his practice not to divulge his true objective at first, and to keep preparations as secret as possible. But this time there was no attempt at secrecy, and orders were

[1] XXX, 4. [2] T 1568.

sent to Mecca and to the allied tribes that they must send at once to Medina all their available armed and mounted men for the Syrian campaign.

It was the beginning of October in the year AD 630. The season was always a hot one, but that year there was a drought and the heat was more oppressive than usual. It was also the time when there was much ripe fruit to be eaten, so that there were two reasons for not wanting to take part in the expedition; and a third reason was the formidable reputation of the imperial legions. The hypocrites and many of the less devout amongst the Muslims came to the Prophet with various excuses, asking his permission to stay behind, and many of the Bedouin did the same. There were also four men of good faith, Ka'b ibn Mālik and two others of Khazraj and a man of Aws, who did not deliberately decide to remain at home, nor did they proffer excuses; but it seemed to them so undesirable to leave Medina at that season that they could not bring themselves to make preparations, and they put off the task from one day to the next until the day dawned when it was too late and the troops had gone. But the majority set about making ready with all speed, and the richer men vied with each other in their contributions of money. 'Uthmān alone gave enough for the mounting and equipment of ten thousand men. Even so, there was not enough for all those who wished to go, and a subsequent Revelation[1] has enshrined in memory "the seven weepers" – five needy Helpers and two Bedouin of Muzaynah and Ghaṭafān – whom the Prophet turned reluctantly away because he was unable to mount them, and tears filled their eyes as they left his presence.

When all the Bedouin contingents had arrived the army was thirty thousand strong, with ten thousand horse. A camp was made outside the town, and Abū Bakr was put in charge of it until, when all was ready for the march, the Prophet himself rode forth and took command.

He had left 'Alī to look after his family, but the hypocrites spread the rumour that the Prophet found him a burden and was relieved to be rid of his presence. Hearing this, 'Alī was so distressed that he put on his armour, seized his arms and overtook the Prophet at his first halt, intending to beg his permission to accompany him. He told him what the people were saying, and the Prophet said: "They lie. I bade thee remain for the sake of what I had left behind me. So return and represent me in my family and in thine. Art thou not content, O 'Alī, that thou shouldst be unto me as Aaron was unto Moses, save that after me there is no Prophet."[2]

During the northward march it happened one day at dawn that the Prophet was delayed in making his ablution. The men were in lines for the prayers and they waited for him until they feared that the sun would rise before they had prayed. Then it was agreed that 'Abd ar-Raḥmān ibn 'Awf should lead them, and they had already prayed one of the two prayer cycles when the Prophet appeared. 'Abd ar-Raḥmān was about to draw back, but the Prophet motioned him to remain where he was, and he himself joined the congregation. When they had uttered the greeting of Peace which ends the prayer the Prophet rose and prayed the cycle he had missed. When he had finished he said: "Ye have done well, for verily a Prophet dieth not until he hath been led in prayer by a pious man of his people."[3]

Meantime in Medina, about ten days after the army had marched out,

[1] IX, 92. [2] I.I. 897. [3] W. 1012.

one of the four believers who had stayed behind, Abū Khaythamah of Khazraj, went out into his garden amid the shade of the trees on a day of great heat. There were two huts there, and he found that his wives had sprinkled each one with water, and in each a meal was prepared for him, and water had been cooled in earthenware jars for him to drink. He stood at the threshold of one of the huts and said: "The Messenger of God is in the glare of the sun, blown on by hot winds, and Abū Khaythamah is in cool shade with food made ready for him, and two fair women, abiding at rest on his own estate!" Then he turned to his wives and said: "By God, I will not enter either of your huts until I have first overtaken the Messenger, so make ready provisions for me." They did so, and saddling his camel, he set off with all speed in the wake of the army.

About half-way between Medina and Jerusalem, the Prophet said one night: "Tomorrow, God willing, ye will come unto the spring of Tabūk. Ye will not reach it until the sun be hot. And whoso cometh unto it, let him not touch its water until I myself be come." But two of the first men to reach it drank from the spring, and when the main part of the army arrived the water had become less than a trickle. The Prophet severely rebuked the two men, and then told some of the others to scoop up what water they could in the hollows of their hands and to empty it into an old skin. When enough had been collected he washed his hands and face in it and poured it over the rock which covered the mouth of the spring, passing his hands over it and praying as God willed him to pray. Then with a sound as of thunder the water gushed forth; and it continued to flow undiminished after all the men had satisfied their needs. He turned to Mu'ādh[1] who was beside him and said: "It may be, O Mu'ādh, that thou shalt live to see this place as a vale of many gardens." And it was as he had said.

He had been disappointed and saddened by the default of the four believers who had failed to march out with the army, not least as regards Abū Khaythamah, who overtook them a few days after they had reached Tabuk. When the lone rider was seen approaching, but before he was distinguishable, the Prophet said, as it were in prayer: "Be Abū Khaythamah!" Then, when the man rode up and greeted him, he said: "Alas for thee, Abū Khaythamah!"; but when told what had happened, he blessed him.

The army stayed for twenty days in Tabūk. It was evident that the rumours of danger from the Byzantines had been quite unfounded. Nor was it yet time on the other hand, for the promised conquest of Syria. But during those days the Prophet made a treaty of peace with a Christian and Jewish community who lived at the head of the gulf of 'Aqabah and along its eastern coast. In return for a yearly tribute they were to be guaranteed protection by the Islamic state. He then returned to Medina with the main part of the army, having sent Khālid with four hundred and twenty horse to Dūmat al-Jandal, to the north-east of Tabūk. This important stronghold was on the road to Iraq from Medina, as well as being on one of the roads to Syria. Ukaydir, its Christian ruler, was surprised when out hunting by Khālid, who took him prisoner and brought him to Medina, where he made an alliance with the Prophet, and entered Islam.

[1] See p. 304.

# LXXX

# *After Tabūk*

LIKE the return from Badr, the return from Tabūk was fraught with sadness: another daughter of the Prophet, Umm Kulthūm, had died during his absence; and this time her husband also had been absent. The Prophet prayed at her grave; and he said to 'Uthmān that if he had had another unwedded daughter he would have given her to him in marriage.

Those of the hypocrites who had not taken part in the expedition now went to the Prophet and made their excuses, which he accepted, while reminding them that God knew their most secret thoughts. But he told the three believers who had stayed behind to depart from him until God should decide their case, and he gave orders that no one should speak to them. For fifty days they lived as outcasts; but after the dawn prayer on the fiftieth day, the Prophet announced in the Mosque that God had relented to them. In the words of the Revelation which had just come: *When the earth for all its vastness was straitened for them and when their souls were straitened, and they had come to think there is no refuge from God except in Him, then turned He unto them that they might turn in repentance unto Him. Verily God, He is the Ever-Relenting, the Merciful.*[1] The congregation rejoiced, and many of them hastened from the Mosque to inform the three men of the good news. The youngest of them, Ka'b ibn Mālik, had pitched a solitary tent for himself outside the town, and he told in after years how he had heard a horse galloping towards him and a voice that shouted "Good tidings, Ka'b," whereupon he had thrown himself down in prostration to God, for there could be no good tiding except one. Then he went to the Mosque. "When I greeted the Prophet," he said, "his face shone with gladness as he said to me: 'Rejoice in the best day that hath come upon thee since thy mother bore thee.' I said: 'Is this from thee, O Messenger of God, or is it from God?' 'Nay, it is from God,' he answered. When the Messenger was glad on account of good tidings, his face would ever have the brightness of a moon."[2]

Since his entry into Islam, Mālik, the leader of Hawāzin, had not been idle. The Bani Thaqīf might still pride themselves on the impregnability of Ṭā'if; but they were now surrounded on all sides, far and wide, by Muslim communities, and any caravan they sent out was liable to be attacked and despoiled. They could not even send camels and sheep out to pasture without the risk that they would be captured by Mālik's men, who moreover let it be known that they would put to death any man of Thaqīf

[1] IX, 118. [2] I.I. 912.

who fell into their hands unless he abandoned his polytheism. After some months they decided that they had no option but to send a delegation to the Prophet saying that they would accept Islam, and asking for a document which would guarantee the safety of their people and their animals and their land.

The return from Tabūk had been at the beginning of Ramaḍān, and in that same month the delegation arrived from Ṭā'if. They were hospitably received and a tent was pitched for them not far from the Mosque. It followed as a matter of course that if they entered Islam their territory would be under the protection of the Islamic state. But the Prophet did not agree to some of their secondary requests. They asked him to let them keep al-Lāt undestroyed for three years, and when he refused they asked for two years and then one, until finally they were reduced to asking for a month's respite, which also met with a refusal. They then begged him not to make them destroy their idols with their own hands, and to give them a dispensation not to say the five daily prayers. He insisted that they should pray, saying: "There is no good in a religion that hath no canonical prayer." But he agreed to excuse them from destroying their idols with their own hands; and he ordered Mughīrah, 'Urwah's nephew, to return with the delegation and to destroy al-Lāt, taking with him Abū Sufyān from Mecca to assist him.

After their entry into Islam the delegates fasted the remainder of Ramaḍān in Medina, and then returned to Ṭā'if. Abū Sufyān joined the party in Mecca, but it was Mughirah single-handed who destroyed the idol. His clan took certain measures to protect him, fearing that he might suffer the same fate as 'Urwah; but no one sought to avenge the goddess, despite the lamentations of a multitude of women who bewailed her loss.

Two of the men who most deplored the surrender of the city were neither citizens nor devotees of its "lady". When the Prophet had marched on Mecca, Abū 'Āmir, the father of Ḥanẓalah, and Waḥshī the javelineer had both taken refuge in Ṭā'if, which seemed an impregnable fortress. But where could they now take refuge? Abū 'Āmir fled to Syria, and it was there that he died, "a fugitive, lonely and homeless", thus fulfilling the curse he had unwittingly laid upon himself.[1] Waḥshī was still hesitating where to go when a man of Thaqīf assured him that the Prophet would put no man to death who entered Islam. So he went to Medina, and going to the Prophet, he made his formal attestation. Even as he did so one of the believers who was present recognised the slayer of Ḥamzah and said: "O Messenger of God, this is Waḥshī." "Let him be," said the Prophet, "for one man's Islam is dearer to me than the slaying of a thousand disbelievers." Then his eyes rested on the black face in front of him. "Art thou indeed Waḥshī?" he said, adding at the man's assent: "Be seated, and tell me how thou slewest Ḥamzah." When the javelineer had finished, the Prophet said: "Alas, take thou thy face from me, let me not look upon thee again."[2]

As to the cousin of Abū 'Āmir, Ibn Ubayy, in the month after Tabūk he fell seriously ill, and after a few weeks it was clear that he was dying. The

[1] See p. 128. [2] I.I. 566.

traditional accounts differ as to the state of soul in which he died, but all are unanimous that the Prophet led the funeral prayer for him, and prayed beside his grave when he had been buried. According to one tradition, when the Prophet had already taken his stand for the prayer, 'Umar went to him and protested against the bestowal of such grace upon a hypocrite, but the Prophet answered him, saying with a smile: "Stand thou behind me, 'Umar. I have been given the choice, and I have chosen. It hath been said unto me: *Ask forgiveness for them, or ask it not, though thou ask forgiveness for them seventy times, yet will not God forgive them.*[1] And did I know that God would forgive him if I prayed more than seventy times, I would increase the number of my supplications."[2] Then he led the prayer and walked beside the bier to the cemetery and stood beside his grave. Not long afterwards the verse was revealed, with reference to the hypocrites: *And never pray the funeral prayer over one of them who dieth, nor stand beside his grave, for verily they disbelieved in God and His Messenger, and died in their iniquity.*[3] But according to other traditions[4] this verse had been already revealed as part of the Revelation which came immediately after the return from Tabūk. Nor was it any longer applicable to Ibn Ubayy, for the Prophet visited him in his illness and found that the imminence of death had changed him. He asked the Prophet to give him a garment of his own in which he could be shrouded, and to accompany his body to the grave, which the Prophet agreed to do. Then again he spoke, saying: "O Messenger of God, I hope that thou wilt pray beside my bier, and ask forgiveness of God for my sins." Again the Prophet assented, and after his death he did as he had promised. The dead man's son 'Abd Allāh was present on all these occasions.

Thaqīf were not the only tribe to send envoys to the Prophet. Many other envoys came to Medina from all over Arabia in this "year of deputations", as the ninth year of the Hijrah is called. Amongst others were those which came from different parts of the Yemen, including letters from four Himyarite princes who announced their acceptance of Islam and their repudiation of polytheism and its adherents. The Prophet replied cordially; he stressed the obligations of Islam, bidding them treat well his messengers whom he would send to collect the taxes incumbent upon Muslims, Christians and Jews, and specifying that "a Jew or a Christian who keepeth his religion shall not be turned away from it but shall pay the poll tax . . . and shall have the protection of God and His Messenger".[5] A recent Revelation had said, with regard to religious differences: *For each We have appointed a law and a path; and if God*[6] *had wished He could have made you one people . . . So vie with one another in good works. Unto God ye will all be brought back and He will then inform you of those things wherein ye differed.*[7]

Not all the deputations were conclusive. 'Āmir ibn Ṭufayl, the man responsible for the massacre at Bi'r Ma'ūnah, was now chief of the Bani

[1] IX, 80. [2] I.I. 927. [3] IX, 84.
[4] Mirkhond, *Rawḍat aṣ-Ṣafā'*, II, vol. 2, pp. 671–2, citing earlier sources. See also B. XXIII, 76.
[5] I.I. 956. [6] See p. 48, note 3. [7] V, 48.

'Āmir, and under pressure from his tribe he came to Medina. But he himself was an arrogant man, and in return for his Islam he asked the Prophet to name him as his successor. "It is not for thee nor thy people," said the Prophet. "Then give me the tent-dwellers and keep thou the villagers," said 'Āmir. "Not so," said the Prophet, "but into thy hand will I put the reins of the cavalry, for thou art an excellent horseman." This was not enough for the Bedouin chief. "Am I to have naught?" he said disdainfully, adding as he turned away: "I will fill all the land with horsemen and footmen against thee." When he had gone, the Prophet prayed: "O God, guide the Bani 'Āmir, and rid Islam of 'Āmir the son of Ṭufayl"; and 'Āmir was smitten with an abcess and died before he reached home. His tribe sent another deputation, and a pact was at last concluded. The poet Labīd was one of the envoys, and he now entered Islam. He is reported to have had some intention of abjuring poetry thereafter. "In exchange, God hath given me the Koran," he said. But he none the less continued to compose poems until his death, placing his gifts at the service of his religion.

The time of the Pilgrimage was approaching, and the Prophet appointed Abū Bakr to take charge of it. He set off from Medina with three hundred men, but not long after they had gone there came a Revelation which it was important that all the pilgrims to Mecca, both Muslims and polytheists, should hear. "None shall be a transmitter from me but a man of the people of my house," said the Prophet, and he told 'Alī to set out with all speed and overtake the pilgrims. He was to recite the revealed verses in the valley of Mina and he was also to make it clear that no one after that year would be allowed to go round the Holy House naked, and that idolaters were making the Pilgrimage for the last time.

When 'Alī overtook the others, Abū Bakr asked him if he had come to command the expedition, but he replied that he was under his command, so they went on together and Abū Bakr led the prayers and preached the sermons. On the day of the Feast, when all the pilgrims were assembled in the valley of Mina to sacrifice their animals, 'Alī proclaimed the Divine Message. The gist of it was that the idolaters were given four months' respite to come and go as they pleased in safety, but after that God and His Messenger would be free from any obligation towards them. War was declared upon them, and they were to be slain or taken captive wherever they were found.[1] Two exceptions were made: as regards those idolaters who had a special treaty with the Prophet and had kept it faithfully, the treaty was to be held as valid until its term ran out; and if any individual idolater sought protection he was to be granted it and conveyed to a place of safety, having first been instructed in Islam. There was also a revealed verse which seemed to be addressed especially to the recent converts of Mecca who might fear that the exclusion of idolaters would not only deprive them of opportunities for trade but also of many rich gifts: *O ye*

[1] The absence of the Names of Mercy stresses the rigorous nature of this message, which starkly opens the Sūrah of Repentance (IX), the only sūrah in the Koran that does not begin with *Bismi Llāhi r-Raḥmāni r-Raḥīm*.

*who believe, the idolaters are unclean. Therefore let them not come nigh unto the inviolable mosque after this their year. And if ye fear poverty, God will enrich you of his Bounty. Verily God is All-Knowing, Infinitely Wise.*[1]

The Prophet remained at home for nearly the whole of the following year, which was the tenth since his emigration. Ibrāhīm could already walk and was beginning to talk. Ḥasan and Ḥusayn had now a small sister named after her aunt Zaynab, and Fāṭimah was expecting a fourth child. Other intimates of the household were the three sons of Ja'far. They were now the stepsons of Abū Bakr, who had married their mother Asmā', and she also was expecting a child. Particularly dear to the Prophet was her sister Umm al-Faḍl. In Mecca it had been his custom to visit her often, and since 'Abbās's move to Medina he was once more a frequent visitor at their house. Their eldest son, after whom she was named, had now grown to manhood and received many signs of favour. On at least one occasion, when it was Maymūnah's turn to house the Prophet, she invited her nephew Faḍl to stay with her.

Deputations still continued to come as in the previous year, and one of these was from the Christians of Najrān, who sought to make a pact with the Prophet. They were of the Byzantine rite, and in the past had received rich subsidies from Constantinople. The delegates, sixty in number, were received by the Prophet in the Mosque, and when the time for their prayer came he allowed them to pray it there, which they did, facing towards the east.

At the audiences which they had with him during their stay, many points of doctrine were touched on, and there were some disagreements between him and them concerning the person of Jesus. Then came the Revelation: *Verily the likeness of Jesus with God is as the likeness of Adam. He created him of dust,*[2] *then said to him "Be!", and he was. This is the truth from thy Lord, so be not of the doubters. And whoso contendeth with thee about him after the knowledge that hath reached thee, say: Come ye, and let us summon our sons and your sons and our women and your women and ourselves and yourselves. Then we will imprecate, putting God's curse on those who lie.*[3] The Prophet recited this Revelation to the Christians and invited them to meet with him and his family and to settle their dispute in the way here suggested. They said they would think about it, and the next day when they came to the Prophet they saw that 'Alī was with him, and behind them were Fāṭimah and her two sons. The Prophet was wearing a large cloak and he now spread it wide enough to enfold them all in it, including himself. For this reason the five of them are reverently known as "the People of the Cloak". As to the Christians, they said they were not prepared to carry their disagreement so far as imprecation; and the Prophet made with them a favourable treaty according to which, in return

[1] IX, 28.

[2] The words "in his mother's womb" are to be understood, for there is no question of Jesus having been created fully grown as Adam was. The parallel between the two creations lies in the direct Divine intervention for both.

[3] K. III, 59–61.

for the payment of taxes, they were to have the full protection of the Islamic state for themselves and their churches and other possessions.

The untroubled happiness of the early months of this year came to an end with the illness of Ibrāhīm. It was soon clear that he would not survive. He was tended by his mother and her sister Sīrīn. The Prophet visited him continually, and was with him when he was dying. As the child breathed his last, he took him in his arms, and tears flowed from his eyes. His forbidding of vociferous lamentation had made prevalent the notion that all expressions of woe at bereavement were to be discouraged, and the mistaken idea still lingered on in many minds. "O Messenger of God," said 'Abd ar-Raḥmān ibn 'Awf, who was present, "this is what thou hast forbidden. When the Muslims see thee weeping, they too will weep." The Prophet continued to weep, and when he could find his voice he said: "Not this do I forbid. These are the promptings of tenderness and mercy, and he that is not merciful, unto him shall no mercy be shown. O Ibrāhīm, if it were not that the promise of reunion is sure, and that this is a path which all must tread, and that the last of us shall overtake the first, verily we should grieve for thee with a yet greater sorrow. Yet are we stricken indeed with sorrow for thee, O Ibrāhīm. The eye weepeth, and the heart grieveth, nor say we aught that would offend the Lord."[1]

He spoke words of comfort now to Māriyah and Sīrīn, assuring them that Ibrāhīm was in Paradise. Then, having left them for a brief while, he returned with 'Abbās and Faḍl. The young man washed the body and laid it out, while the two older men sat and watched him. Then it was borne forth to the cemetery on its little bier. The Prophet led the funeral prayer and prayed again for his son at the edge of the grave after Usāmah and Faḍl had laid in it the body. When the earth had been heaped over it, he still lingered at the graveside, and calling for a skin of water he bade them sprinkle it over the grave. Some unevenness had been left in the earth, and noticing this he said: "When one of you doeth aught, let him do it to perfection." And smoothing it over with his hand, he said of his own particular action: "No harm it doth nor good, but it giveth relief unto the soul of the afflicted."[2]

He had already stressed more than once the need to make perfection one's aim in every earthly act, and many of his sayings indicate that this aim must be unworldly and detached. 'Alī is said to have summed up the Prophet's guidance in this respect as follows: "Do for this world as if to live for ever and for the next as if to die upon the morrow." To be always ready to depart is to be detached. "Be in this world as a stranger or as a passer-by,"[3] the Prophet said.

On the day of Ibrāhīm's death, not long after his burial, there was an eclipse of the sun; but when some of the people attributed it to the Prophet's bereavement he said: "The sun and the moon are two signs of the signs of God. Their light is not dimmed for any man's death. If ye see them eclipsed, ye should pray until they be clear."[4]

[1] I.S. I/1, 88–9. [2] ibid. [3] B. LXXXI, 3. [4] I.S, ibid.

# LXXXI
# *The Degrees*

SPIRITUAL motives were poorly represented in many of the conversions which now took place; and it was not long before there came the following further Revelation: *The Arabs of the desert say: We have faith. Say thou: Faith ye have not, but say "we submit", for faith hath not yet entered your hearts. And if ye obey God and His Messenger, He will in no wise withold from you your meed for what ye do.*[1]

This verse completed the hierarchy of Islam, submission without faith being the lowest degree. The higher degrees, that is the degrees of faith, are the theme – or rather one of the themes – of the Verse of Light which had been revealed to the Prophet some months before the truce of Ḥudaybiyah. God is *the Light*, and this Name is partly equivalent to His Names *the Truth* and *the Knower*. Truth is the object of Knowledge, and both are Light as opposed to the darkness of error and ignorance. The Light is One, but it is manifested with different degrees of intensity throughout creation, degrees of guidance which radiate from Truth, and degrees of faith which radiate from Knowledge.

The Koran constantly affirms, both of itself and other revealed Messages, that they are "Light", and it could indeed be named "the Book of Light" in virtue of its continual reference to the illumination of guidance which it gives, and to the illumination of faith which it kindles in the souls of men. The Verse of Light, which describes a series of receptacles lit by the Divine Light, may be interpreted as a definition of four degrees of enlightenment:

> *God is the Light of the heavens and of the earth. His light is as a niche wherein is a lamp. The lamp is in a glass; the glass is as it were a shining planet. It is kindled from a blessed tree, an olive neither of the east nor of the west. The oil thereof wellnigh blazeth in splendour even though the fire have not touched it. Light upon light. God guideth to His light whom he will; and God citeth symbols for men; and God is of all things the Knower.*[2]

There is firstly, in ascending order, the niche, that is illuminated but not in itself luminous. Then there is the crystalline glass, above which is the splendour of the oil; and finally there is the flame itself. The mention of symbols recalls another verse which begins with the same sentence: *God citeth symbols for men*, but which adds the reason: *that they may meditate*.[3]

[1] XLIX, 14. [2] XXIV, 35. [3] LIX, 21.

Many of the commentators of the Koran, including some of the earliest, have said that the niche is the breast of the believer and that the glass is his heart. 'Abd Allah, the son of 'Abbas, possibly repeating something that his father had heard from the Prophet himself, is quoted as having said: "God's guidance in the heart of the believer is like pure oil which shineth before the fire hath touched it and when the fire hath touched it increaseth in splendour upon splendour. Even so is the heart of the believer: he acteth by guidance until knowledge come to him."[4]

In the Verse of Light the different degrees are indicated symbolically rather than directly. But elsewhere, starting from some of the earliest Revelations, the Koran is more explicit. In one of these[5] mankind is divided into three groups, *those of the right, those of the left* and *the foremost. Those of the right* are the saved, *those of the left* the damned. As to *the foremost*, that is, those of the highest degree, who are also called *the slaves of God*,[6] it is said of them that they are *brought near to God*, this epithet being also used of the Archangels to distinguish them from the Angels. Other early Revelations introduced a third degree into the hierarchy of the faithful, *the righteous*, who are between *the foremost* and *those of the right*. The relationship between these three degrees may be inferred from what the Koran says about their blessings in Paradise. Whereas *those of the right* are given *pure flowing water* to drink, it is *the foremost* alone who have direct access to the highest fountains, but *the righteous* are given a draught which has been blended at one or another of these fountains,[1] which suggests that they are those who follow in the footsteps of *the foremost*.

Degrees of superiority are also implied by the Revelation in its mention of the heart. In speaking of the majority, it says: *Not blind are the eyes, but blind are the hearts within the breasts.*[2] The Prophet on the other hand, like Prophets before him, said that his heart was awake, which means that its eye was open; and the Koran indicates that this possibility can be shared, if only in some measure, by others also, for it sometimes addresses itself directly to *those who have hearts.*[3] It is reported that of Abū Bakr the Prophet said: "He surpasseth you not through much fasting and prayer but he surpasseth you in virtue of something that is fixed in his heart."[4]

The Prophet often spoke of the superiority of some of his followers over others; and in Mecca, at the time of the victory, when in his presence Khālid retorted angrily against 'Abd ar-Raḥmān ibn 'Awf, who had rebuked him, he said: "Gently Khālid, let be my Companions; for if thou hadst Mount Uḥud all in gold and didst spend it in the way of God thou wouldst not attain unto the merit of any man of my Companions."[5]

According to the Revelation the differences between one degree and

[4] Tab., Tafsir. [5] LVI, 7–40.

[6] LXVI, 6; LXXXIX, 29. The Koran uses the term *slaves of God* in two senses, one altogether inclusive – even Satan is His slave – and the other exceedingly exclusive, as in the above verses, and also in the following, which is addressed to Satan: *As to My slaves, over them thou hast no power.* (XVII, 65).

[1] LXXVI, 5; LXXXIII, 27. [2] XXII, 46. See also p. 89.

[3] XII, 111; XIII, 19, etc. [4] al-Ḥakīm at-Tirmidhī, *Nawādir al-uṣūl*.

[5] I.I. 853.

another are vaster in the next world than in this: *Behold how We have favoured some of them above others; and verily the Hereafter is greater in degrees and greater in hierarchic precedences.*[6] And the Prophet said: "The people of Paradise will behold the high place that is above them even as they now behold the bright planet[7] on the eastern or western horizon."[8] The disparities between man and man were also reflected in the manner of his teaching, some of which was reserved for the few who would understand it. Abū Hurayrah said: "I have treasured in my memory two stores of knowledge which I had from the Messenger of God. One of them have I divulged; but if I divulged the other ye would cut this throat,"[9] and he pointed to his own throat.

During the return march to Medina after the victories of Mecca and Ḥunayn the Prophet said to some of his Companions: "We have returned from the Lesser Holy War to the Greater Holy War." And when one of them asked: "What is the Greater Holy War, O Messenger of God?" he answered: "The war against the soul."[10] The soul of fallen man is divided against itself. Of its lowest aspect the Koran says: *Verily the soul commandeth unto evil.*[11] The better part of it, that is the conscience, is named *the ever-upbraiding soul*;[12] and it is this which wages the Greater Holy War, with the help of the Spirit, against the lower soul.

Finally there is *the soul which is at peace*, that is the whole soul no longer divided against itself, after the battle has been won. Such are the souls of those who have reached the highest degree, at the level of *the foremost, the slaves of God, the near*. The Koran addresses this perfect soul in the words: *O thou soul which art at peace, return unto thy Lord with gladness that is thine in Him and His in thee.*[1] *Enter thou among My slaves. Enter thou My Paradise.*[2] The twofold nature of this blessing recalls the Koran's promise of two Paradises for the blessed soul, and also the Prophet's reference to his own ultimate state as "The meeting with my Lord and Paradise". For *the soul which is at peace*, the entry into *My paradise* corresponds to "the meeting with my Lord", whereas the entry *among My slaves* corresponds to "Paradise", that is the second accompanying Paradise. The Supreme Paradise, that of God, "the meeting with my Lord", is none other than *Riḍwān*. The following verse had recently been revealed: *God hath promised the believers, the men and the women, gardens that are watered by flowing rivers wherein they shall dwell immortal, abodes of excellence in the Paradises of Eden. And Riḍwān from God is greater. That is the Infinite Beatitude.*[3]

The Prophet also spoke of the supreme degree insofar as it can be reached during life on earth, and this saying is one of those which are called holy traditions because they transmit the direct words of God: "My slave ceaseth not to draw near unto Me with devotions of his free will until I love him; and when I love him I am the hearing with which he heareth and the sight with which he seeth and the hand with which he graspeth and the foot

[6] XVII, 21. [7] Venus. [8] M. LI, 4.
[9] B. III, 42. [10] Bayhaqī, *Zuhd.* [11] XII, 53. [12] LXXV, 2.
[1] That is, with mutual *Riḍwān* (see p. 95).
[2] LXXXIX, 27–30. [3] IX, 72.

on which he walketh."[4]

The chief of the voluntary devotions is *dhikr Allāh*, which may be rendered "remembrance of God or calling upon God". In one of the first Revelations the Prophet was commanded: *Invoke in remembrance the Name of thy Lord, and devote thyself to Him with an utter devotion.*[5] A later Revelation says: *Verily the ritual prayer preserveth from iniquity and abomination; but the remembrance of God is greater.*[6] With reference to the heart's blindness and its cure the Prophet said: "For everything there is a polish that taketh away rust, and the polish of the heart is remembrance of God."[7] And when asked who would rank highest in God's esteem on the Day of Resurrection he answered: "The men and the women who invoke God much in remembrance." And when asked if they would rank even above the man who had fought in God's path he answered: "Even though he wielded his sword amongst infidels and idolaters until it was broken and smeared with blood, yet would the rememberer of God have a more excellent degree than his."[8]

[4] B., LXXXI, 37. [5] LXXIII, 8. [6] XXIX, 45.
[7] Bayhaqī, *Da 'awāt.* [8] Tir. XLV.

# LXXXII

# *The Future*

THE Prophet said: "The best of my people are my generation; then they that come after them; then they that come after them";[1] and he rejoiced in the outstanding members of his generation, that is in those whom he considered as his Companions. To ten of them who visited him on one occasion he promised Paradise. These were Abū Bakr, 'Umar, 'Uthmān, 'Alī, 'Abd ar-Raḥmān ibn 'Awf, Abū 'Ubaydah, Ṭalḥah, Zubayr, Sa'd of Zuhrah, and Sa'īd the son of Zayd the Ḥanīf. He had already given the same assurance to some of them before, and the books of his sayings have recorded much of his great praises of the Promised Ten, and of others to whom he also gave good tidings of Paradise, as when he affirmed: "For three doth Paradise long, for 'Alī, 'Ammār[2] and Salmān."[3] To Fāṭimah he said: "Thou art the highest of the women of the people of Paradise, excepting only the Virgin Mary, daughter of 'Imrān."[4] In prediction of the great part to be played by 'Alī as one of the chief transmitters of his wisdom to future generations, he said: "I am the city of knowledge, and 'Alī is its gate";[5] and he said in general: "My Companions are even as the stars: whichsoever of them ye follow, ye shall be rightly guided."[6]

When the men returned from Tabūk they had said amongst themselves that their days of fighting were now at an end; and this idea was so strengthened by the coming of the various delegations, which continued throughout the tenth year, that many of the believers set about selling their arms and their armour. But when the Prophet heard of this he forbade them to do so, saying: "A body of my people will not cease to fight for the truth until the coming forth of the Antichrist." He also said: "If ye knew that which I know, ye would laugh little and weep much"[7] and "No time cometh upon you but is followed by a worse."[8] He warned them that his people would surely follow the Jews and the Christians upon the path of degeneration: "Ye will follow them that were before you span by span and cubit by cubit until if they went down the hole of a poisonous reptile ye would follow them down."[9] And, in speaking of the lowest ebb which would be reached by mankind in general before the end, he said: "Islam began as a stranger and will become once more as a stranger."[10] Yet he

[1] B. LXII, 1. [2] See p. 79. [3] Tir. XLVI, 33.

[4] A. H. III, 64. The Koran tells how the Angels said to Mary: *He (God) hath chosen thee above all the women of the worlds* (III, 42).

[5] Tir. XLVI, 20. [6] F. XXVI, Manāqib aṣ-Ṣaḥābah.

[7] B. LXXXI, 27. [8] B. XCII, 14. [9] M. XLVII, 6. [10] M. I, 232.

promised that God would not abandon them: "God will send to this community, at the head of every hundred years, one who will renew for it its religion."[1] On another occasion those of his Companions who were with him heard him exclaim more than once: "O my brethren!" They said to him: "O Messenger of God, are we not thy brethren?" and he answered: "Ye are my companions. But my brethren are amongst those who have not yet come" – in other versions "who will come in the last days". The way he spoke suggested that he was referring to persons of great spiritual eminence.

He also prophesied that despite the evils of the latter days there will arise a caliph whom men will speak of as the Mahdī, which means the rightly guided: "The Mahdī will be of my stock and he will be broad of forehead and aquiline of nose. He will fill the earth with right and with justice even as it hath been filled with wrong and oppression. Seven years will he reign."[2]

But finally, towards the end of his reign or after it, the Antichrist would come, "a man blind in his right eye in which all light is extinguished, even as it were a grape",[3] and he would cause great corruption on earth, and by his power to work marvels he would win more and more men to his side. But there would be a body of believers who would fight against him. "When they are pressing on to fight," said the Prophet, "even while they straighten their lines for the prayer when it is called, Jesus the son of Mary will descend and will lead them in the prayer. And the enemy of God, when he seeth Jesus, will melt even as salt melteth in water. If he were let be, he would melt unto perishing; but God will slay him at the hand of Jesus, who will show them his blood upon his lance."[4]

He also spoke of many of the signs by which men might know that the coming to pass of these final things was near; and as one of the signs he mentioned the excessive height of the buildings that men would build. But that prophecy was made on a great occasion which must be chronicled more fully, on the authority of 'Umar's son 'Abd Allāh, repeating the words of his father.

'Umar said: "One day when we were sitting with the Messenger of God there came unto us a man whose clothes were of exceeding whiteness and whose hair was of exceeding blackness, nor were there any signs of travel upon him, although none of us knew him. He sat down knee unto knee opposite the Prophet, upon whose thighs he placed the palms of his hands, saying: 'O Muḥammad, tell me what is the surrender (*islām*)'. The Messenger of God answered him saying: 'The surrender is to testify that there is no god but God and that Muḥammad is God's Messenger, to perform the prayer, bestow the alms, fast Ramaḍān and make, if thou canst, the pilgrimage to the Holy House.' He said: 'Thou hast spoken truly,' and we were amazed that having questioned him he should corroborate him. Then he said: 'Tell me what is faith (*īmān*).' He answered: 'To believe in God and His Angels and His Books and His Messengers and the Last Day, and to believe that no good or evil cometh but by His Providence.' 'Thou hast spoken truly,' he said, and then: 'Tell me what is

[1] A.D. XXXVI, 1. [2] A.D. XXXV, 4. [3] M. LII, 20. [4] M. LII, 9.

excellence (*iḥsān*).' He answered: 'To worship God as if thou sawest Him, for if thou seest Him not, yet seeth He thee.' 'Thou hast spoken truly,' he said, and then: 'Tell me of the Hour.' He answered: 'The questioned thereof knoweth no better than the questioner.' He said: 'Then tell me of its signs.' He answered: 'That the slave-girl shall give birth to her mistress;[1] and that those who were but barefoot naked needy herdsmen shall build buildings ever higher and higher.' Then the stranger went away, and I stayed a while after he had gone; and the Prophet said to me: 'O 'Umar, knowest thou the questioner, who he was?' I said: 'God and His Messenger know best.' He said: 'It was Gabriel. He came unto you to teach you your religion.' "[2]

[1] A woman giving birth to a daughter will thereby become merely a slave-girl to her by reason of latter-day children's disrespect for their parents. The second part of the saying predicts not only a chaos in the social order but also the ultimate triumph of the sedentary way of life over the nomadic way, that is, the final seal set upon Cain's murder of Abel.

[2] M. I, 1.

# LXXXIII

# *The Farewell Pilgrimage*

WHEN the Prophet was in Medina during Ramaḍān it was his wont to make a spiritual retreat in the Mosque during the middle ten days of the month, and some of his Companions would do the same. But this year, having kept the ten appointed days, he invited his Companions to remain in retreat with him for another ten days, that is until the end of the month, which they did. It was in Ramaḍān every year that Gabriel would come to him to make sure that nothing of the Revelation had slipped from his memory; and this year, after the retreat, the Prophet confided to Fāṭimah, as a secret not yet to be told to others: "Gabriel reciteth the Koran unto me and I unto him once every year; but this year he hath recited it with me twice. I cannot but think that my time hath come."[1]

The month of Shawwāl passed; and in the eleventh month of the year it was proclaimed throughout Medina that the Prophet himself would lead the Pilgrimage. The news was sent to the desert tribes, and multitudes flocked to the oasis from all directions, glad of the opportunity of accompanying the Messenger at every step of the way. The Pilgrimage would be unlike any that had taken place for hundreds of years: the pilgrims would all be worshippers of the One God, and no idolater would desecrate the Holy House with the performance of any heathen rites. Five days before the end of the month the Prophet set out from Medina at the head of over thirty thousand men and women. All his wives were present, each in her howdah, escorted by 'Abd ar-Raḥmān ibn 'Awf and 'Uthmān ibn 'Affān. Abū Bakr was accompanied by his wife, Asmā', and at one of the first halts she gave birth to a son, whom they named Muḥammad. Abū Bakr was for sending her back to Medina, but the Prophet told him to tell her to perform the greater ablution and then to consecrate herself for the Pilgrimage, and to go with them as she had planned.

At sunset on the tenth day after leaving Medina the Prophet reached the pass through which he had entered Mecca on the day of the victory. There he spent the night, and the next morning he rode down to the Hollow. When he came within sight of the Ka'bah he raised his hands in reverence,

[1] B. LXI, 25.

letting fall the rein of his camel, which he then took up in his left hand, and with his right hand held out in supplication he prayed: "O God, increase this House in the honour and magnification and bounty and reverence and piety that it receiveth from mankind!"[1] He entered the Mosque and made the seven rounds of the Ka'bah, after which he prayed at the Station of Abraham. Then going out to Ṣafā he went seven times between it and Marwah, and those who were with him did their best to record in their memories the exact words of praise and prayer that he uttered at every station.

Returning to the Mosque, he now entered the Ka'bah with the keeper of its keys, 'Uthmān of 'Abd ad-Dār, taking with him also Bilāl and Usāmah as before. But that evening when he visited 'Ā'ishah in her tent she noticed that he was sad and asked him why. "I have done a thing today," he said, "that I would I had not done. I entered the House; and it may be that a man of my people" – he meant in years to come – "will not be able to enter it and that he will therefore feel some disquiet in his soul. And we were only ordered to go round it, not ordered to enter it."[2]

Again he refused to lodge in any house in Mecca despite the plea of Umm Hāni' that he would stay with her; and on the eighth day of the new moon he rode to the valley of Mina followed by the rest of the pilgrims. Having spent the night there, he rode on after daybreak to 'Arafah, a broad valley about thirteen miles east of Mecca, just outside the sacred precinct. 'Arafah is on the road to Ṭā'if and is bounded north and east by the mountains of Ṭā'if. But separate from these, and surrounded on all sides by the valley, is a hill which is also named 'Arafah or the Mount of Mercy. It is the central part of this pilgrimage station, which extends none the less over most of the lower ground; and it was on this hill that the Prophet took up his station that day.

Some of the Meccans expressed surprise that he had gone so far, for while the other pilgrims went on to 'Arafah Quraysh had been accustomed to remain within the sacred precinct saying: "We are the people of God." But he said that Abraham had ordained the day on 'Arafah as an essential part of the Pilgrimage, and that Quraysh had forsaken his practice in this respect. The Prophet stressed that day the antiquity of the Pilgrimage, and the words "Abraham's legacy" were often on his lips.

To impress on all the tribes that henceforth blood feuds were at an end throughout the whole community of Islam and that each man's life and possessions were sacrosanct, he sent as crier throughout the multitude Ṣafwān's brother Rabī'ah, who had a powerful voice, and told him to proclaim: "The Messenger of God saith: See ye what month this is?" They were silent, and he answered: "The holy month." Then he asked: "See ye what land this is?" Again they were silent and he answered: "The holy land." Then he said: "See ye what day this is?" And again it was he who gave the answer: "The day of the Greater Pilgrimage." Then he proclaimed according to the Prophet's instructions: "Verily God hath made inviolable for you each other's blood and each other's property, until ye meet your Lord, even as He hath made inviolable this your day, in this your land, in this your month."

[1] W. 1097. [2] W. 1100.

When the sun had passed its zenith the Prophet preached a sermon which he began, after praising God, with the words: "Hear me, O people, for I know not if ever I shall meet with you in this place after this year." Then he exhorted them to treat one another well and gave them many reminders of what was commanded and what was forbidden. Finally he said: "I have left amongst you that which, if ye hold fast to it, shall preserve you from all error, a clear indication, the Book of God and the word of His Prophet. O people, hear my words and understand." He then imparted to them a Revelation which he had just received and which completed the Koran, for it was the last passage to be revealed: *This day the disbelievers despair of prevailing against your religion, so fear them not, but fear Me! This day have I perfected for you your religion and fulfilled My favour unto you, and it hath been My good pleasure to choose Islam for you as your religion.*[1]

He ended his brief sermon with an earnest question: "O people, have I faithfully delivered unto you my message?" A powerful murmur of assent, "O God, yea!", arose from thousands of throats and the vibrant words *Allāhumma na'm* rolled like thunder throughout the valley. The Prophet raised his forefinger and said: "O God, bear witness!"[2]

The ritual prayers were then prayed and the rest of the Day of 'Arafah, as it is called, was spent in meditation and supplication. But as soon as the sun had set the Prophet mounted his camel, and bidding Usāmah mount behind him he rode down from the hill and across the valley in the direction of Mecca, followed by his fellow pilgrims. It was the tradition to ride quickly at this point, but at the first signs of excess he cried out: "Gently, gently! In quietness of soul! And let the strong amongst you have a care for the weak!" They spent the night at Muzdalifah, which is within the sacred precinct, and there they collected small pebbles with which to stone Satan, who is represented by three pillars at 'Aqabah in the valley of Mina. Sawdah asked the Prophet's permission to leave Muzdalifah in the small hours. Being large in stature and heavier than most of the women, she had suffered more from the heat and from the exertions of travel, and she was anxious to perform the rite of stoning before the multitude arrived. So he sent her on ahead in the company of Umm Sulaym, escorted by 'Abd Allāh, one of the sons of 'Abbās.

The Prophet himself prayed the dawn prayer in Muzdalifah, and then led the pilgrims to 'Aqabah, with Faḍl mounted behind him on his camel. It was at this very spot on this very day twelve years previously that he had met the six men of Khazraj who had pledged their allegiance to him, thus preparing the way for the First and Second 'Aqabah pacts. After the stoning, the animals were sacrificed, and the Prophet called for a man to shave his head. The pilgrims gathered round him in the hopes of obtaining some locks of his hair. Abū Bakr remarked afterwards on the contrast between the Khālid of Uḥud and the Trench and the Khālid who now said: "O Messenger of God, thy forelock! Give it unto none but me, my father and my mother be thy ransom!"[3] And when the Prophet gave it him he pressed it reverently against his eyes and his lips.

[1] V, 3. [2] I.I. 969. [3] W. 1108.

The Prophet now bade the pilgrims visit the Ka'bah and return to spend that night and the two next nights in Mina. He himself waited until the late afternoon. Then his wives accompanied him to Mecca, all but 'Ā'ishah, who was not in a state of ritual purity. A few days later, as soon as she was able, he sent her outside the sacred precinct, escorted by her brother 'Abd ar-Raḥmān. There she consecrated herself afresh, and going to Mecca she made the rounds of the Ka'bah.

Having finished the campaign in the Yemen, the troop of three hundred horse that the Prophet had sent out in Ramaḍān was now approaching Mecca from the south. 'Alī had ridden on ahead of his men, eager to meet the Prophet as soon as possible and to make with him the Pilgrimage, which he now had done. Amongst the state's fifth of the spoils there was enough linen to clothe the whole army, but 'Alī had decided that it must be handed over to the Prophet untouched. In his absence, however, the man he had left in charge was persuaded to lend each man a new change of clothes out of the linen. The change was much needed for they had been away from home for nearly three months. When they were not far from entering the city, 'Alī rode out to meet them and was amazed to see the transformation that had taken place. "I gave them the garments," said the deputy commander, "that their appearance might be more seemly when they entered in among the people." The men all knew that everyone in Mecca would now be wearing their finest clothes in honour of the Feast, and they were anxious to look their best. But 'Alī felt he could not countenance such a liberty and he ordered them to put on their old clothes again and return the new ones to the spoils. Great resentment was felt throughout the army on this account, and when the Prophet heard of it he said: "O people, blame not 'Alī, for he is too scrupulous in the path of God to be blamed." But these words were not sufficient, or it may be that they were only heard by a few, and the resentment continued.

On the way back to Medina one of the troops bitterly complained of 'Alī to the Prophet, whose face changed colour. "Am I not nearer to the believers than their own selves?" he said; and when the man assented, he added: "Whose nearest I am, his nearest 'Alī is." Later on the journey, when they had halted at Ghadīr al-Khumm, he gathered all the people together, and taking 'Alī by the hand he repeated these words, to which he added the prayer: "O God, be the friend of him who is his friend, and the foe of him who is his foe"; and the murmurings against 'Alī were silenced.[1]

One of the deputations of the previous year had been from a Christian tribe in Yamāmah, the Bani Ḥanīfah, whose territory lay along the eastern boundary of Najd. They had agreed to enter Islam; but now one of their men, Musaylimah by name, claimed that he too was a Prophet, and not long after the return of the pilgrims from Mecca the following letter was brought to Medina by two envoys from Yamāmah: "From Musaylimah the Messenger of God to Muḥammad the Messenger of God, peace be on thee! It hath been given me to share with thee the authority. Half the earth is ours, and half belongeth unto Quraysh, although they are a people who

[1] Ibn Kathīr, *al-Bidāyah wa n-nihāyah*, V, 209.

transgress." The Prophet asked the envoys what they thought of the matter and they said: "Our opinion is even as his." "By God," said the Prophet, "if it were not that envoys may not be slain I would cut off your heads." Then he dictated a letter for them to give to their master: "From Muḥammad the Messenger of God to Musaylimah the liar. Peace be on him who followeth the guidance! Verily the earth is God's; He causeth whom He will of His slaves to inherit it; and the final issue is in favour of the pious".[1]

Two other impostors arose about this time, Ṭulayḥah, a chief of the Bani Asad, and Aswad ibn Ka'b of the Yemen. The Yemenite had a brief success and rapidly gained control over a wide area, but his pride soon turned many of his followers against him; and after a few months he was assassinated. Ṭulayḥah was finally defeated by Khālid, and renouncing all his claims he became a strength for Islam. As to Musaylimah, it was his destiny to be pierced by a javelin from the hand of Waḥshī, while 'Abd Allāh, the son of Nusaybah, struck him a mortal blow with his sword. But this defeat took place several months later. For the moment, as the moon of the Pilgrimage waned and as the eleventh year of the Hijrah opened, all these impostors were potential dangers to Islam; and there was also a woman of Tamīm named Sajāḥ, who claimed to be a prophetess. But the Prophet was not disposed to take immediate action against any of them. His attention was turned towards the north, and in the last days of Ṣafar, the second month of the year, that is the end of May in AD 632, he decided that the time had come to reverse the defeat of Mu'tah. Having ordered preparations to be made for a campaign against those Arab tribes of Syria which had flanked the imperial legions on the day when Zayd and Ja'far were killed, he called Zayd's son Usāmah to him and put him, despite his youth, in command of the three-thousand-strong army.

[1] I.I. 965.

# LXXXIV

# *The Choice*

THE Prophet continually spoke of Paradise, and when he did so it was as a man who sees what he describes. This impression was confirmed by many other signs, as for example when he once stretched out his hand as if to take something, and then drew it back. He said nothing, but some of those who were with him noticed his action and questioned him about it. "I saw Paradise," he said, "and I reached out for a cluster of its grapes. Had I taken it, ye would have eaten of it as long as the world endureth."[1] They had grown accustomed to thinking of him as one who is already in a sense in the Hereafter. Perhaps it was partly for this reason that when he spoke of his death, and when he inferred indirectly, as sometimes now he did, that it might be imminent, his words made little impression on them. Moreover, despite his sixty-three years, he still had the stature and grace of a much younger man, his eyes were still bright, and there were only a few white hairs in his black hair. Yet on one occasion a remark of his when he was with his wives was sufficiently ominous to prompt the question as to which of them would be the first to rejoin him in the next world. He replied: "She of the longest reach will be the soonest of you to join me,"[2] whereupon they set about measuring their arms, one against another. Presumably, though it is not recorded, Sawdah was the winner of this contest, for she was the tallest of them and in general the largest. Zaynab, on the other hand, was a small woman, with an arm to match. But it was Zaynab who died first of them all, some ten years later. Only then did they realise that by "she of the longest reach" the Prophet had meant the most giving, for Zaynab was exceedingly generous, like her predecessor of the same name who had been called "the mother of the poor".

One night, not long after the Prophet had ordered preparations for the Syrian campaign and before the army had left, he called to a freedman of his in the small hours, Abū Muwayhibah, and said: "I have been commanded to pray forgiveness for the people of the cemetery, so come thou with me." They went out together, and when they reached the Baqīʿ the Prophet said: "Peace be on you, O people of the graves. Rejoice in your state, how much better it is than the state of men now living. Dissensions come like waves of darkest night, the one following hard upon the other, each worse than the last." Then he turned to Abū Muwayhibah and said: "I have been offered the keys of the treasuries of this world and immortality therein

[1] B. XVI, 8. [2] I.S. VIII, 76–7.

followed by Paradise, and I have been given the choice between that and meeting my Lord and Paradise." "O dearer than my father and my mother," said Abū Muwayhibah, "take the keys of the treasuries of this world and immortality therein followed by Paradise." But he answered him saying: "I have already chosen the meeting with my Lord and Paradise." Then he prayed for forgiveness for the people of the Baqī'.[1]

It was at dawn that day, or perhaps the next day, that his head ached as he had never known it to ache, but he none the less went to the Mosque and after leading the prayer he mounted the pulpit and invoked blessings on the martyrs of Uḥud, as if – so it was said afterwards – he were doing it for the last time. Then he said: "There is a slave amongst the slaves of God unto whom God hath offered the choice between this world and that which is with Him, and the slave hath chosen that which is with God." When he said this Abū Bakr wept, for he knew that the Prophet was speaking of himself and that the choice meant imminent death. The Prophet saw that he had understood, and telling him not to weep, he said: "O people, the most beneficent of men unto me in his companionship and in that which his hand bestoweth is Abū Bakr; and if I were to take from all mankind an inseparable friend he would be Abū Bakr – but companionship and brotherhood of faith is ours until God unite us in His Presence." It was on that occasion that he said, looking round at the multiple entrances into the Mosque from the private houses which surrounded it: "Behold these doors that intrude upon the Mosque. Let them be walled up, save only the door of Abū Bakr."[2] Before leaving the pulpit he said: "I go before you, and I am your witness. Your tryst with me is at the Pool,[3] which verily I behold from here where now I stand. I fear not for you that ye will set up gods beside God; but I fear for you this world, lest ye seek to rival one another in worldly gains."[4]

From the Mosque he went back to the apartment of Maymūnah, whose turn it was to house him. The effort of speech to the congregation had increased his fever; and after an hour or two, wishing to let 'Ā'ishah know that he was ill, he went briefly to visit her. She also was suffering from a headache, and when he entered her room she moaned: "Oh my head!" "Nay, 'Ā'ishah," said the Prophet, "it is oh *my* head!" But he looked at her searchingly, as if to seek some sign of mortal sickness in her face, and finding none he said: "I wished that it might be" – he meant her death – "whilst yet I was alive, that I might ask forgiveness for thee and invoke mercy upon thee and shroud thee and pray over thee and bury thee." 'Ā'ishah could see that he was ill and she was alarmed at the tone of his voice, but she tried to make light of it, and succeeded in bringing a brief smile to his face. Then he repeated: "Nay, but it is oh *my* head,"[5] and returned to Maymūnah.

He tried to do as he did when he was well, and continued to lead the prayers in the Mosque as usual; but his illness increased, until the hour

[1] I.I. 1000. [2] I.I. 1006.

[3] Fed by Kawthar, the celestial river given to the Prophet, the Pool is a lake where the believers quench their thirst on their entry into Paradise.

[4] B. LXIV, 17. [5] I.S. II/2, 10.

came when he could pray only in a sitting position, and he told the congregation that they also should pray seated. On his return to the apartment of the wife whose day it was, he asked her "Where am I tomorrow?" and she named the wife to whom he would go. "And where the day after tomorrow?" he asked. Again she answered; but struck by his insistence, and sensing that he was impatient to be with 'Ā'ishah, she told the other wives, whereupon they all came to him and said: "O Messenger of God, we have given our days with you unto our sister 'Ā'ishah."[1] He accepted their gift, but was now too weak to walk unaided, so 'Abbās and 'Alī helped him to 'Ā'ishah's apartment.

Word came to him that there was much criticism of his choice of so young a man as Usāmah to command the army for the Syrian campaign, and that there was in consequence a certain slackening in the preparations. He felt the need to answer his critics, but his fever was intense, so he said to his wives: "Pour over me seven skins of water from different wells that I may go out unto the men and exhort them." Ḥafṣah brought a tub to 'Ā'ishah's room and the other wives brought water, and he sat in the tub while they poured it over him. Then they helped him to dress and bound up his head, and two of the men took him between them to the Mosque, where he sat in the pulpit and addressed those who were assembled there, saying: "O people, dispatch Usāmah's troop, for though ye question his leadership even as ye questioned the leadership of his father before him, yet is he worthy of the command,[2] even as his father was worthy of it." He descended from the pulpit and was helped back to 'Ā'ishah's house. Preparations were hastened on, and Usāmah went out with his army as far as Jurf, where they encamped, about three miles to the north of Medina.

At the next call to prayer the Prophet felt he could no longer lead it even though he remained seated, so he said to his wives: "Tell Abū Bakr to lead the people in prayer." But 'Ā'ishah feared that it would greatly pain her father to take the place of the Prophet. "O Messenger of God," she said, "Abū Bakr is a very sensitive man, not strong of voice and much given to weeping when he reciteth the Koran." "Tell him to lead the prayer," said the Prophet, as if she had not spoken. She tried again, this time suggesting that 'Umar should take his place. "Tell Abū Bakr to lead the prayer," he reiterated. 'Ā'ishah had thrown a glance of appeal at Ḥafṣah, who now began to speak, but the Prophet silenced her with the words: "Ye are even as the women that were with Joseph.[3] Tell Abū Bakr to lead the people in prayer. Let the blamer find fault and let the ambitious aspire. God and the believers will not have it otherwise."[4] He repeated the last sentence three times, and for the rest of his illness Abū Bakr led the prayer.

The Prophet lay much of the time with his head resting on 'Ā'ishah's breast or on her lap; but when Fāṭimah came 'Ā'ishah would withdraw a little to allow the father and daughter some privacy together, and at one of these visits 'Ā'ishah saw him whisper something to his daughter, who

[1] I.S. II/2, 30.

[2] When, after some delay, the campaign took place, Usāmah proved the truth of these words.

[3] Referring to Potiphar's wilful wife and her friends; see K. XII, 31–3.

[4] I.S. II/2, 20.

thereupon began to weep. Then he confided to her another secret and she smiled through her tears. As she was leaving, 'Ā'ishah asked her what he had said, and she answered that they were secrets she could not divulge. But later she said to her: "The Prophet told me he would die in that illness whereof he died, and therefore I wept. Then he told me that I would be the first of the people of his house to follow him, and therefore I laughed."[1]

He suffered much pain in his illness, and one day when it was at its worst his wife Ṣafiyyah said to him: "O Prophet of God, would that I had what thou hast!" whereupon some of the other wives exchanged glances and whispered one to another that this was hypocrisy. The Prophet saw them and said: "Go rinse your mouths." They asked him why, and he said: "For your maligning of your companion. By God, she speaketh the truth in all sincerity."[2]

Umm Ayman was in constant attendance, and she kept her son informed. He had already resolved to advance no further and to remain in his camp at Jurf until God should decide. But one morning the news was such that he came to Medina and went in tears to the Prophet, who was too ill that day to speak, though he was fully conscious. Usāmah bent over him and kissed him, and the Prophet raised his hand, palm upwards, to ask and to receive blessings from Heaven. Then he made a gesture as if to empty the contents of his hand upon Usāmah, who returned sadly to his camp.

The next day was Monday the twelfth of Rabī' I in the eleventh year of Islam, that is, the eighth day of June in the year AD 632. Early that morning the Prophet's fever abated, and although he was exceedingly weak the call to prayer decided him to go to the Mosque. The prayer had already begun when he entered, and the people were almost drawn away from it for joy at the sight of him, but he motioned them to continue. For a moment he stood to watch them and his face shone with gladness as he marked the piety of their demeanour. Then, still radiant, he made his way forward, helped by Faḍl and by Thawbān, one of his freedmen. "I never saw the Prophet's face more beautiful than it was at that hour," said Anas. Abū Bakr had been conscious of the stir throughout the ranks behind him. He knew that it could only have one cause, and that the man he now heard approaching must be the Prophet. So without turning his head, he stepped back, but the Prophet placed his hand on his shoulder and pressed him forwards again in front of the congregation, saying "Lead thou the prayer," while he himself sat on the right of Abū Bakr and prayed seated.

Great was the rejoicing at this apparent recovery, and not long after the prayer Usāmah arrived again from his camp, expecting to find the Prophet worse and overjoyed to find him better. "Set forth, with the blessings of God," said the Prophet. So Usāmah bade him farewell, and rode back to Jurf, where he told his men to make ready for the northward march. Meantime Abū Bakr had taken leave to go as far as Upper Medina. Already before his marriage to Asmā', he had long been betrothed to Ḥabībah, the daughter of Khārijah, the Khazrajite with whom he had lodged ten years ago on his arrival in the oasis, and they had recently been married. Ḥabībah still lived with her family at Sunḥ, where he now went to visit her.

[1] B. LXII, 12. [2] I.S. VIII, 91.

The Prophet returned to 'Ā'ishah's apartment helped by Faḍl and Thawbān. 'Alī and 'Abbās followed them there, but did not stay long, and when they came out some men who were passing asked 'Alī how the Prophet was. "Praise be to God," said 'Alī, "he is well." But when the questioners had gone on their way 'Abbās took 'Alī's hand and said: "I swear I recognise death in the face of God's Messenger, even as I have ever been able to recognise it in the faces of our clansmen. So let us go and speak with him. If his authority is to be vested in us, then we shall know it; and if in other than us, then will we ask him to commend us unto the people, that they may treat us well." But 'Alī said: "By God, I will not, for if the authority be withheld from us by him, none after him will ever give it us."[1]

The Prophet had now returned to his couch and was lying with his head upon 'Ā'ishah's breast as if all his strength had been used. None the less, when her brother 'Abd ar-Raḥmān entered the room with a tooth-stick in his hand, she saw the Prophet looking at it in such a way that she knew he wanted it. So she took it from her brother and gnawed upon it to soften it. Then she gave it to the Prophet, who rubbed his teeth with it vigorously despite his weakness.

Not long afterwards he lost consciousness, and 'Ā'ishah thought it was the onset of death, but after an hour he opened his eyes. She then remembered his having said to her: "No Prophet is taken by death until he hath been shown his place in Paradise and then offered the choice, to live or to die." And she understood that this had been accomplished, and that he had returned from a vision of the Hereafter. "He will not now choose us!" she said to herself. Then she heard him murmur: "With the supreme communion in Paradise, *with those upon whom God hath showered His favour, the prophets and the saints and the martyrs and the righteous, most excellent for communion are they.*"[2] Again she heard him murmur: "O God, with the supreme communion,"[3] and these were the last words she heard him speak. Gradually his head grew heavier upon her breast, until the other wives began to lament, and 'Ā'ishah laid his head on a pillow and joined them in lamentation.

1 I.I. 1011. 2 K. IV, 69. 3 I.S. II/2, 27.

# LXXXV

# *The Succession and the Burial*

THE signs which 'Abbās had been the first to see had soon become apparent to others; and before the advent of death Umm Ayman had sent word to her son that the Prophet was dying. Camp had already been raised for the northward march but Usāmah immediately gave orders for the return to Medina. Many of the older Companions were with the army, including 'Umar, and when they were met on their arrival in the city with the news that the death had taken place 'Umar refused to believe it. He had misinterpreted a verse of the Koran which he had thought to mean that the Prophet would outlive them all and other generations to come, and he now stood in the Mosque and addressed the people, assuring them that the Prophet was merely absent in the Spirit and that he would return. While he was speaking thus, Abū Bakr arrived on horseback from Sunḥ, for news had quickly spread over the whole oasis. Without pausing to speak to anyone, he went straight to his daughter's house and drew back from the Prophet's face the cloak with which they had covered him. He gazed at him, and then kissed him. "Dearer than my father and my mother," he said, "thou hast tasted the death which God decreed for thee. No death after that shall ever befall thee." Reverently he drew the cloak over his face again, and went out to the throng of men whom 'Umar was still addressing. "Gently, 'Umar!" he said as he approached. "Hear me speak!" 'Umar paid no attention and persisted, but recognising the voice of Abū Bakr the people left 'Umar and turned to hear what the older man had to tell them. After giving praise to God, he said: "O people, whoso hath been wont to worship Muḥammad – verily Muḥammad is dead; and whoso hath been wont to worship God – verily God is Living and dieth not." Then he recited the following verses which had been revealed after the battle of Uḥud: *Muḥammad is but a messenger, and messengers have passed away before him. If he die or be slain, will ye then turn upon your heels? Whoso turneth upon his heels will thereby do no hurt unto God; and God will reward the thankful.*[1]

It was as if the people had not known of the revelation of this verse until Abū Bakr recited it that day. They took it from him, and it was on all their

[1] III, 144.

tongues. 'Umar said afterwards: "When I heard Abū Bakr recite that verse, I was so astounded that I fell to the ground. My legs would no longer carry me, and I knew that God's Messenger had died."

'Alī had now withdrawn to his house, and with him were Zubayr and Ṭalḥah. The rest of the Emigrants gathered round Abū Bakr and they were joined by Usayd and many of his clan. But most of the Helpers, of Aws as well as Khazraj, had assembled in the hall of the Bani Sā'idah of whom Sa'd ibn 'Ubādah was chief, and word was brought to Abū Bakr and 'Umar that they were debating there the question as to where the authority should lie, now that the Prophet was dead. They had gladly accepted his authority; but failing him, many of them were inclined to think that the sons of Qaylah should be ruled by none except a man of Yathrib, and it appeared that they were about to pledge their allegiance to Sa'd.

'Umar urged Abū Bakr to go with him to the hall, and Abū 'Ubaydah went with them. Sa'd was ill and he was lying in the middle of the hall, wrapped in a cloak. On behalf of him another of the Helpers was about to address the assembly when the three men of Quraysh entered, so he included them in his speech, which began, after praise for God, with the words: "We are the Helpers of God and the fighting force of Islam; and ye, O Emigrants, are of us, for a group of your people have settled amongst us." The speaker continued in the same vein, glorifying the Helpers, and while giving the Emigrants a share of that glory, deliberately failing to recognise the unique position that they held in themselves as the first Islamic community. When he had finished 'Umar was about to speak, but Abū Bakr silenced him and spoke himself, tactfully but firmly, reiterating the praise of the Helpers, but pointing out that the community of Islam was now spread throughout Arabia, and that the Arabs as a whole would not accept the authority of anyone other than a man of Quraysh, for Quraysh held a unique and central position amongst them. In conclusion he took 'Umar and Abu 'Ubaydah each by a hand and said: "I offer you one of these two men. Pledge your allegiance to whichever of these ye will." Then another of the Helpers rose and suggested that there should be two authorities, and this led to a heated argument, until finally 'Umar intervened, saying: "O Helpers, know ye not that the Messenger of God ordered Abū Bakr to lead the prayer?" "We know it," they answered, and he said: "Then which of you will willingly take precedence over him?" "God forbid that we should take precedence over him!"[1] they said, whereupon 'Umar seized the hand of Abū Bakr and pledged allegiance to him, followed by Abū 'Ubaydah and others of the Emigrants who had now joined them. Then all the Helpers who were present likewise pledged their allegiance to Abū Bakr, with the exception of Sa'd, who never acknowledged him as caliph,[2] and who eventually migrated to Syria.

Whatever they had decided in the hall, it would have been unacceptable for anyone to have led the prayers in the Mosque in Medina except Abū Bakr, so long as he was there; and the next day at dawn, before leading the prayer, he sat in the pulpit, and 'Umar rose and addressed the assembly,

[1] I.S. II/2, 23.

[2] In Arabic *Khalīfah*, the full title being *Khalīfat Rasūl Allāh*, Viceregent for the Messenger of God.

bidding them pledge their allegiance to Abū Bakr, whom he described as "the best of you, the Companion of God's Messenger, *the second of two when they were both in the cave*."[1] A recent Revelation had recalled the privilege of Abū Bakr to have been the Prophet's sole Companion at this crucial moment;[2] and with one voice the whole congregation swore fealty to him – all except 'Alī, who did so later.[3]

Then Abū Bakr gave praise and thanks to God and addressed them, saying: "I have been given the authority over you, and I am not the best of you. If I do well, help me; and if I do wrong, set me right. Sincere regard for truth is loyalty and disregard for truth is treachery. The weak amongst you shall be strong with me until I have secured his rights, if God will; and the strong amongst you shall be weak with me until I have wrested from him the rights of others, if God will. Obey me so long as I obey God and His Messenger. But if I disobey God and his Messenger, ye owe me no obedience. Arise for your prayer, God have mercy upon you!"[4]

After the prayer the Prophet's household and his family decided that they must prepare him for burial, but they were in disagreement as to how it should be done. Then God cast a sleep upon them all, and in his sleep each man heard a voice say: "Wash the Prophet with his garment upon him." So they went to 'Ā'ishah's apartment, which for the moment she had vacated, and Aws ibn Khawlī, a Khazrajite, begged leave to represent the Helpers, saying: "I adjure thee by God, O 'Alī, and by our share in His Messenger!," and 'Alī allowed him to enter. 'Abbās and his sons Faḍl and Qitham helped 'Alī to turn the body, while Usāmah poured water over it, helped by Shuqrān, one of the Prophet's freedmen, and 'Alī passed his hand over every part of the long woollen garment. "Dearer than my father and my mother," he said, "how excellent art thou, in life and in death!" Even after one day, the Prophet's body seemed to be sunken merely in sleep, except that there was no breathing and no pulse and no warmth.

The Companions now disagreed as to where he should be buried. It seemed to many that his grave should be near the graves of his three daughters and Ibrāhīm and the Companions whom he himself had buried and prayed over, in the Baqī' al-Gharqad, while others thought he should be buried in the Mosque; but Abū Bakr remembered having heard him say "No Prophet dieth but is buried where he died," so the grave was dug in the floor of 'Ā'ishah's room near the couch where he was lying.

1 K. IX, 40.

2 See p. 119.

3 After the death of Fāṭimah some months later, 'Alī said to Abū Bakr: "We know well thy pre-eminence and what God hath bestowed upon thee, and we are not jealous of any benefit that He hath caused to come unto thee. But thou didst confront us with a thing accomplished, leaving us no choice, and we felt that we had some claim therein for our nearness of kinship unto the Messenger of God." Then Abū Bakr's eyes filled with tears and he said: "By Him in whose hand is my soul, I had rather that all should be well between me and the kindred of God's Messenger than between me and mine own kindred"; and at noon that day in the Mosque he publicly exonerated 'Alī for not yet having recognised him as caliph, whereupon 'Alī affirmed the right of Abū Bakr and pledged his allegiance to him (B. LXIV, 38).

4 I.I. 1017.

Then all the people of Medina visited him and prayed over him. They came in relays, and each small gathering prayed the funeral prayer – firstly the men, group after group, and then when all the men had visited him the women came, and after them the children. That night he was laid in his grave by 'Alī and the others who had prepared him for burial.

Great was the sorrow in the City of Light, as Medina now is called. The Companions rebuked each other for weeping, but wept themselves. "Not for him do I weep," said Umm Ayman, when questioned about her tears. "Know I not that he hath gone to that which is better for him than this world? But I weep for the tidings of Heaven which have been cut off from us."[1] It was indeed as if a great door had been closed. Yet they remembered that he had said: "What have I to do with this world? I and this world are as a rider and a tree beneath which he taketh shelter. Then he goeth on his way, and leaveth it behind him."[2] He had said this that they, each one of them, might say it of themselves; and if the door had now closed, it would be open for the faithful at death. They still had in their ears the sound of his saying: "I go before you, and I am your witness. Your tryst with me is at the Pool." Having delivered his message in this world, he had gone to fulfil it in the Hereafter, where he would continue to be, for them and for others, but without the limitations of life on earth, the Key of Mercy,[3] the Key of Paradise, the Spirit of Truth, the Happiness of God.

*Verily God and His angels whelm in blessings the prophet. O ye who believe, invoke blessings upon him, and give him greetings of Peace.*

[1] I.S. II/2, 83–4. [2] I.M. XXXVII, 3.

[3] This and the other titles which follow it are taken from the traditional litanies of the names of the Prophet.

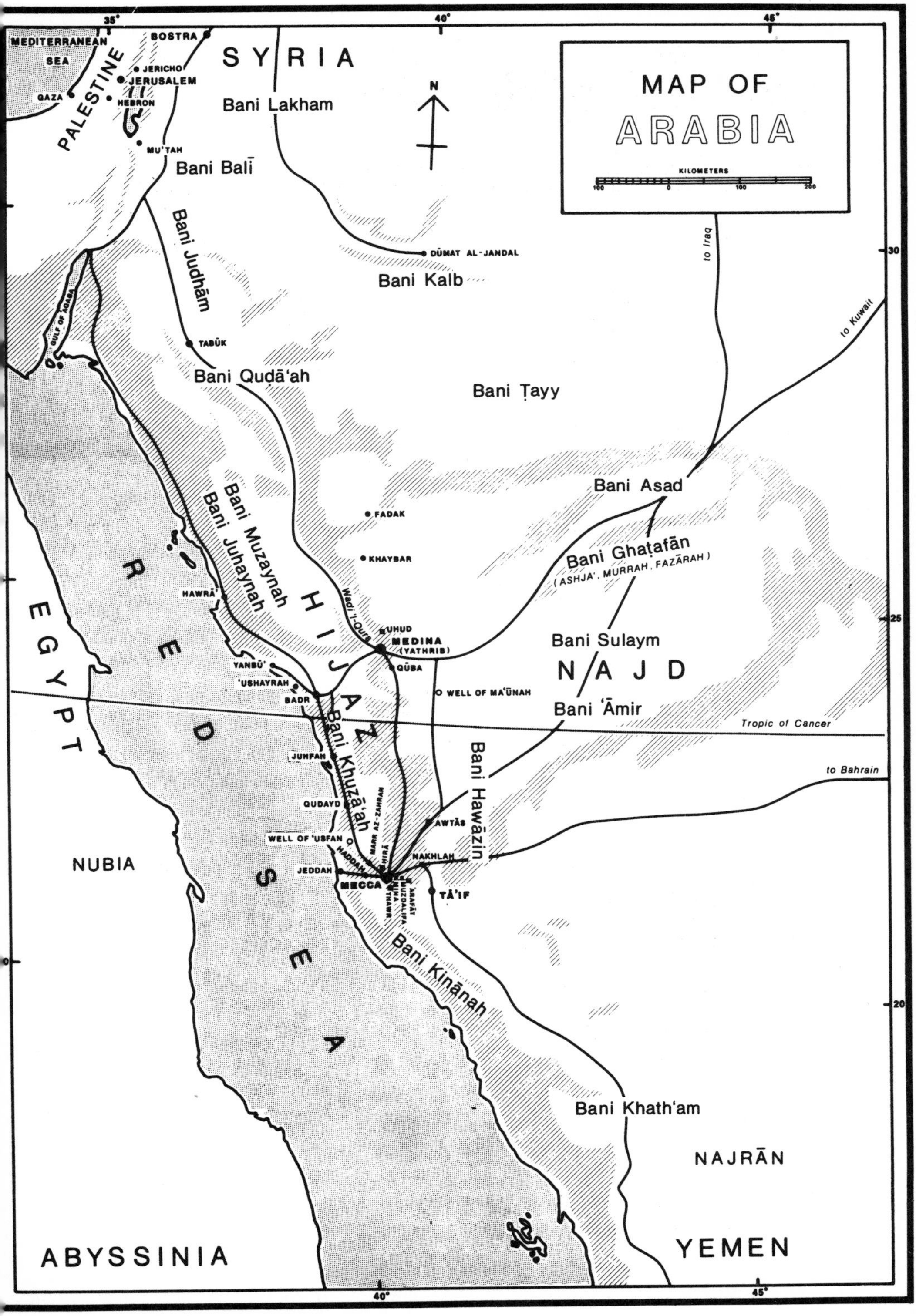
MAP OF
ARABIA
KILOMETERS
100 0 100 200
MEDITERRANEAN
SEA
GAZA
PALESTINE
JERICHO
JERUSALEM
HEBRON
BOSTRA
MU'TAH
SYRIA
Bani Lakham
Bani Balī
Bani Judhām
DŪMAT AL-JANDAL
Bani Kalb
to Iraq
to Kuwait
TABŪK
Bani Quḍā'ah
Bani Ṭayy
GULF OF AQABA
Bani Asad
FADAK
KHAYBAR
Bani Ghaṭafān
(ASHJA', MURRAH, FAZĀRAH)
Bani Muzaynah
Bani Juhaynah
HIJAZ
Wadi'l-Qura
UHUD
MEDINA
(YATHRIB)
QUBA
HAWRĀ'
EGYPT
RED SEA
YANBU'
'USHAYRAH
BADR
WELL OF MA'ŪNAH
Bani Sulaym
NAJD
Bani 'Āmir
Tropic of Cancer
to Bahrain
Bani Khuzā'ah
JUHFAH
QUDAYD
Bani Hawāzin
AWTĀS
WELL OF 'USFAN
MARR AZ-ZAHRAN
HIRĀ
HADDAH
NAKHLAH
NUBIA
JEDDAH
MECCA
ARAFĀT
MUZDALIFA
MINA
THAWR
TĀ'IF
Bani Kinānah
Bani Khath'am
NAJRĀN
YEMEN
ABYSSINIA
35°
40°
45°
30
25
20

# *Quraysh of the Hollow*

(Fihr is directly descended from Ishmael in the male line. The descendants of Fihr who came to be known as Quraysh of the Outskirts are not shown in the following tree)

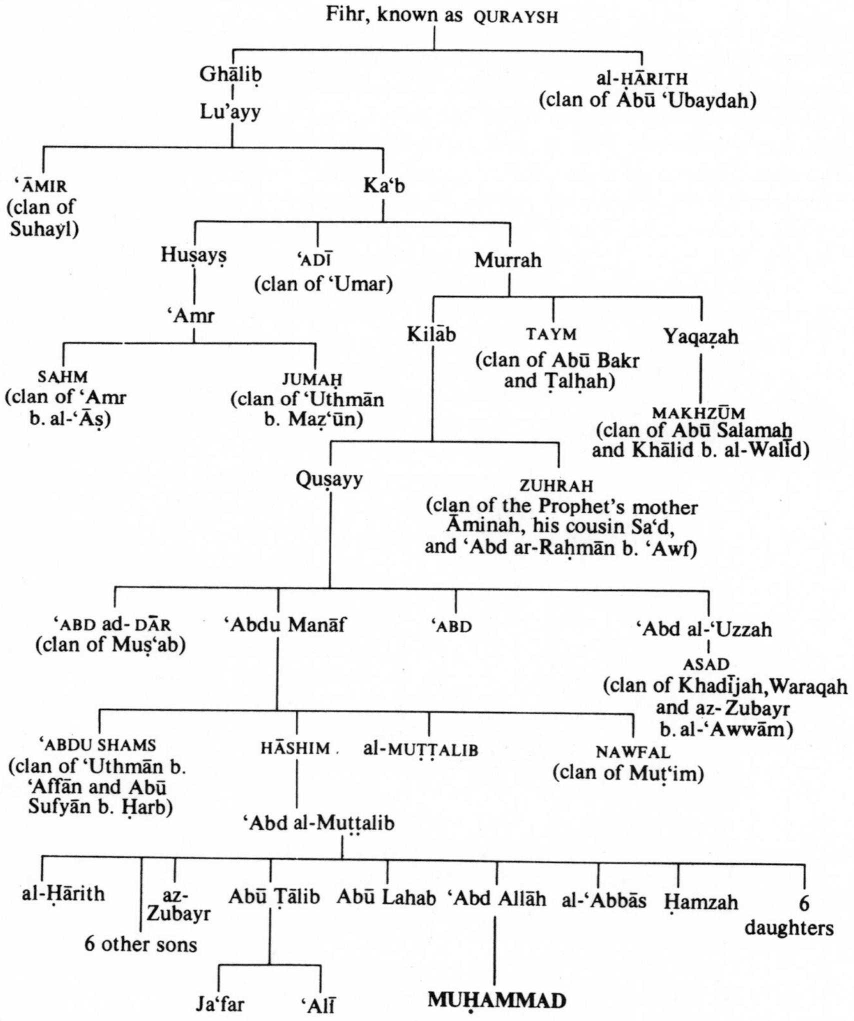


The names of founders of clans are given in small capitals. These are followed by the names of one or more of their descendants who were closely connected with the Prophet or else of historical importance.

# *A Note on the Pronunciation of Arabic Names*

The Arabs sometimes call themselves "the people of Ḍād" because they claim that they alone possess the letter *ḍād*, which sounds like a heavy "d" pronounced far back in the mouth. It is normally transcribed, as here, by *ḍ*. Analogously, *ṣ*, *ṭ* and *ẓ* stand for other characteristic heavy back consonants, whereas *d*, *s*, *t*, and *z* stand for the corresponding front consonants, which are pronounced more or less as in English. The letter *ḥ* is a tensely breathed *h* sound; *q* is a guttural k sound; *th* is to be pronounced as these letters are in *think*, *dh* as they are in *this*, *gh* like a French *r*, *kh* like *ch* in Scottish *loch*. The asper ' denotes the letter *'ayn*, which is produced by narrowing the passage in the depth of the throat and then forcing the breath through it. The apostrophe ' denotes the "*hamzah* of discontinuity," which means a slight catch in the breath. Since in English initial vowel sounds are regularly preceded by this catch, the initial *hamzah* has not been transcribed here, e.g. *Aḥmad*, not *'Aḥmad*. The "*hamzah* of continuity" indicates the running of two words into one by the elision, at the beginning of the second word, of the first letter of the definite article *al-*, the *a* of which is always elided except at the beginning of a sentence. This elision is shown here simply by the omission of the letter in question, e.g. *Abu l-'Āṣ*, not *Abū al-'Āṣ*; the continuity has the effect of shortening any long vowel which immediately precedes this *hamzah*. The first letter of the Divine Name *Allāh* is also elided except at the beginning of a sentence, or when it stands alone, e.g. *bismi Llāh*. But for the sake of simplicity, in the many compound names which begin with the word *'Abd* (slave), the elided *a* is written to replace the sound of the unelided short vowel at the end of *'Abd* which, according to the general principle of not transcribing final short vowels, is not transcribed here, e.g. *'Abd Allāh* not *'Abdu Llāh*, and *'Abd al-Muṭṭalib* not *'Abdu l-Muṭṭalib*. On the other hand, where the second element of the compound name begins with a consonant, the final short vowel of 'Abd is exceptionally transcribed, since transcription here throughout is a guide to pronunciation, and the syllables of a compound name must be pronounced as if they were the syllables of a single word, e.g. *'Abdu Manāf* not *'Abd Manāf*.

The short vowels *a*, *i*, *u* are like the vowel sounds of *sat*, *sit*, *soot*; *ā* (or *à*, so written to indicate a difference of Arabic spelling but not of pronunciation) is like the vowel sound of bare, but back consonants next to it attract it to that of *bār*; *ī* and *ū* are like the vowel sounds of *seen* and *soon*; *ay* is between those of *sign* and *sane*; *aw* is like that of *cow*.

# *Key to References*

K. – The Koran

*Biographical and Historical Works*
This book is mainly based on the writings of the three following authors of the eighth and ninth centuries AD:

| | | |
|---|---|---|
| I.I. | = Ibn Isḥāq | The references are to Wüstenfeld's edition of *Sīrat Rasūl Allāh*, a life of the Prophet by Muḥammad ibn Isḥāq in the annotated recension of 'Abd al-Malik ibn Hishām (I.H.). |
| I.S. | = Ibn Sa'd | The references are to the Leyden edition of *Kitāb aṭ-Ṭabaqāt al-Kabīr* by Muḥammad ibn Sa'd. |
| W. | = Wāqidī | The references are to Marsden Jones's edition of *Kitāb al-Maghāzī*, a chronicle of the Prophet's campaigns, by Muḥammad ibn 'Umar al-Wāqidī. |

Besides these, there are occasional references to:

| | | |
|---|---|---|
| A. | = Azraqī | Wüstenfeld's edition of *Akhbār Makkah*, a history of Mecca, by Muḥammad ibn 'Abd Allāh al-Azraqī. |
| Ṭab. | = Ṭabarī | The Leyden edition of *Ta'rīkh ar-Rusul wa 'l-Mulūk*, "The History of the Messengers and the Kings," by Muḥammad ibn Jarīr aṭ-Ṭabari, whose Koranic commentary, *Tafsīr*, is also quoted. |
| S. | = Suhaylī | The Cairo edition of *ar-Rawḍ al-unuf*, a commentary on Ibn Isḥāq, by 'Abd ar-Raḥman ibn 'Abd Allāh as-Suhaylī. |

*Collections of Sayings of the Prophet*
The references to the following eight traditionists of the ninth century AD are made according to the system used by Wensinck in his *Handbook of Early Muḥammadan Tradition.*

B. = Muḥammad ibn Ismā'īl al-Bukhārī
M. = Muslim ibn al-Ḥajjāj al-Qushayrī
Tir. = Muḥammad ibn 'Īsà at-Tirmidhī
A.H. = Aḥmad ibn Muḥammad ibn Ḥanbal
N. = Aḥmad ibn Shu'ayb an-Nasā'ī
A.D. = Abū Dā'ūd as-Sijistānī
D. = 'Abd Allāh ibn 'Abd ar-Raḥmān ad-Dārimī
I.M. = Muḥammed ibn Mājah

There are also occasional references to the following eleventh century AD traditionists whose collections are not included in Wensinck's handbook.

Bay. = Aḥmad ibn al-Ḥusayn al-Bayhaqī, *Kitāb as-Sunan al-Kubrà*
F. = Ḥusayn b. Maḥmūd al-Farrā' al-Baghawī, *Mishkāt al-Maṣābīḥ*

# *INDEX OF PERSONS (except Muḥammad), PLACES (except Arabia, Ka'bah Mecca and Medina), TRIBES (except Quraysh), BOOKS (except Koran), etc.*



1. Unlike the text, the index gives the definite article *al-* in all those cases where it is normally prefixed to a name (see p. 8 note). The letter *b* stands for *ibn* (son) or *bint* (daughter).
2. *Abī* is the genitive of *Abū*.

1. Place-names are in italics.

1. This Qudayd, due west of Medina on the Red Sea, is not marked on the map.

MARTIN LINGS took an English degree at Oxford and later lectured at Cairo University, mainly on Shakespeare, for twelve years. In 1952 he returned to England and took a degree in Arabic at London University. From 1955 he was in charge of the Arabic library at the British Museum where, in 1970, he was appointed Keeper of Oriental Manuscripts and Printed Books. In 1973, when the British Library was formed, he was transferred there in the same capacity together with his whole Department. From 1974-6 he acted as consultant to the World of Islam Festival Trust and was also a member of the Arts Council Committee for their exhibition 'The Arts of Islam'. In 1977 he went to Mecca at the invitation of King Abd al-Aziz University to participate in the Conference on Islamic Education.

In addition to his three works on Islamic mysticism, which have been published in many languages, he is the author of *The Secret of Shakespeare, Ancient Beliefs and Modern Superstitions,* and the splendidly illustrated *Quranic Art of Calligraphy and Illumination.* His latest publications are *The Eleventh Hour (The Spiritual Crisis of the Modern World in the Light of Tradition and Prophecy), Symbol & Archetype (A Study of the Meaning of Existence)* and his *Collected Poems.* He is also the author of the chapter on 'Mystical Poetry' in volume 2 of the *New Cambridge History of Arabic Literature*, and he has written numerous articles for *Studies in Comparative Religion*, *The Islamic Quarterly*, as well as for *The New Encyclopaedia of Islam* and for *Encyclopaedia Britannica.*